THE JEWISH LAW ANNUAL

The Institute of Jewish Law
Boston University School of Law
765 Commonwealth Avenue
Boston, MA 02215
Publication No. 29

# THE JEWISH LAW ANNUAL

VOLUME FOURTEEN

THE INSTITUTE OF JEWISH LAW
BOSTON UNIVERSITY SCHOOL OF LAW

Routledge
Taylor & Francis Group
LONDON AND NEW YORK

First published 2003
by Routledge

2 Park Square, Milton Park, Abingdon, Oxon, OX14 4RN
711 Third Ave, New York, NY 10017, USA

*Routledge is an imprint of the Taylor & Francis Group, an informa business*

First issued in paperback 2016



Typeset in Palatino by
Newgen Imaging Systems (P) Ltd, Chennai, India



*British Library Cataloguing in Publication Data*
A catalogue record for this book is available
from the British Library

*Library of Congress Cataloging in Publication Data*
A catalog record for this book has been requested

ISBN 978-0-415-30913-4 (hbk)
ISBN 978-1-138-97378-7 (pbk)

This volume is dedicated to the memory of
Isaac Hecht ז"ל
who joyfully devoted his life to serving his Creator
and helping his fellow man

*The Jewish Law Annual* is published under the auspices of The Institute of Jewish Law, Boston University School of Law, in conjunction with the Oxford Centre for Hebrew and Jewish Studies and the International Association of Jewish Lawyers and Jurists.



*Editorial communications* should be addressed to Prof. Berachyahu Lifshitz, Institute for Research in Jewish Law, Faculty of Law, The Hebrew University of Jerusalem, Mount Scopus, 91905 Jerusalem, Israel. All communications should be clearly marked "Attention: Editor, Jewish Law Annual." Contributors should consult the style sheet that appears at the end of the volume; it is also available from the editor upon request. Submissions are welcome from all. Neither the editor nor members of the Board of Editors are to be associated with the views expressed by contributors.


This book is part of a series. The publisher will accept continuation orders, which may be canceled at any time, and provide for automatic billing and shipping of each title in the series upon publication. Please write for details.

## CONTENTS

PART ONE

## PART TWO

## CHRONICLE



## PART THREE

# PART ONE

# DOUBT, CHOICE AND CONVICTION: A COMPARISON OF THE *KIM LI* DOCTRINE AND PROBABILISM

HANINA BEN-MENAHEM*

Coercion is in the nature of all legal systems. Coercion is also one of the main concerns of legal theory. Specifically, legal theory attempts to delineate the foundations and limits of coercion. In this context, theories of consent, despite their fictitious nature, are often put forward. Some such theories argue that the alleged consent of the governed — the participation of the ruled in the evolution and determination of the law — is the principal justification for legal coercion. This is so even where insistence on the acceptance of the law by the governed is not motivated directly by the desire to justify legal coercion, but by other concerns. Consider the following doctrine from the area of religious law: where the law is controversial, legal coercion cannot be exercised unless agreed upon by the litigants, lest the doubtful law fail to represent the will of God. While motivated by theological considerations, it may provide some moral justification for legal coercion.

In this article, I compare two doctrines of this genre, one found in Jewish law, the other in Catholic theology; doctrines that, despite differences in origin, underlying assumptions and historical context, share several pivotal features. Discussion of the jurisprudential implications of these doctrines is left for another occasion.

The doctrines in question originated independently, with an interval of almost a hundred and fifty years between them. In both cases, the doctrines constituted an innovation, albeit an innovation based on familiar concepts, and had significant impact on the systems within which they emerged, provoking clamorous opposition and generating much literature. In both cases, controversy and diversity of opinion characterize the social contexts within which the doctrines gained acceptance. To be sure, the Jewish doctrine developed in the sphere of

* Hanina Ben-Menahem teaches at The Hebrew University of Jerusalem, and is Gruss Visiting Professor of Talmudic Civil Law at Harvard Law School.

law, whereas its Catholic counterpart developed in the sphere of theology. Important as this distinction may be, it does not detract from the interest in comparing the doctrines, as Catholic theology itself constitutes a coercive normative system much like a legal system.

The similarities between the two doctrines are striking, as are their differences. However, I do not claim, or even mean to suggest, a historical link between the two institutions. Similarities that evolve independently in two different systems are more instructive than cases of historical influence, pointing, it would seem, to common conceptual structures across different systems, with all this entails.

## *The* Kim Li *Doctrine in Jewish Law*

Let me begin by presenting a schematic description of the legal argument known as the *kim li* plea.[1] The centrality of this plea in Jewish law is attested both by the frequent recourse to it in actual litigation, up to the present day, and by the constant attempts of halakhic scholars to provide theoretical justification for the plea and to clarify its nature.[2] The essence of the argument, without the mass of technical detail that has evolved around it over the centuries, is as follows. In a given monetary case, the judge, on the basis of his understanding of the law, seeks to rule according to an opinion that supports the plaintiff. Yet by appealing to the *kim li* doctrine, the defendant can invoke an opinion more congenial to his case, thereby repelling the judge's ruling.

An example will clarify this. The validity of an unspecified obligation is a matter of controversy among the Early Authorities. Maimonides (Spain-Egypt, 1138–1204) contends that such an obligation is not valid.[3]

1 '*Kim li*' is a talmudic expression meaning, 'I am certain that....' In the Talmud, it is used almost exclusively to make factual assertions. See bShabat 136a; bYoma 83a; bHagiga 5a; bKetubot 8a; 85a; bBaba Metzia 23b; bSanhedrin 25b; 72b; bAvoda Zara 76b; bNida 44b. The innovation of the *kim li* plea, we will see, is its use to make legal assertions.

2 See e.g., R. Jacob Castro (Egypt, 1525–1610), *Responsa Ohalei Yaakov*, #93; R. Aaron Sasson (Greece and Turkey, 1550–1616), *Responsa Torat Emet*, #207; R. Joseph b. David ibn Lev (Greece and Turkey, 1505–1580), *Responsa Maharibal*, part 3, #102; and the numerous references to *kim li* in the *sifrut haklalim*.

3 "He took upon himself an indefinite obligation, e.g., I will pay for your maintenance or clothing for five years — the transaction is valid, but there is no obligation" (*Code*, Laws concerning Sales 11:16).

R. Abraham b. David (France, ca. 1125–1198),[4] Nachmanides (Spain, 1194–1270),[5] and R. Solomon b. Adret (Spain, ca. 1235–ca. 1310)[6] disagree. The following case came before the courts: someone who had agreed to meet the medical expenses of his associate's son retracted this commitment. The judge ruled in accordance with the authorities who disagree with Maimonides, and obliged the man to fulfill his duty. Using the *kim li* plea, the defendant could have argued thus: "I am certain (*kim li*) that the law is in accordance with the view of Maimonides, who says that an indefinite obligation is void." Under these circumstances, the judge could not have forced him to pay.[7]

The *kim li* argument, then, is a type of plea employed by a defendant, and hence quite distinct from the halakhic principle that money cannot be expropriated on the basis of an uncertainty, which is derived from the talmudic rule "the burden of proof is on the one who has a claim against his fellow."[8] This latter rule is invoked on the initiative of the judge, when he cannot decide, regarding an earlier legal controversy, which opinion to uphold. Lacking proof, or rather, decisive legal support for either opinion, he cannot order anyone to give up his possessions. The *kim li* plea, on the other hand, is directed against the judge. The defendant pleads that he does not accept the ruling, which is based on one opinion, because he would rather follow another. In such a case, the judge is in no doubt, but is nonetheless immobilized by the defendant. Direct evidence that the *kim li* argument is indeed a defense plea is to be found in the halakhic discussion of whether such a plea is admitted at all, and in particular, on behalf of a woman or an ignoramus.[9] Such opposition to the doctrine makes no sense if we construe the doctrine as signifying a state of legal doubt on the part of the judge,[10] since in that case the talmudic principle favoring the possessor would, without question, be applicable.

4 *Glosses*, ad loc.
5 *Responsa Ramban*, #38, #64, #65.
6 "The words of our master Maimonides are nothing if not puzzling" (*Responsa Rashba*, part 4, #145).
7 *Code*, loc. cit.; *Mishne Lamelekh* ad loc.
8 bBaba Kama 46a. See *Encyclopedia Talmudit* (Hebrew) s.v. *hamotzi mihavero alav hareaya*.
9 See, e.g., *Responsa Maharik Hadashim*, #2 (p. 13); *Responsa Ohalei Yaakov*, #93.
10 As has been suggested, e.g., by M. Elon, *The Principles of Jewish Law* (Jerusalem: 1975), 134–135.

Thus, the *kim li* argument, as I understand it, upsets the almost universally-accepted 'triangle' model of the juridical process. On this model, the juridical process pivots around three points: prosecution, defense, and a third party who decides the case. As the decision is always made by the third party, this role is off-limits to the litigants.[11] The *kim li* argument upsets the triangle model in that it enables one of the litigants to introduce and impose his own reading of the law in opposition to that of the supposedly-decisive third party.

Three responses to this conflict between the triangle model and the *kim li* doctrine are possible: (1) *kim li* is upheld and the model rejected; (2) the model is upheld and *kim li* rejected; (3) the doctrine of *kim li* is integrated into the judge's decision-making process, thereby neutralizing the special status accorded the defendant if the *kim li* plea is admitted. It is important to be clear about the meaning of the third response, and how it differs from simple acceptance of the *kim li* plea.

The third response assumes that the legal controversy in question creates an objective doubt unresolvable even by the judge. The judge is therefore forced, by the standard legal principles covering cases of doubt, to rule in favor of the possessor. On this reasoning, an objective doubt exists regardless of the judge's subjective opinion of the matter. The judge's reading of the law is superseded by the system's determination that a state of doubt exists, and the judge cannot impose his understanding of the law. Thus, the decision favoring the defendant is reached, not at the defendant's behest, but due to the system's independent determination. It should be noted, however, that it is not the case that on this view, all legal controversies generate a state of objective doubt. Which controversies have this quality is left to the halakhic scholar judging the case.

### *Historical Development of the Plea*

Jewish sources present two conflicting pictures of the sages' self-perception. On the one hand, the sages are self-effacing with respect to their status relative to that of their predecessors, demonstrating meekness and reluctance to assume decision-making responsibility. This approach is reflected in the talmudic saying, "If the ancients were

11 M. Shapiro, *Courts* (Chicago: 1981), 1.

angels, we are but men; if they were men, we are but beasts."[12] On the other hand, some sages attribute both to themselves and to scholars of all times exceedingly great power and authority. These opposing tendencies have vied with each other in the past and continue to do so in the present.

The Geonim, heads of the talmudic academies in Babylonia from the sixth to the tenth centuries, were fully aware both of the importance of their great enterprise, the inculcation of the Babylonian Talmud, and of their tremendous authority. For them, anything close to the *kim li* plea would have been unacceptable, as the following query shows. A Gaon was asked, "what should the ruling be in a case where responsa by two Geonim differ, and each of the litigants ... chooses one; what are we to do?"[13] The Gaon replies that the judge has full authority to decide between the proffered responsa as he sees fit, adding, "If the litigant tries to rely on the opinion of the other Gaon, he is ignored."[14] Conversely, the halakhic authorities of fifteenth century Germany seem to have been characterized by an unparalleled sense of humility and apprehension about assuming juridical responsibility. And, indeed, we find that the *kim li* plea first appears in halakhic discussions in the schools of the latter scholars. External factors encouraged the rhetoric of self-effacement employed by these scholars, which was undoubtedly conducive to the establishment of the *kim li* doctrine.

The radical change in the rabbis' self-perception can be directly linked to the traumatic effects of the Black Death of 1348–1350 and the persecutions endured by the Jews of Germany in its wake: the German Jewish population was reduced by two-thirds, and 300 communities were destroyed. The halakhic authorities of this period, regarding themselves as inferior to their predecessors, adopted a rhetoric of meekness,

12 Literally, donkeys; bShabat 112a; see Ben-Menahem et al., *Controversy and Dialogue in the Halakhic Sources* (Hebrew), (Jerusalem: 1991), vol. 1, 326–327.

13 The reality underlying this situation, where two different responses to a given question have been tendered, reflects the fact that in some cases questioners sent queries to the two leading Geonic academies. See S. Abramson, "One question and two answers" (Hebrew), *Shenaton Hamishpat Haivri* 11–12 (1984–1986), 1–40, and the literature there cited.

14 *Geonic Responsa* (Harkavy), #347. The respondent is Rav Hai Gaon. See *Geonic Responsa* (Assaf), (Jerusalem: 1942), 180–181.

which pervades their writings.[15] Given that in halakhic works, engagement in historical and psychological self-reflection is quite rare, we can hardly expect to find explicit support for this conjecture in the primary sources themselves. Furthermore, the deterioration was so profound as to almost completely stifle awareness that the crisis even existed. However, remarks in a responsum by R. Jacob b. Moses Moellin (Germany, ca. 1360–1427) explicitly link the persecutions to the contemporary decline in learning and the hesitancy of contemporary sages to take issue with the rulings of their predecessors.[16] The same sentiment is also voiced by his student, R. Jacob b. Judah:

> Alas, nowadays, owing to our sinfulness, generations have become corrupted, hearts impoverished, and judges warped. In the entire world there is no learned man who can be deemed an expert. The same is written in *Sefer Haaguda*[17] on the talmudic passage which states that a slaughterer who does not present his knife to a learned man for periodic inspection is to be banned: "In our times learned men forgo this honor; furthermore, there are no scholars who are versed even in the minor tractate Kala." Now [the author of] *Sefer Haaguda* speaks of his own times, before the persecution, and even so he says that in that period there were no scholars versed even in the minor tractate Kala. How much more so is it true in our own, since compared to them, we are nothing — their fingernails were wider than our bellies! For this reason, my teacher, R. Jacob Moellin, wrote that the fine of a pound of gold, imposed for shaming a learned man, has lapsed, and he supports this ruling with numerous precedents.[18]

One of the central figures to emerge in the world of Jewish law after the Black Death, embodying the collective trauma that had been experienced, was the influential R. Israel Isserlein (Germany, 1390–1460). Indeed, the plea, as it is described here, makes its first

15 See I. Yuval, "*Rishonim veaharonim, antiqui et moderni*: periodiation and self-awareness in Ashkenaz," *Zion* 57 (1992), 392.

16 *Responsa Maharil*, ed. Satz, #67. On the far-reaching consequences of the Black Death in the spheres of culture, higher education and religion in the Christian context, see D. Herlihy, *The Black Death and the Transformation of the West* (Cambridge, MA: 1997), especially ch. 3. Herlihy emphasizes the rupture in the authority of those in professional positions, such as physicians.

17 By R. Alexander Zusslein Hakohen of Frankfurt, one of R. Asher b. Jehiel's teachers. The quote is from his commentary on the first chapter of tractate Hulin.

18 *Responsa Mahari Weil*, #146. See also #129 and #163, and *Responsa Maharam Mintz*, ed. Domb (1991), #63 (4).

appearance in his responsa. Had this development not been recognized, discussed, and adopted in subsequent halakhic writings, it might well have eluded us, for it is still quite embryonic in Isserlein's responsa, and Isserlein himself may not have been fully aware of the move he initiated, or at least advanced markedly. Certainly, it is only in the writings of R. Israel Isserlein's younger contemporary, R. Joseph Colon, the Maharik, that the new doctrine is fully articulated.

The difficulty in pinpointing the emergence of the new move arises from the fact that it is not always easy to distinguish between the older principle that money cannot be expropriated on the basis of an uncertainty, and the novel doctrine of *kim li*. Nevertheless, careful examination of R. Isserlein's theoretical work demonstrates that the core elements of the new doctrine are indeed present. In particular, we see that the problem of an opposed opinion's being advocated is raised in the context of the defendant's argumentation: Isserlein focuses on the nature and admissibility of the litigant's plea, rather than on the quandary facing the judge who confronts uncertainty. For example, one theoretical question pondered by R. Israel Isserlein was whether it was possible for a litigant to hold two contrary views on a given halakhic issue. Elaborating on an existing legal precedent, he constructed an example in which an individual who was a defendant in two different cases could benefit from holding an opposite view in each case. R. Isserlein held that a litigant need not be consistent in the legal convictions he espoused in separate cases.[19] Furthermore, we also find

19 *Responsa Trumat Hadeshen*, #310. R. David b. Zimra, the Radbaz, writing in Egypt almost a century later, was well aware of the innovativeness of the *kim li* doctrine and, objecting to R. Isserlein's view, argued as follows:

> I do not agree with the ruling of R. Israel, of blessed memory, on this particular case, because the words of scholars would be the subject of mockery and ridicule, and we would be "a parable in the mouths of fools" (Prov. 26:9), who would say that an hour ago he argued that he upheld the law in accordance with the view of the Raban, and we ruled along with that, and now he will argue that he upholds the law in accordance with the view of the Rabia, and we will have to rule along with that. And surely the litigant himself will say that there is partiality here....
>
> Furthermore, let us suppose that someone is being sued by two, Reuben and Shimon — surely he cannot argue against Reuben that he upholds the opinion of the Raban, and against Shimon that he upholds the opinion of the Rabia. Rather, he must be consistent in his claims, always upholding the opinion of the one or of the other.

in his responsa analysis of some of the points that dominate later discussions of the plea.[20]

R. Israel Isserlein's legal opinions have come down to us in two collections, *Pesakim Ukhtavim* and *Trumat Hadeshen*. The received opinion is that the latter work contains pseudo-responsa — the author's responses to hypothetical queries he himself is raising, as opposed to questions presented to him to solicit his opinion on matters of actual litigation.[21] It is noteworthy that the *kim li* doctrine is proposed in the pseudo-responsa, and is totally absent from the other collection. This may suggest that R. Israel Isserlein, aware of its innovative nature, was hesitant to apply it in actual litigation.

A contemporary of R. Israel Isserlein, R. Israel b. Haim Bruna (1400–1480), sensing the emerging new attitude, sought to thwart this development, and, commenting on a legal ruling that had been presented to him, wrote as follows:

> **The learned master speaks the words of the Lord, and presents the true law. He substantiates his opinion by citing several chapters of the**

---

> The Talmud (bEruvin 6b) says that one who adopts the leniencies of dissenting teachers is a wicked person, while one who adopts their strictures is a fool, as Scripture states, "But the fool walketh in darkness" (Eccles. 2:14). This is also applicable to the subject under discussion. I can accept someone's claim that he upholds the view of a certain scholar only if he follows it consistently; but if today he says that he upholds the view of A, and tomorrow, that of B, who argues the reverse, this is unacceptable, and I do not think that the rule was meant to be applied in the way it was explained by our teacher and rabbi R. Israel, of blessed memory.
>
> Moreover, this rule is in itself highly novel. If the judge has sufficient evidence to arrive at a ruling that is in line with the dissenting view, or has evidence that inclines him to rule in favor of one of the views, why should the litigant be able to declare that he upholds the opposed view? And since it is a novel innovation, it should not be seen as more than that, and should not serve litigants as a means of reversing anything they object to.
>
> (*Responsa Radbaz*, #825)

20 See *Trumat Hadeshen*, #309, #310, #321, #340, #341, #235, #241.

21 Note the title of this work: '*trumat hadeshen*' is the talmudic term for removal of the ashes from the Temple altar. R. Israel Isserlein, with characteristic humility, refers to his legal opinions as ashes. Note also that *hadeshen* in gematria equals 359 (5 + 4 + 300 + 50), the number of queries in the book.

> Talmud.... and one of the Maharam's responsa. But in order to preempt any argument over this on the part of the litigant, I must elaborate. If one suggests that the ruling is wrong, since there is a controversy of the halakhic authorities over the issue under consideration, quoted in the *Mordekhai*[22]...and on every occasion when there is an unresolved controversy of the authorities, money cannot be expropriated, as the *Mordekhai* states in the following places... — this argument is baseless. Whatever would happen to our law were it accepted? There is no law that does not generate dissenting views and argumentation in this manner. We cannot allow the litigant to choose the opinion of anyone at all to negate conclusive arguments and the words of eminent scholars. The expression "a controversy of the halakhic authorities" applies to controversies such as those between Alfasi and the Tosafists.[23]

This attempt to counter the plea was not successful, however, and R. Israel Isserlein's younger contemporary R. Joseph Colon (ca. 1420–1480), uses the doctrine in his legal opinions — though sometimes critically, demarcating its limits[24] — leading to its dissemination throughout the Diaspora. Balkan scholars of the sixteenth and seventeenth centuries, who lived in a very different social environment, found the doctrine difficult to grasp, and invested much intellectual energy in its explication and justification.

Though aware of the novelty of *kim li*, not all scholars emphasized this aspect of the plea. Some of the Later Authorities sought to anchor it in earlier sources, attempting to identify talmudic grounds for the argument, an idea that is by no means farfetched, as the Talmud endorses various legal principles that can be regarded as anticipating the *kim li* plea. By the same token, the Talmud also admits various principles and strategies that militate against recognition of the *kim li* plea. But I leave this for another occasion.[25]

22 On Ketubot ch. 13.

23 *Responsa Mahari Bruna*, #236.

24 One such qualification is discussed in "Probabilism and *kim li*," below.

25 In addition to various specific institutions that militate against recognizing the *kim li* plea, the main argument, from the talmudic perspective, against the philosophy embodied in the *kim li* doctrine, is the Talmud's fundamental affirmation of judicial liberty from legal constraints, to the point where judicial deviation from the law is countenanced. See my *Judicial Deviation in the Talmud; Governed by Men, Not by Rules* (Chur, Switzerland: 1991). Indeed, the position of Jewish law on the judicial process and the rights of litigants vis-a-vis the courts is complex and sophisticated.

The talmudic source that most directly anticipates the plea, although it was not utilized in this context, is mEduyot 1:5. In one of the very few self-reflective passages in the Mishnah, we find the following remark about the Mishnah's methodology:

> And why do they record the opinion of the individual against that of the majority, since the law may only be decided according to the opinion of the majority? So that if a court approves of the opinion of the individual, it may rely on him.

This passage suggests a strategy for dealing with legal controversies. While the opinion of the majority determines the law, the opinion of the minority, though repudiated, is not completely expunged, but preserved for future reference. This strategy thus sanctions possible future implementation of dissenting views.

Underlying the Mishnah here is a conception of the law as an open-ended, dynamic order that changes spontaneously as its players change, without recourse to formal procedures, an enterprise characterized by flexibility and sensitivity to minority points of view. Admittedly, there is a considerable gap between the mishnaic passage and the *kim li* plea — the Mishnah authorizes reliance on a minority view by a court of law, not by a litigant, and only under certain circumstances.[26] But despite these differences, the conception of the law as open-ended is presupposed by both.

A less relevant source, though one often cited in discussions of the plea, is the dictum of the Babylonian Amora, Samuel, that, notwithstanding the well-established talmudic principle that the law follows the majority, we do not follow the majority with regard to factual findings.[27] Rabbenu Tam, commenting on this view, uses language identical to that of the yet-to-be-articulated *kim li* plea: he explains that the behavior of the majority is not considered to be circumstantial evidence regarding an individual, who can claim, "I am certain that I am from the minority."[28] In so doing, however, Rabbenu Tam is simply following the talmudic usage of the *kim li* formula, viz., to make factual assertions. Nevertheless, this phraseology may account for the fact that some

26 The Talmud and the halakhic literature make frequent use of the principle embodied in this Mishnah, known as "so-and-so is to be relied on in a case of exigency"; see the discussion in "Probabilism and *kim li*" below.

27 bBaba Kama 46a, 27b; bBaba Batra 92b.

28 Rabbenu Tam (France, ca. 1100–1171), *Tosafot* on bBaba Kama 27b.

authorities saw in Samuel's principle anticipation of the *kim li* plea, despite the evident differences between the two contexts, differences that did not go unmentioned, even by those who cite Samuel's dictum as a source of the plea.[29]

Others sought its origin in the writings of the Early Authorities. Most frequently cited in this context is R. Meir of Rothenburg (1215–1293), the Maharam, and specifically, remarks such as the following:

> The issue was not resolved but is a controversy of the halakhic authorities… and whenever our masters are divided and we do not know whose view the law is in accordance with — in such a case of doubt, we cannot make the possessor relinquish his money.[30]

It should be noted that here, as in similar statements to this effect, the emphasis is on the legal doubt that precludes an unequivocal decision, and not on the litigant's contention, constitutive of the *kim li* plea, that the law is on his side.

The same sentiment is voiced by the Maharam's students: R. Mordekhai b. Hillel (1240–1298),[31] R. Asher b. Jehiel (Rosh)

29 *Responsa Radakh*, bayit 2, sec. 10; *Responsa Maharashdam*, 2:61; *Responsa Maharibal* 1:854. Interestingly, the rather enigmatic dictum, "Samuel was known to take notice of individual opinions" (bMegila 18b; bJebamot 83a), which might be Samuel's principle regarding findings of fact as applied to the legal domain, and as such, much more relevant than the original principle to the *kim li* doctrine, is nonetheless not referred to in the *kim li* context.

30 *Responsa Maharam* (Berlin ed., 1891), #25. Another source, even earlier than the Maharam, that has been cited as the origin of the plea, is a tradition reported in the *Mordekhai* on Ketubot, ch. 4, sec. 154. According to this tradition, R. Samuel b. Barukh, one of the Maharam's teachers, was, in the context of a specific controversy, unwilling to appropriate money from its possessor, because he did not wish to contravene the view that does not sanction such appropriation. See *Responsa Maharik*, #94.

31 *Mordekhai* on Baba Batra, ch. 10, sec. 649; Ketubot, ch. 4, sec. 154; ch. 7, sec. 194; ch. 10, sec. 245. The formulation closest to *kim li* in the *Mordekhai*, is in the glosses on Ketubot, sec. 290: "I found that regarding cases on which the great authorities were divided, R. Meir used to rule as follows: If one of the litigants made a seizure, the other is powerless to compel him to relinquish it, for the seizer can argue: 'Bring proof that the law is in accordance with the authority whose ruling favors your claim.'"

(1250–1327),[32] R. Haim Or Zarua (d. 1260)[33] and R. Meir Hakohen of Rothenburg (late 13th century).[34] It is clear, however, that the reference here is to what I termed earlier 'objective doubt.' The Maharam does not intend to include cases where he has decided the law, but is indicating that the fact of legal controversy (again, not all legal controversies generate objective doubt) could interfere with his rendering a decision. Where, despite the existence of a legal controversy, he has managed to decide the law, the defendant cannot block the ruling.

Shortly, we will note that some halakhic authorities construed the *kim li* doctrine itself as simply denoting a state of objective doubt. This may explain references to the Maharam and his students as anticipating the doctrine. The plea, however, was never articulated prior to the fifteenth century.

In the research literature, it has been argued that R. Jacob b. Asher (Germany-Spain, ca. 1270-ca. 1343), in his introduction to the *Tur*, Hoshen Mishpat, refers to the *kim li* plea.[35] This contention is based on the following passage:

> And when I, Jacob, son of R. Asher, of blessed memory, realized that our Temple had been destroyed on account of our sins ... and there is no righteous judge ... judges are themselves judged, constables themselves arrested, auxiliaries aided, supporters supported, redeemers redeemed, preachers admonished, and everyone does as he sees fit. And who can tell them how they ought to act? They have gone astray and caused corruption. Consequently, the law has become twisted. Some expound the law, but the law evades them, as their intelligence is too limited. And on others the law shines, but they deliberately ignore its illumination, due to their fear of failing to reach the strict law, which hinges on them. They say, 'I will choose an opinion at random, in line with one of the authorities; on

---

This formulation, however, clearly implies that the dispute among the "great authorities" was one that the judge could not resolve, and hence, the principle that 'the burden of proof is on the one who has a claim against his fellow' would apply here.

32 *Responsa Rosh*, 1:8, 45:11, 84:3, 94:5.

33 *Responsa R. Haim Or Zarua*, #53, #250, #251, #252.

34 *Teshuvot Maimoniot*, Laws concerning Neighbors 12:37–38; Laws concerning Pleading 1:37; Laws concerning Marriage 35.

35 M. Elon, *Jewish Law: History, Sources, Principles* (Philadelphia: 1994), vol. 3, 1281–1282.

> his authority I will base my judgment, and I will be relieved of responsibility. My stick [alluding to a magic rod] will direct me.'[36]

However, it is evident that this passage, in its entirety, does not refer to litigants who try to utilize the *kim li* plea, but rather, to judges who do not discharge their judicial responsibilities faithfully. Such judges resort to randomly choosing from among previous rulings as the basis for their own rulings, even when these rulings are clearly unwarranted. R. Jacob b. Asher's opposition to such judges simply reiterates that of his father, the renowned R. Asher b. Jehiel, expressed in his well-known statement: "In cases where two authorities disagree regarding a ruling, the judge should not say, 'I will rule as I choose,' and if he does so, his ruling is false."[37]

The passage, then, describes the collapse of the judicial system, and in particular, the corruption of judges.[38] It distinguishes two categories of inadequate judges, the unintelligent and the cowardly.

Elon argues against this reading, misinterpreting the latter category as a reference to litigants who fear losing their cases, and on the basis of this erroneous construal, reading the passage as describing recourse to the *kim li* plea. The passage, however, manifestly refers to judges who are afraid to rely on their own understanding, lest they err in interpreting the law. R. Jacob b. Asher is clearly alluding to the following talmudic passage: "R. Samuel b. Nahmani further said, reporting [the words of] R. Jonathan: A judge should always think of himself as having a sword hanging over his head, and Gehenna gaping under him" (bSanhedrin 7a). Elon also argues that since *kim li* is only applicable in monetary law, and this passage appears only in the introduction to Hoshen Mispat, which deals with monetary law, and not in the introductions to Orah Haim and Yore Deia, which deal with ritual law, his reading must be correct. The truth, however, is that these two sections of the *Tur*, on R. Jacob's own account, refer to the conduct of the

36 Based on bPesahim 52b, which alludes to Hosea 4:12: "My people ask counsel of a piece of wood, and their staff declareth unto them." Both the talmudic passage and R. Jacob are making a pun here: the word for rod, differently pointed, means 'one who rules leniently.'

37 Rosh on bSanhedrin, ch. 4, sec. 6.

38 See Freimann's "Ascher Ben Yechiel, sein Leben und Wirken," cited by Elon, n. 35 above, 1252.

individual, and not to the conduct of courts. Hoshen Mishpat, on the other hand, deals precisely with the conduct of courts, and that is why the passage appears only there.

From the time of its introduction, halakhic authorities have evinced a range of attitudes to the *kim li* plea. There is clearly a correlation between acceptance of *kim li* and the assertiveness of the halakhic scholar in question: the more inclined he is to assume judicial responsibility openly, the less likely he is to tolerate the *kim li* plea, and vice versa. The three possible responses posited above have, indeed, all been expressed. One response has been acceptance of *kim li* as a privilege of the defendant, with all the implications for the juridical process this entails. A more modest variant of this approach has been to regard the plea as an exercise of the defendant's right to self-help, and the judge's recognition of it as valid only provisionally, and not a final legal settlement of the larger issue. On this view, the judge's decision to accept the plea is subject to subsequent judicial review on the basis of the accepted principles applicable to cases of self-help.[39]

Another response has been to reject the plea as an offense against the dignity of judges. The most vehement rejection came in the form of an enactment prohibiting appeal to the plea:

> They sent us a ruling signed by R. Moses Saragossi, R. Judah Cohen, R. Menahem Cohen, R. Israel Romano and R. Nathan Gueta, may they be remembered for eternal life, all concurring that the *kim li* argument should not be admitted, and cases must be decided according to the Torah. And at the time, we were told by reliable persons that in the past, in the town of Safed, may it be speedily rebuilt, all the rabbinical authorities there had agreed to impose a strict ban: no judge was to rule on the basis of the *kim li* plea, but rulings were to be in accordance with the Torah, that is, by following the majority view, or the view of the local authority. Quite recently, about four or five years ago, there passed through these parts a traveling scholar from the land of Israel, may it be speedily rebuilt, with whom I spoke, and in the course of our conversation, the subject of *kim li* came up. The scholar said to me, "In Safed, I saw this agreement, which had been drawn up in the days of R. Joseph Caro, may he be remembered for eternal life, with the concurrence of all the other rabbis there, and all were signatories to it. They all agreed that no judge would admit a *kim li* plea, and agreed to a strict ban on any judge who did. Rather, judges had to rule according to the view of the local authority, and if they did not have a local

39 See, for example, *Responsa Ohalei Yaakov*, #93, and *Responsa Darkhei Noam*, HM #15.

> rabbinical authority, then, as is decreed by the Torah, they are to 'follow the majority' (*aharei rabim lehatot*) (Exod. 23:2)."[40]

This total opposition to the doctrine also has a milder variant. To lessen recourse to the *kim li* plea, a new doctrine was introduced: the claim that the community or the litigants have accepted upon themselves the jurisdiction of a given authority. The effect of this move was that while the *kim li* doctrine remained intact, it was stripped of any applicability.[41]

A far more common response, however, has been to integrate the plea into the complex of factors taken into account by the judge in arriving at a decision, by regarding legal controversies — once again, not all legal controversies — as instances of objective doubt. This move transforms it from a defense plea into a legal consideration taken into account by the judge at his own initiative. It is imperative to bear in mind the distinction between the first response, namely, acceptance of the doctrine, and the third response, namely, integration of the doctrine into the legal system as a decision-making rule. The former construes the plea as an independent legal move, whereas the latter construes it

40 *Responsa Maharif*, R. Jacob Faraji (Egypt, 17th century), #61, but see *Taalumot Lev*, R. Elijah b. Joseph Rafael Hazan (Turkey-Israel-Egypt, 1848–1908), "Kuntres Haklalim," on *kim li*, which disputes this:

> And I would say that the testimony of the scholar from the land of Israel is not reliable. Had there been such an agreement backed by a ban in Safed, may it be rebuilt and reestablished, it would have been mentioned by the rabbinical decisors, of blessed memory, particularly by R. Joseph Caro, of blessed memory, since it happened during his time, and he is said to have agreed to it and to have been one of the signatories. And he would have mentioned it in his *Beit Yosef*. As it happens, to this very day the *kim li* argument is admitted in the courts of the great communities of Tograma [Turkey], and no disdain is expressed by anyone.

41 See, for example, *Responsa Radbaz*, part 4, #115: "Furthermore, in my opinion, R. Joseph Colon, who supports the use of the *kim li* plea on the authority of the *Mordekhai*, does so only where the community has not accepted the jurisdiction of a given authority." The doctrine of "acceptance of a given authority," while rooted in talmudic discussions, came to the fore as a means of combating the spread of the *kim li* doctrine, and in a way, constitutes a radical reversal of the *kim li* doctrine: here, it is not the individual's acceptance of halakhic authorities that is respected and given precedence, but rather, the community's.

as indistinguishable from objective doubt. Failure to appreciate the distinction obscures an important element of the judicial process in Jewish law.

This discretionary admission of the plea as a legitimate consideration had a salutary, if surprising, effect. While it might have been predicted that recourse to the plea would tend to highlight classic rulings, to the detriment of innovative interpretations, this did not transpire. The selective admission of the plea, far from promoting a rigid, dogmatic administration of the law, injected into the legal system a not insignificant measure of flexibility. By admitting the defendant's *kim li* plea on a selective basis, the judge could finesse his way to the desirable legal outcome without challenging existing halakhic principles. Thus a legal instrument that had its origins in conservative tendencies is used to promote innovation, without sacrificing conservative rhetoric.[42]

To illustrate this adequately would take us far into the textual and legal analysis of the responsa literature, an endeavor we cannot undertake here. It must suffice for the present to point out that this observation attests to an important distinction. The analysis of the *kim li* doctrine can be conducted on two different levels: the theoretical level, where the doctrine is studied in terms of its underlying assumptions, and the level of its actual application in real-life situations. Not attending to the gap that exists between the two can lead to serious misconceptions as to the role of the doctrine in the history of Jewish law. This paper, however, deals only with the former dimension.

### *Catholic Theology*

Let us now turn to probabilism, the Catholic analogue of the *kim li* doctrine. Some historical background is useful.

Doubt is a major concern in Catholic theology. What is to be done if the performance of an action is a matter of dispute among the authorities? That is, what is to be done if there are opinions both permitting and prohibiting a given action? Four different ethical doctrines were formulated to address this problem. In logical, rather than chronological,

42 This thesis, first put forward in a paper I delivered at Stanford in 1988, is illustrated in an examination of the responsa of R. Joseph ibn Lev carried out by Samuel Morell in his *Precedent and Judicial Discretion* (Atlanta: 1991).

order, they are: (1) following the stricter opinion — tutiorism; (2) following the most probable opinion — probabiliorism; (3) allowing choice between two equally probable opinions — equiprobabilism, associated with Alphonsus Liguori (1696–1787); and (4) following any opinion, even if it is less probable than another — probabilism.

The background to the development of the fourth doctrine, probabilism, is described by Ian Hacking.

> What is to be done if authorities, especially the Fathers of the Church, are found to disagree? The problem became pressing in the Renaissance, as more and more texts were discovered and more and more interpretations of existing texts were invented.[43]

The doctrine of probabilism enabled the individual, in applying the law to himself, to benefit from doubt, and to free himself from the burden of laws that lacked absolute certainty. But as we will see, the doctrine was also applied to confessors, who were instructed to condone conduct based on opinions with which the confessor disagreed.[44]

Probabilism was first formulated by Bartholomeo Medina (1528–1580), a Dominican who served as professor of theology in Salamanca, in his 1557 commentary on the works of Thomas Aquinas.[45] Although the idea appears almost incidentally in the commentary, it introduces a completely novel form of reasoning.

The starting point for the discussion is a question posed by Medina concerning the morally required course of action in a situation where two opposing opinions exist: "Whether we are obliged to follow the more probable opinion, abandoning the probable one, or is it sufficient that we follow the probable opinion?"[46] The standard reply to this

43 I. Hacking, *The Emergence of Probability* (Cambridge: 1975), 24; J. Mahoney, *The Making of Moral Theology* (Oxford: 1987), 135ff.

44 "In the tribunal of penance the confessor is never permitted to refuse absolution to any penitent who holds and follows an opinion proposed by prudent and learned moralists, even though the confessor himself looks upon it as false" (Bernard Haring, *The Law Of Christ* [Westminster, MD: 1969], vol. 1, 187).

45 Medina, *Expositiones in primam secundae Divi Thomae*, Venetis: 1602 (1st ed. Salamanca: 1557). The Latin is reproduced in J. de Blic, "Barthelemy de Medina et les origines du Probabilisme," *Ephemerides Theologicae Lovanienses* 7 (1930), 65–73.

46 Medina, *Expositiones*, q. 19, a. 6, in Blic, 70.

question was that one is morally obliged to follow the more probable opinion. Soto (1494–1560), cited by Medina, held that if both opinions are equally probable, the individual should follow the opinion most convincing to him. That is, the individual must decide for himself, after thorough deliberation, which opinion, to the best of his understanding, accords with right reason. This view endows the system with a significant degree of subjectivity and pluralism, as different individuals will reach different conclusions, all of equal merit. The only constraint is that the individual must adopt the opinion that emerges from his moral reflection — he cannot follow any opinion at random.

Nevertheless, Medina puts forward his own idea: "It seems to me that if an opinion is probable, it is licit to follow it even though the opposite opinion is more probable."[47] The probability of an opinion is determined by the fact that it is sustained by wise men (moral authorities) and supported by compelling arguments. These two elements will later be distinguished as **extrinsic** and **intrinsic** probability. For Medina, however, they constitute but a single criterion determining the probability of an opinion. The formulation of Medina's thesis clearly indicates that he allows for a range of opinions with different probabilities, and that one is not obliged to follow the most probable opinion.

Medina offers five arguments for his novel thesis. His first argument elaborates upon and adapts a thesis formulated by earlier theologians. These thinkers distinguished between speculative reasoning, which addresses theoretical questions, and practical reasoning, which addresses concrete concerns. They then claimed that in speculative reasoning, one is allowed to entertain a probable opinion even though a more probable one exists, but not in practical reasoning, where the most probable opinion must always be followed. Medina argues, however, that the two spheres are analogous, and just as one can entertain a probable opinion without scruple about being mistaken, so one can follow it in practice without scruple about committing a sin. That is, being sinful in the sphere of the practical is analogous to being mistaken in the sphere of speculative reasoning.

Medina's second argument is that to hold otherwise — to maintain that one is not allowed to follow a probable opinion where a more probable opinion exists — involves us in a contradiction, as the probability of an opinion entails permission to follow it, otherwise it is not probable.

47 Ibid., 71.

Thirdly, as we saw, the probability of an opinion is determined by the fact that it is sustained by wise men (moral authorities) and supported by compelling arguments. This means that a probable opinion is part of right reason, and as such, can be followed. Medina recognizes that following the more probable opinion leads one to perfection, but argues, "no one is obligated to that which is better and perfect."[48]

The fourth argument derives the validity of a probable opinion from the fact that its teaching is unequivocally authorized. What may be taught in colleges may be advised and acted upon. On this basis Medina infers that a confessor cannot force a confessant to follow the more probable opinion if the latter chooses to follow the probable opinion.

The final argument for allowing reliance on the probable opinion is that to hold otherwise — to hold that one is always obligated to follow the more probable opinion — would mean that each individual must make his own evaluation of which existing opinion is the most probable, an endeavor God-fearing people are reluctant to undertake. When a probable opinion is identified, the individual is not duty-bound to reflect on it and examine whether or not it makes sense to him, but is allowed to follow it without any deliberation. Medina does not mandate personal identification with the endorsed opinion, or deep conviction. What we have here, according to Medina, is a formal principle allowing reliance on a probable opinion. I will return to the question of conviction at the end of the paper.

Medina's doctrine was meant to be applied not only by the individual contemplating his own course of action, but also, as I mentioned, by the confessor in granting penance for confessed sins: if the confessant could ground his action in a probable opinion, the confessor could not dismiss it, even if he did not approve of it. A similar idea had already been advanced by Soto, who had claimed that the confessor must not pass judgement in accordance with what he opines, but rather in accordance with what speculative reasoning holds to be probable. If the individual is convinced by and committed to a probable opinion different from the confessor's, his action is legitimate nonetheless. Medina's position is that the same holds true whenever an individual can base his action on a probable opinion even though a more probable one exists, even if the individual does not hold this view as a result of thorough deliberation.

48 Ibid.

This idea was later extended, in theory, to apply to judges as well, as the following passage indicates:

> May a judge, on a point of law, judge according to a probable opinion, setting aside the most probable opinion? Yes, and even against his own opinion: "*imo contra propriam opinionen.*" And that is what our Father Escobar (1589–1669) quotes also in tr. 6 ex. 6 n. 45.[49]

Probabilism was much discussed.[50] It became an accepted tenet of Catholic theology, and flourished for about eighty years without any serious challenge.

In light of the application of probabilism to confessors, it might be suggested that an explanation for the establishment of probabilism be sought in the need to respond to Lutheran arguments against the Church and its conduct of confessions. At the time, penances for confessed sins made up a substantial portion of Church income. It is possible that probabilism was appealing because it presented the confessor with wide scope for absolution without selling the harshly-criticized indulgences and other pecuniary penances. This is the spirit in which the following remarks should be understood: "These multiple opinions are a sign of salvation.... many who might be damned, are saved by a probable opinion";[51] "diversity of opinions in moral matters renders the yoke of the Lord more sweet and His burden more light."[52]

If this explanation is correct, the main motivation for the doctrine is the flexibility it introduces into the application of the law. This contrasts with the main motivation for the *kim li* doctrine: a sense of modesty and reluctance to assume legal responsibility. Yet, this is the point at which we find most resemblance between the doctrine of probabilism and that of *kim li*. Both instruct the deciding party — the judge or the confessor — to uphold the opinion favored by the defendant.

Though the doctrine was introduced and adopted by the Dominicans, it was developed by the New Jesuits. The three individuals

49 Pascal, *The Provincial Letters*, trans. A.J. Krailsheimer, letter 8.

50 A recent study of probabilism, Ilkka Kantola, *Probability and Moral Uncertainty in Late Medieval and Early Modern Times* (Helsinki: 1994) has a comprehensive bibliography. Kantola's discussion of Medina, however, is incomplete, covering only the first three arguments.

51 Caramuel (1606–1682), quoted in A.R. Jonsen and S. Toulmin, *The Abuse of Casuistry* (Berkeley: 1989), 168.

52 Escobar (1589–1669), quoted in Jonsen and Toulmin, ibid.

who contributed most to this process of elaboration were Gabriel Vasquez (1551–1604), a Jesuit; Francisco Suarez (1548–1617), also a Jesuit; and John of St. Thomas (1589–1644), a Dominican.

Gabriel Vasquez, a commentator at the University of Salamanca, is best known for distinguishing two subtypes within Medina's notion of probability: an opinion could be intrinsically probable, that is, based on "excellent arguments," or extrinsically probable, that is, based on the authority of "wise men." Intrinsic probability soon gave way to extrinsic probability, and head-counting replaced reasoned debate. This development drew probabilism closer to the *kim li* model, which was, from the very beginning, a matter of extrinsic probability in this sense. A further point of resemblance in the doctrines' histories, then, is the fact that ultimately both became a matter of the preponderance of experts.

Francisco Suarez's treatment of the doctrine reflects his legal training. He brought to the discussion two legal principles, first, that in cases of doubt the presumption favors the side in possession, and second, that laws are not binding unless properly promulgated. Taken together, they imply that one in moral doubt is free to act as he wishes: since he has possession of his liberty, and there is no properly-promulgated law restricting it, his freedom to act on his convictions remains intact.

John of St. Thomas limited the doctrine of probabilism to cases that did not involve the property of another individual. This limitation is related to issues having to do with the separate jurisdictions of the secular and ecclesiastical courts. As a result of this qualification, the doctrine was not applied in monetary litigation.

The doctrine's inapplicability in civil courts is illustrated in a sarcastic account of the doctrine given by Blaise Pascal, one of its bitterest adversaries, in his *Provincial Letters*. He presents a description of probabilism in the form of an anecdote proffered by an adherent to a skeptical listener. One Jean d'Alba, who was in the service of the fathers of the College de Clermont, feeling dissatisfied with his wages, stole something to make up the difference. The unfortunate man, when interrogated, confessed that he had taken a few pewter plates, but insisted that he had nonetheless not stolen them. In his defense, he cited the doctrine of Father Bauny (1564–1649), a French Jesuit, which he presented to the judges. Bauny had declared, "If servants complain about their wages, they can, in certain circumstances, increase their wages themselves by laying their hands on as much of their master's property as they deem necessary to make their wages equal to their toil." The court, however, was not impressed with the said doctrine, which it found to be "contrary to all laws, natural, divine and human, [and] capable of disrupting every family and authorizing any domestic theft," and gave judgment against the defendant.[53] On the basis of this anecdote, the listener raises the following objection to probabilism:

> You have certainly safeguarded those who follow your probable opinions with regard to God and their conscience. You also have given them safeguards as regards confessors; for you have obliged priests to absolve them on the basis of a probable opinion on pain of mortal sin. But you have not safeguarded them as regards judges; so that they find themselves liable to the lash and the gallows if they follow your probabilities.

To this objection, the doctrine's supporter can only respond by saying, "we do not have as much power over magistrates as over confessors."[54]

### *Probabilism and* Kim Li[55]

After the eighty-year period in which the doctrine of probabilism was sanctioned, it came under heavy criticism, first by Pascal,[56] then by others. In 1680, a decree issued by Pope Innocent XI stated that instruction opposing the doctrine was not erroneous, and arguments against the doctrine were not to be suppressed. Subsequently, the doctrine underwent a number of limitations in scope and validity.

Interestingly, the *kim li* plea was also subjected to heavy criticism, but the two doctrines were censured on different grounds. Arguments against the Catholic doctrine center on the individual who evades his religious duties by exploiting theological controversies. The arguments critical of *kim li* focus more on its institutional repercussions: the law will lose its unity; the Torah will be abandoned; the status of judges will suffer; courts will be held in contempt.[57]

53 For the historical records of the trial of Jean d'Alba, see *Oeuvres de Blaise Pascal*, ed. L. Brunschvigg, P. Boutroux, F. Gazier (Paris: 1929), 26.

54 Pascal, *The Provincial Letters*, letter 7.

55 I am indebted to Prof. Antonio Ferrari for his useful comments and suggestions.

56 *The Provincial Letters*, letters 5 and 6.

57 A contemporary example. R. I. Herzog relates the case of a contested estate that came before the civil courts in Bombay. The sides, both Jewish,

We must now consider an important difference, already touched upon, between the Jewish and Catholic doctrines. The *kim li* plea is not applied to ritual precepts, where the more stringent opinion is always adopted. It is only admitted in monetary cases, and consequently, it can impact on third parties. This position was articulated at the time the doctrine was first introduced. In a passage that has since been much quoted, R. Joseph Colon, the Maharik, makes this point in speaking of a controversy that had arisen regarding the ritual duty of fringes (*tzitzit*):

> It was a great mistake and blunder on the part of the one who said that the owner of the *kafa* [a garment] could argue, 'I uphold the law according to R. Simha, who says that a garment with five corners is exempt from the duty of fringes.' ... We surely do not compare monetary and ritual law, for, as every child knows, according to the halakha doubts in the area of ritual law are to be decided in accordance with the stricter view, while those in monetary law are decided in accordance with the more lenient view. The two areas are quite distinct. To be sure, on a monetary question the individual in possession may argue in favor of upholding the law as reflected in a ruling of a great authority, even though others ruled differently, as in the case cited in the *Mordekhai* concerning the disagreement of Rabbenu Tam and Rashi. The individual in possession could argue, 'If you want to [take away what I have], prove that the law is in accord with the view of Rabbenu Tam rather than that of Rashi,' for the side that seeks to claim something in the possession of another must substantiate its claim. But, here, in the case of the garment, it is a matter of ritual prohibition, and who would be so irresponsible as to permit something because of an uncertainty? Let us be saved from such a thing in Israel.[58]

The doctrine of probabilism, by contrast, is not, we saw, applied in monetary cases, but restricted to the realm of ecclesiastical ritual law. Indeed, the doctrine of probabilism, which emerged and evolved within the sphere of Catholic theology, never made its way into canon law, let alone civil law.

---

invoked the *kim li* plea throughout the litigation. R. Herzog then comments: "The complication that originated from the application of the *kim li* plea was much discussed amongst gentile judges and lawyers and *kim li* soon became a mockery and the Tora — the laughing stock of all" (Isaac Herzog, *Constitution and Law in a Jewish State according to the Halacha* [Jerusalem: 1989], vol. 2, 137).

58 *Responsa Maharik*, #149.

One possible explanation for this difference, namely, that *kim li* is operative in legal disputes whereas probabilism is applied only to moral questions, points to the issue of codification. Throughout the formative years of the *kim li* doctrine, Jewish law had no supreme legislative body. Hence, it could be argued, controversies remained unresolved, promoting the emergence of the doctrine. Canon law, by contrast, was under the authority of the Church, whose legal hierarchy enabled all controversies to be resolved. But this explanation is unsatisfactory, since the same could be said with regard to theology, which was likewise under the authority of the Church. It seems that a better explanation can be found in the different attitudes of the Church and the Jewish sources to spiritual perfection, on the one hand, and interpersonal dealings, on the other. The Church, placing considerable importance on achieving moral perfection, could not permit the decline of individuals into mortal sin. It therefore widened the scope for morally legitimate courses of action by regarding all probable opinions as valid.

The Catholic doctrine is motivated by the desire to introduce some flexibility into Church law in order to save sinners from perdition. Not viewing interpersonal legal affairs as decisive in the domain of moral perfection, the Church was under less pressure to save individuals from committing offenses in this arena. Consequently, in the context of interpersonal dealings, a rigid standard was acceptable. On this reasoning, the doctrine of probabilism is adopted in the sphere most crucial in the eyes of the Church.

Jewish thinking goes in the opposite direction. The notion of saving mortal souls is less pronounced, and the area where flexibility is deemed imperative is that of interpersonal dealings. Thus it was said that it is much easier to allow a woman whose matrimonial status is doubtful to remain married to her husband, than to force someone to pay under a doubtful law.[59] In the same vein, Maimonides asserts that we are less concerned with the accuracy of the factual basis used in reaching a legal determination in cases concerning religious prohibitions than in matters of monetary law.[60] That is to say, the system reflects greater sensibility in the context of interpersonal dealings than in the context of God–man relations, where decisions, their reflection of divine truth being less crucial, can be almost arbitrary.

59 *Responsa R. Joseph ibn Lev*, vol. 3, #33.

60 Maimonides, *Code*, Laws concerning Divorce, end of ch. 7.

The same idea emerges from the following passage, which deals with the talmudic principle allowing reliance on a minority view in cases of exigency, based on mEduyot 1:5, quoted above. The passage limits the applicability of this principle to ritual law only:

> All but the Rashbam share the same opinion; how can we relinquish the well-established law accepted by the great authorities and rely on the view of an individual? This is out of the question. And as for the argument that the Rashbam is to be relied on in a case of exigency — this principle has never been applied in monetary law. It could only have been put forward by individuals who are unlearned, and make false analogies. We, however, follow a great principle: the burden of prove is on the one who has a claim against his fellow. And this is explicitly stated in the Mishnah.... Hence, the principle, 'So and so is to be relied on in a case of exigency' is not applicable to monetary law.[61]

The principal factor underlying the emergence of the *kim li* plea was, we saw, rabbinical diffidence and reluctance to decide between venerated authorities of the past. Yet in the sphere of ritual law no such reluctance is voiced. Admittedly, the principle of following the stringent view in ritual law (which makes no sense in the context of monetary law) might indicate a philosophy of taking the safest road. However, it is significant that no hesitancy is manifested in this sphere regarding the very fact of deciding between venerated authorities of the past.

There seems to be something paradoxical about allowing the *kim li* plea, and thereby making it possible to avoid passing judgement, only in the monetary realm, generally considered of lesser gravity than the ritual realm. This sense of paradox is reflected in the words of an opponent of the *kim li* doctrine:

> With regard to our contemporaries, however, if the judge has good reasons for deciding in accordance with one of them, and he is sure that the other master was wrong, then — in my opinion, and I am fully aware of my limitations — since, according to the law, the judge must be guided by what he perceives, he should not rule against his own better judgment.
>
> And should we wish to claim that the virtues of modesty and humility compel us to say that due to our limitations we cannot be decisive, there is clear evidence to the contrary — judges have the authority to rule on serious matters, on marital and dietary law, so why should they have any qualms at all when the issue at stake is only money?[62]

61 *Responsa Yakhin Uboaz*, 2, #33.

62 *Hikrei Lev*, HM #38.

Yet, in the opinion of those who accept the *kim li* doctrine, the paradox remains, and in their view, at least, in order to resolve it, we must say that ritual law is of less consequence than monetary law. On this understanding of the relationship between ritual and monetary law, the remarks of the Maharik quoted above, despite their vigorous style, are no more than rhetoric aimed at elevating the inferior status of ritual law vis-a-vis monetary law by claiming that ritual law is not subject to the *kim li* plea.

What is the source of this assignment of greater gravity to possible judicial errors in matters of interpersonal dealings? Is it merely an outcome of a certain socio-economic situation? Or does it, perhaps, reflect a 'Calvinistic' notion that the material status of an individual is determined by divine providence and hence human intervention should be undertaken only with caution? The presumption favoring the possessor seems to rest on the conception that human decision-making interferes with the divine order and thus can be justified only if well-grounded.

Another important distinction between the two doctrines is hinted at by their names — '*kim li*' points to the plaintiff's conviction, whereas 'probabilism' highlights a quality of the belief held. In making the *kim li* plea, the defendant is declaring, 'I want to uphold the law according to A, because it is my conviction that the law is indeed in accordance with A's opinion, which happens to support me.' The doctrine would lose its force were the defendant to concede that the opposite opinion was more probable, or more correct, but that he nonetheless wished to follow the less probable opinion for reasons of convenience. To be sure, the defendant need not hold the chosen opinion as a result of thorough deliberation. And his commitment to it is of a temporary nature: regarding a different legal matter, he is entitled to endorse the opposite opinion. The *kim li* plea is a declaration that, for the time being at least, one believes a certain opinion to embody the legal truth. This dimension is absent in the case of probabilism, where, as we saw, the endorsement of an opinion by the defendant need rest only on formal considerations.

*The Jewish Law Annual*, Vol. XIV

# HALAKHIC ALTERNATIVES IN IVF-PREGNANCIES: A SURVEY

YITZCHOK A. BREITOWITZ*



* Yitzchok A. Breitowitz is Associate Professor of Law at the University of Maryland School of Law and Rabbi of the Woodside Synagogue in Silver Spring, Maryland.

## 1 *Introduction*

The advent of assisted reproductive technologies such as in vitro fertilization, egg and sperm donation, and gestational surrogacy offers hope to many infertile couples. But they also present a bewildering array of choices, many of which raise difficult ethical dilemmas. A married couple who participate in an IVF-program, for example, will have a number of options regarding the disposition of fertilized ova: implantation of all or some of the preembryos[1]; destruction or at least non-implantation; experimentation; or donation to an infertile couple

1 "Preembryos" is the term used by the American Fertility Society (now called the American Society for Reproductive Medicine) to describe a fertilized egg not yet implanted in the uterine wall. Where fertilization occurs within a woman's body, implantation generally occurs 0–14 days after fertilization. (In the case of an IVF-frozen embryo, implantation cannot occur until transfer to a uterus, perhaps years later.) Upon implantation, the embryonic stage begins. It lasts for about eight weeks, by which time there is at minimum rudimentary development of differentiated organs. From here on, the organism is termed a "fetus." See American Fertility Society, *Ethical Considerations of Assisted Reproductive Technologies* (Nov. 1994), henceforth ECART, 295–315.

or possibly to an unmarried woman desirous of being a mother. The couple must also grapple with the issue of whether or not to use third-party contributions of sperm, egg, embryo, or even uterus (a gestational surrogate) to enhance their reproductive efforts.

With the possible exception of gestational surrogacy, under the laws of most US states all these options are legitimate, though some are subject to varying degrees of governmental regulation.[2] As a result, the courts have generally validated whatever decisions the parties make — by formal contract or otherwise — and have faced difficulties only when the parties have not come to an agreement and are in a state of deadlock.[3] In an earlier article,[4] I tried to provide a halakhic answer to the problem of deadlock based on the principles of partnership law. It must be noted, however, that in a pure halakhic system the problem of decisional deadlock is less pressing simply because there are far fewer choices that are allowed.

The issue of "who decides" in the context of Anglo-American jurisprudence is indeed a major concern in many fields of medical ethics, from abortion to advance directives for the care of the terminally-ill. It is fair to say that American law is more preoccupied with **who** makes the decision than with **what** the decision should be. This is so because once the legal system identifies the individual entitled to make the decision, his authority is in many cases well-nigh absolute. Thus, the case reports and statutes focus on matters such as informed consent, delegation of surrogate decision-making, hierarchies of persons to consult where no surrogate has been designated, ethics committees, institutional review boards, and procedures in the event of deadlock.

---

The relatively recent introduction of the term "preembryo" has been criticized, as some argue that its usage is a veiled attempt to curtail the protections these potential lives should otherwise enjoy; they insist that once an ovum is fertilized, it is an embryo and should be treated as such. Usage within the medical profession is not consistent, and with respect to preimplantation fertilized ova, both terms are often used interchangeably.

2 See text at nn. 236–238 below.

3 See, e.g., *Davis v. Davis*, 842 S.W. 2d 588 (Tenn. 1992) (recognizing the validity of advance directives of the gamete providers).

4 See Breitowitz, "Halakhic approaches to the resolution of disputes concerning the disposition of preembryos," reprinted in Feldman and Wolowelsky (eds.), *Jewish Law and the New Reproductive Technologies* (NY: 1997) (henceforth JLNRT), 155–186.

The focus on **who** rather than **what**, and the concomitant validation and encouragement of private agreements, are a reflection of the core values of autonomy, privacy, and bodily integrity that underlie much of Anglo-American law, circumscribing the state's authority to interfere with or override the individual's right to choose.

Halakha, a religious system premised on subservience to the Divine will, makes different assumptions. Rather than ask who decides, it focuses directly on what may be decided. It makes little difference who has the right to make dispositional decisions if halakha does not permit a decision to be made. Only if halakha legitimates a given course of action where both parties agree do we face the question of what is to be done where there is a dispute.

The purpose of this article is to address this question of permissible choice; it thus constitutes a "prequel" to my earlier piece. Using a standard IVF protocol as an example, this article, after summarizing the basic halakhic rules governing IVF, will address the following questions: may surplus preembryos be destroyed or allowed to thaw?; may such preembryos be utilized for experimentation and research?; may such preembryos be donated to other infertile couples?; may a Jewish couple utilize donated sperm, egg, or embryos of Jewish or non-Jewish origin in their own IVF protocol?; does halakha allow the use of a gestational surrogate, and if so, under what conditions?; does the halakhic system recognize a right of compensation to the egg and sperm (gamete) providers if preembryos are wrongfully destroyed without their consent?; do preembryos have inheritance rights, and do they "count" for purposes of *yibum, halitza,* and *pidyon haben*? To facilitate comparison to the secular legal system, an Appendix to this article describes the status of the preembryo under American law.

## 2 *General Halakhic Principles Governing a Standard IVF Protocol*

Before proceeding to a discussion of preembryos, it is important to present the rules governing the basic IVF procedure. All IVFs require procurement of semen from the donor or the husband, generally not through marital intercourse. By definition, some form of artificial insemination is necessary. Focusing for now on a "garden variety" IVF with the husband's sperm only, there is a vast halakhic literature on artificial insemination with the husband's sperm (AIH), and virtually all the halakhic concerns about AIH, particularly those involving the methods by which sperm is procured, apply equally to standard in vitro fertilization.[5]

In my earlier article, I noted that "subject to careful supervision of the physician, waiting periods, and exploration of alternatives, AIH is generally regarded as a halakhically permissible procedure through which paternity can be established .... By and large, most *poskim* have assimilated IVF to AIH and have permitted its utilization subject to the same limitations."[6] R. Eliezer Waldenberg and R. Moses Sternbuch are notable exceptions;[7] they deny paternity in IVF-pregnancies and prohibit IVF outright on the grounds of its being *hotzaat zera levatala* (wasteful emission or destruction of male seed).[8] A somewhat intermediate position is taken by R. Judah Gershuni who, although denying paternity, nonetheless permits IVF on the grounds that because it does, or can, result in the birth of a human being, albeit one without a technical

5 See A. Steinberg, "Artificial insemination in the light of halakha," *Sefer Assia* 128–141 (1982) and R. A. Cohen, "Artificial insemination," *Journal of Halakha and Contemporary Society* 43 (1987), 13. These articles also discuss the myriad issues that arise when donor semen (AID) is employed.

6 See Breitowitz, n. 4 above, n. 7, and the sources cited there. Parts of this section are based on that paper.

7 See R. Waldenberg, *Tzitz Eliezer* 15:45. R. Sternbuch's ruling is quoted in *Beshvilei Harefua* 8 (1987), 33.

8 The prohibition against the wasteful emission of male "seed" (*hotzaat zera levatala*) is based on bNida 13a and codified in *Shulhan Arukh* (henceforth *SA*), EH 23:1. See also Genesis 38:7 and Rashi's comments. The prohibition is often referred to as *hashhatat zera* (destruction of seed) and the two phrases are generally regarded as synonymous. But cf. R. Moses Feinstein, *Igrot Moshe* EH 2:70, who attempts to identify a distinct additional prohibition called *niuf beyad* (adultery by the hand).

It should be noted that on their view, IVF is prohibited even if AIH is allowed, as it indeed is, by most decisors. Unlike AIH, where all sperm is deposited into the vagina or uterus, IVF transfers only the fertilized ovum, with the rest of the sperm being discarded. This alone constitutes a waste of "seed." Second, where fertilization occurs outside the woman's body, it is their view that one does not fulfill the commandment of procreation, nor is there a paternal bond with the resulting offspring. As such, IVF serves no halakhically recognized procreative purpose, and thus violates the prohibition against destroying seed. It should further be noted that R. Waldenberg would deny even a **maternal** relationship with an IVF baby even where the egg donor and birth mother are the same person.

There is a variation of IVF termed Gamete Inter-Fallopian Transfer (GIFT), where the egg and the sperm are mixed in a petri dish, then

father, the emission of the seed cannot be characterized as being "in vain" (*levatala*).[9]

In any event, the views of rabbis Waldenberg, Sternbuch, and Gershuni are definitely in the minority. Virtually all contemporary decisors have concluded that a sperm provider has a paternal relationship with IVF-generated offspring; and that the procedure, if undertaken for procreation by an otherwise infertile couple, does not violate the prohibition against destroying seed, at least to the extent AIH in general does not.[10] This article will be premised on this majority position.

It is, however, a matter of dispute whether AIH or IVF may be used where the husband and wife already have a son and daughter.[11] It is also unclear whether the birth of IVF-generated offspring constitutes fulfillment of the Torah commandment of *pru urvu* — "be fruitful and multiply," or just the "lesser" prophetic injunction of *lashevet*.[12]

---

placed in the woman's fallopian tube, where fertilization takes place. See text at nn. 136–140 below. It would be interesting to see how rabbis Waldenberg and Sternbuch (as well as R. Gershuni) would rule in cases of GIFT, since fertilization does take place "in accordance with the natural way" (*kederekh kol haaretz*), although not through marital intercourse. GIFT seems nearly indistinguishable from AIH injected directly into the uterus.

9 *Kol Tsofayikh*, 361–367. Technically, he asserts there can be fulfillment of the commandment of settling (*lashevet*), even with children to whom one has no genealogical connection. See n. 12 below.

10 See, for example, R. Ovadia Yosef, *Tehumin* 1 (1980), 287; R. Avigdor Nebenzal, *Assia* 34 (1983); R. Shmuel Wozner, *Shevet Halevi*, 5:47.

11 The birth of a son and a daughter fulfills the Torah commandment to "be fruitful and multiply." While it is meritorious and perhaps obligatory to attempt to have a larger family, the basic commandment has been fulfilled. As such, there may be less justification for the obtaining of sperm outside marital intercourse, thereby making it "in vain." See Breitowitz, n. 4 above, n. 15; *Nishmat Avraham* EH 23:1 (citing R. S.Z. Auerbach as inclined, though with reservations, to permit sperm testing even where couples have already fulfilled the commandment of procreation). Contra: *Igrot Moshe* EH 4:73 (prohibiting sperm **testing** once the commandment of procreation has been fulfilled; it is not entirely clear how this applies to actual procreative use).

12 *Lashevet* is the shorthand expression for the verse, "He did not create the world to be desolate but rather inhabited" (Isa. 45:18). This is understood as a prophetic exhortation to populate the world that may be binding even on men who have already fulfilled the basic precept of procreation, and even on those not obligated to fulfil it, such as women. It may be

### 3 *May Surplus Preembryos be Destroyed or Discarded?*

The parties may, for various reasons, decide not to implant embryos. These reasons include health concerns of the mother; genetic abnormalities in all or some of the preembryos; the incremental risk to a successful pregnancy of implanting multiple preembryos; and changes in family dynamics (divorce, marital discord, and so on). Does halakha permit either the active destruction of these preembryos, or passive neglect until they disintegrate naturally?

In the early days of IVF, this was a pressing concern: before the discovery of techniques for freezing the preembryos, they could not be stored for future use. Any preembryos not implanted during a particular cycle would be discarded. Because of this, some halakhic authorities

amenable to fulfillment in ways other than those that fulfill the commandment of procreation. See *Tosafot*, bHagiga 2a and bBaba Batra 13a, both s.v. *kofin*; and *Minhat Hinukh*, end of commandment 1.

Whether one fulfills the Torah commandment of procreation, or only the lesser prophetic exhortation of *lashevet*, through either AIH or IVF, appears to remain unresolved. R. Auerbach in *Noam* 1 (1958), states that the matter is unclear. R. Jacob Ettlinger in *Arukh Laner* on bJebamot 10a explicitly rules that one does not fulfill the commandment of procreation in the absence of a sexual act. But see *Minhat Hinukh*, commandment 1, noting that the commandment of procreation is not marital intercourse per se, but the actual having of children; the act which generates those children is nothing more than *hekhsher mitzva* (a necessary preliminary). On this analysis, it would seem that whether children are created through intercourse, AIH, or IVF is irrelevant to fulfillment of the commandment.

It should also be noted that the opinions that permit AIH or IVF only to those who do not yet have a son and daughter obviously presuppose that procreation via these procedures does fulfill the commandment of procreation, *pru urvu*. If the most that could be accomplished through AIH or IVF was fulfillment of *lashevet*, there would be no difference between those with two children and those with none.

Finally, there can be a possibility of fulfilling *pru urvu* only if the sperm provider has a paternal bond to the offspring. On the view of rabbis Waldenberg, Sternbuch, and Gershuni that sperm contributors do not have paternity in IVF cases, it is clear that the commandment of procreation cannot be fulfilled, though R. Gershuni would maintain that the *lashevet* commandment is fulfilled.

permitted IVF only if all fertilized eggs were implanted.[13] Since, however, the implantation of multiple preembryos could jeopardize the prospects of a successful pregnancy, this meant that only a few eggs could be extracted, generally no more than four. This in turn reduced the probability of successful fertilization, necessitating repeated IVF attempts. Since insurance plans did not, as a rule, cover IVF after two or three failed attempts, IVF was not very feasible for observant Jews.

Two developments have lessened these concerns. The development of cryopreservation (embryo freezing) allows fertilized ova to be stored for future use.[14] Second, use of specialized ova penetration techniques, such as intracytoplasmic sperm injection (ICSI), greatly increases the probability of fertilization, even with a small number of eggs.[15] Yet though the said concerns are less pressing, the problem of determining the disposition of preembryos remains: must a fertilized egg be implanted in an attempt to achieve a pregnancy?

### a Abortion

The destruction of embryonic or fetal life falls within the halakhic strictures against abortion. The basic guidelines concerning abortion have been detailed in a number of places and need not be covered in depth here.[16] Briefly, they are as follows:

1. The killing of a fetus is not a capital crime, at least for a Jew.[17]
2. Notwithstanding (1), most halakhic authorities regard the killing of a fetus as a violation of Torah law. A small minority views the prohibition as purely Rabbinic.[18]

13 See R. J. David Bleich, *Judaism and Healing* (NY: 1981), 90 (suggesting this as a possibility).

14 See ECART, n. 1 above, 54S–59S.

15 See Van Steirteghem et al., "High fertilization and implantation rates after intracytoplasmic sperm injection," *Human Reproduction* 8 (1993), 1061 and ECART, n. 1 above, 61S.

16 The most complete English-language study of the halakhic aspects of abortion is R. J.D. Bleich, "Abortion in the halakhic literature," in Bleich (ed.), *Contemporary Halakhic Problems*, vol. 1 (NY: 1977), 325. See also *Nishmat Avraham*, HM 425.

17 Mekhilta, Exodus 21:12; bSanhedrin 84a.

18 An isolated reference in *Tosafot*, bNida 44a s.v. *ihu*, seems to suggest that the killing of a fetus may be permitted even Rabbinically, but most

3. Feticide is committed not only by the physician performing the procedure, but also by the woman who hires him and undergoes the operation. At minimum, making oneself available for an abortion violates the prohibition against aiding and abetting a transgression (*lifnei iver*), whether the physician is Jewish or not.[19]
4. The source of the Torah prohibition is controversial. Some view abortion as a form of murder (*retziha*), albeit one that does not carry the death penalty, akin to the killing of a *treifa*, where the prohibition against murder is transgressed, though the corresponding punishment is not incurred.[20] Others see it as falling

---

commentators have concluded that it is either a scribal error, or should not be taken literally. See, e.g., the comments of R. Jacob Emden; *Igrot Moshe*, HM 2:69. See also *Ahiezer* 3:65 (14); *Beit Shlomo*, HM 132.

19 It is not entirely clear who the transgressor is — the physician who actually kills the embryo or fetus, or the woman (and perhaps the husband) who requests the service and, (in the case of the woman), makes herself physically available for the operation. If the former, the woman violates only the prohibition against causing another to transgress: "Thou shalt not put a stumbling block before the blind" (*lifnei iver lo titen mikhshol*) (Lev. 19:14), which is equally applicable to causing non-Jews to violate the Noahide laws; if the latter, the woman is a direct and primary transgressor, not merely an aider and abetter in someone else's sin. The resolution of this question may depend on how the prohibition against feticide is conceptualized. Deeming the woman a direct violator is logical if the reason abortion is proscribed is the affirmative obligation of saving lives (*hatzala*) — facilitating fetal destruction is as inconsistent with this duty as is actual destruction. This may also follow if abortion is conceived as non-capital murder, since, as Maimonides rules, one who hires a murderer is, at least in the eyes of Heaven, guilty of murder; see *Code*, Laws concerning Murder 2:1. On the other hand, it is difficult to regard the woman as a primary offender if the offense is defined as destruction of seed, since merely **allowing** seed to be destroyed does not appear to be an act of destruction. (And many maintain that a woman is generally not subject to the destruction of seed prohibition.) The same conclusion follows if abortion is prohibited as a form of wounding (*havala*), since the woman is not the "wounder."

It must be reiterated, however, that even if an woman is not a primary violator, she is prohibited from obtaining an abortion from either a Jewish or non-Jewish physician because of the prohibition against causing another to transgress.

20 See R. Meir Simcha Hakohen, *Meshekh Hokhma*, Exodus 35:2; *Igrot Moshe*, HM 2:71.

under the destruction of seed prohibition, in that it wastefully destroys that which could have blossomed into life.[21] A third view sees abortion as an unjustified act of wounding (*havala*), violating the prohibition of Deuteronomy 25:3.[22] Some who hold this view regard the wounding as wounding of the mother, others, as wounding of the fetus.[23] Another opinion prohibits abortion as inconsistent with the obligation to protect and preserve life and well-being, an obligation derived from the prohibition against standing idly by the blood of one's neighbor (Lev. 19:16), or the obligation to return lost articles (*hashavat aveida*), which includes 'returning a lost person' (*hashavat gufo*).[24]

5. The halakhic rationale for the prohibition will determine which, if any, extenuating circumstances suffice to justify its violation. If, for instance, the prohibition against abortion is based on its being construed as murder, abortion can be sanctioned only if the fetus qualifies as a "pursuer" (*rodef*)[25]; general considerations of mortal danger (*pikuah nefesh*) would not suffice. On the other hand, the prohibition against wounding may be set aside by lesser concerns, perhaps maternal health in general, or even psychological well-being. The injunctions pertaining to the destruction of seed and the saving of life can arguably be set aside in a case of mortal danger, even where the fetus does not qualify as a "pursuer," but nothing short of mortal danger will suffice.[26]
6. The foregoing refers to abortions performed by Jews (on Jewish or non-Jewish fetuses).[27] Abortion performed by

21 R. Yair Haim Bakharakh, *Havot Yair*, #31. See also n. 8 above.

22 R. Joseph Trani, *Responsa Maharit* 1, #97, #99. Cf. *Sridei Eish* 3:127 (who understands Maharit to refer to wounding of the fetus) and R. A. Lifschutz, *Aryei Devei Ilai*, YD:14 (who sees it as wounding of the mother).

23 See Abraham, *Nishmat Avraham*, HM 425.

24 See bSanhedrin 73a; Maimonides, *Commentary on the Mishnah*, Nedarim 4:4.

25 See the discussion in Bleich, n. 16 above, 337–339.

26 See ibid., 354–361.

27 A Jew is not permitted to perform an abortion on a non-Jew, but the reason is uncertain. If Jews are prohibited to perform abortions because feticide is regarded as a kind of murder, albeit non-capital, then just as a Jew is not permitted to murder a non-Jew, he is not permitted to abort a non-Jewish fetus. If, however, the abortion prohibition is grounded in the prohibition against the destruction of seed, the prohibition against wounding the child or mother, or the obligation to sustain life, none of which are obligations due non-Jews, why is it not permissible for a Jew to perform

non-Jews (whether on Jewish or non-Jewish fetuses) is a capital offense under the seven Noahide laws.[28] There is considerable debate over whether Noahides may perform abortions even where there is mortal danger to the mother, or the fetus qualifies as a "pursuer," and many authorities take a strict position.[29]

---

an abortion on a non-Jew? The answer is that the Jew would be transgressing the injunction against causing another to transgress. If the woman herself would be committing the equivalent of an act of murder (indeed, in the case of a Noahide, capital murder), it would be prohibited for the Jewish doctor to facilitate such a transgression. Even if there are other doctors willing to perform the abortion if he declines to do so, his assistance is prohibited, because these others are themselves subject to the same proscription. (See R. Judah Rosanes, *Mishne Lamelekh,* Laws concerning Creditor and Debtor 4:2, who asserts that the existence of alternative facilitators obviates the prohibition against causing another to transgress only where such facilitators are **allowed** to extend assistance.)

Thus, if abortion is viewed as murder, the Jewish physician performing it on a non-Jew is the primary transgressor; if it is not viewed as murder, the physician is aiding and abetting a transgression of Noahide law committed by **the patient.** (This is so, however, only if the woman seeking the abortion can be characterized as the primary offender, see nn. 19 and 30).

28 bSanhedrin 57b, based on Genesis 9:6.

29 *Tosafot,* bSanhedrin 59a, remain in doubt as to whether the Noahide prohibition against feticide may be set aside where there is danger to the mother's life. R. Moses Feinstein rules that because of this doubt, the non-Jewish doctor should not perform the abortion, *Igrot Moshe,* HM 2:69. Indeed, decisors have indicated that even if the endangered patient is Jewish, it is preferable for a Jewish physician to perform the procedure. See *Nishmat Avraham,* HM 420:1(22).

At first glance, the uncertainty of the *Tosafot* appears problematic. Because Noahides are not obligated to observe the commandment of santification of the Divine name (*kidush hashem*), the Talmud in bSanhedrin 74b concludes that a Noahide need never submit to martyrdom, and may even violate the prohibition against idolatry if facing mortal danger. Why then should not the prohibition against abortion be waived to save the mother's life?

Three distinct explanations have been suggested. (1) Although mortal danger indeed serves to waive observance for Noahides, a Noahide may transgress the law only to preserve his own life, not that of another. See *Minhat Hinukh,* 296. Thus, mortal danger to the **mother** does not provide the **physician** with a dispensation to abort the fetus. (2) Although a Noahide may violate Noahide law if someone threatens to kill him if he does not do so, he may not violate Noahide law to extricate himself from

It is not entirely clear if this stringency should apply to a Jewish physician.[30]

### b Abortion Prior to 40 Days

The Talmud states in several places that fetal development prior to the 40th day is "mere water." Thus, a miscarriage within 40 days carries no

---

a life-threatening **illness**, since one's response to illness is an autonomous choice, as opposed to having a third party's will forced upon one. See *Minhat Hinukh*, 296; Maimonides, *Code*, Laws concerning the Fundamental Principles of the Torah 5; R. Meir Simcha Hakohen, *Or Sameiah* ad loc. (3) Although Noahides may, where there is mortal danger, violate any of their commandments, including the prohibitions against idolatry and sexual offenses, they may not violate the prohibition against murder. Since for Noahides abortion is equivalent to murder, and one soul cannot be set aside to save another, the procedure cannot be allowed even to preserve the mother's life (unlike the situation for Jews, for whom the fetus either lacks full personhood, or is deemed a "pursuer.") A good summary of these explanations appears in Bleich, "Fetal tissue research: Jewish tradition and public policy," *Tradition* 24 (1989), 87–88, n. 47.

In effect, therefore, a Noahide physician is prohibited from performing an abortion even to save the life of the mother, whether she is Jewish or non-Jewish. Paradoxically, however, from the perspective of the Jewish patient who indeed has a dispensation to abort due to mortal danger, the only possible transgression is the injunction, "Thou shalt not put a stumbling block" (*lifnei iver*), a "lesser prohibition" that is unequivocally waived to preserve her life. This leads to the anomalous result that while a Jewish woman is permitted to request and encourage a non-Jew (as well as a Jew) to abort her life-threatening pregnancy, the non-Jew — from the perspective of Noahide law — should decline to do so.

30 While it is clear in light of *Tosafot*'s uncertainly that a non-Jew should not perform a life-saving abortion on either a Jewish or a non-Jewish patient, an interesting question not addressed by R. Feinstein is whether a Jewish physician can perform an abortion on a non-Jewish patient whose life is in danger. This may depend on whether the Jewish physician is a primary offender or the aider and abetter of the Noahide; see n. 19 above. If the Jewish physician is a primary offender, because abortion constitutes non-capital murder, under no circumstances could a Jew perform an abortion on a non-Jew, since there is no obligation to save the patient's life that would override the prohibition against homicide. If, on the other hand, the sole reason a Jew cannot abort a non-Jewish fetus is because he would facilitate a transgression on the part of the woman, and hence would

impurity of childbirth, nor does it necessitate the bringing of an offering.[31] A widowed daughter of a priest (*kohen*) who was married to a *yisrael* is allowed to eat the heave offering in her father's house for 40 days after her husband's death, because even if she is pregnant, the embryo does not disqualify her.[32] Based on these teachings, some decisors have concluded there is no prohibition against abortion within 40 days of conception.[33]

To the extent that it is absolutely permissible to abort an under 40-day old embryo, there would obviously be a dispensation to destroy or discard a preembryo (regardless of how many days may have passed from fertilization), since its development has certainly not reached the 40-day point. However, the 40-day limit is highly controversial. The argument that an embryo of under 40 days is "mere water" is relevant to the abortion issue only if abortion is predicated either on its being **murder**, that is, the taking of life, or on its being wounding (*havala*) of the embryo — arguably, one cannot "wound" that which does not have the status of an existent person. The 40-day cut-off is clearly irrelevant insofar as wounding of the mother is concerned (though by definition this could not be a basis for prohibiting the destruction of an externalized preembryo). "Destruction of seed" is equally irrelevant — after all, it is prohibited even prior to fertilization.

Moreover, the obligation to preserve and protect life may well apply at all stages of embryonic development. There is a disagreement among the *rishonim* as to whether one is permitted to desecrate the Sabbath or otherwise violate the law to save or prolong the life of

---

violate the prohibition against causing another to transgress, then if the woman is permitted to seek the abortion, the Jew would be allowed to supply it. Of the three explanations cited in n. 29, the first explanation would allow the endangered Noahide to seek the abortion; the second and third explanations would not. This would have direct bearing on whether the Jewish physician could perform the procedure at the patient's request.

31 bNida 30a.

32 bJebamot 69b.

33 See *Beit Shlomo*, HM 132; *Torat Hesed*, EH 42 (33); *Sridei Esh*, 3:127. See also *Ahiezer* 3, end of 65 ("perhaps" there is no Torah prohibition). A stricter view is taken by R. I.J. Unterman, *Shevet Miyehuda* 1:9, and R. Moses Feinstein, *Igrot Moshe* HM 2:69.

a fetus where the mother's life is not endangered.[34] According to some authorities, the "he shall live by them" (*vehai bahem*) (Lev. 18:5) dispensation applies only to those who have been born, and not to fetuses. The *Baal Halakhot Gedolot* seems to concede that the verse does not cover a fetus, but maintains that the potential for life and future observance of the commandments brings into play the principle that "it is better that one Sabbath be violated, so that many Sabbaths may be kept." The Behag apparently utilizes this concept as a justification for *pikuah nefesh* that is independent of the verse "he shall live by them." Nahmanides makes clear that according to the Behag, no distinction should be drawn between the pre- and post-40-day point. It is the **potential** for human life, not its actualization, that justifies the "mortal danger" dispensation to violate the law.

The law is in accordance with the view of the Behag.[35] Moreover, even on the view of those who disagree with it, it might still be argued that the obligations to save life and restore lost property obtain even with respect to a fetus, and even before the 40-day point, but do not fall within the parameters of *pikuah nefesh* when such obligations conflict with other prohibitions, such as the Sabbath prohibitions. In the absence of conflict, all might concede the duty to save life. Be that as it may, according to the Behag, one can clearly violate the Sabbath prohibitions for a fetus under 40 days old. Now it would be incongruous to permit — and apparently mandate — violation of the Sabbath to save a life that one is permitted to extinguish. Thus, the permissibility of desecrating the Sabbath to preserve such life should entail a prohibition against taking it away.[36] Note, however, that the converse is not necessarily true: the impermissibility of desecrating the Sabbath does not automatically imply that active termination is permitted.

34 See Nahmanides, bYoma 82a and *Torat Haadam* (Shaar Hasakana); *Noda Biyehuda* 2, HM 59.

35 See *Shmirat Shabat Kehilkhata* 36:2, but see Noda Biyehuda 1, HM 59; *Magen Avraham*, 330:15.

36 Indeed, *Havot Yair*, #31, utilizes this very point to prove that abortion prior to 40 days is prohibited. This argument is rejected by *Sridei Esh*, who argues that **even according to the Behag** abortion within 40 days may be permissible. The dispensation to desecrate the Sabbath to save a life does not, in his judgment, automatically entail a prohibition against terminating it. As noted by R. Weinberg himself, however, his assertion is contradicted by *Havot Yair*. See R. Bleich, n. 16 above, 340, n. 31.

Conceding, however, that abortion within 40 days is not murder or wounding of the fetus, does permit consideration of factors and mitigating circumstances that would otherwise be ignored. Thus, genetic defects or medical reasons falling short of "pursuit" or mortal danger, may, according to some views, justify abortion.[37]

### c Abortion Prior to 40 Days under Noahide Law

The source of the Noahide ban on abortion is the verse "Whoso sheddeth man's blood, by man shall his blood be shed" (Gen. 9:6), which is interpreted as, "He who sheds the blood of a person within a person, his blood will be shed." As the Talmud points out, "person within a person" aptly describes a fetus.[38] Since, however, the Noahide prohibition refers to a "person," and an embryo of less than 40 days does not have the status of "personhood," some decisors have concluded that there is no Noahide ban on feticide before 40 days,[39] Noahides being enjoined only against the taking of actual life (even fetal), not potential life. The latter is proscribed only by dint of the "destruction of seed," procreation, wounding (of the mother) or "desecrate one Sabbath so that many other Sabbaths may be kept" injunctions, none of which non-Jews are obligated to observe.

This gives rise to two questions. Can a Jew perform an abortion on a Noahide if the embryo is less than 40 days old? Assuming the stringent view that Jewish law prohibits abortion even before 40 days, can a Jewish woman procure such an abortion from a non-Jewish physician? The answer to the first question appears to be in the affirmative. While a Jew may not take the life of a non-Jew, there is no positive duty to protect potential life. Nor is there the problem of causing another to transgress in aiding the woman to obtain the abortion, since the non-Jew herself is not subject to the affirmative commandment of saving life (*hatzala*). Thus, though a Jewish physician could normally not abort the fetus of a non-Jew, he is permitted to abort an under 40-day old Noahide fetus even according to the authorities who prohibit such an abortion for a Jew.[40]

37 See, e.g., *Tzitz Eliezer*, 9:51(3).
38 bSanhedrin 57b.
39 R. I.J. Unterman, *Shevet Miyehuda*, 1:9.
40 For reasons that are not clear to me, R. Bleich, n. 16 above, 343, limits this dispensation to "giving advice or rendering indirect assistance."

The answer to the second question, however, is negative. Given that the abortion prohibition applies not only to the physician performing the procedure, but also the woman who makes herself available for the operation and hires the physician, her obligation to preserve even potential life would preclude her utilizing a non-Jewish physician for this purpose.[41] Thus whatever leniencies may exist under Noahide law for the termination of a less than 40-day old pregnancy do not extend to a Jewish woman enlisting the assistance of non-Jews. (At the very least, this would also be prohibited Rabbinically under the rubric of *amira leakum*,[42] but in all probability would be a direct violation of the prohibition against standing idly by the blood of one's neighbor, or the obligation to return lost articles, certainly on the view of the Behag, and possibility even on the dissenting view.)

### d Preembryo Disposition

Most contemporary decisors who have considered the issue allow the destruction, or at least passive discarding of, unwanted embryos, ruling that the strictures against abortion are inapplicable.[43] A number of rationales for this ruling have been offered:

1. As noted, some opinions permit aborting a less than 40-day old embryo because its status is that of "mere water." The preembryo's physiological development is far less advanced.

41 The statement in the text is premised on R. Unterman's analysis that the prohibition of abortion on an under 40-day embryo is not a matter of proscribing murder, but rather, it proscribes violation of the affirmative duty to protect and preserve even future life. Hence, it is clear that the woman is a **primary** offender and not merely an aider and abetter of the physician.

42 This refers to the general principle that a Jew may not ask a Gentile to do something for him that the Jew cannot do himself. This applies even where the activity is not prohibited to the Gentile, and is therefore to be distinguished from *lifnei iver*. This principle is not limited to the laws of the Sabbath; see *SA* YD 297:4, and *Shakh* ad loc.

43 See R. Mordechai Eliyahu, "Discarding fertilized eggs and fetal reduction," *Tehumin* 11 (1991); R. Chaim David Halevi, "On fetal reduction," *Assia* 12 (1990), 47–48; R. Moses Sternbuch, *Beshvilei Harefua* 8 (1987), 29; R. Ezra Bick, "Ovum donations: a rabbinic conceptual model of maternity," reprinted in JLNRT, n. 4 above, 83, 93.

2. The prohibitions against abortion, even if applicable to less than 40-day old embryos, apply only to procedures destroying life already implanted within the womb, and not to living cells **in vitro**. Since the cells are not in an environment in which they can achieve human viability, they are not considered a potential person (*nefesh*) entitled to protection.
3. Regardless of the 40-day rule, until implantation within the body of a human being, no human life can be said to exist even *in potentia*.[44]
4. Since the preembryo is microscopic, that is, invisible to the unaided human eye, the Torah does not invest its existence with any significance, just as microscopic insects are not deemed "creeping things" (*shratzim*).
5. At least where implantation of all preembryos poses a pregnancy risk to the successful development of any one of them, the law permits selective implantation; indeed, even actual reduction of fetuses already in utero may be permissible.[45]

Examining the inner logic of these rationales, it appears that only the first is conceptually unassailable. Clearly, if one may abort embryos in the womb that are under 40 days old, one may do the same to an externalized preembryo whose development is far below the 40-day point. The fifth argument, however, is essentially a non sequitur. While it is true that halakha would undoubtedly permit selective implantation to maximize the chances of a successful pregnancy, it is hard to see how nonimplantation would justify preembryo destruction, particularly in view of the possibility of cryopreservation for later use. Arguments (2), (3) and (4) all focus on the preembryo's attenuated

44 This differs from rationale (2). On (2), the laws governing abortion are inapplicable here because the externalized preembryo is not in an environment in which its life potential can be brought to fruition. In the event technology ever devises a self-sufficient artificial womb, a halakhic dispensation based on nonviability would lose its force. By contrast, on (3), any human cells that have not undergone uterine implantation do not qualify as human life, regardless of how far along their development is. Indeed, were a child "hatched" in an incubator, it might not be human at all. See Bick, n. 43 above, 92–93.

45 See generally, Grazi and Wolowelsky, "Multifetal pregnancy reduction and disposal of untransplanted embryos in contemporary Jewish law and ethics," *American Journal of Obstetrics and Gynecology* 165 (1991), 1268–1271.

humanity or lack of personhood as a basis for permitting its destruction, even where destruction of under 40-day old implanted embryos is prohibited. But even conceding the relevance of these arguments to the definition of "personhood," the conclusion that destruction is permitted does not necessarily follow.

If indeed one accepts the rule that abortions are prohibited where the pregnancy is under 40 days, but nevertheless attempts to distinguish the preembryo from the implanted early embryo, the distinction might be difficult to defend. Ultimately, the validity of the distinction depends on why abortions are prohibited in the first place. Because a preembryo is outside a woman's body, wounding (*havala*) of the mother is obviously not an issue. Nor is murder (*retziha*) at issue, since the preembryo, not being in an environment in which it can be brought to term and live, arguably does not have the status of a living being, even on the view of those who might accord such status to an under-40-day old (implanted) embryo. Nor is it likely that destruction of a preembryo could be regarded as a wounding of the preembryo, since no existent living being is being "wounded."

It must be remembered, however, that there are two additional halakhic grounds adduced for the prohibition of abortion. To the extent that abortion restrictions rest on "destruction of seed" considerations, these concerns should apply equally to the preembryo. The preembryo's lack of "present" humanity should be irrelevant, since even sperm, which is not "human" at all, cannot be destroyed.

Thus, at least on the reasoning of *Havot Yair*, there would be no justification for the indiscriminate destruction of preembryos. As noted, however, many authorities do refuse to equate abortion of any embryo or fetus with the sin of "destruction of seed," arguing that the latter occurs only at the time of seminal emission, and not after an ovum has been fertilized. They nonetheless maintain that early abortion is prohibited, not because it is the termination or wounding of an existing life, but because it constitutes failure to protect and preserve **future** life — not life that is, but life that could be, if not interfered with. If indeed there is a duty to protect the future potential of life, it is not at all clear why the present "diminished humanity" of the preembryo should be a mitigating factor.

I have already noted the view of the Behag and the argument of *Havot Yair* that whenever there is a dispensation to desecrate the Sabbath, there is a duty to sustain life and a corresponding prohibition not to diminish it. The fundamental question would therefore be: is there in fact a religious obligation to preserve the life of a preembryo? If there is, that alone would prohibit its destruction and indeed, compel its implantation. Do the directives of "not standing idly by the blood of your neighbor," returning lost objects, and "it is better that one Sabbath be transgressed, so that many Sabbaths may be kept" apply to the externalized preembryo? While it may be true that the preembryo lacks some of the elements of personhood, recall that the Behag permitted Sabbath desecration for the pre-40 day embryo not on the grounds of its **present** personhood, but on the grounds of its **future** potential. Should not the identical standard apply to the preembryo, regardless of its present status?

In a recent responsum, R. Samuel Wozner of Bnei Brak ruled that even according to the Behag, one may not desecrate the Sabbath on behalf of a preembryo.[46] Since justified Sabbath desecration is based not on the presence of **actual** human life, but on the potential for it, where such potential is very remote or improbable (as it is here, given the present percentage of IVF pregnancies brought to term), there is no dispensation to desecrate the Sabbath or otherwise transgress. If we take this ruling to mean that there are no duties that mandate sustaining preembryo life, surplus embryos may indeed be discarded with impunity. If, however, as is more likely, R. Wozner's ruling is limited to cases where there are conflicts with other prohibitions, but in the absence of such conflict, there would indeed be an obligation to protect potential life, the unlimited right to discard unwanted preembryos cannot be assumed.[47]

46 *Shevet Halevi,* 5:47.

47 Two peripheral points that may seem to warrant leniency should be rejected. First, the fact that the preembryos are likely to be destroyed by a non-Jew would not in and of itself justify the procedure. Even if the non-Jew is free of transgression, as R. Unterman argued, the Jewish parents who authorize the embryo destruction are considered to be primary violators of their halakhic obligation to protect and sustain even potential life (on the view that a Jew may not abort an under 40-day old embryo). From the perspective of the "do not stand idly" injunction, there is no distinction between commission and omission. Moreover, should we view the prohibition against a Jew's aborting an under 40-day old embryo as based on recognition of the embryo's **actual** life rather than its **potential** to **become** life, in which case it is a form of noncapital murder, Maimonides makes clear that at least insofar as Heavenly judgment is concerned, hiring the murderer (even if for him — the Noahide — it is not murder) renders the hirer culpable. See *Code,* Laws concerning Murder 2:1.

I would suggest, however, an alternative basis for leniency. It must be kept in mind that what is involved in preembryo disposition is not necessarily active destruction, but simply allowing them to thaw out or disintegrate in storage. Thus, we are not dealing with active homicide (*retziha beyadaim*), but with omitting to act (*shev veal taase*) to save life. Moreover, given that the preembryo is "mere water" (*mayim bealma*), even active destruction would at worst violate only the duty to protect potential life, and would under no circumstances constitute murder.[48] Certainly, from the perspective of the couple, they are at worst authorizing the cessation of actions that would culminate in embryo transfer and implantation.

Assuming that in the abstract there is an obligation to sustain life based on "do not stand idly," "rescuing a lost person" (*hashavat gufo*); and "it is better that one Sabbath be transgressed" — at what cost? The halakha is very clear that one need not endanger one's life to preserve or protect even the existing life of another.[49] While it is permitted and

---

A second argument for leniency might be that, in many cases, the preembryos will not be physically destroyed, but thawed out or left in storage, which will cause their inevitable spoilage and deterioration. Death will occur only via *gerama* (indirect causation). This too should not make a difference. Whether destruction is active and direct or merely indirect and gradual, it still constitutes failure to affirmatively preserve life. The gravamen of "do not stand idly" is not **how** the death occurs, but the fact that no steps were taken to prevent it. Moreover, even if the abortion prohibition is based on the prohibition against murder, Maimonides rules that indirect homicide violates the prohibition against murder though the perpetrator is not subject to capital punishment, see ibid.

48 This follows R. Unterman's analysis that pre-40 day abortions are proscribed because they constitute failure to preserve potential life, and not because they constitute murder.

49 The *Beit Yosef*, HM 426, quotes the Jerusalem Talmud as stating that one is obliged to expose oneself to **possible** danger to extricate another from **certain** danger. This rule is not quoted by either the *SA* or Rema. According to *Sema* and *Pithei Teshuva*, the Babylonian Talmud disputes the Jerusalem Talmud's premise, and the law is in accordance with the former. See also *Teshuvot Radbaz*, #627, who states that it is forbidden to endanger oneself to save another, and one who does exhibits "foolish piety." Others permit (but do not require) self-endangerment if the person to be rescued is a scholar or otherwise worthy personage, but prohibit such endangerment if the rescuer is more learned still (*Pithei Teshuva*, YD 252:1 in name of *Responsa Yad Eliyahu*, #43). In practice, altruistic

perhaps encouraged, there is no duty. It is also clear that the process of childbirth is a life-threatening condition that justifies Sabbath desecration.[50] Thus, a woman should not be halakhically compelled to receive a fertilized ovum in order to possibly preserve its life, because in that process she would be endangering her own.[51] Accordingly, fertilized eggs do not have to be implanted.[52]

Admittedly, this argument might prove too much. After all, it is clear that a healthy woman may not abort a viable pregnancy merely because childbirth per se is life-threatening. Because it is normal, common and natural, and the risk of danger is ordinarily low, the life of the fetus must be respected. Moreover, though a woman is technically not obligated to fulfil the precept of procreation, she certainly could not insist on contraception or abstinence on the grounds that pregnancy per se is a dangerous condition. The obligations and responsibilities of the marital bond, including sexual relations (*ona*), populating the world (*lashevet yetzara*), and the duty to facilitate the husband's obligation to procreate cumulatively neutralize the element of danger, which is in any event remote. However, where the prospect of rescue is in itself very remote, even remote dangers may justify inaction. Insofar as sexual relations and populating the world are concerned, these obligations do not require consent to an IVF procedure, nor would the wife be required to complete the procedure once begun.[53] (*Ona* can also be waived by mutual consent.)[54] In the absence of countervailing

volunteering is permitted, but not obligatory, regardless of the rescuer's status. See *Igrot Moshe*, YD 2, 174:4 re kidney transplants, and *Arukh Hashulhan*, HM 421:4, who cautions that one should not be overly solicitous of one's own safety and thus decline to render assistance. See *Nishmat Avraham*, YD 156:4 and 252:1.

50 See *SA* OH 330:1.

51 See *Meshekh Hokhma* on Genesis 9:7, who offers this as an explanation of why women are exempt from the "be fruitful and multiply" commandment.

52 Even according to the Jerusalem Talmud, it is possible that there is no obligation to put oneself in danger here, for the obligation might be imposed only if it is fairly certain that the rescue will succeed. In view of the small percentage of implanted IVF embryos that are brought to term, the prospects of rescue are at best doubtful. See *Kesef Mishne*, Laws concerning Murder 1:14.

53 See *Nishmat Avraham* 5, EH 1 (App.).

54 See generally *SA* OH 240.

concerns, therefore, the woman's claim of danger, at least in the context of preembryo implantation, should be given credence.

The conclusions that emerge from this analysis are the following:

1. All extracted eggs that are fertilized should, optimally, be implanted.
2. The wife has the right to refuse implantation on the grounds that all pregnancies present some danger (*sakana*).
3. If the wife is willing, the husband has no right to abort the process.
4. Since preembryos are at best potential life and not actual life, to the extent there is no duty to sustain them because of danger to the mother, they can be actively destroyed. "Passive v. active" is an immaterial distinction when we are only considering an unrealized potential.[55]
5. Although the danger to the woman could be averted by donation of the preembryo to an infertile woman willing to assume the risks, the halakhic problems of such donation rule it out as an acceptable alternative.[56]

### e Propriety of Initiating the Procedure

One question remains: given that a woman has the right to refuse the receipt of fertilized eggs, on the grounds that it poses a danger, is it proper to perform or authorize an IVF procedure that may result in more preembryos than the woman is willing to receive either now or later? Must the IVF protocol be structured so that only a very limited number of eggs are retrieved, to guarantee that all fertilized eggs will be "rescued"? Freezing for later implantation minimizes the problem, but does not eliminate it. If, for example, twenty eggs are retrieved and six fertilized, a woman may be unwilling to have all the embryos implanted even over a period of several years.

55 One difficult question may be, what if the woman's desire not to implant is not due to "danger," but some unrelated reason, for example, preimplantation genetic testing that revealed a defect, or because the woman was divorced from her husband? Whatever her reason for not wanting the procedure, halakha gives her the right to decline it.

56 See the discussion in sec. 6 below.

This question can be connected to a well-known dispute between Nahmanides and R. Zerahiah Halevi (Baal Hamaor).[57] In talmudic times, babies needed warm water after circumcision. If the circumcision was taking place on the Sabbath, the water had to be prepared before the Sabbath, because it is only a *makhshir mila* — something necessary for but not part of the circumcision ceremony. If the water was spilled after the circumcision, it is clear that more water could be boiled, due to the threat of mortal danger. But what if the water spilled before the circumcision? Is one allowed to perform the circumcision knowing that a dangerous situation will thereby be generated, necessitating desecration of the Sabbath, or is it preferable to defer the circumcision until the next day? Baal Hamaor rules that it should be postponed, while Nahmanides rules that the commandment should be carried out even with the knowledge that a situation of mortal danger will be generated.[58] While this dispute is not explicitly addressed in the *Shulhan Arukh*, the halakhic consensus follows Baal Hamaor: the circumcision must be deferred.[59]

If we can extrapolate from the Sabbath to other areas, the governing principle appears to be that one is not allowed to engage in conduct that is permissible in and of itself with the knowledge that a situation of mortal danger necessitating transgression will thereby be engendered. Applying this to the disposal of surplus embryos, while the in vitro fertilization may be halakhically permissible in and of itself — removal of eggs is not problematic, and the emission of sperm was for procreative purposes and not "in vain" — it would be halakhically improper to utilize the procedure in such a manner that there are likely to be surplus fertilized eggs that will then have to be discarded. Even if halakha permits those eggs to be discarded once they are generated (because of considerations of maternal health and mortal danger), it would be improper to bring about a life-threatening situation that will necessitate what would in other circumstances be a halakhic violation. In effect, therefore, unless the mother is willing to have fertilized ova

57 See *Sefer Hamaor* on Alfasi, bShabat 53a (standard Vilna edition). Nahmanides' view is cited by R. Nissim Gerondi.

58 For a full discussion, see R.M. Pirutinsky, *Sefer Habrit*, 266:6.

59 See *Mishna Brura*, 331:24, citing this as the position of "most *aharonim*"; if the circumcision does take place, however, one is certainly obligated to desecrate the Sabbath to extricate the child from danger.

cryopreserved for future use, extraction would have to be limited to the number of eggs that the mother is able and willing to have implanted.

The analogy to circumcision on the Sabbath may not be exact. Circumcising on the Sabbath in the absence of warm water will **inevitably** necessitate desecration of the Sabbath due to the threat of mortal danger, but the extraction of multiple eggs will not necessarily result in transgression. Presumably, even according to the Behag, the obligations of rescue, "do not stand idly," restoring lost objects, and so on, come into effect only upon fertilization. It may be that out of eight, ten, or even twelve eggs, only one or two, if any, will be fertilized. It is **possible**, of course, that multiple fertilizations will occur, thereby necessitating their disposal, but since this is only a possibility, not a certainty, the parties are permitted and indeed encouraged to proceed in any way that will enhance the efficacy of the procedure, regardless of what consequences **might** ensue.

This conclusion, which distinguishes between certainty and possibility, finds support in another law concerning circumcision on the Sabbath. The Rabbis of the Talmud had a tradition that for the first three days following circumcision (according to some, only the third day) the baby's health may be especially precarious, permitting violation of the Sabbath due to mortal danger. Some decisors have concluded that it is improper to perform a circumcision on Thursday or Friday (unless it is the eighth day), since this may necessitate desecration of the Sabbath.[60] The majority of decisors rule, however, that Thursday or Friday circumcision is permitted, and it is in fact improper to delay the performance of a mitzva.[61] While it is indeed true that purely elective surgery should not be performed after Wednesday given the mere possibility the Sabbath will have to be violated,[62] such possibilities carry no weight where a mitzva is being performed.

60 *Tashbetz*, 1:21, quoted in *Beit Yosef*, YD 268; *Birkhei Yosef*, YD 262; *Maharsham*, 5:7; *Yabia Omer*, 5, YD 23.

61 *Shakh*, YD 266:18; *Magen Avraham*, 331:9; *Eliyahu Rabbah*, 331:10; *Noda Biyehuda* 2, YD 166; *Hakham Tzvi, Additional Responsa*, #9; *Mishna Brura*, 331:73; *Shmirat Shabat Kehilkhata*, 32 (96). See also *Nishmat Avraham*, YD 262:3, quoting R. S.Z. Auerbach.

62 Some opinions prohibit this because of the prohibition against engendering situations of mortal danger. Others prohibit it merely because it is improper to cause unnecessary pain and suffering over the Sabbath. On the latter view, this halakha is of no relevance to the *pikuah nefesh* issue under discussion here. See *SA* OH 248, and commentaries ad loc.

IVF falls somewhere between a mitzva like circumcision, where only the **certainty** of desecration warrants postponement, and an optional medical procedure, where even the **possibility** of Sabbath desecration necessitates rescheduling. On the one hand, the obligations of procreation and "settling the world" (*lashevet*) have never been understood as compelling resort to any type of surgical procedure to achieve procreation.[63] At the same time, most decisors do consider the offspring produced from IVF as having a familial bond to the biological parents.[64] The father fulfils either the obligation of procreation, or at least the prophetic injunction of *lashevet*.[65] As such, the mitzva that one may achieve may be sufficiently great that one is permitted to pursue whatever avenues carry the greatest prospects of success, even if there is a possibility (not a certainty) that, because of mortal danger, violation of prohibitions, specifically, disposal of surplus eggs, may ensue.

In fact, one might argue that to the extent IVF is permissible only because the sperm was procured for purposes of reproduction, the "destruction of seed" prohibitions **require**, not only permit, that IVF be implemented in the manner most likely to produce a successful pregnancy and thus eliminate the need for repeated semen procurement. Since multiple egg retrieval greatly increases the chances of success, its utilization may actually be preferable, notwithstanding the "risk" of surplus embryos that will not be implanted.[66]

63 See n. 53 above.

64 See sources cited in Breitowitz, n. 4 above, nn. 7–16.

65 Breitowitz, n. 4 above, n. 16.

66 A more subtle analysis lends further support to this argument. If destruction of a fertilized ovum is prohibited, it is not because it is a "life," but because it is an organism that has the potential to develop into life. Justification of the obligation to rescue it is predicated on its future existence, not its present reality. The "sin" of destruction is not abortion or feticide, but rather, failure to actualize a certain potential. This failure obtains whether the fertilized ovum is discarded or the egg was not retrieved in the first place. Limiting ova retrieval to a small number of eggs does not eliminate this dereliction, hence there is no reason such limitation should be halakhically mandated. Ultimately, however, I believe this subtlety is unconvincing, because it would suggest that the failure to retrieve an egg, and the act of destroying or discarding an already fertilized egg, are morally and halakhically equivalent — a dubious proposition at best. I thus prefer to rest my conclusion on considerations of maternal danger (*sakana*).

## 4 *Experimentation*

Although the authorities disagree as to whether an aborted fetus or stillborn requires burial, it is clear that the "mere water" status of an under 40-day implanted embryo, and certainly any preembryo, renders burial totally unnecessary.[67] Nor does a preembryo transmit any impurity due to contact with a corpse (*tumat met*),[68] hence burial is not needed for that purpose. For the same reason, the prohibition against deriving benefit from a cadaver, which is the basis for prohibiting various forms of dissection and experimentation on fetuses and stillborns, should be inapplicable to preembryos that will not be implanted.[69] In short, to the extent the preembryo can be destroyed or discarded, it can be used for research or experimentation.[70]

Note, however, that halakha may impose two significant restrictions on such experimentation. First, nontherapeutic experimentation **followed by implantation** may very well be forbidden because of the potential harm it may cause to a future human being. Even if the preembryo itself is "mere water," there may be an obligation not to "stand idly by," that is, an obligation to prevent harm, not to the embryo, but to the person the preembryo might become. This approach parallels the recommendation of the American Fertility Society (now the American Society for Reproductive Medicine) that experimentation be permitted on embryos not destined for implantation, but prohibited on embryos that will be implanted.[71]

Second, current ethical guidelines specifically permit the creation of preembryos exclusively for research purposes, at least where there is

67 See, e.g., *Responsa Maharsham*, 4:146 (even a stillborn need not be buried if the miscarriage occurs in the first trimester).

68 R. Judah Rosanes, *Mishne Lamelekh*, Laws concerning Corpse Impurity 2:1.

69 I have not found an explicit source, but this appears to be an obvious corollary of their "mere water" status. See *Binyan Tzion*, #119 (no prohibition against benefit from a corpse when there is no obligation of burial).

70 Indeed, it might conceivably be argued that experimentation is preferable to disposal insofar as it minimizes "destruction of seed," but this line of reasoning has not, to my knowledge, been utilized by any halakhic authority.

71 ECART, n. 1 above, 79S. A similar concept exists under common law, which affords little or no protection to the embryo, but awards compensation to live human beings who suffered damages in vitro. See text at nn. 219–225 above.

the informed consent of the gamete providers and certain other conditions are met.[72] Since IVF involves the emission of seed outside the confines of marital intercourse, the only halakhic justification for it is procreation.[73] Seminal emission for the express purpose of generating an embryo that will **not** be implanted is a clear violation of the prohibition against "destruction of seed," and cannot be sanctioned.[74] For a Jewish doctor to facilitate such a protocol may constitute causing someone else to sin, or violate the Rabbinic prohibition against assisting in the commission of a transgression (*mesayeia lidvar aveira*).[75] Since, however, many authorities maintain that the prohibition against destruction of seed does not hold for non-Jews,[76] the physician would be

72 This is the consensus of the two major medical organizations dealing with this problem — the American Fertility Society (American Society for Reproductive Medicine), and the American College of Obstetrics and Gynecology. See ECART, n. 1 above, 79S. An identical position was taken in a 1994 report of a US government sponsored Human Embryo Research Panel. See National Institutes of Health, *Final Report of the Human Embryo Research Panel* (September 22, 1994). Note, however, that at least with respect to federal funding, the Panel's recommendations were never implemented. See below, text following n. 255.

73 Interestingly, certain types of preembryo generation may not involve the emission of seed at all, e.g., cloning. May an embryo be created by cloning for the purpose of experimentation? This is an especially important question given that so-called "therapeutic cloning" can be used to obtain genetically-compatible stem cells. See nn. 256–260 below. I plan to address this problem in a future work.

74 Moreover, in light of the analysis presented earlier, that predicates the permissibility of discard on considerations of danger, there would clearly be no justification for creating life potential with absolutely no intention of bringing it to fruition. Indeed, this could very well apply to a cloned embryo as well.

75 Technically, the biblical transgression of causing another to transgress only applies if the sin could not be committed without the aider and abetter. See bAvoda Zara 6a. But see n. 27 above. Nevertheless, even if there are others who could have enabled this sin, violation of the Rabbinic prohibition against assisting in the commission may be involved. See *SA* YD 151; comments of *Shakh*, sec. 6.

76 See *Tosafot*, bSanhedrin 59b s.v. *venahzor*. In point of fact, even if non-Jews were subject to the prohibition, it would not be a sin for a Jew to facilitate commission of the act. The prohibition against causing another to sin is inapplicable, because there are other physicians who can enable the sin to be carried out, and with respect to the Rabbinic law against "assistance" (*mesayeia*), the *Shakh*, ibid., rules that it is inapplicable vis-a-vis a non-Jew.

allowed to facilitate the emission of seed from non-Jewish donors even for experimental use. But where the IVF procedure is undertaken for procreation, and the parties later decide to donate the preembryo for research, this is nothing more than a decision to discard — an option that is halakhically valid.

### 5 *Preembryo Donation*

A fourth alternative to implantation, destruction or experimentation is the donation of the embryo to infertile couples. IVF clinics often encourage the exercise of this option, and some clinics even require that surplus preembryos be donated.

Embryo donation raises a number of halakhic problems, first and foremost, the identity of the mother. Where the woman who carries a baby to term is not the woman whose egg was fertilized, there is halakhic disagreement as to who the mother is.[77] If, for example, the embryo recipient is non-Jewish, is the child non-Jewish, based on the status of the birth mother, or Jewish, based on the status of the egg donor? Maternity is also important for establishing which relationships

77 One of the midrashic sources often cited in this context is the Aggada that Dina was originally conceived in Rachel's womb but miraculously transferred to the womb of Leah as a result of Leah's prayer; i.e., Joseph and Dina were switched embryos. See Targum Yonatan on Genesis 30:21. In effect, Rachel was the genetic mother of Dina, while Leah was the birth mother. Apart from the question of whether Midrash can serve as a halakhic source, the implications of this Aggada are not unequivocal. We might say that since Dinah is consistently described as the "daughter of Leah," motherhood must be defined by birth, rather than genetic origin. However, in light of another Midrash, which that teaches that Shimon married Dinah, an act that would be prohibited even under Noahide law if they shared a common maternal bond, we might conclude that Dina was halakhically regarded as **Rachel's** child. See *Tur* on Genesis 46:10. (The *Tur* assumes that Shimon and Dinah were Noahides, who are permitted to marry siblings with the same **father**.) As R. E. Bick, n. 43 above, points out, Rachel's "motherhood," which the *Tur* assumes, might be based on the fact that conception took place in her womb, and not on the fact that she was the egg donor. Hence the *Tur*'s remarks do not resolve the question of maternity for the case where eggs are fertilized in vitro and then donated to a recipient. A similar point can be made with respect to bHulin 70a. And see n. 78 below.

are incestuous. In a comprehensive study, R. J. David Bleich notes that the majority of authorities regard maternity as based on birth;[78] one minority view regards the egg donor as the sole mother.[79] Yet a third opinion maintains that although the woman giving birth will be deemed the exclusive mother where both the egg donor and the birth mother are Jewish, the genetic egg donor establishes maternity if one is

78 See R. Bleich, "In-vitro fertilization: questions of maternal identity and conversion," reprinted in JLNRT, n. 4 above, 46. See also R. Ezra Bick, n. 43 above, and R. Bleich's rejoinder, JLNRT, 10, as well as volume 5 of *Tehumin* (1984), in which rabbis Z.N. Goldberg, Avraham Kilav, and Zerah Warhaftig discuss this issue.

A text that is sometimes cited **against** this majority view is bHulin 70a, which discusses the case of an animal that is removed from the womb of its mother and transplanted into the womb of a second animal, from which it is eventually born. It is clear to the Talmud that the first animal is deemed to have had a calf, so that any other offspring it has in the future will be exempt from the law of the firstling (*bekhor*) — the first-born animal that must be given to a priest and brought as a sacrifice. The question is the status of the second animal. See Maimonides, *Code*, Laws concerning Firstlings 4:18. Taken alone, this passage might indicate that maternity is definitely assigned, at least in part, to the genetic mother, particularly since the Talmud refers to the fetus, vis-a-vis the first animal, as "hers" (*dida*), and vis-a-vis the second animal, as "not hers" (*lav dida*).

As R. Z.N. Goldberg convincingly argues, however, the animal from which the fetus was removed was far more than a mere egg contributor or genetic parent; it was the animal in whose body conception took place. It was also a "birth mother," since the fetus was removed at a point of fetal development that would qualify as a birth — the differentiation of limbs and organs — for otherwise its removal could not exempt a subsequent birth from the law of firstlings. As such, the most the Talmud teaches us is that once maternity is established in animal A via conception, gestation, and/or birth, it is not terminated by transfer to and (re)birth from animal B (though the latter may acquire attributes of maternity). The passage does not establish that mere egg donation or genetic connection, in and of itself, suffices to establish maternity.

In short, the Talmud does not really address the question of "genetic mother" v. "birth mother," but rather, that of whether the existence of a prior birth mother rules out a later firstling exemption for the second birth mother. Accordingly, it is not relevant to our concerns here. And see n. 212 below.

79 R. Shlomo Goren, *Hatzofe*, 7 Adar 1 (1984). See also R. Warhaftig in *Tehumin* 5 (1984), who seeks to demonstrate this from the law of *dmei vladot*.

a Jew and the other is not.[80] R. Bleich even asserts the possibility of dual maternity. R. S.Z. Auerbach concludes that the matter is uncertain, and one would have to be strict in considering the various possibilities.[81]

In light of this uncertainty, the following conclusions emerge. Donation of a preembryo to a non-Jewish couple (or to the IVF clinic, which, at least in the United States, will probably give it to a non-Jewish couple) cannot be countenanced, for if in fact the resulting child is Jewish, in light of the egg donor, he ought not be raised as a non-Jew. Moreover, even on the majority view that the child is non-Jewish, in light of his gestation, birth, or both, within the body of a non-Jew, embryo donation may be prohibited on the grounds of "giving birth to a child for idolatry."[82] It is also possible that if donation of the embryo will produce a child who is halakhically

80 This is the position of R. Avraham Kilav. See *Tehumin* 5 (1984), 260, 267.

81 See *Nishmat Avraham* (App.), EH 22:2, 186. In an entirely different context (the laws of meat and milk), R. Akiva Eiger, *SA* YD 87, suggests that a maternal bond may be forged during gestation, i.e., even prior to birth. This does not fully resolve the maternity problem of ovum donations for two reasons. First, in IVF using donated ova, there is no gestational process within the donor's body. Thus, even R. Akiva Eiger might well concede exclusive maternity to the birth mother. Even in uterine lavage, where fertilization does occur within the donor's body, R. Akiva Eiger's remarks seem to limit maternity to gestation beyond the first trimester. (His comments would become germane should technology ever develop the capacity to carry out full-fledged fetal transfers. If a fetus is transferred from one woman to another woman **after** the first trimester, R. Akiva Eiger might consider the first woman the halakhic mother, but IVF or uterine lavage are currently far from that point.)

Second, and more importantly, R. Akiva Eiger's recognition of a maternal bond on the basis of gestation does not preclude recognition of birth as a superseding indicator of maternity, nor does it preclude dual maternity. In short, his brief comments do not resolve the fundamental halakhic uncertainties.

82 R. Bleich notes that such a procedure is at the very least "contrary to the ideological norms of Judiasm." The Gemara in bAvoda Zara 26a permits assistance in birthing idolatrous children only where the withholding of such services will promote enmity or hatred towards Jews (*eiva*). While "enmity" may justify the practice of obstetrics, it certainly could not permit ovum or preembryo donation. It is, however, questionable whether the talmudic interdiction applies to non-idolatrous religions.

non-Jewish, as most would maintain, the Jewish sperm donor may be in violation of a different Torah prohibition, that against impregnation of a non-Jew.[83] Finally, even if such a child has dual maternity and is a "half Jew, half Gentile," it would still be forbidden to have him

83 Whether or not such a prohibition exists, apart from the general ban on intermarriage, is apparently a matter of dispute. The Mishnah in Megila states that one who interprets the verse "And of your seed you shall not give over to Molech" (Lev. 18:21) to mean: you shall not give of your seed to impregnate an Aramean woman, is silenced with a reprimand." Rashi understands this to mean that the verse in Leviticus is concerned exclusively with idol worship and **not** with the impregnation of a Gentile woman. However, *Targum Yonatan Ben Uziel* (a variant of *Targum Yerushalmi*) and the *Arukh* interpret the verse precisely in the manner the Mishnah seems to condemn. Indeed, the Gemara ad loc. cites R. Yishmael, who quotes the supposedly discredited teaching approvingly. (But cf. Rashi, who interprets R. Yishmael as telling us what we should **not** do.) Various explanations have been offered to reconcile this conflict, e.g., the Mishnah condemns any implication that such impregnation would be a capital offense, as true Molech worship is, but concedes that the prohibition of impregnation of a non-Jew is a valid secondary meaning of the verse. Alternatively, the Mishnah rejects limiting the verse to Arameans who are Molech worshippers when in fact it should be applied to all non-Jews. See *Tosafot Yom Tov, Tiferet Yisrael*, and *Maharsha* on bMegila 25a.

In any event, on the view of the *Arukh* and *Targum Yonatan*, it follows that the insemination of a non-Jew with Jewish sperm may be a direct violation of the prohibition against Molech, even if insemination as such is normally not deemed a sex act. Note, however, that neither Rambam nor SA cite the reading of *Targum Yonatan*, suggesting that it is not halakhically definitive.

In discussions with rabbinical colleagues, I have heard it said that to the extent the child is not Jewish and bears no relationship to the Jewish father, the act of preembryo donation constitutes "destruction of seed" — the seed is literally going to waste, since it will not produce a child related to the sperm donor. This position is untenable. Given that most decisors permit even the physical destruction of a preembryo (see nn. 43–45 above), donation to a non-Jew obviously is no more destructive of the seed than actual destruction. The point is that as long as the seed was procured for purposes of procreation, and the emission was legitimate, what happens later is governed by the rules governing abortion, not those governing "destruction of seed." (But cf. *Havot Yair*, who prohibits abortion on grounds of "destruction of seed.") It is true, however, that the emission of sperm for the purpose of donating to a non-Jewish woman would unquestionably be "destruction of seed." See also n. 90 (use of a non-Jewish gestational surrogate may indeed involve "destruction of seed" if the child is deemed non-Jewish), but cf. the view of R. Gershuni, cited in n. 9.

raised as a Gentile, as his Jewish half is obligated to observe the commandments.[84]

Donation of a preembryo to a Jewish couple raises additional problems. At minimum, it would, of course, be improper to donate the embryo to a couple who will not raise the child according to the laws of the Torah. Even assuming the best case, an observant infertile couple, donation raises serious questions of adultery and *mamzeirut* (illegitimacy). By causing a married woman other than his wife to carry and bear his child, the sperm donor may be committing adultery and producing a (halakhically) illegitimate child (*mamzer*).[85] To the degree the identities of the donor couple are kept secret (as is common), there

84 See Bleich n. 78 above, 94, 94; Goldberg, *Tehumin* 5 (1984), 248. On R. Kilav's minority position that the child is Jewish because of the identity of the egg donor, the paternal relation is also maintained. Accordingly, embryo donation would not be "destruction of seed," and it is probable that it would not be deemed impregnation of a Gentile, though this is less clear. The only basis for prohibition would be the impropriety of raising a Jew as a non-Jew, an issue that would not arise in the case of, say, gestational surrogacy, since the non-Jewish surrogate returns the baby to the Jewish couple.

85 The issues of adultery and *mamzeirut* arising from the utilization of reproductive technologies were the subjects of a long-standing debate between the Satmar Rav, R. Joel Teitelbaum, and R. Moses Feinstein, in the context of an impregnation with donor semen (AID). The Satmar Rav took the position that any married Jewish woman who is impregnated with the semen of a Jewish man other than her husband has committed adultery, and the child born from such a procedure is a *mamzer*. Interestingly, he ruled that even the (male?) doctor mechanically introducing the semen into a married woman's body was guilty of adultery. See *Hamaor* 15(9) (1954), 3–13. See *Igrot Moshe*, EH 1:71; 2:11; 3:14; 4:32(5) for R. Feinstein's view to the contrary. Despite R. Feinstein's eminence, a number of decisors have stated that a child born to a Jewish couple from Jewish donor semen is at least a possible *mamzer*. See R. Auerbach in *Noam* 1 (who points out, however, that the woman is not forbidden to her husband); *Tzitz Eliezer*, 9:51. Even those who do not impose the stigma of illegitimacy conclude that such impregnation may violate Torah law. See *Shevet Halevi*, 3:175; *Maarakhei Lev*, #73; *Bnei Ahuva*, Ishut ch. 15 (citing Lev. 18:20).

R. Feinstein himself concludes that AID from a Jewish donor is forbidden not because of adultery or *mamzeirut* but because of the concern over the possibility of incest with paternal relatives. Accordingly, provided the donor semen is from a non-Jew, where there will be no paternity, he permitted the procedure in cases where the woman was suffering terribly from her infertility. He stated, however, that only an expert scholar and decisor was to make a determination as to when this condition was met.

is also the possibility of incest with unknown paternal and, on the view that the egg donor is the mother, maternal relatives as well.[86]

While donation to a single Jewish woman raises neither the problem of non-Jewish impregnation nor the issues of adultery and

---

In his final pronouncement on the subject, he wrote that the decision should not be implemented, but, after the fact, the child is certainly not a *mamzer* and, if a girl, could even marry a *kohen*. (Nor does the wife become prohibited to her husband even if he is a *kohen*). See *Igrot Moshe*, EH 4:32(5). Contra: *Tzitz Eliezer*, 9:51, who absolutely condemns use of non-Jewish sperm, characterizing it as a "terrible spiritual catastrophe"; he concludes that a daughter so produced could **not** marry a *kohen*.

Whether the Satmar Rav's ruling applies only to direct insemination of a married woman, or includes IVF-fertilization of her egg outside her body, is debatable. Moreover, it could be argued that *mamzeirut* and adultery issues do not arise at all when a fertilized embryo, as opposed to sperm, is donated, since the donor sperm did not fertilize the ovum of another man's wife. Given, however, that there is at least a possibility of *mamzeirut*, this is reason enough to discourage embryo donation. See discussion at nn. 141–142.

86 The possibility of incest with unknown relatives of one's parents is the basis for the law that every widowed or divorced woman must wait at least 90 days before remarrying, to determine whether she is pregnant. Any marriage before that point could result in the birth of a child who might be raised as a premature child of the second husband but is in fact the full-term child of the first. Not knowing who his true father is, the child may wind up marrying forbidden relatives, e.g., his sister. See bJebamot 41a and *SA* EH 15:26.

On the view of most decisors, the child has no maternal tie to the genetic egg donor. Even R. Kilav, who accords maternity to the egg donor in Jewish–non-Jewish cases, concedes that birth is the exclusive determinant in "same religion" cases. Thus, the only potential incest problem would be with unknown **paternal** relatives. If, on the other hand, we adopt the position of R. Goren, who considers the egg donor to have exclusive maternity in all cases, or R. Bleich's view that there may be dual maternity, the fear of incest could arise with respect to maternal relatives as well, e.g., a maternal half-sister.

Note that if we accept R. Waldenberg's position that the use of IVF cuts off paternal relationships (see n. 7 above), the preembryo has no father or mother, and its subsequent transfer to a recipient generates no problems with respect to adultery, *mamzeirut*, or potential incest with unknown paternal relatives. (R. Waldenberg's reference to *mamzeirut* in *Tzitz Eliezer* 9:51 must be limited to AID where sperm is deposited directly into the woman's body. In light of *Tzitz Eliezer* 15:45, this could have no application to IVF outside the woman's body, since the sperm donor has no paternity. In any case, R. Waldenberg's position is not generally accepted.)

*mamzeirut*, it would generally be contrary to Jewish ethical norms to facilitate a woman's bearing children out-of-wedlock. And even if the recipient is single, the problem of future incest with unknown paternal or maternal (if the egg donor is the mother) relatives remains.

In sum, donation of preembryos, whether to Jewish or non-Jewish couples or to single women, raises numerous halakhic problems. It cannot be regarded as an acceptable option, at least as long as the gamete providers are alive.[87] Whether these concerns apply to pure egg donation will be discussed below.[88]

## 6 *Use of a Gestational Surrogate*

If a woman is capable of producing eggs but incapable of carrying them, she may desire to employ a surrogate who, pursuant to some agreement, will carry the baby to term and (hopefully) deliver it back to the sperm and egg contributors.[89]

87 The possibility of embryo donation after the father's death is discussed below in the text following n. 142.

88 A point that calls for further elucidation is whether, notwithstanding the halakhic difficulties, donation is nonetheless preferable to destruction. Many decisors have indeed permitted virtually indiscriminate destruction of preembryos. See text at nn. 43–45 above. Nevertheless, if we uphold the view of the Behag, n. 34 above, it may be a mitzva to try to sustain even pre-embryonic life, on the grounds of the "it is better that one Sabbath be transgressed" principle. If there is in fact an obligation to observe the "rescue" precept and "protect" preembryonic life, should that not override concerns such as possible future incest, generating *mamzeirim*, "giving birth to a child for idolatry," and the other problems mentioned? Are we dealing with something akin to sexual transgressions where the law is that one must kill himself or let himself be killed rather than commit such a crime (*yehareg veal yaavor*)? See Maimonides, *Code*, Laws concerning the Fundamental Principles of the Torah 5:2. It is also possible that, in light of R. Wozner's ruling prohibiting desecration of the Sabbath on behalf of the preembryo (see text at n. 46 above), intervention to protect it would not justify any transgressions, even of Rabbinic strictures not deemed to fall into the category of the three precepts never to be transgressed. This indeed entails the counterintuitive notion that destruction or at least passive neglect is preferable to donation.

89 The term "surrogate motherhood" actually describes two very different types of situations. Type 1 involves a woman who contributes both egg and womb; it is exemplified by the notorious Mary Beth Whitehead-Elizabeth Stern case in New Jersey, see 537 A.2d 1227 (NJ: 1988).

The issue of "who is the mother?" in gestational surrogacy is identical to that arising from embryo donation. If the surrogate is non-Jewish, the child may — and probably will — require conversion. The sperm contributor may be violating a prohibition against the impregnation of a Gentile.[90] If the surrogate is a Jew married to a Jew, the surrogacy arrangement may be tantamount to adultery, and the child a *mamzer*, depending, again, on who is deemed the mother. The same would be true if the surrogate is single but the relationship is halakhically incestuous, e.g., a woman carrying her sister's embryo. To the extent the identity of the Jewish surrogate is concealed from the child, there is the possibility of incest with unknown maternal relatives.

While surrogacy arrangements have been roundly condemned by many leading decisors on both halakhic and ethical grounds,[91] the Israeli Chief Rabbinate has given its qualified approval to the use of surrogates, subject to the following conditions:[92] (1) the gestational

---

The American Fertility Society report was sharply divided on the ethics of such an arrangement; see ECART, n. 1 above, 76S–77S. From the halakhic perspective, maternity in type 1 cases is not an issue; the surrogate is unequivocally the mother (except on R. Waldenberg's decidedly minority view, see n. 7). Type 2 involves a woman who is simply the incubator of another woman's egg. She is termed a gestational surrogate mother. The AFS viewed this arrangement slightly more favorably, see 69S–70S. It is the gestational surrogate that poses the halakhic uncertainties discussed in this article.

90 It is also probable that the emission of sperm with the express intention of fertilizing an egg (even that of a Jewish spouse) that will be carried by a Gentile surrogate constitutes emission of seed in vain, since the resulting offspring has no relation to the Jewish father. (But cf. the view of R. Gershuni, n. 9 above.) According to R. Kilav, however, since the child is halakhically Jewish and does bear a relation to the Jewish sperm provider, such an arrangement might be permitted. Note, however, that even according to R. Kilav, who maintains that the child is Jewish, the use of a non-Jewish gestational surrogate might be strongly discouraged on spiritual grounds. See *SA* YD 81:7 (against use of a non-Jewish nurse for a Jewish baby) (Rema).

91 See *Nishmat Avraham*, (App.) EH 5(2).

92 As reported in *Haaretz*, February 14, 1995.

surrogate must be a single woman who does not bear a prohibited relationship to the father;[93] (2) accurate records must be kept detailing the identities of both the surrogate and the egg donor, that is, the mother who will raise the child, so that the child will not marry relatives of either; (3) to emphasize the surrogate's maternal status (at least as a matter of doubt), the parents who will to raise the child must go through formal adoption procedures; (4) each case must be individually evaluated and approved by a special commission with at least one member representing a halakhic perspective; (5) authorizations will be limited to demonstrated cases of need; and (6) surrogacy cannot be legitimized by public statute, but must remain under administrative regulation.[94]

In essence, while it is regarded as ethically inappropriate for a single woman to be the recipient of sperm, egg, or embryo in order to bear an out-of-wedlock child she will raise, the Rabbinate views the matter somewhat differently when the single woman functions as a facilitator enabling a married couple to raise a child and the husband to fulfill his obligation to procreate. Whether the Rabbinate's ruling will be accepted by other decisors, and what effect it will have on the growth of surrogacy, remain to be seen.[95]

93 There are actually two distinct reasons for prohibiting the use of **married** surrogates. First, the possibility of adultery and *mamzeirut*. In addition, R. Wozner cites the Sages' interpretation of "He shall cleave unto his wife" (Gen. 2:24) — his wife, and not the wife of his friend. Interestingly, in a discussion of the permissibility of AID, the *Bnei Ahuva* cites another verse — Leviticus 18:20 — as a basis for not giving one's seed to another's wife; see n. 85 above. Why this verse would not be equally applicable to gestational surrogacy is unclear (One reason might be that in gestational surrogacy, the husband's sperm is fertilizing his wife's egg). In any event, at most, these verses prohibit use of a married surrogate. The use of an unmarried surrogate who bears an prohibited degree of family relation to the sperm provider could only be proscribed on a theory akin to the Satmar Rav's, a stringency that R. Auerbach, for one, was willing to consider.

94 Although the Rabbinate did not explicitly address this point, there should presumably also be a requirement that the surrogate be Jewish in order to avoid the problems mentioned in n. 83.

95 It is not clear whether the Rabbinate's guidelines are limited to gestational surrogacy or can be extended to type 1 surrogates as well, and if not, why not? In any case, even the rabbinical courts under the Rabbinate's jurisdiction have continued to condemn surrogacy. See the authorities cited in *Nishmat Avraham*, (App.) EH 5(2).

To summarize, the range of halakhically acceptable options for pre-embryos includes implantation, cryopreservation for later implantation, destruction, experimentation, and possibly gestational surrogacy along the lines approved by the Chief Rabbinate. Donation of embryos to other infertile couples — Jewish or non-Jewish — would appear to be improper.[96]

### 7 *Utilization of Third Party Sperm, Eggs or Embryos*

The previous section focused on the Jewish couple who have generated embryos from their own egg and sperm and face various options with regard to the embryos' disposition. This section will examine the extent to which a Jewish couple can utilize the third party contributions of others — egg, sperm, or embryo — in their own reproductive efforts. In many cases of infertility, a woman may be capable of carrying a baby to term, but not of producing eggs that can be fertilized, or perhaps her chromosomes have a serious genetic defect. There may also be a factor in the male sperm which hinders reproduction. Third party contributions can often help the couple out, but, as to be expected, the halakhic obstacles may be formidable.

#### a Sperm or Embryo Receipt from Non-Jews

Obviously, to a considerable degree the issues raised by receipt mirror those raised by donation. Nevertheless, because of the configuration of

96 At least one US state seems to require that unwanted preembryos be donated. See Louisiana Revised Statutes 9:124–9:133. This may be the case in Illinois and Minnesota as well. See n. 218 below. This creates a serious problem for an Orthodox couple in these states, since the requirements of state law may contravene halakha. The couple would accordingly have to limit egg retrieval to the number of eggs that can be implanted in the wife's womb, although this may drastically reduce the efficacy of the procedure. A strong case can safely be made, however, that mandatory donation statutes are unconstitutional under *Roe v. Wade* and, to the extent they violate religious belief, inconsistent with the First Amendment. But cf. Robertson, n. 215 below, 453, n. 46. (*Roe v. Wade* does not rest on a constitutional right **not** to be a biological parent, but on protection of a woman's bodily integrity. Accordingly, as long as the state does not force a woman to carry a child, her constitutional right of privacy is not violated.)

Jewish family law, and its technical definitions of maternity and paternity, certain types of transfers that would be prohibited in one direction may be permissible in the other direction.[97]

This will be particularly true in the case of contributions from non-Jewish sources. As noted previously,[98] R. Moses Feinstein was willing, in cases of great emotional distress, to allow impregnation with non-Jewish donor sperm; the female recipient is not deemed to have cohabited with a non-Jew, and is consequently permitted to remain with her husband even if he is a *kohen*. Although he expressed reservations about implementing this ruling in practice, he never retracted its basic permissibility. Presumably, the Satmar Rav, who equated Jewish donor insemination with adultery, would similarly construe non-Jewish donor insemination as forbidden intercourse with a non-Jew. As a result, the act would not only be sinful in and of itself, but would render the recipient forbidden to marry a *kohen* (assuming his rule applies to IVF procedures and not just uterine sperm deposits).[99] There would clearly be no problem of incest with unknown paternal relatives, because a non-Jew who impregnates a Jewish woman has no paternal bond with the offspring.

How would this work in the case of embryo transfer? An embryo is nothing more than a combination of egg and sperm, and it might be assumed that whatever dispensation or lack thereof may exist with regard to sperm donation would apply equally to embryo transfer. Embryo transfers are more complicated, however, because they involve the question of split maternity: who is the mother — the egg donor, birth mother, or both?

It is here that there is some asymmetry in the halakha, at least according to some authorities. It was noted above that if a Jewish embryo, that is, a fertilized ovum from a Jewish woman, is transferred to a non-Jewish woman, the children that result will, on most views, be regarded as non-Jews, because only the birth mother bears a maternal

97 One example, by way of analogy, involves organ donation. Although many decisors maintain that a Jew cannot authorize the removal of his heart for transplantation, he may be allowed to put his name on a waiting list of potential recipients. See R. Aaron Soloveitchik, "Death according to the halacha," *Journal of Halacha and Contemporary Society* 17 (1989), 41, 45–47.

98 See n. 85 above.

99 See text at nn. 141–142.

bond to them. This should lead to the conclusion that, for the very same reason, children resulting from an embryo transfer from a non-Jew to a Jew do **not** need conversion. Since maternity is defined by the birth mother, who is Jewish, the children should automatically acquire the status of Jews. However, on the basis of bJebamot 78a, R. Z.N. Goldberg argues that this is not the case. Children born of a Jewish birth mother do indeed need conversion. Paradoxically, however, once they do convert, they are deemed related to their birth mother (though, of course, not to the birth mother's Jewish husband).[100] R. A. Kilav regards such children as altogether non-Jewish, and thereby requires conversion, the children being deemed to have no relation to their birth mother.[101] Presumably, R. Bleich's suggestion of dual maternity would similarly necessitate a conversion, but the child would retain his tie to his birth mother by virtue of his pre-conversion half-Jewish status. While the conversion and maternal identity issues are serious, these uncertainties alone seem to pose no particular impediment to utilization of the procedure.[102]

100 *Tehumin* 5 (1984), 248.

101 Ibid., 260. R. Kilav's position has the virtue of consistency. In transfers from Jew to non-Jew, he accords maternity to the egg donor. He does exactly the same in transfers from non-Jew to Jew, thereby necessitating conversion.

102 Without repeating the extensive analysis in R. Bleich's article, the essence of the problem is that the Gemara in bJebamot 78a makes clear that when a pregnant woman converts, the fetuses undergo conversion as well, and are thus considered converts, not born Jews. According to Nahmanides (bJebamot 47b), if they are male, they do not acquire the status of Jews until circumcision. (But cf. *Nimukei Yosef*, commentary on Alfasi, Jebamot 16a (Vilna, ed.), in the name of R. Aaron Halevi, who rules that they are Jews even prior to circumcision.) This alone rules out the possibility that birth is the exclusive determinant of maternity since, were this so, conversion would be unnecessary. At the same time, bJebamot 97b informs us that halakhically speaking, brothers born of such a convert share a fraternal relationship and common mother. R. Kilav understands this to mean that initially, religious identity and genealogical (maternal) affiliation are determined at the moment of conception, i.e., a fertilized ovum of a non-Jewish woman is non-Jewish. However, the bond that in effect renders the embryo or fetus non-Jewish is erased or transformed by conversion. The embryos now become Jewish; once Jewish by virtue of conversion, a new post-conversion maternal bond is created by birth from a Jewish mother, a bond that creates a maternal relationship. By contrast, where a non-Jewish embryo is transferred to a Jewish recipient and no

Since the babies produced from non-Jewish preembryos will bear no relationship to the non-Jewish egg and sperm providers, at least after the conversion, the problems of secret incest that can arise with Jewish donor sperm are nonexistent. Other than the need for a conversion, "receiving" a non-Jewish preembryo seems analogous to "receiving" non-Jewish donor sperm, which R. Feinstein was in theory willing to permit, at least in cases of anguish. It may be that even the reservations he eventually expressed concerning implementation of the ruling would apply only to a married Jewish woman impregnated with the semen of a non-Jew, and not to the implantation of an already-fertilized embryo.

Note, however, that the Satmar Rav's construct equating insemination with a forbidden sex act **might** mean that the receipt of a fertilized non-Jewish embryo is equivalent to impregnation with non-Jewish sperm, which in turn is tantamount to intercourse with a non-Jew.

---

conversion process takes place, the old maternal connection arising from conception has never been severed. As a result, no new bond can be created by birth. The children are born, and remain, non-Jewish, unless and until they convert. Not only do such children need conversion, but even after conversion, the birth mother is not deemed to have a maternal bond with them. (As R. Bleich notes, R. Kilav's position is difficult to sustain in light of Nahmanides' view that circumcision is required for conversion if the children are born male. If no conversion occurred before birth, how can birth establish a bond to the birth mother? R. Kilav's opinion does fit well with the view of R. Aaron Halevi cited in *Nimukei Yosef*.)

R. Z.N. Goldberg analyzes the text very differently. His position is that for genealogical purposes, maternal bonds are generated exclusively by birth, even if the embryos were non-Jewish. Thus, whether the birth mother converted during pregnancy, or non-Jewish embryos were implanted in a Jewish woman, she is deemed to have a maternal bond with the children. This is true even when their conversion takes place after their birth, as in the scenario envisaged by Nahmanides. Conversion is nonetheless required, however, because of the need to establish *kedushat yisrael* and obligation to observe the commandments. Conversion achieves that limited purpose, and does **not** erase prior relationships.

Thus, virtually all authorities agree that the children born from non-Jewish embryos implanted in a Jewish birth mother must be converted. The authorities disagree as to whether, after the conversion, the mother is deemed to have a maternal bond with the children. The relevance of this text to IVF is open to question. See text at nn. 109–114.

This would indeed furnish a substantive halakhic basis for prohibiting embryo transfer.[103]

In any event, a non-Jewish embryo transfer is no more problematic than the use of non-Jewish semen (except for the need for conversion) and, on the logic of R. Moses Feinstein, may be justified when other alternatives have been exhausted.[104] It is also clear that even if halakha does not prohibit the practice, the husband has fulfilled neither the precept of procreation, nor that of "settling the world," so there may be little point in proceeding.

### b Ovum from a Non-Jew

With respect to a donated ovum from a non-Jew (which would then be fertilized in vitro), the conversion and lineage problems are identical to those arising in the case of the preembryo. The children would need conversion by virtue of their genetic origin; according to R. Goldberg, their birth mother would retain her maternal ties to them, but whether they would be related to their Jewish biological father is questionable.[105] Indeed, it is probable, though not certain, that there is no filial connection to their biological Jewish father. On the view of R. Kilav, the Jewish parents would be deemed unrelated to them. At least according to R. Kilav, and probably according to R. Goldberg as well, the utilization of non-Jewish egg donation may involve potential violation of the

103 See the discussion in the text at nn. 141–144 below.

104 I speak, of course, in theory. In practice, R. Feinstein did not permit use of donor semen. See n. 85.

105 If the children are genealogically Jewish by virtue of the birth mother, and if their later conversion does not sever that tie, one might assume that there is a paternal relationship as well. I believe this is incorrect. Paternity arises upon fertilization, not birth. At the time of fertilization, the ova were of non-Jewish origin, thereby severing the paternal bond. Once severed, it is not reestablished by the children's Jewish birth. Thus, we are presented with an anomalous situation of children born from a Jewish mother and a Jewish father who are halakhically Jewish (in the genealogical sense) despite their genetic origin, yet nonetheless, their father has no paternal bond to them. Indeed, it would appear that even on the minority opinion, cited above, that transplanted non-Jewish embryos under 40 days old do not need conversion **for any purpose**, a paternal relationship may not exist.

prohibition against destruction of seed, since the Jewish partner will have no paternal relation to the child.[106]

Ironically, therefore, the use of a non-Jewish ovum, fertilized by the husband via IVF, may be more problematic than use of a non-Jewish embryo, or even use of non-Jewish sperm.[107] It is also possible, though unlikely, that use of a non-Jewish ovum to be fertilized by Jewish sperm constitutes an impermissible act of intercourse between Jew and non-Jew (on the approach of the Satmar Rav), since "egg" and "sperm" unite in a prohibited attachment.[108]

### c Conversion Issues in Embryo/Ovum Donation from Non-Jews

As indicated, a number of decisors require the conversion of children born to a Jewish mother where the egg/embryo was obtained from a non-Jewish source. Their proof-text is bJebamot 78a, which states that where a non-Jewish mother converts while pregnant, the embryos also undergo a conversion process.[109] By the same token, any transfer of a non-Jewish embryo to a Jewish birth mother would necessitate some conversion, and, if not undergone by the birth mother (because she is already Jewish), would have to be undergone by the children after birth. The text, however, is equivocal, for at least three reasons. First, the presumptive non-Jewish status of the embryos that necessitates their conversion in utero may stem from their being conceived and implanted within the body of a Gentile. Where no such conception or implantation occurs, viz., an IVF fertilization outside the Gentile's

106 Even on the dual maternity thesis of R. Bleich, he would lack paternity, since at the time of fertilization, the ova were not Jewish. See text at nn. 181–186. Note, however, that on the analysis of R. Gershuni, n. 9 above, even if the Jewish sperm contributor lacks paternity, it would not be considered "emission of sperm in vain."

107 The problem of emission of sperm in vain could be resolved in some cases by exposing the sperm to the Jewish spouse's eggs along with the non-Jewish donor's. Even if the sperm fertilizes the non-Jewish eggs, its emission has not been in vain, as there was potential for a paternal relationship with an offspring.

108 See text at nn. 152–153 below.

109 See n. 102 above on the disagreement between R. Kilav and R. Goldberg regarding the scope of the conversion.

body, the resulting children may indeed be deemed Jewish by birth, not conversion, since there is no other event that would confer on them the status of being non-Jewish.[110] There is no direct proof from the passage that a **genetic tie** alone can give rise to a maternal relationship.

Second, even embryos conceived **within** the body of a Gentile may not require their own conversion (that is, they are deemed "born Jews") where the mother converts within 40 days of their conception, since at the time they became an "actual life," the mother was already Jewish.[111] This too would suggest that where an IVF-embryo that has not reached the 40-day point is implanted into the uterus of a Jewish woman, the child does not require a conversion after birth.

Third, the talmudic passage in question necessitating conversion of the embryos in **utero** upholds the view that a fetus or embryo is not part of the mother's body (*ubar lav yerekh imo*). On the view that the fetus or embryo is part of the mother's body (*ubar yerekh imo*), if the mother is Jewish, by conversion or otherwise, the fetus is automatically Jewish.[112] By extension, any embryo transfer to a Jewish woman would **automatically** make the embryo and the resulting child Jewish.[113] Since many decisors do in fact rule that the fetus or embryo is part of the mother's body,[114] conversion may not be necessary at all.

Assuming, however, that conversion of the children is required because of their non-Jewish origin, a number of questions arise. The Talmud in Jebamot 78a clearly indicates that if the mother is non-Jewish, her immersion in the *mikve* for conversion will constitute a valid immersion for the fetus. (Whether a male child, when born, will need circumcision to complete the conversion process is the subject of dispute between Nahmanides and R. Aaron Halevi.)[115] What if the

110 This is the thesis of R. Bick, n. 43 above.

111 See R. Elchanan Wasserman, *Kovetz Hearot*, no. 73 (in name of R. Chaim Soloveitchik) and *Or Hamizrah* 127 (1981) (in name of R. Aaron Soloveitchik).

112 *Avnei Miluim*, EH 4:3 and 13:4.

113 This argument is advanced by R. Z.N. Goldberg in *Tehumin* 5 (1984), 253–255. But R. Bleich, n. 78 above, 63, disputes this analysis.

114 See, for example, *Shakh*, YD 79:8 and *Taz*, YD 79:5. See also *Sdei Hemed*, *ayin*, rule 62, for a list of sources. (There is a misprint in n. 42 of R. Bleich's article cited in n. 78 above: the references to *Taz* and *Shakh* should be to 79, not 89.)

115 See n. 102.

mother does not convert, that is, is already Jewish? Can she effect a valid immersion for the fetuses by going to the *mikve*, or must their immersion await their birth? R. Bleich convincingly argues that she can, but the contrary view admittedly has strong support.[116]

A second issue is whether the conversion of children in utero constitutes a conversion by dint of Torah law or Rabbinic law. According to a number of authorities, the conversion of minor children, expressly validated by bKetubot 11a, effects conversion only at the Rabbinic level, since by Torah law, benefits cannot be conferred on a minor (*ein zekhiya lekatan*) who by definition is incapable of consent or acquiescence.[117] R. Akiva Eiger argues, however, that where a pregnant woman undergoes conversion on her own behalf, the conversion for the fetus will be effective at the biblical level on the grounds of the principle "that which is effective for oneself can simultaneously be effective for another" (*migo dezakhai lenafshai zakha nami lehavrai*) even where that other is incapable of consent.[118] Invoking the principle of *migo*, however, presumes an efficacious conversion on the part of the mother; where the mother is Jewish and not converting, the immersion might effect valid conversion only at the Rabbinic, and not the biblical,

116 See R. Bleich, n. 78 above, 63–64, who argues that the conclusion of bJebamot 78a-b that the mother's body is not a barrier (*hatzitza*) between the mikve water and the fetus applies not only to "natural mothers," but to host mothers who receive fertilized embryos, and applies whether or not the immersing mother intends to effect a conversion for herself. A contrary view is expressed by rabbis S.Z. Auerbach, A. Nebenzahl and A. Kilav. According to R Bleich, R. Auerbach's reservations were based not on *hatzitza*, but on the lack of parental authority for a host mother to effect a conversion of a minor, since she herself lacks a maternal bond until birth. R. Bleich convincingly argues that a host mother, even before giving birth, is certainly not inferior to an adoptive parent, who generally is authorized to effect a conversion of a minor.

117 See, e.g., *Tosafot*, bKetubot 11a s.v. *matbilin* (first explanation). It is likely, however, that the law is not in accordance with this position. See n. 119.

118 See *Drush Vehidush* on bKetubot 11a s.v. *matbilin* (first explanation). It seems to me that R. Akiva Eiger's analysis can apply only where the child is a girl or, in accordance with the view of R. Aaron Halevi that circumcision is unnecessary to complete the conversion process. See n. 102. According to Nahmanides' view that the conversion for male children immersed **in utero** is not completed until their circumcision after birth, the conversion would remain at the Rabbinic level (according to *Tosafot*).

level.[119] This alone, however, would be no reason to defer immersion until after birth, because even then the conversion may be only of Rabbinic force. Nevertheless, given that there are authorities who do not permit conversion of the embryos where the mother is not undergoing a conversion,[120] it is advisable to defer the conversion until the children are born.

A final issue is whether children from IVF-generated embryos who undergo conversion, though born to a Jewish woman, have the right to renounce it upon reaching adulthood. According to bKetubot 11a, a non-Jewish minor who is converted has the right to renounce his conversion upon attaining adulthood.[121] The matter is much more complicated in cases of egg or embryo donation, where the need for conversion is in itself questionable. Certainly, the views that regard birth as determinative[122] would not permit renunciation; the children are Jews by birth,

119 It is not clear what the practical difference between a Rabbinic and a biblical conversion would be, since the *Tosafot* conclude that even where a conversion is valid only Rabbinically, the convert may marry a Jew. Presumably, however, one whose conversion is only of Rabbinic force would need to "reconvert" as an adult in order to be fully obligated to observe the precepts. Based on my own personal observations, such a reconversion in the case of a non-Jew originally converted as a minor is never required, implying rejection of the construal of such conversion as merely Rabbinic.

120 See n. 116.

121 This rule clearly applies when non-Jewish children are converted after birth. (But see *Responsa Hatam Sofer*, YD 253, who rules there is no right of renunciation if one or both of the parents converted along with the child). Whether the right of protest applies where the conversion of the minor was effected by the mother during pregnancy is a matter of dispute. See *Pithei Teshuva, SA* YD 268:8 quoting *Tiferet Lemoshe*. Such a distinction may be based on R. Akiva Eiger's ruling that conversion effected during pregnancy has biblical rather than Rabbinic force (see n. 118 above), with the protest rule applying only to Rabbinic conversions. But see n. 119 above (we apparently rule that the conversions of all minors, even after birth, are of biblical force). It should also be noted that, according to R. Chaim Soloveitchik, if a woman converts within 40 days of conception, it is clear that the child could not renounce the conversion, because he would be a Jew by birth, not conversion. See n. 111.

122 See discussion at nn. 111–112. I would note, however, that on R. Goldberg's position, although the children are related to their mother through birth, to terminate their precept obligation, renunciation would still be possible. The statement in the text is limited to those authorities who maintain that conversion is unnecessary for any purpose whatsoever.

not conversion. Similarly, on R. Bleich's dual maternity approach, where the children are half-Jewish–half-non-Jewish,[123] practically-speaking, renunciation would be impossible, since the children would, even after renunciation, retain the status of half-Jew by virtue of their birth mother. While it is true that in light of these uncertainties, we follow the stricter view and advise that conversion take place, this surely cannot be the basis for a leniency allowing renunciation. In effect, one would have to treat the progeny of an IVF where the eggs are of non-Jewish origin as falling into the category of doubtful Jews by birth or Jews by conversion, and impose the stringencies of both categories.

It should also be noted that because of halakhic uncertainties, it would be essential that the progeny of an IVF-pregnancy who underwent a conversion due to uncertainty (*giyur misafek*) be informed of his status, though, in the unlikely event of repudiation, his status as Jew or non-Jew would be highly uncertain.[124] This is an important point to keep in mind since many parents using egg donation prefer to keep the process undisclosed even to their own children.[125]

### d Embryo or Ovum Receipt from Jewish Donors

As mentioned, these cases generally raise a number of serious halakhic concerns, including the potential for unknown incest with relatives of the egg donor (since the egg donor may be deemed the mother),[126] and, in the case of embryo receipt, the father, as well as immodesty and the undermining of domestic peace if the donor's identity were made known. In the case of an embryo transfer, if we equate embryo transfer with donor insemination, there is also the possibility of adultery and *mamzeirut*, on the Satmar Rav's position.[127] A pure ovum donation

123 See R. Bleich, n. 78 above, 53–57.

124 On the view of R. Moses Feinstein, in the case of a minor convert who was not informed of his conversion, the right to renounce or protest remains even afer adulthood; failure to renounce cannot be deemed acquiescence when the person did not know there was anything to renounce; see *Igrot Moshe*, YD 1:162. How this would play out in an undisclosed IVF-pregnancy is anyone's guess.

125 The author is personally familiar with a number of these cases. Egg donation, by definition, is a more discreet procedure than, say, gestational surrogacy, and many parents seek to keep it that way.

126 See n. 79 above.

127 See text at nn. 141–142 below.

from a married woman is less likely to constitute adultery or generate *mamzeirut* even on the view of the Satmar Rav, but uncertainty remains.[128] It would thus seem that a single, unmarried unrelated donor is preferable, though even here, if her identity is unknown, there is still the problem of future incest.

### e Ovum Receipt via Uterine Lavage

In garden-variety IVF using donor gametes, the egg is fertilized by sperm in a petri dish, then transferred to the uterus of the infertile woman. It is possible, however, for fertilization to take place **within** the body of the egg donor, with the preembryo then being transferred to the uterus of the recipient either immediately after removal, or after a period of cryopreservation. In uterine lavage (UL), a woman is inseminated at the predicted time of ovulation with sperm from the husband of an infertile woman. Five to six days later (before implantation), the preembryo is flushed from her uterus and transferred to the uterus of the infertile woman.[129] Despite some early indicators of success, the American Fertility Society report regards uterine lavage as an experimental procedure not recommended for general use.[130]

The "split motherhood" issue appears to be more acute in UL than in standard IVF using ovum donation. In UL, the ovum donor is not only the genetic mother of the child, but the woman in whose body conception took place. Thus, whether UL is employed from Jew to Jew or non-Jew to Jew, a strong argument can be made that in either case the egg donor should have **a** maternal tie, if not the exclusive one. Nevertheless, the halakhic authorities who have debated the matter have not differentiated between IVF and UL. R. Goldberg's conclusion that in Jew to Jew transfers the birth mother is the sole mother was articulated in the context of an intrauterine transfer, and a fortiori

128 See text at nn. 149–153 below.

129 See Buster, Bustillo et al., "Non-surgical transfer of in-vitro fertilized donated ova to five infertile women: report of two pregnancies," *Lancet* 1983 (2), 223 and Buster, "Embryo donation by uterine flushing and embryo transfer," *Journal of Clinical Obstetrics and Gynecology* 1985 (12), 815.

130 ECART, n. 1 above, 52S.

would apply to IVF. R. Kilav's conclusion that the identity of the ovum donor is determinative where one of the parties is non-Jewish applied even to IVF, and a fortiori would apply to UL. Thus, at least as reflected in most contemporary rabbinic writing, the questions pertaining to maternal identity appear to be identical in both procedures.[131]

Nevertheless, UL does pose distinct halakhic problems, particularly on the view of the Satmar Rav. If the ovum donor is Jewish and married, direct insemination within her body is more likely to be adulterous than the insemination of the donor's egg in a petri dish.[132]

If the ovum donor is not Jewish, the general prohibitions against intercourse with non-Jews, and the possible prohibition against impregnation of non-Jews,[133] may be germane as well. The emission of semen to impregnate a non-Jewish woman may also be "emission of seed in vain," even where the embryo is then flushed out and transferred to a Jewish woman, viz., the sperm provider's wife.[134] In short,

131 A notable exception is R. Ezra Bick, n. 43 above, who accords great significance to where conception takes place. At present, UL can only be employed at a very early, pre-implantation stage. We can imagine, however, a "brave new world" in which implanted embryos, or even developed fetuses, could be transferred into another woman's uterus. At some point in the gestational process, it may become increasingly difficult to accord sole maternity to the birth mother. Moreover, at some stage of embryonic or fetal development (40 days? end of first trimester?), the woman from whose uterus the embryo or fetus was removed would herself have the status of a birth mother, since the removal of the child would be a birth. Surely a 9-month fetus that is transplanted to another woman would not lose its filial connection to the woman who first carried it. R. Auerbach alludes to this conceptual difficulty. See *Nishmat Avraham* (App.), EH 1:15. Fortunately, these issues as yet are of no practical importance. See n. 81 above regarding R. Akiva Eiger's views as to the status of the embryo in the first trimester, and M. Broyde, "The establishment of maternity and paternity in Jewish and American law," at http://jlaw.com/Articles/maternity1.html.

132 Indeed, at least with respect to adultery, UL is no different from AID, which the Satmar Rav expressly condemned as adultery. On whether UL may result in *mamzeirut* as well, see below at n. 154.

133 See n. 83 above.

134 I do not mean to suggest that every time a Jew has intercourse with a non-Jew, he is guilty of violating the prohibition against "wasteful emission of seed." Even though he will not have a paternal bond to any resulting child, the act of intercourse, though prohibited, is nonetheless not "wasteful" (*levatala*), since the semen was emitted in the course of normal sexual relations. See, e.g., *Tosafot*, bJebamot 12b s.v. *shalosh*.

UL is certainly no less problematic than other forms of ovum donation, and may be considerably more so.[135]

### f Ovum Receipt via GIFT

GIFT is essentially the opposite of uterine lavage. As an alternative to traditional IVF, where fertilization takes place in a petri dish, physicians in the mid-1980's developed a procedure known as GIFT ("Gamete Intra Fallopian Transfer") where ova are mixed with sperm and deposited directly into the fallopian tube, where fertilization occurs (if it does) as it would naturally.[136] Passage of the fertilized egg through the tubes is thought to increase the probability of successful uterine implantation in ways not yet fully understood. (As IVF has improved, however, its success rate has become as good as or better than GIFT.) The disadvantage of GIFT is that it necessitates **two** surgical procedures in the very delicate area of the fallopian tubes and ovaries — one to remove the eggs from the ovaries, the other to insert them into the fallopian tubes.[137] Moreover, GIFT can be employed only if there is no tubal blockage, while IVF is helpful precisely where blockage exists. From the perspective of halakha, GIFT may have certain advantages over IVF. Consider R. Waldenberg's minority position that

However, in cases of IVF or artificial insemination, the sperm was by definition not emitted in the course of sexual relations. To the extent it is permitted at all, the emission is permitted only because it is a vehicle to produce a child. If the child will not bear any relationship to the sperm provider, the entire justification loses its force. But cf. R. Gershuni's view cited in n. 9 above.

135 Theoretically, UL could be employed without using the sperm of the recipient's husband: a woman could be impregnated with donor sperm, then undergo UL. The issues here, from the perspective of the Jewish woman **receiving** the embryo, are identical to those discussed above in the text at nn. 97–102. As far as I know, this variant of the procedure has not been employed, perhaps because it is too close to outright baby selling.

136 See ECART, n. 1 above, 38S.

137 GIFT can be used **without** ovum donation, in which case both procedures are performed on the same woman, but here we consider the case where the eggs are removed from one woman and inserted into the body of another.

would deny paternity and maternity to IVF participants because fertilization occurs outside of the woman's body.[138] Could it not be argued that GIFT essentially replicates natural reproduction and should thus be halakhically sanctioned even on this minority view?

As to the question of maternity, let us consider whether GIFT might resolve the problem of "split" maternity that arises in ovum donation. Presumably, an ovum, which is simply inert human tissue incapable of reproduction, becomes part of the body onto which it is engrafted. Even the opinions that seem to regard the egg donor as the sole (or joint) mother may concede that where fertilization occurs within the body of the woman who gives birth, she is the sole mother despite the lack of a genetic connection. Accordingly, a non-Jewish ovum transferred to a Jewish woman via GIFT might **not** require conversion; an ovum from a married Jewish woman would be totally free of the stigma of *mamzeirut* even according to the Satmar Rav; and since the egg donor would have no maternal relationship with the child, potential incest with relatives of the Jewish egg donor would not be a concern.[139] Ovum donation coupled with GIFT does not appear to raise the traditional fears associated with AID.[140]

### *Excursus: The Satmar Rav on Third Party Facilitators — Sperm, Egg and Embryo Donation*

The foregoing has discussed issues that arise when third parties contribute eggs, sperm, or embryos to a married couple. Repeated reference has been made to the Satmar Rav's ruling on AID. It may be helpful to briefly summarize some of the uncertainties this position raises. According to the Satmar Rav, a married Jewish woman who is

138 See text at n. 9 above.

139 This also appears to be the position of R. Bick, n. 43 above, 38, who draws an analogy from responsa dealing with ovarian transplants, where it is clear that the recipient is regarded as the mother of any resulting offspring notwithstanding the lack of any genetic connection. See also R. Zahn, *Birkhat Banim*, 11:27 and *Tzitz Eliezer*, 7:48.

140 Note, however, that alternatives to GIFT such as ZIFT (Zygote Intra Fallopian Transfer) continue to raise problems, since fertilization does take place in vitro, with the preembryo placed in the fallopian tube rather than directly into the uterus. Halakhically, ZIFT appears to be indistinguishable from standard IVF.

impregnated with the sperm of a Jewish man other than her husband has committed adultery, and is forbidden to her husband. A child born from such an insemination is halakhically a *mamzer*. The generation of *mamzeirut* does not depend on the occurrence of a sex act, and can be effected simply by sperm penetrating a woman's body. The implications of this very stringent position on the range of options for third party assistance in reproduction are unclear. Consider the following problems:

1. **AID with IVF** While the Satmar Rav clearly regards AID into the recipient's uterus as adulterous, would his ruling apply to donor sperm that fertilizes the recipient's egg in vitro, with the fertilized egg then being transferred? At that point, it is not "seed" that is penetrating the woman's body, but a new living being. Is there a difference between a pure AID procedure and one that is coupled with an IVF? My assumption would be that there is no difference, at least as regards the *mamzeirut* problem, since a child was born from the union of sperm with the egg of a Jewish woman who was married to someone else. On the other hand, it is less likely, though possible, that the implantation of a full-blown embryo — even one from the woman's own ovum — would constitute an act of adultery rendering a woman prohibited to her husband.[141] (It should also be noted that on the minority view of *Tzitz Eliezer*, which denies paternity in IVF-pregnancies, the child would presumably not be a *mamzer*, because halakhically he has no father, and thus could not be regarded as the progeny of adultery.)[142]
2. **AID with or without IVF after donor's death** Assume a married Jewish woman is impregnated with donor sperm after the donor has died. Or, assuming the Satmar Rav's ruling applies to IVF, the donor sperm fertilizes her eggs in vitro and the embryos are then

141 It could be argued that where impregnation, i.e., fertilization, did not take place within a woman's body, no adultery has occurred. A new living embryo is being implanted, not seed (semen). See M. Halperin, "In-vitro fertilization, embryo transfer and embryo freezing," *Jewish Medical Ethics* 1 (1988), 25–30. After suggesting this, Halperin concludes that IVF using donor sperm may be preferable to direct artificial insemination from a donor.

142 This is analogous to a non-Jew's impregnating a married Jewish woman, where the non-Jew lacks paternity and the child is not a *mamzer*. See *SA* EH 4:19.

transferred to her uterus. Indeed, the donor could even be the woman's first husband. Are the children illegitimate? Do they have a paternal bond to the now-deceased sperm donor? On the one hand, we could not regard the impregnation of a woman after the death of the donor as a prohibited sex act. On the other, is it not the essence of the Satmar Rav's position that *mamzeirut* is predicated on the fact of a married Jewish woman's giving birth to a child from a Jewish man who is not her husband, whether or not prohibited intercourse took place?[143]

3. **AID from non-Jewish source** While neither *mamzeirut* nor paternity is an issue, is the woman guilty of intercourse with a non-Jew? Is the woman forbidden to her husband as a result of the impregnation? May the woman marry a *kohen*? Although the Satmar Rav does not explicitly treat these matters, presumably the same parameters that define adultery and *mamzeirut* between Jews will define prohibited intercourse with non-Jews. Here too there may be a distinction between direct deposit of sperm and transfer of an embryo after IVF.[144]

143 Whether there can be a *mamzeirut* problem after the sperm contributor died is uncertain. Arguably, once the first husband has died, he is incapable of committing adultery — "once a man is dead, he is free of religious obligations" (bShabat 151b, bNida 61b) — and hence, incapable of generating *mamzeirut* even on the view of the Satmar Rav. On the other hand, it may also be the case that *mamzeirut* does not depend on the commission of a technical act of adultery, but merely on the fact that a married woman bears a child from a Jewish man who is not her husband. As such, the problem of *mamzeirut* exists whether the first husband is dead or alive. See Maharsha on bJebamot 77a s.v. *ketnai*; but see *Shaar Hamelekh*, Laws concerning Levirate Marriage and Release 6:11 (at the end).

Note too that on R. Shaul Yisraeli's view (see text at n. 175 below) — as interpreted by Makhon Eretz Hemda — a sperm contributor who died even after fertilization of the embryo but before its implantation bears no paternal relationship to the resulting child. This would clearly preclude *mamzeirut*, since given that the child has no father, the recipient is not bearing the child of a man other than her husband. As will be discussed, both R. Yisraeli's definition of *klita* and his extension of the *Noda Biyehuda*'s ruling beyond the area of *yibum* are problematic. Most authorities fully recognize a paternal bond to the sperm donor even where fertilization does not occur until after the donor's death. (On the view of R. Waldenberg, who denies paternity to **any** IVF-offspring, there could not, of course, be *mamzeirut* even if the sperm donor were alive.)

144 Even though it is the Jewish woman's own egg.

4. **AIH with embryo transfer after woman remarries** Indeed, even implantation of an embryo generated from the husband's sperm could create a halakhic problem. This is obviously the case where the first husband's sperm fertilizes his ex-wife's egg after their divorce and her subsequent remarriage, since the first husband is then like any other sperm donor.[145] But consider the following scenario: IVF-embryos are generated from a husband and wife. They divorce. The wife remarries and desires implantation of those embryos. Maybe the first husband consents, maybe he does not.[146] Are the children illegitimate? Has the wife committed adultery with her ex-husband? On one hand, there was an embryo transfer involving the sperm of a Jewish man other than her present husband. Is this analogous to a new impregnation after divorce or remarriage to a new husband, which is unquestionably adulterous? Or, given the fact that at the time of the fertilization the first husband was married to the wife, is it tantamount to a pregnancy predating the second marriage, in which case the child could not be a *mamzer* regardless of when it was born?

Is there a distinction between *mamzeirut* and adultery? Is it possible that the child is not illegitimate, because its fertilization was not the result of an incestuous or adulterous union of egg and sperm, but the transfer of the embryo after remarriage is nonetheless an act of adultery, rendering the woman prohibited to her second husband? Can embryo transfer itself be a prohibited sex act?[147] Can a child become a *mamzer* through embryo transfer and birth if *mamzeirut* was not created at conception?[148]

145 If such fertilization takes place after the first husband's death, this would raise the question of postmortem adultery, point (2) above.

146 Recall that in *Davis v. Davis*, n. 3 above, the sperm provider, in the absence of an advance directive, was given a presumptive veto to assert his right not to be a biological parent. On the other hand, another case, in the 1996 *Nahmani v. Nahmani* decision, CA5587/93, 50(4)PD661, the Israeli Supreme Court gave greater recognition to the wife's right to bear a child, at least where it might be her last chance. *Nahmani*, however, did not consider the potential rights of the second husband, who might well object to his wife's bearing a child from her first husband.

147 This issue can, and was, raised before with respect to AID combined with IVF. See (1). However, even if it is accepted that an embryo transfer **may** constitute an adulterous act, this might not be the case where, at the time of fertilization, the sperm and egg providers were married.

148 As in gestational surrogacy, discussed in (9) below.

5. **Ovum donation from a Jew** The Satmar Rav regarded AID as tantamount to adultery. Assuming that his ruling applies to AID coupled with IVF (see (1) above), how would this play out in ovum donation? Assume, for example, that a woman is capable of carrying a baby to term, but either does not ovulate, or her eggs are genetically defective. An egg is donated by a married woman or a woman who is a close relative, such as her sister or mother. The husband's sperm fertilizes the donor egg, which is then transplanted into his wife. Obviously, his wife has committed no act of adultery by receiving a married woman's egg. By definition, adultery cannot be committed between two women. The question, however, is whether the husband's act of fertilizing the donor's egg is an act of adultery with the egg donor, and whether the resulting child is therefore a *mamzer*. In other words, does ovum donation raise the same concern as sperm donation? In sperm donation, the possibility of adultery exists between male donor and female recipient, whereas in egg donation the adultery would be between the husband of the infertile woman and the egg donor.

Given that the man's sperm never entered the egg donor's body, either directly or through the transfer of an IVF-generated embryo, it is intrinsically improbable that the union of sperm and donor egg in a petri dish, which is transferred **into his own wife's body**, could ever be regarded as an act of adultery with the egg donor. It is, I believe, safe to conclude that the married egg donor need not leave her husband.

The absence of adultery, however, does not necessarily resolve the *mamzeirut* problem. If indeed it is the essence of the Satmar Rav's position that *mamzeirut* can arise even where no prohibited sexual act was committed, as long as the child is a product of a union that would be adulterous or incestuous, the child born from an ovum donation could conceivably be tainted **if** the egg donor is deemed the mother. However, since, according to most decisors,[149] maternity in egg donation cases is assigned exclusively to the birth mother, not the egg donor, the child is not deemed the progeny of an adulterous or incestuous union, but rather, the progeny of his

149 It should be reiterated that where both donor and recipient are Jewish, most decisors conclude that the birth mother is the sole mother. The argument between rabbis Goldberg and Kilav applies only to **Jewish–non-Jewish** situations.

father and birth mother. On this view, with respect to the issue of *mamzeirut*, there would be no reason to insist that egg donors be single or unrelated to the husband and wife.

If, on the other hand, maternity is assigned to the genetic egg donor (a decidedly minority position), or, as R. Bleich suggests, there can be dual maternity, illegitimacy is indeed a potential problem. At least one of the mothers — the egg donor — has an adulterous or incestuous relationship with the sperm provider, thereby generating *mamzeirut* (or partial *mamzeirut*), despite the absence of a prohibited sexual act. On the basis of R. Auerbach's ruling that because maternity is uncertain, we must be strict in considering all possibilities, the child would be of doubtful legitimacy (*safek mamzer*).[150]

In short, egg donation probably does not involve adultery even where the donor is related or married. On the majority view that assigns maternity to the birth mother, there would also be no problem of illegitimacy, even on the strict position of the Satmar Rav. However, because of the other views, which assign maternity in whole or part to the egg donor, one would have to be strict about not permitting married or related persons to donate. Note that here I am addressing only the issues of adultery, incest, and illegitimacy. Other reasons for restricting egg donation, even from single women, were discussed above.[151]

6. **Ovum donation from a non-Jew** As noted, the child will need to be converted, and there is a dispute regarding the maternal relationship after the conversion.[152] Here too it is unlikely that the use of a Jewish husband's sperm to fertilize a non-Jewish egg which is then transferred to his Jewish wife could be construed as an act of prohibited intercourse with a non-Jew, since his sperm never penetrated her body. There may, however, be violation of other prohibitions, such as "destruction of seed" and, though this is less likely, impregnation of a Gentile.[153]

150 See text at n. 81 above. Note that the status of *safek* (or half)-*mamzer* is actually more restrictive than that of a definite *mamzer*. One who is illegitimate may marry someone illegitimate, whereas one of doubtful or partial legitimacy may not (though he may marry a convert). See *SA* EH 4:24.

151 See text at nn. 82–88 above.

152 See text at n. 102 above.

153 See text at n. 83 above.

7. **Ovum donation coupled with GIFT** Where fertilization occurs within the wife's fallopian tubes, rather than in the petri dish, the assignment of maternity to the recipient is much stronger. It probably gives rise to neither *mamzeirut* nor adultery. Any dispensation that would cover egg donation in general would clearly cover GIFT, though R. Auerbach's caution may apply even here, barring the use of married or related ovum donors.
8. **Ovum donation via uterine lavage** Uterine lavage starts off identically to AID. The depositing of sperm in the body of a married woman would clearly be adulterous, and the married woman impregnated in such a way prohibited to her husband. However, this would not necessarily result in *mamzeirut*. Given the fact that most decisors rule that in Jew to Jew transfers, maternity is established through birth, the child's "mother" is the woman who is married to the sperm provider. In the halakhic sense, the child is not the **product** of an adulterous or incestuous union. This creates a paradox: a child conceived from a adulterous union will not be a *mamzer* if he is born to a woman whose connection to the sperm provider is not adulterous and that woman is deemed his sole mother.

   Once again, however, if we adopt R. Auerbach's position, a UL child (from a married Jewish woman) would be of uncertain illegitimacy, or, if we accept R. Bleich's notion of dual maternity, partial illegitimacy. It is also possible that the case for the maternity of the egg donor is stronger in UL cases, increasing the probability of *mamzeirut*.[154]
9. **Gestational surrogacy (Jewish surrogate)** Assume a woman's ovulation is in order, but she cannot carry a baby to term. Her egg may be fertilized with her husband's sperm in vitro and then transferred to a gestational surrogate who agrees to deliver the baby to the couple upon its birth. Assume further that the gestational mother is a married Jewish woman. Would the transfer of the fertilized embryo be an act of adultery? Would the child born from the embryo transfer be illegitimate? Here, we face the opposite of the egg donation quandary. Instead of the husband's sperm fertilizing the donor's egg, which is then transferred to his wife, the husband's sperm fertilizes his wife's egg, which is then transferred to a surrogate. On the view of most authorities, maternity will be

154 See R. Ezra Bick, n. 43 above.

assigned to the birth mother, probably in whole, and at least in part. The child is thus the progeny of a union that is adulterous or, if the surrogate is a sister or mother, incestuous. There is thus more reason to require that a gestational surrogate be single and unrelated than there is to impose such a requirement on an egg donor, and indeed, the Israeli Chief Rabbinate has so ruled.[155]

Nevertheless, theoretically speaking, it is still possible that adultery occurs only when the man's sperm enters a married woman's body as sperm, or at least fertilizes her egg, which is then transplanted into her body. When it fertilizes his wife's own egg, which is then transferred to a married woman's body, no prohibited sex act can be said to have occurred, since the union of egg and sperm occurred neither within a married woman's body (unlike UL), nor with her egg. What is transferred is a separate living being. Adultery can occur only at the moment of union, not at the moment of transfer. Thus, the argument could be made that a gestational surrogate has not committed adultery, even technically, and would not be prohibited to her husband.

Notwithstanding this, in light of the assignment of maternity to the surrogate, the *mamzeirut* problem remains a concern (but see (2) above). This too creates a paradox, though the converse of that discussed in (8): a child could be **conceived** in a union that is neither adulterous nor incestuous, and nevertheless be illegitimate because it is born to a woman whose connection to the sperm provider is adulterous (and possibly incestuous), and that woman is deemed to be his mother in whole or in part.

10. **Gestational surrogate (non-Jew)** Illegitimacy will not be a concern here even if the surrogate is married, since the child will need a conversion after birth. Whether the sperm provider is committing a forbidden sexual act with a Gentile depends on whether embryo transfer, as opposed to sperm injection, is the equivalent of intercourse — an issue discussed in (1), (4), and (9). The two additional halakhic problems would be impregnation of a Gentile and wasteful emission of seed.[156] It should be noted that on the view of

155 See text above at nn. 89–96, and in particular n. 93, for additional reasons a married surrogate should not be used.

156 See nn. 83, 90 above. The Rabbinic prohibition against "giving birth to a child for idolatry" clearly does not arise, since the surrogate agrees to return the child to the Jewish couple at birth.

R. Kilav, who assigns maternity to the egg donor in Jew to non-Jew cases, neither of these problems arise, and it is possible that a non-Jewish surrogate would be **permitted.**[157] His, however, is a minority view.

11. **Embryo donation from a Jewish couple** Donation of a fertilized embryo to a married Jewish couple seems to raise the same concerns as gestational surrogacy, namely, a married woman is carrying an embryo that was fertilized by the sperm of a Jewish man who is not her husband. Embryo donation may or may not be an act of adultery on the part of the recipient (see (9)), but in either case, the assignment of maternity to the recipient will raise the problem of illegitimacy, in that a child has been born to a woman married to someone other than the father.

    A possible distinction between gestational surrogacy and embryo donation should be noted. In surrogacy, although the husband's sperm initially fertilized his own wife's egg, it was done with the intention of transfer to a surrogate. Perhaps this renders the "union" adulterous in a way that embryo donation is not. In embryo donation, the fertilization is not initially undertaken to impregnate a third party. If this subtle distinction is accepted, a married woman cannot consent to be a gestational surrogate, but could perhaps be a recipient of an embryo donation, at least where the transfer was not contemplated at the time of the fertilization. However, this distinction does not appear to be relevant to the problem of illegitimacy. As long as maternity is assigned to a birth mother who is married to someone other than the sperm provider, the illegitimacy problem exists, again highlighting the paradox of non-adulterous fertilization resulting in *mamzeirut* through embryo transfer and birth.

    If it is assumed that embryo transfer to a married Jewish woman constitutes adultery, embryo transfer to a non-Jewish woman would similarly constitute prohibited intercourse with a Gentile. The two other problems noted in (10) would also apply.

To summarize this excursus, the resolution of these various hypotheticals essentially hinges on two problems. **First**, what is the definition

157 In light of R. Wozner's argument, however, the non-Jewish surrogate would have to be unmarried. See n. 93 above.

of adultery once we extend it beyond the parameters of physical intercourse, as does the Satmar Rav? Assuming that AID is a prohibited act of adultery, is this prohibition limited to the direct deposit of sperm in a married woman's body, or does it include the transfer of an embryo fertilized outside her womb? If adultery does include embryo transfer, does it make a difference whether the transferred egg is her own or that of another woman (the sperm provider's wife) which she receives and brings to birth? Conversely, does the fertilization of a married woman's egg either inside (UL) or outside (IVF) her body constitute adultery where the fertilized egg is transferred to the sperm provider's wife? Determining the precise parameters of adultery is significant, because a woman who commits adultery may not remain with her husband.

The second issue is the relationship between adultery (or incest) and *mamzeirut*. The Satmar Rav asserts that the insertion of donor sperm, at least within the body of a married woman, constitutes an act of adultery, and that it generates illegitimacy. He does not clarify whether these two outcomes are dependent or independent, that is, whether the second outcome is a function of the first. Are the resulting offspring illegitimate **because** AID constitutes a prohibited adulterous sex act, in which case, in the absence of such an act, *mamzeirut* cannot arise?[158] Or alternatively, does *mamzeirut* arise whenever a child is born of parents whose union **would have been** incestuous or adulterous, whether or not a prohibited sex act took place? Can a child whose conception was non-adulterous (IVF with husband's sperm and wife's egg) nonetheless acquire the status of *mamzer* by virtue of later implantation in a married gestational surrogate, who gives birth to the child? Conversely, can a conception that was arguably adulterous (UL) and prohibited nevertheless not generate illegitimacy upon later implantation in the sperm provider's wife? The apparent paradox of the uncoupling of two ordinarily inextricably-linked phenomena (adultery without *memzeirut* and *mamzeirut* without adultery) merits further investigation and analysis.

158 I speak of the original creation of *mamzeirut*. Once the status of *mamzer* is established, it will automatically be passed on to the *mamzer*'s offspring, even if the *mamzer*'s relationships are fully permissible, e.g., if he marries a convert.

## 8 *Jewish Law Tort Remedies Against Unauthorized Preembryo Destruction*

American law has recognized that gamete providers may have a tort remedy against third parties who destroy preembryos without consent.[159] Would halakha recognize such a remedy? The Torah provides that if one hits a woman and as a result, causes a miscarriage, the perpetrator must pay compensation (*dmei vladot*) to the woman's husband (*baal haisha*).[160] Assuming, for a moment, that the principles of *dmei vladot* apply to preembryos, the following conclusions emerge:

1. The father is entitled to compensation.
2. According to most authorities, this entitlement exists even if the father was not married to the woman at the time of the accident.[161]
3. The right to compensation passes to the father's heirs if he dies after the wounding takes place.
4. If the father died before the wounding, the compensation goes either to his heirs (Raavad) or to the mother (Rambam).[162]

The application of *dmei vladot* liability to Noahides, however, may be somewhat problematic. First, does it apply to non-Jews at all? After all, this is a particular law found in the Book of Exodus, and like many particularistic laws in the Torah, may be limited to Jews. There is no textual evidence that liability for *dmei vladot* represents a universal

159 See *Del Zio v. Columbia Presbyterian Hospital*, No. 71-3588 (SDNY 1978). A jury awarded a couple $50,000 damages for intentional infliction of emotional distress when a physician who objected to their efforts at IVF without prior Institutional Review Board approval destroyed the preembryo. But cf. *Doe v. Irvine Scientific Sales Co.*, 7 Fed. Supp. 2d 737 (1998), which imposed no liability for negligent infliction of emotional distress resulting from contamination of embryos with virus.

160 Exodus 21:22.

161 The Talmud in bBaba Kama 43a clearly states this to be the case. R. Saul Yisraeli has attempted to demonstrate that according to Maimonides, if the father and mother were not married, or if they were divorced before the accident, *dmei vladot* would be payable to the mother. *Minhat Hinukh*, #49, seems to reject this understanding of Maimonides. See Breitowitz, n. 4 above, 165–166.

162 Maimonides, *Code*, Laws concerning Wounding and Damaging 4:2, and Raavad's comments.

principle applicable to non-Jews under the Noahide laws.[163] Second, in Jewish law compensation can exist only in the absence of a capital crime.[164] To the extent injury results in a homicide for which capital punishment can be imposed, there is no monetary liability. Feticide committed by Jews is not a capital crime, but feticide committed by Noahides is.[165] If destruction of fetal or embryonic life by non-Jews incurs capital punishment, this alone may preclude any liability for fetal damage.[166] If, on the other hand, the destruction of an externalized preembryo is not a capital offense under Noahide law, financial liability may indeed arise.[167]

It is probable, however, that even for Jewish tortfeasors, halakha does not recognize liability for the destruction of preembryos. First, it is doubtful whether liability can ever attach to wounding incurred by

163 Whether Noahides are subject to *dmei vladot* liability may depend on the scope of the Noahide commandment of *dinim*. If, as Maimonides says, it simply necessitates the establishment of a court system to enforce the other six Noahide commandments, the various civil liabilities of the Torah would generally not apply to Noahides (except, perhaps, to the degree that halakha would place its imprimatur on self-imposed legislative or judicial expansion of rights by the non-Jewish societies themselves). See Maimonides, *Code*, Laws concerning Kings 9:14. According to Nahmanides, at least as he was understood in *Responsa Rema*, #1 and *Responsa Hatam Sofer*, 6:14, *dinim* encompasses virtually all the Torah's interpersonal laws and obligations, except where Scripture specifically excludes them. Thus, Noahides might indeed be liable for *dmei vladot*. But see *Haamek Sheeila*, sheilta 2:3; *Even Haazel*, Creditor and Debtor 27:1; and *Arukh Hashulhan Heatid*, Sanhedrin 79:15, who interpret Nahmanides differently.

164 Indeed, the law of *dmei vlalot* is one of the sources for this principle; see bKetubot 36b. (By emphasizing that there is monetary liability because no one has been killed, the Torah implies that had a homicide occurred, e.g., had the mother been killed, no compensation would be imposed.)

165 See text at nn. 27–30 above.

166 My hesitation stems from the fact that it is not entirely clear that the "a lighter penalty is not imposed where a heavier penalty is imposed for the same offense" (*kam lei bidraba minei*) rule, which precludes monetary liability in the event of a capital offense, applies to Noahides. See *Minhat Hinukh*, #49. It is also possible that even if the halakhic rule exempts Noahides from financial liability where there is a capital crime, Noahide society could adopt a contrary rule by dint of its authority to establish laws (*dinim*).

167 See text at nn. 31–33 above.

an embryo under 40 days old. The principle of "mere water" may mean that functionally speaking, such an embryo is considered nonexistent. Second, regardless of its level of development, no monetary liability should arise from destruction of an externalized embryo. The amount awarded as *dmei vladot* is calculated not on the basis of damage to the fetus, but on the basis of damage to the woman's person.[168] The perpetrator pays the difference in value between a pregnant woman and a non-pregnant woman. While this measure may indeed suggest liability for the destruction of an **implanted** embryo even if it is under 40 days old, it precludes liability for the destruction of an externalized preembryo, no matter how developed.[169]

## 9 *Parentage of the Preembryo for Purposes of* Yibum, *Inheritance and* Pidyon Haben

Although maternity in the event of a donated preembryo or ovum is a matter of sharp controversy, the standard IVF protocol, where the fertilized egg is transferred back to the woman from whose womb it was removed, poses no such problem. In such a case, virtually all decisors

168 See Maimonides, *Code*, Laws concerning Wounding and Damaging 4:2. This position, however, is not universally accepted. See bBaba Kama 48b–49a; *Tosafot*, bBaba Kama 47a s.v. *vekhen*; *Lehem Mishne*, Laws concerning Wounding and Damaging 4:2. If there is indeed separate compensation for the destruction of the fetus, such compensation might be available even for the destruction of preembryos.

169 There are three additional points that might rule out *dmei vladot* liability for the destruction of externalized preembryos: (1) R. Shaul Yisraeli has argued, based on a responsum of the *Noda Biyehuda*, that no paternal relationship can exist until uterine implantation, a stage that preembryos have not achieved. As such, there is no "father" who might have a right to recover. (Could the mother recover?) As explained below, this may be a misinterpretation of the *Noda Biyehuda*'s ruling. (2) A passage in bSanhedrin 69a can be construed as suggesting that paternity arises only upon completion of the first trimester. R. Akiva Eiger, *SA* YD 87, applies this to maternity as well. See n. 81 above. If so, the preembryo has neither father nor mother. However, none of the codes limit *dmei vladot* liability to fetal miscarriages after the first trimester. (3) On R. Waldenberg's view, IVF-generated embryos, even after birth, have no halakhic father or mother. Accordingly, there may be no *dmei vladot* liability even for wounding that occurs after implantation. This too is a minority position that has been rejected by most decisors. See n. 7 above.

accord full parental status to the couple involved.[170] Assuming that a preembryo transfer back to the ovum donor results in full maternity and paternity rights — a relatively uncontroversial position — there are a number of implications.

## a Yibum

### 1 *Postmortem Implantation*

Consider the mitzva of *yibum*: The Torah states that if someone dies without children, his brother is obliged to either marry the widow or release her through the ceremony of *halitza* (Deut. 25:5–10). If someone dies leaving no brothers, but his mother had a frozen preembryo, which was later implanted, resulting in a pregnancy and birth, would the deceased's widow need *yibum* or *halitza*? Is she allowed to get married if such a preembryo exists? This would appear to pose no halakhic difficulty. The Mishnah in Jebamot lays down the rule that any brother born after the death of his sibling does not perform *yibum* and *halitza*, nor can he prevent the widow from remarrying. Thus, even were the deceased's mother pregnant at the time of his death, there would be no *yibum*. Obviously, an unimplanted preembryo whose development is clearly not beyond "mere water" cannot have a status greater than that of a fetus in its ninth month.

The *yibum* question does become more difficult, however, if we look at the widow herself. Assume her husband died but left either frozen sperm or fertilized preembryos. What is her status regarding *yibum* or *halitza*? Unlike the laws pertaining to the term "brother" (*ah*), those where the term "son" (*ben*)[171] appears are more expansive. The Torah says there is *yibum* if one brother dies "and has no child" (*uben ein lo*): if "*ein*" here is read "*ayen*," it means "you must investigate," implying that even an unborn son may obviate the duty of *yibum*. Consequently, the law is very clear that if a woman is pregnant at the time of her husband's death, whether or not she will need *yibum* depends on whether the child is born dead or alive.[172] If the child is born alive (even if he or she dies shortly after birth), the widow is

170 See text above at nn. 6–10.

171 The term "*ben*" in this context includes "daughter" as well as "son."

172 See *SA* EH 164:2.

permitted to marry without *yibum* or *halitza*. If the child is born dead, the widow requires *yibum* or *halitza* (There is an argument in the Gemara between R. Johanan and R. Shimon b. Lakish over whether *halitza* received **while** she was pregnant would suffice in the event the child is stillborn).[173] It is equally clear that the live birth of a child after the husband's death would qualify as a "son" for purposes of obviating *yibum* even if the pregnancy at the time of the husband's death was **under** 40 days old. Its status as "mere water" is irrelevant. This is evidenced by the fact that a widow cannot get married before a minimum of 90 days have elapsed, 90 days being the amount of time after which a pregnancy is recognizable.[174] If a pregnancy is not treated as a "son" until it is at least 40 days old, the only question that would be relevant would be whether the woman was carrying such an embryo at the moment of her husband's death, which could be discovered after 50 days.

Since any pregnancy that eventually results in a live birth terminates the obligations of *yibum* and *halitza*, the status of a frozen preembryo must be addressed. Little has been written on the subject, but R. Shaul Yisraeli has ruled that a postmortem implantation of a preembryo (and certainly sperm) does not confer posthumous paternity on the deceased, and the widow would require *halitza* even if the baby is brought to term.[175] His primary source is a responsum of the *Noda Biyehuda*.[176] According to the law, the "absorption of seed" (*klitat zera*) may take place up to 72 hours after intercourse.[177] If so, asks the *Noda*

173 bJebamot 35b. The law is in accordance with R. Shimon b. Lakish's view that a second *halitza* is necessary; *SA* EH 164:2.

174 bJebamot 41a; *SA* EH 164:1.

175 See *Torah Shebeal Pe* 33 (1992), 41–46.

176 *Noda Biyehuda*, 1, EH 69.

177 See *Tosafot*, b.Jebamot 37a s.v. *rov*. *Klita* seems to be understood by R. Yisraeli as referring to implantation of a fertilized ovum in the uterine wall. This is problematic, however, since implantation could actually occur up to 10–14 days after fertilization. See n. 1 above. An alternative explanation of *klita* would be penetration and fertilization of the egg. The halakha would thus reflect the idea that sperm are capable of fertilizing an egg up to 72 hours after ejaculation, a concept articulated in other contexts as well; see e.g., *SA* YD 196:11. If so, the *Noda Biyehuda* never intended to require implantation as a condition for paternity. This interpretation of *klita* casts serious doubt on R. Yisraeli's ruling regarding preembryos.

*Biyehuda*, why is a childless widow permitted to have *halitza* or *yibum* after 90 days? Perhaps she had intercourse immediately before her husband's death, and the seed was not "absorbed" until 72 hours later. As a result, the pregnancy would not be recognizable until 93 days after death. Therefore, if a woman received *halitza* between days 90 and 93 and proceeded to marry, such a marriage would turn out to be sinful in the event the child is stillborn (because the interim *halitza* given to a pregnant woman is invalid). Conversely, in the event she elected to have *yibum* after day 90, the union with the levir would be sinful if the child is later born alive. To avoid these problems, the Rabbis should have enacted a 93-day waiting period, after which the absence of a pregnancy could be definitively established. The *Noda Biyehuda's* answer is that if *klitat hazera* did not occur by the time of the husband's death, halakhically speaking he did not have a son on the date of his death. Paternity cannot be established by postmortem *klita*, though it can certainly be established by a postmortem birth. Thus, on day 91, assuming no visible pregnancy, the widow may undergo levitate marriage in any event. She is either not pregnant at all, or any pregnancy is a result of postmortem *klitat hazera*. Either way, the "has no child" requirement is fulfilled. The *yibum* is valid even if she eventually gives birth to a child. She would need *halitza* to marry anyone else even if she gives birth to a child. By the same token, any *halitza* given after day 90 will suffice to permit her to remarry, even if the child is ultimately stillborn. R. Yisraeli argues that these considerations certainly apply to frozen preembryos and (a fortiori) to sperm.

It appears to this writer, however, that the analogy may not be apt. While R. Yisraeli's analysis is unquestionably correct in the case of frozen sperm that is not utilized until after the husband's death, extending the *Noda Biyehuda*'s ruling to preembryos would be justified only if the term *klitat hazera* refers to uterine implantation. If, as is likely, *klita* refers to penetration and fertilization of the egg by the sperm, in the case of a preembryo a *klitat hazera* has indeed occurred during the lifetime of the husband, even where transfer and implantation take place after his death. Accordingly, in the event of a postmortem embryo transfer that culminates in a live birth, the widow would not require *halitza* to be able to remarry.

If the above assumption, viz., that a preembryo is a child for purposes of *yibum*, is correct, problems may arise concerning the timing of *halitza*. In accordance with the view of R. Shimon b. Lakish, *halitza* performed while a woman is pregnant is invalid.[178] This has two consequences: she is not permitted to receive *halitza* and marry during her pregnancy, lest she miscarry. In the event she did receive *halitza* while pregnant and then miscarried, she would need a new *halitza*. (If the baby is born alive, the widow may of course marry without *halitza*.) How would this apply to a preembryo? One possibility might be that even if a preembryo is a child for purposes of *yibum*, the widow is not considered pregnant for the purpose of invalidating her *halitza*. As such, in the event the woman decided not to have the embryos implanted, she could undergo *halitza* any time after the 90th day following her husband's death.[179] If, on the other hand, the woman is deemed to be pregnant at the time of her husband's death, no *halitza* can take place unless the embryos are implanted into her body and then stillborn or (spontaneously) aborted, or else destroyed and not implanted (assuming this is halakhically permissible).

In any event, even where the *klitat hazera* clearly occurred after the husband's death, not all the decisors have followed the *Noda Biyehuda*.[180]

178 bJebamot 35b; *SA* EH 164:2.

179 She would still have to wait 90 days to rule out the possibility of another pregnancy.

180 See e.g., *Noam* 1, 155 (1958). In this early article exploring the halakhic problems of artificial insemination, R. Auerbach ruled that sperm with which the wife is inseminated after the death of the husband cannot produce a child for purposes of *yibum*. Accordingly, the woman must undergo *yibum* or *halitza* even if the insemination produces a live birth. This also means that any *halitza* the woman undergoes while pregnant will immediately permit her to marry even if the pregnancy eventually results in a stillbirth. (This ruling appears obvious, since sperm alone is not deemed a child.)

R. Auerbach was in doubt, however, with regard to the case where the sperm was placed in her body before her husband's death but there was no *klita* until afterwards. Thus, if she underwent *halitza* while she was pregnant, but the baby was stillborn, a new *halitza* should be carried out due to the uncertainty.

(If the baby is born alive, there is no need for a second *halitza*: if posthumous *klita* cannot produce a child even if it culminates in a live birth, the *halitza* she underwent while pregnant was valid, since the pregnancy does not count. If posthumous *klita* can produce a child, a live birth exempts her from *halitza*, and she can marry for that reason alone. The validity of *halitza* during such a pregnancy becomes important only where there is a later stillbirth. If the pregnancy does not count as a potential child (as in the case of posthumous insemination), there is no need for another *halitza*. If, however, such a pregnancy is deemed a child for purposes of *yibum*, the *halitza* would be invalidated due to her pregnancy (*halitzat meuberet*).)

## 2 *Third-Party Contributions*

If an otherwise childless woman bears a child via a donated embryo of Jewish or non-Jewish origin, such a child is obviously not a child (*ben*) for purposes of *yibum*, because the woman's husband clearly has no paternity. Conversely, if a woman gave birth to a child through IVF and ovum donation from a Jewish donor, and the egg is fertilized by her husband's sperm, *yibum* or *halitza* (assuming a live birth) would clearly not be necessary, because regardless of whether maternity resides with the birth mother or egg donor, the husband is the father and that is all that matters. For purposes of exemption from *yibum* and *halitza*, the existence of paternity suffices.[181]

If the ovum came from a non-Jewish source and was fertilized by the husband's sperm and then transferred to his wife's uterus, it would appear that such children would **not** exempt their mother from *halitza*. According to R. Kilav, such children are non-Jews who must undergo conversion, after which they have no filial connection with either the mother or the father.[182] According to R. Goldberg, the peculiarities of their conversion would not sever their filial bond to their Jewish birth mother, but there would appear to be no basis for the father to claim paternity.[183] Indeed, even on the view that conversion is not necessary and the children are born Jews,[184] there would probably be no **paternity** on the part of the Jewish father, since paternal bonds are generated, if at all, at the time of conception, and at that time, the ovum was of non-Jewish origin. If a paternal relation was severed at the time of fertilization, it can probably not reestablish itself later. For the same reason, the dual maternity analysis of R. Bleich[185] (half born Jew–half convert) would probably not suffice to generate a filial bond to the father.

As a consequence, children born from non-Jewish egg donation do not exempt their mother from *yibum* or *halitza* regardless of how one resolves the maternity/religious status issue. Conversely, if years later,

181 Of course, if one accepts the minority views of R. Waldenberg and R. Sternbuch that no paternity exists in IVF-pregnancies, obviously the preembryo would not count as a *ben* for *yibum* purposes. As noted, this view is not widely accepted. See text at nn. 6–12 above.

182 The notion that paternity arises from conception is the basis of the ruling in bJebamot 97b. But cf. R. Akiva Eiger, *SA* YD 87, and n. 81 above.

183 See n. 102 above.

184 See nn. 111–112 above.

185 See R. Bleich, n. 78 above.

a "natural sibling" (born without egg donation) dies without children, his widow could not receive *halitza* from an IVF-generated brother, and if he were the only brother, would not have to receive *halitza* at all. This is yet another reason why parents of IVF-generated children from donated eggs should inform their children of this fact.[186]

Where a child is born from a non-Jewish gestational surrogate but from his wife's egg, the analysis is a bit more complicated. Here, paternity very much depends on maternity. One could argue that a proper paternal relationship was in fact generated at the moment of conception/fertilization. The question then becomes whether that paternity is forfeited by transfer of the embryo to the non-Jewish woman who becomes the birth mother. According to R. Kilav, the child is deemed a Jew by virtue of his genetic origin, without any need to convert. Hence, the paternal relationship which arose upon conception has not been severed. The same is true on R. Bleich's dual maternity approach: if the child is indeed half Jew–half non-Jew, the paternal bond remains by virtue of the "half" of the child that remained Jewish.[187] Hence, the widow would be exempt from *yibum* and *halitza*. On R. Goldberg's view, the child is a definite non-Jew, conversion is required, and the child does not exempt its genetic mother from *halitza*. On R. Auerbach's view, this would be a "doubtful case" (*safek*), and *halitza* would be required as a stringency (*lehumra*).

### b Inheritance

#### 1 *Postmortem Implantation*

A child who is born after the death of his parent clearly has inheritance rights, and may compel a reallocation of the parent's estate even after the other heirs have already taken possession.[188] There is considerable disagreement among the decisors as to whether he inherits as a fetus or

186 See text at nn. 124–125 above.

187 This is not true in the case of non-Jewish egg donation, for although here too the child might be half Jew–half non-Jew, the paternal bond was already severed at the time of conception, since the egg was, at the time, of totally non-Jewish origin.

188 If one accepts the minority view of R. Waldenberg that no paternity exists in IVF pregnancies, then obviously the embryo will not have inheritance rights even if it is implanted and then born in the lifetime of the father.

owns nothing until he is born, but it is indisputable that once he is born, he has a share of the parental estate.[189] R. Auerbach has ruled that these principles apply not only to fertilized preembryos that are implanted subsequent to the father's death, but even to sperm.[190] R. Yisraeli argues (without citing R. Auerbach) that the same definitions that exist for *yibum* should be determinative for inheritance purposes.[191] As such, postmortem implantation cannot establish paternity.[192] In support of R. Yisraeli's position, it should be noted that the phrase "has no child" (*ben ein lo*) appears in connection with both *yibum* and inheritance.[193]

### 2 *Third-Party Contributions*

If the egg donor is Jewish (whether married or not), the child is a born Jew. Assuming that full paternity exists in IVF-pregnancies, the child has a Jewish father, namely, the sperm provider. As such, the child will clearly have rights of inheritance in his father's estate regardless of the identity of his mother. Whether he would share in the distribution of his birth mother's estate depends on the question of maternity, discussed

---

The issue of posthumous implantation would be moot. Ironically, however, on his approach direct implantation with the husband's sperm after his death could result in a later child having inheritance rights while a child who is born from a IVF-transfer in the lifetime of his father would not.

189 See generally *Tur*, HM 210 and YD 331 and commentary of the *Beit Yosef*. See also Maimonides, *Code*, Laws concerning Heave Offerings 8:4; *Biur Hagra*, HM 275; *Or Sameiah*, Nahalot 1:13; *Hidushei Rabeinu Haim Halevi*, Terumot 8:4. For a complete discussion, see R. Binyamin Rabinowitz-Teumim, *Hukat Mishpat* (1976), 1:5 and 2:9–10.

190 See article cited in n. 180 above. Indeed, this seems to be the position of the *Noda Biyehuda* despite his ruling on *yibum*. See *Noda Biyehuda*, I, EH 69.

191 See *Tora Shebeal Pe* 33 (1992), 44, where R. Yisraeli writes that the ruling cited in n. 190 is a legal error (*taut behoraa*), and children born from postmortem implantation do not have inheritance rights.

192 This again rests on R. Yisraeli's assumption that in cases of a preembryos, no *klitat zera* has occurred. If *klita* is conceived as fertilization, the most the comparison to *yibum* could do is negate paternity in cases of postmortem insemination, not embryo transfer.

193 It must be admitted, however, that the *Noda Biyehuda* himself clearly assumed that his ruling applied only to *yibum* and not to inheritance, and that a child could inherit from his father even if the *klitat zera* took place after the father's death.

earlier.[194] It will be recalled that in Jew to Jew transfers, a majority of decisors would indeed assign maternity to the birth mother.[195]

Where the egg donor is not Jewish, it would appear that the children would not inherit from their biological father for the same reasons they do not constitute children for purposes of *yibum*.[196] According to R. Kilav, such a child is born a non-Jew, and must undergo conversion, and thus, has no filial bond with either his birth mother or his biological father. While R. Goldberg recognizes the maternity of the birth mother, notwithstanding the fact that the child must undergo a conversion for *kedushat yisrael*, there appears to be no basis to establish the paternity of the biological father, since at the time of fertilization, the ovum was "non-Jewish." The same is true on R. Bleich's position, and indeed, on the view that does not require conversion at all.

Whether the child could inherit from his birth mother in the event the biological father predeceases or divorces his wife depends on the various approaches discussed above. R. Kilav would deny such a right. R. Goldberg and R. Bleich would recognize it, for different reasons.[197]

194 Normally, when a married woman dies, her assets are inherited by her husband and not her children; *SA* EH 90:1. Maternity as such, therefore, will have no direct impact on inheritance rights. If, however, the husband predeceased his wife or divorced her, upon her death, her assets would go to her children.

Even where the wife predeceases her husband and her estate passes to him, maternity may be important due to the law that upon death of a father, the male children of a previously-deceased wife take the value of their mother's *ketuba* before the rest of the estate is divided among all the heirs (*ketubat banin dikhrin*); see bKetubot 52b and *SA* EH 69:1–2. To the extent the IVF-child is not a child of the mother, the *ketubat banin dikhrin* law would benefit her other children.

195 In light of R. Auerbach's ruling that the situs of maternity is unresolved (see text at n. 81 above), it appears that the children generated from donated ova of Jewish origin would have no right to inherit from either mother, because the heirs of each woman can assert that maternity resides with the other (*hamotzi meihaveiro alav hareaya*). Conversely, on R. Bleich's dual-maternity view, perhaps the child could inherit from both!

196 See nn. 182–185 above.

197 Note, however, that the right to inherit the mother's estate will not carry with it the entitlement of *ketubat banin dikhrin* if their mother dies first. See n. 194 above. That right exists only if the children are also the children of her deceased husband. If halakhically they are not (notwithstanding the biological reality that they were conceived from his sperm), this right would not arise.

R. Auerbach would treat the right of inheritance as a "doubtful monetary case" (*safek mamon*) and as such, apply the rule of *hamotzi meihaveiro alav hareaya* (the burden of proof falls on the one who asserts a right to recover).

Where the child is born from a non-Jewish gestational surrogate, the inheritance rights from the biological father depend on the assignment of maternity.[198] R. Kilav would grant full inheritance rights, as would R. Bleich. R. Goldberg would deny them. R. Auerbach would apply the rules for doubtful monetary cases.[199]

In the case of AID or embryo transfers, there will, of course, be no inheritance from the recipient's husband, as he is not the father of those children. With respect to inheriting their birth mother's estate, children produced from AID (Jewish or not) where the birth mother's own eggs were fertilized, would clearly inherit. Children resulting from embryo transfer raise the same issues of split maternity as do ovum donations.

### 3 *Preembryos and the Law of Primogeniture*

The foregoing section dealt with the inheritance rights of preembryos that are implanted after the father's death. Even where implantation and indeed live birth took place in the father's lifetime, the ability to freeze and preserve embryos may raise questions concerning the definition of "first-born" (*bekhor*). A male child who is his father's first-born is entitled to a double portion of inheritance (Deut. 21:17). Assume an embryo is frozen, but another child is born first (either naturally or through IVF). Which child is deemed the first-born for purposes of the law of primogeniture? In spite of the fact that the Torah describes the first-born as "the beginning of his [the father's] strength" (Deut. 21:17), the consensus of most decisors is that the double portion goes to the first male child of the father that is actually born, not the first to be conceived.[200]

198 See the explanation for *yibum* in the text at n. 187 above.

199 The positions of rabbis Kilav and Goldberg are reversed with respect to egg donation and gestational surrogacy. It is only R. Bleich who would recognize inheritance rights in both, due to his dual maternity construct.

200 See *Shoel Umeishiv*, 3:52; *Haamek Davar* on Deuteronomy 21:15. But see the fascinating comments of the Vilna Gaon in *Kol Eliyahu* to Deuteronomy 21:15, suggesting that the double portion be awarded to the first **conceived**. Even the Vilna Gaon, however, might concede the contrary position with respect to an embryo fertilized outside the womb.

If both children were born after their father's death, for instance, if two frozen preembryos were transplanted to the wife at different times, the law of primogeniture does not apply at all and both children inherit equally.[201]

### c Pidyon Haben

Assuming the fertilized egg is implanted into the Jewish woman from whom it was taken, there is no question that if a male child is later born from the IVF and would otherwise qualify as the first-born, as the child who "opened" his mother's womb (*peter rehem*) — there is an obligation of redemption of the first-born son (*pidyon haben*). Whether the obligation devolves on the father, or on the child after he attains adulthood, depends on recognition of paternity in IVF pregnancies, a paternity that virtually all decisors recognize. It is also clear that in the case of frozen preembryos, *pidyon haben* would devolve on the first to be **born** — emerge from the womb — and not the first to be fertilized.[202]

Questions arise, however, when we consider cases of preembryo transfer or ovum donation from either Jewish or non-Jewish sources.

**Recipient Issues** If a Jewish woman is impregnated by a non-Jew and has a male child, that child, if otherwise a *peter rehem*, is subject to the mitzva of *pidyon haben*.[203] Although there is no halakhic father who is obligated to observe the mitzva, the son must do so when he reaches adulthood.[204] What about an embryo transfer from a non-Jew to a Jewish woman? On the view of R. Goldberg, who maintains that the child bears a genealogical connection to his birth mother despite the need for conversion, it would appear that a *pidyon haben* is mandated. The child is a first-born son of a Jewish mother.[205]

201 See *SA* HM 277:4 (assuming, of course, they are both male or both female).

202 This is true regardless of how the double portion law is interpreted, since *pidyon haben* is clearly a matter of "opening the womb."

203 *SA* YD 305.

204 See the comments of *Taz, SA* YD 305 (11) and Shakh in *Nekudot Hakesef* on whether it would be proper for the mother or the court to redeem the child as a minor, or it is best that the *pidyon* be deferred until adulthood.

205 The *SA* rules that if a non-Jewish woman converted while pregnant, the baby that is subsequently born must have a *pidyon haben*. Since R. Goldberg treats every transfer of an embryo from a non-Jew to a Jew as endowing the birth mother with full maternal status (though conversion is necessary), an embryo transfer would be analogous to a fetus not conceived prior to conversion but born afterwards (*horato shelo bikdusha veleidato bikdusha*).

Nevertheless, in view of the absence of a Jewish father, the obligation of *pidyon haben* would not devolve on the father, but on either the child, when he reaches adulthood, or the court (*beit din*). The same result would follow on R. Bleich's dual maternity view.

By contrast, on R. Kilav's view, namely, that the child is a non-Jew who does not bear a relationship to his birth mother, he could not be a first-born, and there is thus be no obligation to redeem him. It seems likely, however, that even according to R. Kilav, the birth of such a child would mean that the birth mother's **next** child would not be a *bekhor*, since he would not be a *peter rehem*.[206] Thus, on R. Kilav's view, there would be no *pidyon haben* at all. This same argument would hold true for ovum donations fertilized with the husband's sperm **in vitro**.[207] For the reasons noted above, it is possible that ovum donation coupled with GIFT would necessitate a *pidyon haben* even on R. Kilav's view.[208]

**Donor Issues** It is also clear that if a Jewish woman donated an ovum that was fertilized and implanted in another woman (Jewish or non-Jewish), or utilized a gestational surrogate, the resulting child would **not** be her *peter rehem*, and a subsequent male birth on the part of the egg donor would indeed be subject to *pidyon haben*. This is definitely the case on the view of the decisors who assign maternity to the birth mother — and even R. Kilav does so in Jew to Jew transfers — and would probably be the case even if the egg donor is deemed the mother, since the child nonetheless did not emerge from her womb. This creates the interesting anomaly of a woman's first-born son's not needing a *pidyon haben* (at least where he is born from a non-Jewish

206 See *SA* YD 305. Even where the child does not bear a genealogical tie to the birth mother, the physical birth of a child from a woman's womb renders subsequent births exempt from *pidyon haben*. Thus, if a non-Jewish woman had children and then converted, her first child with a Jew will not require a *pidyon haben*. On R. Kilav's understanding, embryo transfer appears to be analogous to this situation.

207 The only possible distinction between embryo transfer and ovum donation is the fact that in the latter, husband's sperm fertilized the egg, arguably creating a Jewish father. If, according to R. Goldberg, the child needs a *pidyon haben*, the obligation could possibly devolve on that father. I have already argued, however, that even if the child bears a relationship to its birth mother, it does not bear a relationship to its biological father. See text at nn. 182–185 above.

208 See text at nn. 136–140 above.

birth mother or from a Jewish woman who already had children) but the second-born son's requiring it.[209]

**Uterine Lavage** Even if the Jewish egg donor contributed an embryo via uterine lavage, it is likely that a later male birth will be subject to the obligation of *pidyon haben*. The only difference between a naked ovum donation coupled with IVF, and UL, is that in the latter, conception occurred within the donor's body, the embryo entered the uterus, and it was removed via the vaginal canal. Such removal does not constitute a "birth" for the purpose of exempting a subsequent child from *pidyon* unless the fetus had reached the developmental stage of having differentiated organs[210]; the embryo removed via UL is far below this level of development.

Of course, in the event technology ever makes possible full-fledged inter-uterine fetal transfers, the situation might be different: a second child of the donor mother might be exempt from *pidyon haben* even if the birth mother is deemed the child's sole mother.[211] Conversely, the child might be deemed "born" of its genetic mother — depending on how far along the pregnancy was — but still exempt a second child of the birth mother from *pidyon haben* on the grounds that the second child of the birth mother is not a *peter rehem*, given that the

209 If a woman gives birth to a child via a caesarian, neither that child nor the next one, even if delivered vaginally, requires a *pidyon haben*, the first because it is not a *peter rehem*, the second because it is not a first-born; see *SA* YD 305:24. This may mean that if the ovum donor is deemed the mother — which at best is but a minority position — the preembryo would be deemed akin to a caesarian birth (*yotzei dofen*) and exempt subsequent vaginal births by the egg donor from *pidyon haben*. This rule, however, does not appear to apply where the first child was never carried in the womb at all. See the ruling of R. S. Wozner quoted in R. G. Oberlander, *Pidyon Haben Kehilkhato* 2:21, n. 48 (ectopic or tubular pregnancy). An externalized preembryo is even further removed from the womb than an ectopic pregnancy. Indeed, even a uterine lavage will not constitute a "birth" for the purpose of exempting the next child from redemption. In any case, on the majority view that in Jew to Jew transfers, the birth mother is deemed the sole mother, it is certain that a subsequent male birth on the part of the egg donor will be subject to redemption.

210 See *SA* YD 305:23 (Rema).

211 In such a case, the child might be a *peter rehem* of the birth mother but at the same time exempt subsequent children of its genetic mother from *pidyon haben*.

first child "opened her womb," although genealogically it is not her child.[212]

*Appendix: The Preembryo under American Law*

a Criminal Liability for the Destruction of Embryonic Life

Under American law, the responsibilities owed to preembryos or indeed, embryos or even fetuses, are somewhat limited, though they have undergone expansion in recent decades.[213] For the most of

212 See bHulin 70a; Maimonides, *Code*, Laws concerning Firstlings 4:18; and R. Goldberg, n. 78 above, 257–259. The discussion in Hulin deals, not with *pidyon haben*, but with the sanctified, sacrificial status of a first-born animal. The Tamud discusses the case of an embryo transfer from one animal to another animal, with the second animal giving birth. The question is whether the birth of the fetus from animal 2 qualifies as "birth" to exempt a subsequent birth from animal 2 from the sanctity of the law of the firstling, although animal 2 is neither the genetic mother nor the animal in whose body conception takes place. The upshot of the discussion is that it is clear that the second animal born from animal 1 is not a firstling, but we remain in doubt concerning the second animal born from animal 2. The Talmud does not resolve the question and leaves the matter in doubt. In the case of animals, the doubtful firstling must be treated as though it has sanctity, i.e., one cannot shear or work with the animal, though its uncertain status precludes bringing it as a sacrifice. In the case of humans, however, a doubtful first-born is relieved of the obligation of redemption entirely, because of the principle that doubts in connection with monetary obligations are resolved to the benefit of the obligor. In short, even if in a late-stage uterine transfer, maternity is not assigned to the "birth" mother — as in the case in Hulin — the emergence of that child from her womb will, at least due to the uncertainty, exempt subsequent births from *pidyon haben*.

213 Ironically, this expansion has taken place at a time when the courts have recognized a woman's right to terminate her pregnancy. See *Roe v. Wade*, 410 U.S. 113 (1973) (a woman has a constitutional right to terminate a pregnancy prior to the final trimester; the state may engage in only limited regulation thereafter). While *Roe* has been under severe attack, its basic structure survives. See *Stenberg v. Carhart*, 530 U.S. 914 (2000) (5–4 decision striking down Nebraska's ban on partial-birth abortion).

The principles of fetal/embryonic rights, on the one hand, and a woman's right to choose, on the other, maintain an uneasy coexistence within the universe of our legal system. There will inevitably be some tension between them, and the precise parameters of the balance remain somewhat unclear. See text at nn. 261–267 below.

the history of the common law, and in most American jurisdictions through the mid-19th century, abortion prior to quickening (fetal movement) was not a crime at all and, even after quickening, was at worst a misdemeanor, not a felony.[214] (A preembryo, an entity that in any case was unimaginable during this period, would certainly be at the prequickening stage, and its destruction would therefore not have been punishable under the common law.)[215] The widespread criminalization of even early-stage abortion, a process that rapidly accelerated in the mid-19th century, was motivated, at least in part, by concerns for the mother's health — given the dangerous nature of the procedure — rather than any notion of an inherent "right to life" of the fetus (though the diversity of statutes enacted does reflect multiple objectives).[216] In any case, the general criminalization of early-term abortions — even if it applied to externalized preembryos, which is questionable — was declared unconstitutional under *Roe v. Wade*,[217] and is no longer a source of fetal/embryo protection.

214 See, e.g., Coke, *Institutes* III, *50; I Blackstone, *Commentaries* *129–130; *Commonwealth v. Bangs*, 9 Mass. 387 (1812); *Miller v. Bennet*, 56 S.E. 2d 217 (Va. 1949). Note that some historians have argued that Coke was either mistaken or intentionally misstated the law, and that even a postquickening abortion was not originally a crime under English common law, but only an ecclesiastical offense. See Means, "The phoenix of abortional freedom," 17 *N.Y.L.F.* 335 (1971). Regardless of its accuracy, Coke's declaration that postquickening abortion was a common law crime (albeit not a felony) was accepted in the United States as well as England. See, e.g., *Lamb v. State*, 10 A. 208 (Md. 1887).

215 Note that even under the common law rule, if the fetus was born alive (i.e., died after full expulsion from the womb and some evidence of independent vitality, such as respiration, crying, etc.) and then died of injuries suffered in utero, the perpetrator could indeed be guilty of murder, but only if the injury was inflicted after the quickening stage. See LaFave and Scott, Jr., *Criminal Law* 2nd ed. (West 1986), §7.1(c) at 607–609 and Robertson, "Reproductive technology and reproductive rights: In the beginning — the legal status of early embryos," 76 *Va. L. Rev.* 437 (1990).

216 See the discussion in Justice Blackmun's majority opinion in *Roe v. Wade*, 410 U.S. 113 (1973), 148–149. He also notes that as late as 1840, only eight states had statutes dealing with abortion, and even when abortion statutes were more widely enacted, they continued to differentiate between quickened and nonquickened fetuses, at least in terms of the severity of the punishment. It was not until the end of the 19th century that the quickening distinction began to disappear; by the end of the 1950's, it was largely gone. Ibid., 139–140.

217 410 U.S. 113 (1973).

It is only in the 20th century that we see the full-scale extension of felonious homicide statutes to the intentional or reckless destruction of fetal life, but many of these statutes do not cover early-stage embryos or IVF preembryos.[218]

b Tort Liability

It is equally clear on the civil side that preembryos, embryos and previability fetuses are not "persons" entitled to legal protection, at least under the common law.[219] Whatever protections these entities enjoyed

218 Recently, several states have extended homicide or feticide protection to fetuses even when they are not born alive. In most cases, however, a fetus must have reached viability or at least quickening (movement) to fall within the protection of the law. See *Commonwealth v. Cass*, 392 Mass. 799, 467 NE 2d 1324 (1984) (viable fetus falls within definition of "person" as used in motor vehicle homicide statute); *Commonwealth v. Lawrence*, 404 Mass. 378, 536 NE 2d 571 (1989) (viable fetus is human being for purpose of common law crime of murder): *State v. Horne*, 319 SE 2d 703 (S.C. 1984) (action for homicide may be brought if fetus is viable). To the same effect are statutes in Cal. Penal Code §187; Fla. Stat. Ann §782.09 (willful killing of an unborn child after quickening is first degree manslaughter); Iowa Code Ann. §707.7 (intentional termination of human pregnancy after the end of second trimester is feticide); Oklahoma St. Ann. title 21, §713 (same); Rhode Island Gen. Laws §11-23-5 (same); Wash. Rev. Code §1232.060.

Other states have gone further. Minnesota provides a maximum punishment of life imprisonment for first degree murder of the unborn, defined as existing "from conception." Minn. Stat. Ann. §609.266. See also *State v. Merrill*, 450 NW 2d 318 (Minn. 1990) (upholding the constitutionality of this statute as applied to a man who killed a woman who was only six weeks pregnant). Illinois provides that it is a crime to kill an unborn child, other than by lawful abortion. "Unborn child" includes "an individual of the human species from fertilization until birth." Section 720 ILCS 5/9-1.2 (2000). See also Louisiana Rev. Stat. Ann. §9:129 (bars intentional destruction of embryo).

Except in the cases of Illinois, Louisiana, and Minnesota, the application of any of these statutes or court decisions to externalized preembryos is highly uncertain. See Robertson, n. 215 above; "Prior agreements for disposition of frozen embryos," 51 *Ohio State Law Journal* 414 (1990); "Resolving disputes over frozen embryos," 18 *Hastings Center Report* 7–12 (1989).

219 Although *Roe v. Wade* recognized the state's authority to regulate postviability abortion, this type of regulation did not confer legal rights or personhood on the unborn. Indeed, *Roe* explicitly declared that the "fetus" is not deemed a "person"; whatever regulatory authority the state has is predicated on protecting and nurturing potential for the future.

were based on later claims asserted by or on behalf of the "persons" these entities become after birth.[220] Put differently, while a preembryo, embryo or fetus has historically enjoyed no rights under American law, the human being that is eventually born has a right to be protected against, and compensated for, conduct perpetrated against him at those earlier stages. The post-natal entity, not the embryo, is the repository and possessor of these rights.[221] For example, many courts may permit a child or his parents to recover damages for injuries committed in utero or for wrongful death only if the child was born alive.[222] In some states, this action will lie for tortious conduct committed any time after conception.[223] A minority impose liability only for injuries inflicted after the point of viability.[224] Yet a third group goes to the other extreme and would impose liability even for preconception behaviors that result in harm to a child eventually born, an extension that New York, among other states, explicitly rejects.[225]

220 This was also true of the "born alive" rule originally applicable to homicides. See n. 215 above.

221 See the discussion in Prosser and Keeton, *Handbook of the Law of Torts*, 5th ed. (1984), §55; Note, 22 *Suffolk University Law Review* 717, 754–756, nn. 54–58 (1988); and Dobbs, *The Law of Torts* (2000), 781–801.

222 The original common law rule was that the tortfeasor incurred no liability at all for harm perpetrated on an unborn child, even if the child was later born alive. See, e.g., *Dietrich v. Northampton*, 13 Mass. 14 (1884) (no duty due to lack of legal personhood). This is to be distinguished from criminal law, where the "born alive" rule was always applied; see n. 215 above. The landmark case of *Bonbrest v. Kotz*, 65 F.Supp 138 (D.D.C. 1946) established the "born alive" rule for torts, allowing recovery for injuries inflicted prenatally as long as the child was born alive, albeit momentarily. (If the born child died from the injuries, a wrongful death action could be brought.) By 1972, *Bonbrest* was universally accepted throughout the United States. See Annotation (Chase), "Liability for Prenatal Injuries," 40 ALR 3d 1222 (1972).

223 This is the rule adopted by Restatement of Torts (2nd) §869. **Accord**: *Sylvia v. Gobeille*, 220 A.2d 222 (RI 1966) and *Group Health Ass'n v. Blumenthal*, 453 A.2d 1198 (MD 1983).

224 See, e.g., Ferguson v. District of Columbia, 629 A.2d 15 (District of Columbia Court of Appeals, 1993).

225 See *Renslow v. Mennonite Hospital*, 367 N.E. 2d 1250 (Ill. 1977) (child allowed to maintain action in tort for injuries sustained as a result of a **pre-conception** blood transfusion to mother); *Jorgensen v. Meade Johnson Laboratories*, 483 F.2d 237 (10th ca. 1973) (father as special administrator of the estate of deceased mongoloid child could bring an action based on birth control pills the mother ingested, resulting in the birth defect). As noted, New York rejects the notion of liability for a preconception tort. See *Albala v. City of New York*, 429 N.E. 2d 786 (N.Y. 1981).

The "born alive" rule on its own affords no remedy in cases of fetal life terminated before birth. As occurred in the criminal context, with the enactment of fetal homicide statues, many courts have gone beyond the "born alive" rule of *Bonbrest*, and have been willing to allow wrongful death actions for fetuses killed in the womb anytime after viability.[226] A few decisions — still a minority — have even allowed recovery for the death in utero of a nonviable fetus.[227]

In sum, with few exceptions, even the intentional destruction of preembryos generally entails neither civil nor criminal liability. This was true even prior to *Roe v. Wade*, which constitutionalized the right to terminate a pregnancy in its early states, and after *Roe* would arguably be truer still.[228] Because of quickening and/or viability requirements, the destruction of preembryos is not subject to fetal homicide statutes, nor, in most states, would a wrongful death action lie. Indeed, even one of the few cases that did recognize a cause of action for the wrongful death of a nonviable fetus noted *in dicta* that its ruling may not apply to externalized IVF preembryos.[229]

Two qualifications to the above must be made: first, some states have indeed moved in the direction of protecting preembryonic life. In recent years, sensitized to the ethical problems engendered by assisted reproductive technologies, some states have taken a more protectionist stance, expanding both civil and criminal liability. Louisiana appears to flatly prohibit the discarding of preembryos, and this may be true for Illinois and Minnesota as well.[230] While no woman can be compelled to have them implanted, unwanted embryos must apparently be donated

226 See the cases cited in Dobbs, n. 221 above, 782–783.

227 See, e.g., *Wiersma v. Maple Leaf Farms*, 543 N.W. 2d 787 (S.D. 1996); *Farley v. Sartin*, 466 S.E. 2d 522 (W.Va. 1995) (emphasizing that the decision did not necessarily apply to embryos fertilized outside the womb); *Torigian v. Watertown News Co.*, 225 N.E. 2d 926 (Mass. 1967). It might be argued that these cases are inconsistent with the fundamental premise of *Roe v. Wade*. (*Torigian*, of course, was decided before *Roe*). How can even third parties be liable for the negligent death of a nonviable fetus, if the mother has a constitutional right to terminate its existence? If there is no "life" until viability, how can "wrongful death" occur, at least from the perspective of the fetus?

228 But see text at nn. 261–265 below (*Roe* does not exclude a greater degree of state intervention).

229 *Farley v. Sartin*, 466 S.E. 2d 522 (W.Va. 1995).

230 See n. 218 above.

for the benefit of infertile couples. Whether a "mandatory donation" statute can survive *Roe v. Wade* is discussed below.[231]

Second, although the preembryo as such may possess no legal rights, its unwarranted destruction will often give the gamete providers an independent cause of action for a tort that constitutes an invasion of **their** interests. That is, the action is based not on what was done to the embryo, but on what was done to its parents.[232] Some courts treat the gamete providers as having a "property right" in their cells, which are a "mere bailment" in the hands of the IVF clinic; this would give the gamete providers a conversion claim if their "property" is wrongfully taken or destroyed.[233] Other courts have eschewed the

231 See text at nn. 261–267 below.

232 Dobbs, n. 221 above, 784–785, points out that this is equally true, or more so, in cases of a woman carrying a child, where even under the "born alive" rule that would preclude a wrongful death action, the woman may recover for battery to her person or intentional infliction of emotional distress. This could apply in cases of IVF embryos as well.

233 See, e.g., *York v. Jones*, 717 F.Supp. 421 (E.D. Va. 1989). A doctor and his wife living in New Jersey were infertile due to problems in the wife's fallopian tubes. They originally sought IVF treatment at the Jones Institute in Norfolk (the first and probably most successful IVF clinic in the United States). They later moved to California and eventually wanted to take the frozen embryos from the Virginia clinic to a program in Los Angeles. The Norfolk clinic refused to release them, and the couple brought suit in federal district court in Norfolk. In denying the clinic's motion to dismiss, the court noted the absolute obligation of the clinic to "return the subject matter of the bailment to the bailors when the purpose of the bailment has been terminated." (The case was eventually settled out of court.) Cf. *Davis v. Davis*, n. 3 above, which also recognized that the gamete providers have ultimate decisional authority over the disposition of preembryos, but predicated that authority on the constitutionally-protected right of privacy, which includes both the right to procreate and the right not to.

(*York* was a relatively easy case, because the consent form the Yorks signed made no mention of their giving up dispositional authority to the clinic. What would be the result if such authority were ceded? *York* is silent, but its "property-bailment" analysis suggests that agreements ceding authority to the clinic would be binding and preclusive. *Davis v. Davis*, on the other hand, perhaps because of its constitutional underpinnings, strongly intimates that even an express agreement with the clinic could not override a present mutual consent of the husband and wife to the contrary. *Davis* looks at advance directives for guidance only where the gamete providers are deadlocked, not where they are in agreement.)

property rights analysis, holding that human tissues and cells are not "things" that can be owned.[234] Even without utilizing concepts from property law, courts have been able to protect the rights of gamete providers through alternative theories of tort law, particularly by recognizing actions based on the intentional infliction of emotional distress.[235]

The recognition of such tort actions, however, should not be construed as protection of the rights of the preembryo; it is exclusively for the benefit of the gamete providers.

---

The concept that a person has ownership, i.e., dispositional control, over his body parts and cells, has been recognized by the Uniform Anatomical Gift Act, adopted in all fifty US states, allowing an adult to make a gift of all or part of his/her human body after death for specified purposes, such as transplant, education and research. Note, however, that at least ten states prohibit the purchase or sale of human body parts, with the exception of blood, hair or semen. These states include California, Georgia, Louisiana, Michigan, New Mexico, New York, Pennsylvania, Texas, Virginia and West Virginia. See the references and discussion in Boulier, "Sperm, spleen, and other valuables: the need to recognize property rights in human body parts," 23 *Hofstra Law Review* 693, 713, nn. 144–146 (1995).

234 See, e.g., *Moore v. Regents*, 51 Cal. 3d 120, 739 P. 2d 479 (Cal. 1990). The plaintiff was suffering from leukemia, and had a diseased spleen surgically removed. The doctor noticed unique cellular structures in the spleen. He modified the cells through genetic engineering and was eventually able to create a valuable medical product. The plaintiff brought an action alleging the conversion of his personal property, i.e., severed or removed body parts. In reversing the trial court and dismissing the case, the California Supreme Court ruled that while the plaintiff may have privacy or dignity interests, human cell lines are not "things" that are subject to the laws of property.

*Moore* has had its share of criticism. See Fischer, "Walling claims in or out: misappropriation of human gametic material and the tort of conversion," 8 *Tex. J. Women & Law* 143 (1999). If it is true, however, that "ownership" cannot be applied to human cells, a fortiori ownership concepts cannot be applied to preembryos. Whatever one's view about the origins of life, a preembryo with its capacity for full human development has a greater degree of autonomous personhood than a removed spleen. This being so, the property analogue is even less apt.

235 See, e.g., *Del Zio v. Columbia Presbyterian Hospital*, n. 159 above (unauthorized destruction of preembryos constitutes intentional infliction of emotional distress).

### c Regulation of Experimentation

Starting in the 1970s, a number of states passed laws imposing restrictions on preembryo experimentation.[236] The American Society for Reproductive Medicine (formerly, American Fertility Society) has noted that many of these statutes are disappointingly vague, leaving many questions unanswered.[237] In over three-quarters of the states, there are virtually no restrictions on fetal or embryonic experimentation, though at least some experimentation might be covered by fetal homicide statutes or general tort law. In fact, the only aspects of assisted reproductive technologies (ART) that have received widespread legislative attention are those involving surrogacy or egg or sperm donation.[238]

236 See, for example, Arizona Rev. Stat. Ann. §36-2302; Arkansas Stat. Ann. §82-436; California Health & Safety Code §25956; ILCS 5/9-1.2 (Illinois 2000); Louisiana Rev. Stat. Ann. §9:122; Maine Rev. Stat. Ann, title 22 §1593; Mass. Ann. Laws, Ch. 112 §12J; Mich. Comp. Laws §333.2685-2692; Minn. Stat. Ann. § 145.421-422 and §609.266-2661; North Dakota Cent. Code §14-02.2 -01 to -02; Penn. Cons. Statutes §32163; Rhode Island General Laws §11-54-1; Utah Code Ann. §76-7-310. See also *Margaret S. v. Edwards*, 494 F.2d 494 (5th ca. 1986); *Lifchez v. Hartigan*, 735 F.Supp. 1361 (ND Ill. 1990) aff'd without opinion 914 F.2d 260 (7th ca. 1990) (Illinois ban on nontherapeutic fetal experimentation held an unconstitutional invasion of privacy rights).

237 ECART, n. 1 above, 9S–10S.

238 Even here, the concerns are primarily economic, not moral. Over thirty states have provided, by statute or court decision, that a sperm donor is not financially liable for the support of the child, and has no parental rights. See Eggen, "The Orwellian nightmare reconsidered: a proposed regulatory framework for the advanced reproductive technologies," 25 *Ga. Law Rev.* 625, 681–683, nn. 242–243 (1991). All paternal rights belong to the consenting husband. The situation is less clear where a single woman uses donor sperm. Even an explicit agreement relieving the donor of liability may be unenforceable. See *Jhordan C. v. Mary K.*, No. A27810 (Cal. Ct. of App. 1986). Five states — Florida, North Dakota, Oklahoma, Texas, and Virginia — have parallel legislation covering egg donors; Texas and Florida cover donated preembryos. See the discussion in New York State Task Force on Life and the Law, *Assisted Reproductive Technologies* (1998), henceforth ART, 339–340.

The area that has generated the most controversy, and the most activity, is the "surrogate mother" or "rent-a-womb" problem, particularly in the aftermath of notorious cases such as *Baby M.* See 109 N.J. 396, 537 A.2d 1227 (1988). The states' response to surrogacy

### d Nongovernmental Policy Statements

The relative inaction of state governments does not mean that the status of the preembryo has been ignored. The Catholic Church issued a detailed pronouncement stating that human life begins from the moment of fertilization, and no moral distinctions can be drawn between a zygote, a preembryo, an embryo or a person.[239] This position would, of course, prohibit any preembryo disposal or experimentation. However, it would be an immoral practice even to generate an externalized preembryo, since the Church also condemns AIH, IVF, and quite obviously, the use of third party gamete donors or surrogates. In a conclusion that even many of those who subscribed to its premises found disturbing, the statement called upon governments to pass laws that would criminalize utilization of these fertility therapies (even AIH).

The mainstream medical consensus can be found in the pronouncements of two authoritative bodies, the American Society for Reproductive Medicine (formerly, American Fertility Society)[240] and the American College of Obstetrics and Gynecology (ACOG).[241] In 1986, the ASRM (under its prior name) issued a document entitled "Ethical Considerations of Assisted Reproductive Technologies." This document was updated in 1988, 1990, and 1994. Broadly, it: approves the use of ART, in most of its variants — AIH, AID, IVF, GIFT, ZIFT and ovum donations (expressing reservations only with regard to surrogate

has been varied, ranging from outright prohibition to enforcement, with several positions in between. See ART, 334–339, and an earlier report by the same commission, *Surrogate Parenting: Analysis and Recommendations* (1988).

239 *Instruction on Respect for Human Life in Its Origin and on the Dignity of Procreation* (1987), issued by the Congregation for the Doctrine of the Faith. A detailed critique of the position appears as an Appendix to ECART, n. 1 above.

240 The American Fertility Society changed its name in 1997. See 67 *Fertility and Sterility*, iii (1997).

241 The ASRM has been a very influential voice in ART. Although not legally binding, its ethical standards have been cited with approval by courts. See *Davis*, n. 3 above. Indeed, at least one state has provided that all IVF clinics within the state must comply with ASRM/ACOG standards as a condition of licensure. See Louisiana Rev. Stat. Ann. §9:128. In 1992, the two organizations jointly established the National Advisory Board on Ethics in Reproduction (NABER).

motherhood arrangements and uterine lavage)[242]; recommends that, optimally, third party gamete or embryo providers receive no compensation (beyond time and expenses)[243] for their donations; asserts that preembryos are not the same as human life, but are nonetheless entitled to "special respect" (without spelling out what "special respect" entails)[244]; recognizes that the gamete providers should have ultimate decisional authority over the disposition of their sperm, egg or preembryo; would give effect to any advance agreements the parties would make; and essentially, validates whatever decision the parties come to — implantation, destruction, thawing, donation or research.[245]

242 ECART, n. 1 above, 90S–93S.

243 Ibid., 45S, 49S, 70S.

244 Ibid. ECART noted that some deem preembryos fully human, while others argue that preembryos should be treated no differently than any other severed human tissue. Rejecting both these extremes, the ASRM stated that the "preembryo deserves respect greater than that accorded human tissue but not the respect accorded to actual persons. The preembryo is due greater respect than other human tissue because of its potential to become a person and because of its symbolic meaning for many people. Yet it should not be treated as a person because it has not yet developed the features of personhood, is not yet established as developmentally individual, and may never realize its biologic potential" (33S). The Report concludes that because the preembryo does not have differentiated organs, having no brain, no nervous system, no capacity for sentience, and given the fact that under present US law even fetuses in the first two trimesters of pregnancy may be aborted at will, it would be a logical anomaly to accord the full rights of personhood to the preembryo, see 32S–34S.

The intermediate characterization of the preembryo as entitled to "special respect" echoed earlier reports issued by the Ethics Advisory Board of the Department of Health, Education, and Welfare (1979); the 1984 Warnock Committee in Great Britain; and the 1985 report of the Ontario Law Reform Commission. In articulating the meaning of "special respect," the ASRM guidelines are disappointingly vague. The only definitive position taken is that if the preembryo is to be transferred to a uterus in an attempt to bring it to term, there is a duty not to engage in research or any other intervention that might injure the offspring who might be born after the transfer; see 33S–34S.

245 Ibid., 34S. The guidelines essentially endorse the approach of *Davis*, n. 3 above, recognizing the dispositional authority of the gamete providers and the enforceablility of prior advance directives in the event of divorce, death or other dispute. It is important to note, however, two major issues

Citing a 1979 report of the Ethics Advisory Board of the Department of Health, Education and Welfare (as HHS was then called) the ASRM also concluded that "it is acceptable from an ethical standpoint" to undertake research on preembryos if the gamete providers have given their informed consent, the information is not reasonably obtainable by other means (presumably, including genetic testing), the project is designed to improve the safety and efficacy of embryo transfer or IVF, and the preembryo will not be sustained in vitro beyond the development stage in which it would be ready to implant (14 days after fertilization).[246] Note that there is no requirement that the experimentation be potentially therapeutic to the development of this particular preembryo; indeed, if this preembryo is not to be implanted, by definition the experimentation cannot be therapeutic. Rather, the moral permissibility of experimentation hinges on the potential benefits for other embryos that may be generated in the future. Note too that the ASRM not only validates preembryo experimentation where the gametes were initially extracted for procreative purposes, but would apparently support the creation of preembryos for the specific purpose of such experimentation, provided informed consent was obtained. The guidelines of ACOG are a bit more cautious on this last point, noting that it is ordinarily "preferable" to use "spare" preembryos rather than generate them specifically for research, fearing that the latter step creates a process vulnerable to trafficking in gametes.[247] The ACOG also prohibits the purchase or sale of embryos. Both the ASRM and ACOG wisely provide that preembryos that have been the subject of nontherapeutic experimentation should normally not be transferred.[248]

---

that the guidelines do not address: (1) the standing of an IVF clinic to enforce the terms of the agreement over the objections of the couple; (2) the default rules in the absence of an agreement, which was the issue addressed in *Davis*. See also n. 146 (*Nahmani*).

246 ECART, n. 1 above, 79S–80S.

247 See ACOG Committee on Ethics, Ethical Issues in Human In-Vitro Fertilization and Embryo Placement (1986), reprinted in *American Medical News*, August 28, 1987.

248 There may be a subtle, but significant, difference between the different standards. The ASRM states that its guidelines for experimentation apply to preembryos **not destined for transfer**. This implies that nontherapeutic research can never be performed if the preembryos are to be transferred. Presumably, this is so because any experimentation might create

### e The Federal Moratorium on Human Embryo Research: A History of Vacillation

The federal restrictions on fetal and embryonic research do not directly prohibit or mandate action, but merely specify the conditions allowing the use of federal funds.[249] Given the overwhelming need for such funds in many areas of scientific research, barring the use of federal money for certain activities can often be tantamount to outright interdiction (though in potentially lucrative areas of hi-tech research, the private sector may be more than willing to take up the slack).

The federal government's attitude toward the proliferation of assisted reproductive technologies and embryonic research can best be described as ambivalent, vacillating between extreme caution and generous encouragement. Indeed, at times the two attitudes are evinced simultaneously. It is fair to say, however, that for a variety of reasons (many connected to the politics of the abortion debate), federal funding is quite limited. Some history may be useful.[250]

---

unfair and unreasonable risks to the health and welfare of any offspring born. Nor could these risks be assumed by informed consent, since it is the welfare of the child, not the parents, that is at stake.

The ACOG guidelines are a little less clear. Standard #7 provides that "any preembryo that has undergone research will be transferred to a uterus only if: [1] the research was related to the preembryo's preparation for placement; and [2] there is reasonable scientific confidence in its normal development." This seems to allow a certain degree of "safe" experimentation, provided the risks to the embryo are truly regarded as minimal. Of course, it may turn out that this confidence was misplaced. (I am assuming that confidence merely means belief that the experiment will not impair normal development, but not that in fact there will be normal development, since only a small percentage of IVF's result in a baby.) In any event, it is not clear what type of research the first criterion was designed to exclude.

(It is also possible, though unlikely, that the first prong of Standard #7 requires that the experimentation be potentially beneficial to **this** embryo. If so, it is not clear why implantation would be contraindicated by risks. After all, would not the parents be entitled to make such a medical decision in the case of an in utero pregnancy?)

249 One notable exception to the statement in the text is reproductive cloning. A bill was recently approved by the House of Representatives to criminalize human cloning, and it is likely that the bill will be passed by the Senate and become law. See n. 260 below.

250 This history is described in detail in ART, n. 238 above; the next few paragraphs are based on this report, unless otherwise indicated.

Throughout the 1970s and 1980s, federal funding of IVF and fetal research, including vital research into infertility and the genetic basis of disease, was virtually non-existent.[251] By 1993, Congress, at the urging of the Clinton Administration, evinced a greater willingness to provide funding for much of this research, and directed the National Institutes of Health (NIH) to develop appropriate federal guidelines.[252] The NIH in turn appointed a Human Embryo Research Panel, which issued a final report in 1994.[253] This report essentially validated the conclusions stated in the ASRM and ACOG guidelines, upholding a wide variety of non-therapeutic interventions, provided the embryos experimented upon would not be implanted, and did not progress beyond the 14-day stage of development.[254] Most significantly, the panel, with some dissent, specifically legitimized the deliberate creation of embryos for research purposes, at least where necessary for the validity of a study that is potentially "of outstanding scientific and therapeutic value," and the gamete providers have given their informed consent.[255] The report was approved by the Director's Advisory Committee in December 1994, and in theory should have greatly expanded the use of federal funds in IVF and embryonic research.

Once again, however, the political pendulum swung the other way. Shortly after the Report was issued, President Clinton announced that he would not approve any federal funds for the creation of human embryos solely for research, effectively negating the Panel's most

251 This was largely due to a 1975 regulation promulgated by the Department of Health, Education and Welfare (HEW) that no IVF or embryo experimentation would be federally funded unless the proposal was approved by an Ethics Advisory Board (EAB). The terms of existing EAB members expired in 1980, and no new appointments were ever made.

252 Upset with the failure of five successive secretaries of HEW and (later) HHS to appoint an EAB, and concerned that vital research was not being undertaken, Congress enacted the 1993 NIH Revitalization Act, which removed the requirement that an EAB approve embryo research proposals.

253 National Institutes of Health, Final Report of the Human Embryo Research Panel (September 22, 1994), henceforth Report.

254 See Report, ibid., 59–60, 88–89. The Report did, however, discourage research that would facilitate sex selection (except to the extent necessary to prevent the transmission of sexually-linked genetic diseases); cross-species fertilization; and cloning.

255 Report, 56–57, but see separate statements by Patricia King and Carol Tauer, 97–100.

controversial recommendation. Congress went even further. Since 1996, it has included language in its annual NIH appropriations that bars the use of federal funds for any research in which human embryos will be destroyed or discarded, no matter how or why they were initially created. Concerned that federal funds not be used to encourage abortions, the ban rejects any distinctions between embryos that were originally created for procreation ("spare embryos") and those deliberately created for research. In effect, only interventions that potentially benefit the actual embryo experimented on could be funded.

With the startling advances in stem cell research, attacks on this federal ban greatly increased in the late 1990s.[256] Many of the undifferentiated stem cells are obtained from unimplanted embryos, and in the process of obtaining the cells, the embryos are destroyed. An overly rigorous application of the federal ban would greatly inhibit this medical research. Basing itself on a legal opinion from the Department of Health and Human Services, the NIH tried to circumvent these restrictions by allowing federally-funded research on stem cells as long as the cells were obtained from unfunded sources in the private sector, and only if the embryos were initially created for fertility purposes ("spare embryos"), and not deliberately generated for stem cell retrieval.[257] These guidelines were quite controversial, and were bitterly opposed by prolife members of Congress, who felt that the guidelines encouraged destruction of embryos and trafficking in human life.

In August, 2001, President Bush resolved the issue by way of a compromise that fully satisfied neither side.[258] Declaring that federal

256 Stem cells are undifferentiated cells that can be cultured indefinitely and "directed" to produce virtually any type of specialized cell, e.g., heart, liver, kidney, brain. The use of stem cells offers great promise in treatment of heart disease, Alzheimer's, and spinal cord injuries. Stem cells can be obtained from placentas and even from the bloodstream of mature adults, but many researchers have concluded that embryonic stem cells obtained from preembryos shortly after fertilization are "more flexible," and best suited for therapeutic use. See http://www.nih.gov/news/stemcell, henceforth, stemcell website.

257 See National Institutes of Health, *Guidelines for Stem Cell Research* (August 25, 2000) available at stemcell website, n. 256 above. These guidelines were rescinded in August 2001.

258 The President initially gave a national address on television the evening of August 9, 2001. The text of his talk and follow-up statements are available at stemcell website.

money should not provide sanction or encouragement for the further destruction of embryonic life, he directed the NIH to provide funding only for research on stem cells obtained prior to 9 p.m., August 9, 2001, that is, cells from embryos that had already been destroyed prior to the date of his funding decision.[259] In contradistinction to NIH's earlier position that funding would be available even for newly created stem cell lines, as long as federal money was not used in the actual process of destruction, and the embryo was initially created for procreation ("spare"), the President's directive precluded any funding even indirectly connected with new destruction of embryonic life. The NIH has withdrawn its prior guidelines, and issued new guidelines incorporating the President's directives.

As of this writing, therefore, the use of federal funds for non-therapeutic embryonic research is severely restricted. In this volatile area, however, change is always possible.[260]

### f The Impact of *Roe v. Wade* on Governmental Attempts to Protect Embryonic Life

In *Roe v. Wade*,[261] the Supreme Court recognized a woman's constitutional right to terminate at least a first and second trimester pregnancy at will. It has been convincingly argued that if a woman has the absolute right to abort a fetus, she certainly has the right to dispose of a surplus preembryo; hence, any laws mandating that embryos either be implanted or donated would be unconstitutional. Thus, until *Roe v. Wade* is overturned, state bans on destruction would simply be invalid.[262] One scholar has argued, however, that *Roe v. Wade* does not

259 The Bush directive also incorporated three other requirements: (1) the embryos from which the cells were derived must have been created for reproductive purposes and not for research; (2) the gamete providers gave informed consent without financial inducement; (3) the stemcells will not be used for embryo cloning. These requirements already existed in the superseded NIH Guidelines.

260 It should also be noted that at least one type of embryonic research — cloning — might even be criminalized and not merely defunded. See Annas, "Cloning and U.S. Congress," *N. Eng. J. Med.* 346:20 (May 2002), 1599.

261 410 U.S. 113 (1973).

262 This would invalidate the mandatory donation requirements of Illinois, Louisiana and Minnesota. See n. 218 above.

represent a constitutional right not to be a genetic or biological parent, but rather a right to protect a woman's bodily integrity by not compelling her to carry a baby to term (which is why fathers are not given equal say).[263] As such, while *Roe* would clearly preclude state laws that would require a woman to **receive** the embryos, it would not prevent the state, if it so desired, from extending its protections to preembryonic life. (As noted earlier, however, historically, the state, even before *Roe*, has not done so.[264]) It should also be noted that to the extent parents are given dispositional authority, there is no particular logic to favoring the mother's decision over the father's where the preembryo is externalized. Thus, the statutes of Louisiana, Minnesota and Illinois,[265] which arguably compel implantation or donation, might well pass constitutional muster.

It is also an open question whether *Roe v. Wade* protects a woman's prenatal conduct that results in harm to a person actually born. While a woman may have an absolute right to terminate a pregnancy, once the child is brought to term she may be held legally responsible for injuries that her negligence generated.[266] This would be highly relevant

263 Robertson, n. 215 above. Robertson's analysis, however, seems to be rejected in *Davis v. Davis*, n. 3 above. In according gamete providers ultimate dispositional authority over preembryos, the court emphasized that the right "not to be a parent" was of constitutional dimension. *Davis*, however, is the opinion of only one state supreme court, and not binding on other jurisdictions.

264 Note too that even if *Roe* is read as giving the "parents" the constitutional authority to destroy the preembryo, a third party acting **without their consent** could be criminally prosecuted — see Cal. Penal Code §187; Washington Rev. Code §1232.060 (feticide punishable as murder unless it is a lawful abortion), as well as civilly liable. See nn. 213–235.

265 See n. 213 above.

266 Cf. *Grodin v. Grodin*, 301 NW 2d 869 (Mich. 1980) (pregnant woman's use of tetracycline during pregnancy caused her child's teeth to be discolored. Notwithstanding *Roe*, mother liable to offspring for prenatal injuries) with *Stillman v. Youngquist*, 531 NE 2d 355 (Ill. 1988) (tortious liability for prenatal conduct that results in postnatal injuries cannot be imposed on the pregnant woman herself). Put differently, the rule of *Bonbrest*, n. 222 above, giving born children a cause of action for prenatal injuries, should arguably be applicable to suits against mothers, notwithstanding their constitutional right to have terminated the pregnancy. The right to prevent a life from coming into being is not equivalent to the right to bring a life into existence burdened with suffering and pain, an invasion that cannot be justified by the mother's privacy interests.

if experimentation was authorized, but was followed by embryo transfer, a practice that is in any event discouraged by ASRM and ACOG guidelines.[267]

Thus, while government regulation and protection of the preembryo may be quite limited, there are no definite constitutional barriers (though there may be political barriers) to legislatures and courts taking a more activist, interventionist role.

---

Similar issues arise under child abuse statutes — can mothers be prosecuted for child abuse on the basis of behaviors undertaken during pregnancy at a time when under *Roe*, they had a constitutional right to an abortion? Cf. Myers, "Abuse and neglect of the unborn: can the state intervene?" 23 *Duquesne Law Review* 76 (1984) and Note, "Maternal substance abuse: the need to provide legal protection for the fetus," 60 *Southern California Law Review* 1235 (1987) with Note, "Maternal rights and fetal wrongs: the case against the criminalization of fetal abuse," 101 *Harvard Law Review* (1988). See also Steinbock, *Life Before Birth: The Moral and Legal Status of Embryos and Fetuses* (London: 1992), 127–163.

(But cf. *Automobile Workers v. Johnson Controls*, 499 U.S. 187 (1991), where the Supreme Court struck down an employer policy excluding women from certain positions allegedly hazardous to pregnancy. This was deemed illegal discrimination based on gender under Title VII of the Civil Rights Act. *Johnson* should not be read as giving mothers license to endanger their fetuses; it merely provides that under the employment discrimination laws, the employer is not empowered to assess the risk. If in fact a child is born injured, *Johnson* does not preclude a later action by the child against his mother for that endangerment under the *Bonbrest* rationale. While the Court does suggest that if federal law prohibits the employer from excluding women, the employer may very well be immune from suit, there would be no reason to extend that immunity to the mother who voluntarily and intentionally assumed the risk.)

267 See text at n. 248.

*The Jewish Law Annual*, Vol. XIV

# RECOVERY FOR FRIGHT, SHOCK AND EMOTIONAL DISTRESS UNDER JEWISH LAW, AND SOME COMPARISONS TO THE COMMON LAW

IRWIN H. HAUT, z"l

Irwin H. Haut, z"l, died while this volume was going to press. A longtime contributor to *The Jewish Law Annual*, he was driven by a vision of the halakha as a system of law with the capacity to adapt to life's ever-changing circumstances. He will be greatly missed.

Dedicated to the memory of my beloved in-laws, Esta and Teddy Makowsky.

## 1 *Introduction*

The story of the tortuous path taken by the common law in determining the ambit of liability for fright, shock and emotional distress, whether intentionally or negligently caused, has oft been told and is still unfolding, as reflected in the Appendix to this article. We will, however, focus on the remarkably parallel developments in Jewish law that long preceded their common law counterparts. Indeed, the similarity raises the question of whether there might be a causal connection between developments in these two legal systems; this intriguing question will not be discussed here.

I will focus on recovery of damages for fright, shock and emotional distress under Jewish law, both where they result in mental distress alone, and where such distress results, or manifests itself, in physical or psychological trauma or injury. Aspects of emotional distress include fright, nervousness, grief, anxiety, worry, mortification, shock, humiliation, terror, embarrassment, apprehension and ordeal.[1] Injuries to the

* Irwin H. Haut, z"l, received ordination at RIETS. In addition to practicing law, he wrote numerous works on various aspects of Jewish law.

1 See *Capelouto v. Kaiser Foundlings Hosps.*, 7 Cal. 3d 889, 892–893, 500 P.2d 880, 883, 103 Cal. Rptr. 856, 859 (1979); 4A *Personal Injury: Actions, Defenses, Damages*, [henceforth *Piadd*], "Fright, shock and emotional distress" (NY: 1989), sec. 1.01, n. 1.

nervous system, both with and without physical, emotional or mental consequences, will also be discussed.

My survey and analysis of the position of Jewish law will highlight the self-evident necessity for growth and development within Jewish law in this area, as is the case in related areas of Jewish law, a topic I have dealt with elsewhere.[2] I supplement my analysis of Jewish law by presenting (in the Appendix) a survey of the common law developments in this area in England, America and other common law jurisdictions. The purpose of this juxtaposition of the two systems is to show how the subject was addressed by a legal system that initially shared the basic approach of Jewish law in this area, but under the stress of modern conditions diverged and developed in different directions. A review of the Appendix is therefore vital to a fuller understanding of the problems faced by Jewish law in this as well as in other areas, and can provide a model for change and development, as and where appropriate. While I will make occasional references to the common law in the body of the article, fuller discussion of the common law is reserved for the Appendix.

Candor compels me to admit that a primary purpose in writing this article is to establish that Jewish law, which, I have elsewhere argued, has the capacity to grow, expand and develop, **must do so, if it is to survive and flourish**. By reference to another system of law that is undergoing development and change in the area in question, supported by advances in medical science, I hope to sketch a viable path for such growth, and help establish an appropriate methodology for the development of Jewish law in this rather innocuous area of the law.

My discussion of Jewish law will commence with a presentation of the Talmud of Babylonia, with some references to the Jerusalem Talmud. These talmudic texts, compilation of which was completed in the fifth and fourth centuries CE, respectively, are the basic sources of Jewish law. I will occasionally bring to bear insights gleaned from the English and American cases on point.

2 See my "Some aspects of absolute liability under Jewish law, and particularly, under the view of Maimonides" [henceforth, "Some aspects"], 15 *Dinei Israel* 7, 56 (1989–1990); "Abuse of process and unjust enrichment: a proposed restatement of Jewish law," 2 *Nat'l. Jewish Law R.* 31 (1987); *Divorce in Jewish Law and Life* (NY: 1983); "A problem in Jewish divorce law: an analysis and some suggestions," *Tradition* 16 (1977), 29; "Jewish law of warranties: some comparative aspects," 10 *Is. L.R.* 102 (1975).

As will be seen, the texts construed, and the comments and analysis of the Rabbis and the anonymous redactors (*stamaim*, sing. *stamai*) are sometimes confusing, complex or ambiguous, calling for clarification by the commentators, whose views will also be discussed. It will be seen that the views of the commentators fall into categories somewhat parallel to approaches taken by the common law courts. I will present Jewish law as codified in the various medieval codes as reflecting the state of Jewish law today.

## 2 *The Classical Jewish Texts*

The rule that suddenly surfaced in the common law in the nineteenth century, that there could be no recovery for fright and shock absent physical impact,[3] had already been embedded in Jewish law for many centuries, indeed, almost two millennia. However, as a result of a fundamental difference between the two systems in the area of causation, Jewish law applied this rule quite differently.[4]

Jewish law encompasses two approaches to causation, termed *gerama* and *garmi*, which some authorities see as diametrically opposed, and others attempt to reconcile. The generally accepted view is that there is no liability for indirectly-caused harm under the application of the narrow *gerama* rule. However, under the application of the broader rule of proximate cause termed *garmi*, there is liability for indirectly-caused harm, particularly on the view of Maimonides. In this context, no distinction is made between intentional acts and non-intentional but negligent acts. As will be seen, the rule pertaining to non-liability for emotional distress surfaced in Jewish law in connection with intentional acts, unlike the common law, in which this concept arose in connection with negligent, rather than intentional torts, where liability was imposed irrespective of impact.[5]

3 See Appendix, text at n. 95.

4 An analysis of causation in Jewish law is beyond the scope of this article; the interested reader is referred to the literature, and in particular, to my "Causation in Jewish tort law," 3 *Nat'l. Jewish L. Rev.* (1988), and "Causation in Jewish tort law — part II," 4 *Nat'l. Jewish L. Rev.* (1989).

5 For an excellent discussion of this area of the common law, see *Prosser and Keeton on Torts*, 5th ed. (1984). See also William L. Prosser, "Intentional infliction of mental suffering: a new tort," 37 *Mich. L. Rev.* 874, 878 (1939): "There has been much more readiness to grant a remedy where mental

The talmudic texts, already 2,000 years ago, took as the starting point for their analysis the issue of whether for purposes of tort liability the law measures foreseeability of damage or injury by a person of normal fortitude, or whether the tortfeasor takes the injured party as he finds him.

In the Babylonian Talmud, bBaba Kama 91a, the question whether assessment (*omed*) is required to establish tort liability is raised: as a predicate for tort liability, is it necessary to determine whether the particular instrumentality allegedly causing the injury was capable of so doing to a person of ordinary sensibility? In the discussion of this issue, the related question of whether there is liability for fright and shock is raised.

The anonymous redactor of the discussion (*sugya*, pl. *sugyot*) raises the question of whether tort liability is governed by the same rules that govern criminal liability, as in cases of homicide. In such cases, asserts the redactor, assessment is necessary, since: "this type of instrument is sufficient to cause death; whereas another type of instrument is not."[6] However, continues the *sugya*, "but as to tort liability, do we assume that any instrument is sufficient to cause injury, or is there no difference [between civil and criminal liability]?" Thus, the inquiry becomes an analysis of whether the particular type of injury must have been one that could reasonably have been anticipated. The *sugya* concludes with a statement of the rule that assessment is indeed required in order to establish tort liability.[7]

---

suffering is inflicted intentionally than where it is the result of mere negligence. One reason, of course, is the natural tendency of the courts, which has been apparent elsewhere in the field of torts, to extend liability as the moral guilt of the defendant increases. But perhaps more important is the fact that in such intentional misconduct there is an element of outrage, which in itself is an important guarantee that the mental disturbance which follows is serious, and that it is not feigned."

6 bBaba Kama 91a. See Encyclopedia Talmudit (2nd ed.), vol. 1, 293.

7 In the *Code*, Maimonides articulates this rule in two different contexts, and in a seemingly disparate manner, as pointed out by R. Y.Z. Gustmann, *Kuntresei Shiurim*, Baba Kama (Jerusalem: 1980), 393. In the *Code*'s Laws concerning Wounding and Damaging 1:18–19, Maimonides merely asserts that assessment of the instrument is necessary to ascertain whether it was of sufficient size or weight to have caused the injury, except for metallic objects, which can cause serious injury regardless of their size. However, in the Laws concerning Homicide and Bodily Safety 3:1–4,

The *stamai,* consistent with the usual talmudic methodology, attempts to decide the issue on the basis of an analysis of the Tannaitic sources,[8] which he quotes. One of the Tannaitic sources so utilized is a baraita[9] dealing with the right of a Canaanite slave to obtain his freedom if his master intentionally[10] injured him by deafening or blinding him, or cutting off his arm.[11] The discussion begins as follows:

> Come and hear. 'If he hit him in the eye and blinded him; or on his ear and deafened him; the slave goes out free thereby. If he struck an object that was opposite his eye and blinded him [i.e., he pounded on the wall opposite to the slave's eye, which caused him to become blind][12]; or if he struck an object that was opposite his ear and deafened him, he does not go out

---

Maimonides rules that three elements are taken into consideration in making the assessment, except, again, in the case of homicide by a metallic object: the instrument used and the part of the deceased's body struck; the force of the attack, whether from a distance, or in close proximity; and the strength of the attacker and of the person killed.

It would not appear that Maimonides intended to distinguish between these two areas of law with respect to application of the rule requiring assessment. It can be assumed that it applies to inflicting injury as well as to homicide, and was apparently so understood by R. Solomon b. Yehiel Luria (Maharshal, 1510–1574). See *Yam Shel Shlomo*, Baba Kama 8:38, where, without explicitly referring to Maimonides' codification of the matter, he asserts that various matters are taken into consideration in making this assessment in cases of tort liability, including the points mentioned by Maimonides, as well as other attendant circumstances, such as whether the injury was inflicted in wrath, and whether the deceased was thrown from a height. For further discussion of Maimonides' view, see text at n. 58 below.

8 A Tannaitic source is a teaching transmitted by the Tannaim (sing. Tanna), Sages who flourished at the end of the Second Temple period. The Tannaitic period ends with the death of R. Judah the Prince, redactor of the Mishnah. The later Sages, up to the redaction of the Babylonian Talmud, are termed the Amoraim (sing. Amora).

9 A Tannaitic source not included in the Mishnah.

10 If the act was unintentional, the slave did not go free. See Maimonides, *Code*, Laws concerning Slaves 5:4: "if he struck his slave intentionally, and caused the loss of a limb, he gains his freedom."

11 See Exodus 21:26–27, "When a man strikes the eye of his slave, male or female, and destroys it, he shall let him go free on account of his eye. If he knocks out the tooth of his slave, male or female, he shall let him go free on account of his tooth." See n. 27 below.

12 See Rashi (R. Solomon b. Isaac, 1040–1105) ad loc. s.v. *keneged*.

> free.' Is not the reason for this rule that assessment (*omed*) is required [and it is assumed that the said activity might not have caused the injury to the slave]?[13] No. The absence of tort liability is predicated on the fact that he [the slave] frightened himself. As it was taught, 'if one frightens another he is not liable by the law of man, but he is liable by the law of heaven.[14] If he blew [with a shofar, trumpet, or the like] into his ear and made him deaf, he is not liable.[15] But, if he held him[16] and blew into his ear, and made him deaf, he is liable.'

On this approach, if one directly injured another, as by striking his ear and deafening him, there is, of course, liability. However, if he clapped his hands, or made a noise, or blew, or did some sort of external act, for example, knocked on the wall, and the sound broke the victim's eardrum, or the shock made him deaf, or blind, there is no recovery. But if he held his ear,[17] or held him by the arm, there would be recovery.

13 See Rashi ibid. s.v. *debeinyan umdena*: "and he should not thusly have been blinded, but his bad luck caused his harm."

14 On liability under the laws of heaven, as distinguished from human law, see A. Kirschenbaum, *Equity in Jewish Law* (NY: 1991), vol. 2, ch. 4; "Causation in Jewish tort law," n. 4 above, 20, n. 125. For parallels to Roman law of equity, see Kirschenbaum, vol. 1, 17–19; Cohen, n. 28 below.

15 But cf. mBaba Kama 8:6, quoted by Rashi on bBaba Kama 90a s.v. *hatokeia*, to the effect that for the blowing of a shofar, or the like, in another's ear, there can be recovery of punitive or liquidated damages if humiliation results, although no physical injury ensues, even in the absence of any holding or touching. It is unclear why this is treated differently from liability for fright and shock. R. Menahem b. Solomon Meiri (1249–1316), *Beit Habehira*, Baba Kama, Schlesinger ed., 262, says the following:

> The term [*tekia*, blowing] has been explained as connoting striking with the hand upon the ear. Some explain that he screamed into his ear, and the only damage is that of humiliation (*boshet*). Some commentators explain that he held him as he blew, but if he blew without holding him, there would be no liability. It appears to me that there would be no liability for blowing when the victim was not held, except when he was deafened [by the noise]. But as to liability for damages resulting from humiliation, even where there was no touching and deafness did not ensue, he must pay.

See also Encyclopedia Talmudit, vol. 12, 706.

16 On whether the tortfeasor held the other's ear or his person, see below, the concluding paragraph of this section.

17 See n. 39 below on whether liability follows when the injured party is being held, and the sound is projected directly into his ears, as well as when it is indirect, as where a wall opposite the ear is struck.

The *stamai* thus initially suggests that the reason for the rule that the slave does not gain his freedom by virtue of the injury is that assessment as to whether the act was the cause of the injury is required, and the Rabbis determined that the injury was not an injury that would have occurred as a consequence of this act. The *stamai* concludes, however, that there is a different reason, namely, because "he frightened himself." The case is one of injury allegedly resulting from fright and shock; there is no recovery because he scared himself.[18] It follows that the question of whether assessment is necessary for purposes of tort liability cannot be decided from this ruling regarding the injured slave. The Talmud proceeds to decide the issue, concluding, on the basis of another Tannaitic source, that such a requirement does indeed exist.

A difficulty in this talmudic analysis is the question of why a rule of non-liability for the consequences of emotional distress, conditional upon the absence of physical impact of some sort, such as touching[19] or holding, is enunciated at all. Unlike the common law, these issues received little attention, with a few exceptions, to be considered below.[20] Still, as in the case of the common law, the commentators struggled mightily to explain these somewhat paradoxical rules.

These same principles regarding liability for fright and shock are also discussed in bKidushin 24b. The issue of liability for fright and

18 See R. Moses Feinstein, *Igrot Moshe*, HM 1:98, distinguishing a case where the injury to the victim was, or should have been, anticipated by the tortfeasor, from that involving injuries from fright or shock. In the former case, as where the person injured was known to be a sensitive person and he became ill when spat upon, liability is imposed. In cases involving injuries from fright or shock, there is no liability, reasons R. Feinstein, "since any person is capable of controlling himself to avoid fright and its consequences." Cf. William L. Prosser, n. 5 above, 876: "It is not difficult to discover in the earlier opinions [denying recovery for negligent infliction of emotional distress] a distinctly masculine astonishment that any woman should ever be so silly as to allow herself to be frightened or shocked into a miscarriage."

A view parallel to R. Feinstein's is that of Bohlen, n. 130 below, 147: "No act can be said to be negligent as to the plaintiff, unless the average man if in the defendant's position, knowing what he did or should have known, should have regarded injury to the plaintiff likely to result if care were not taken. The probability of injury raises the duty of care."

19 For the view of Maimonides, see the text below at n. 48.

20 See section 3.

shock is again raised in the context of discussing the type of injuries which, if inflicted on a slave, entitle him to manumission. The Talmud states:

> The Rabbis taught: 'If he hit him on the eye and blinded him; or on his ear and deafened him; the slave goes out free thereby. If he struck an object that was opposite his eye and blinded him [i.e., he pounded on the wall opposite to the slave's eye, which caused him to become blind]; or if he struck an object that was opposite his ear and deafened him, he does not go out free.' Thereupon Rav Shaman said to Rav Ashi: does that mean that sound is of no consequence? Did we not learn to the contrary? Thus, Rami b. Yehezkel stated: 'If a rooster sticks his head into a the neck of a glass pitcher and crows, and the pitcher breaks, the owner of the rooster has to make payment for it in full.'[21] And R. Joseph said: It was learned in the school of Rav: 'If one has a horse that neighed, or a donkey that brayed, and broke vessels in the house, there is liability of one-half.' Thereupon, Rav Ashi[22] answered: 'man is different; he is a rational being (*bar daat hu*), he scared himself.' As we learned: 'if one frightens another he is not liable by the law of man, but he is liable by the law of heaven. If he blew into his ear and made him deaf, he is not liable. But, if he held him and blew into his ear, and made him deaf, he is liable.'

21 Whether full payment is required for the object damaged, or only half payment, depends on whether the view of Symmachus or the Rabbis is accepted in their dispute over damage caused by an animal while kicking up pebbles (*tzrorot*), causing breakage of a nearby vessel, or by the beating of a fowl's wings, generating a breeze sufficient to cause damage (bBaba Kama 17b). Symmachus held that full payment is to be made, with the Rabbis ruling that half payment should be made. For discussion of rule of half-payment, as distinguished from payment in full, under Jewish tort law, see Steven F. Friedell, "Some observations on the Jewish law of torts," 15 *Rutgers L.J.* 897 (1984); Haut, "Some Aspects," n. 2 above, 18. For more on the concept of *tzrorot*, see Gustmann, n. 7 above, lecture 11.

22 From a literary point of view, it is interesting that in Kidushin it is Rav Ashi making this comment, "he scared himself"; in our passage (bBaba Kama 91a), it was not Rav Ashi, but the *stamai*, who makes that point. However, analysis of this issue is beyond the scope of this article. For discussion of this question, see David Weiss Halivni, *Mekorot Umsorot*, Shabat, Introduction, 25–26. He suggests that if the contexts differ and the terminology of the *stamai* is shorter than that of the named author of the statement, and omits the author's name, the *stamai* must be viewed as having effected the changes and having transposed the statement from its original source. Applying this approach to our case, the citation in bBaba Kama 91a can be viewed as a transposition (*haavara*) from bKidushin 24b. But see *Mekorot Umsorot*, Baba Kama, Introduction, 20, n. 22.

It is therefore clear that the Rabbis were aware that sound can cause damage and presumably injury. And yet, despite this knowledge, we find Rav Ashi asserting in Kidushin — echoed by the *stamai* in Baba Kama — that there is no recovery for fright and shock, because the injured party scared himself, and he is an intelligent person. If he was injured, he brought it on himself, a form of contributory negligence, or culpable conduct. But if so, why is liability imposed when he was held?

One possible, but improbable, explanation for this conundrum is afforded by the Jerusalem Talmud in jKilayim 8:2. It presents various sources maintaining that criminal and civil liability can flow from speech alone, without the performance of any physical act. For example, inter alia, the issue is raised of whether a bailment is created where the bailee does not lead the animal out of the bailor's possession, but merely calls out to it, and it follows.[23] In the context of that inquiry, a question is presented from the case of the affrighted slave, which appears to contradict the rule of liability previously established, as follows:

> If he struck the slave opposite to his eye and blinded him; opposite his ear and deafened him, the slave does not go free. R. Leizer b. R. Yosi[24] said before R. Yosi, 'the case of the slave can be distinguished, in that the slave could have run away.' The proof that this is correct is that it is stated, 'if he held him there is liability.'[25]

23 For a parallel source in the Babylonian Talmud, see bBaba Metzia 90b. The issue presented is whether one violates the injunction against muzzling an animal engaged in threshing to prevent it from eating (Deut. 25:4), by growling or grimacing at it. Rashi ad loc. s.v. *havei* refers to the general rule that one does not receive stripes, the punishment for violating a negative commandment in the Torah, **unless an act was performed**. The issue therefore is whether speech or grimacing constitute an act for that purpose. There is a dispute between R. Johanan and Resh Lakish on this point, the former declaring liability for stripes on the grounds that the movement of the lips constitutes an act sufficient for the imposition of the punishment. The latter opines that there is no such liability, "for sound is not an act."

24 Probably Eliezer b. R. Jose II.

25 I have assumed that the concluding phrase of this text, "if he held him there is liability," was uttered by R. Leizer, although it might also be an addition by the *stamai*. This concluding phrase is not found in connection with the case of the slave in bBaba Kama or bKidushin, quoted above, nor in the presentation of this rule in the Tosefta, to be quoted shortly. What then is its source? It is possible that R. Leizer or the *stamai* deduced

On this approach, therefore, the absence of liability for the intentional infliction of emotional distress causing physical injury is, in the case of the slave, due to the fact that the victim brought it upon himself by not seeking to escape the consequences of the sound, for example, by running away and distancing himself from it. However, if he was prevented from avoiding the impact of the sound and its physical consequences, as where he was held by the tortfeasor, liability ensues. If so, the case of the slave does not present an instance of non-liability for fright and shock at all, a rule omitted in the Jerusalem Talmud passage, although it may be implied.

This is a difficult distinction to accept, especially since the text nowhere makes explicit that the holding or touching was intended to prevent escape. Furthermore, how could the injured person have run away, thereby escaping injury, if the tortfeasor suddenly struck the nearby wall, deafening him?

An alternate basis for the rule of non-liability for fright and shock in the classical texts is found in the Tosefta, Baba Kama 9:26, which presents a Tannaitic source parallel to, but having significant differences from, the sources quoted above. The following formulation of the rule is set forth, again in the context of injuries to slaves mandating manumission:

> And he struck him (*vehikahu*) opposite his eye, and he does not see, opposite his ear, and he no longer hears — he does not go free; because it says in the Torah, 'one strikes the other' (Exod. 21:18)[26]; unless he performs a direct act.

The text of the Tosefta diverges considerably from the parallel texts quoted in the Babylonian and the Jerusalem Talmuds. On the view of

---

the rule of liability in the case of the slave who is being held from the text relating to liability for fright and shock generally, the latter text not being explicitly connected to that of the slave in the Jerusalem Talmud. If so, R. Leizer or the *stamai* is conjoining the texts and reading them *in pari materia*, as the Babylonian Talmud does, but without explicitly referring to this, unlike the sources in the Babylonian Talmud. On the other hand, it is quite possible that R. Leizer or the *stamai* had a variant of the text that contained the concluding phrase.

26 The phrase used here, *vehikahu*, "and he struck him," differs slightly from the wording in Exodus 21:18, *vehika*. And see Y. Abramsky, *Hazon Yehezkel*, Baba Kama 9:9, Biurim.

the Tosefta, the non-liability rule is derived directly from a decree of the Torah (*gzeirat hakatuv*). The Torah states that liability attaches only to physical acts, "strikes the other." And the definition of "strike" is to directly injure another. But short of actual physical contact, there is no liability.[27]

There is yet another pertinent distinction between the passages in the Babylonian Talmud and the Tosefta. In the talmudic texts, it is stated that being held is a predicate for liability for fright and shock. However, it is left open whether this refers to holding the limb involved, or any portion of the injured person's body. In the Tosefta, Baba Kama 6:16, the rule is stated as follows: "One who frightens another is not liable by the laws of man, but is by the laws of heaven. Thus, if he screeched into his ear and deafened him, there is no liability; if he held his ear and deafened him, he is liable." On this approach, there is no liability for fright and shock unless there was physical contact not only with the body of the person injured, but with the limb thereof actually injured.

### 3 *Classical Commentaries, Codes and Responsa*

#### a The Classical Commentaries

The classical commentaries, codifiers and other rabbinical authorities, medieval and modern, have taken the following four approaches in explaining the rule of non-liability for fright and shock, even when intentionally caused:

1. **Fright and shock constitute a species of indirect injury, termed *gerama*, for which there is no liability under Jewish law.**

27 This point was already noted by *Tosafot*, Baba Kama 91a s.v. *lo*. For parallel texts reflecting the approach of the Tosefta, see Mekhilta DeRabbi Ishmael, Horovitz ed., 279; Mekhilta DeRabbi Shimon b. Yohai, Melamed ed., 177. The latter source predicated the rule on the term "his eye" (*eino*, n. 11 above), implying that there is no requirement of manumission unless he actually struck his eye. Quaere: might this source be taking the phrase, "opposite his eye," as referring to a portion of his body that is adjacent to the eye? And could the other sources be taking the phrase the same way? And see the text at n. 53 below.

2. There is a conclusive presumption that a causal connection cannot be established between the wrongful act and the resulting injury.
3. The injured person's failure to exercise due care for his own safety precludes recovery.
4. A wrongful act has not been committed, or the injured party has not, in fact, sustained any legally-cognizable injury.

The first and by far most widespread approach is that fright and shock constitute a species of indirect cause, *gerama*, for which there is no liability under Jewish law. On this view, as with tort liability generally, there is no liability absent direct physical contact between the person injured or property damaged, and the wrongdoer, whether the injury is caused intentionally or unintentionally.[28] This approach is exemplified by Maharshal,[29] who suggests applying a test of causation.[30] If the injured party was directly struck on the face or head, causing blindness or deafness, then liability, of course, follows. But if the tortfeasor struck the wall adjacent to his head, causing the injuries from the fright or shock occasioned thereby, there is no liability.

28 See B. Cohen, *Jewish and Roman Law* (NY: 1966), vol. 2, 594–595, which interprets the rule of non-liability under Jewish law, comparing it to parallel developments in Roman law; S. Albeck, *Interpreting Tort Law in the Talmud* (Hebrew), (Tel-Aviv: 1965), 48–49; G. Horowitz, *The Spirit of Jewish Law* (NY: 1993), sec. 329; Encyclopedia Talmudit, vol. 12, 705, nn. 393–396.

29 See n. 7 above.

30 "The Talmud preliminarily seeks to explain the rule of non-liability on the basis that assessment is necessary to establish that the injured person was reasonably susceptible to this injury, and it was established that he should not have suffered or sustained blindness from the act; and it was an instance of pure accident [*ones*, for which there is no liability]. ... However, the Talmud concludes that the basis for the rule is the concept that he scared himself, since he did not touch him, and by virtue of the rule that acts of *gerama* do not give rise to tort liability." (*Yam Shel Shomo,* n. 7 above)

For discussion of the concept of liability for acts deemed *ones* under Jewish law, paralleling absolute liability under common law and American law, see Haut, "Some Aspects," n. 2 above.

The latter case represents a type of indirect injury, *gerama*, for which there is no liability.[31] Others also take this approach.[32]

On this approach, the absence of liability devolves from the notion that the injury was too removed from the act to support the imposition of liability, except where there was some further connection between the two, some type of impact, such as holding or touching. However, the logical difficulties in this approach persist. Even on the narrow view of proximate cause taken by Jewish law, this approach fails to take into account that the same law acknowledges that sound can and does have physical impact, as reflected in the passage from bKidushin discussed above.[33] If so, why does not the physical impact of sound satisfy the requirement of direct physical impact for purposes of tort liability, even under the application of the *gerama* rule?[34]

31 Maharshal suggests that although there is no liability by human law in the cases in question, there would nevertheless be liability under the law of heaven, as with any case of indirect injury, for example, cases of fright and shock. For the contrary view, see R. Jacob b. Joseph Reischer (1670–1733), *Responsa Shvut Yaakov*, 1:180. The case involved a functionary of the court who was over-zealous in administering court-ordered corporal punishment. One of the issues raised was whether he was personally liable where he had no reason to anticipate that the defendant would sustain injury. He concludes that no liability follows under either the laws of man, or of heaven, disagreeing with Maharshal as to liability under divine law in those circumstances. R. Reischer distinguishes liability under divine law in cases of fright and shock, from the case of the court official, in that, "in the former, he should have anticipated that it is in the nature of man to be affrighted when he is frightened, unlike the case of the official, where he was not required to have anticipated that striking the individual with the type of instrument used would have effected the resulting injury." However, if injury from fright or shock was or could have been anticipated under this view, why does not liability follow under the laws of man, as well?

32 See Encyclopedia Talmudit, vol. 12, 705, n. 393. R. Meir of Rothenburg (1215–1293), *Responsa*, 4:300; R. Moses Feinstein, *Igrot Moshe*, EH 4:29 s.v. *vegav iuni*.

33 bKidushin 24b, quoted above following n. 20.

34 R. Isaac Elhanan Spektor (1817–1896) makes this point in *Responsa Ein Yitzhak*, EH #11, asserting that the basis for non-liability in cases of fright and shock cannot be application of the *gerama* rule. He reasons: "If the rationale [for non-liability] that he frightened himself was not supplied [in cases of fright and shock resulting from sound], then the perpetrator

It has been suggested that the difference in legal consequence lies in the distinction between inanimate objects, such as jars and pitchers, which cannot but shatter as a result of certain sounds, and humans, who should not have permitted themselves to become frightened.[35] This is a difficult distinction to uphold, particularly where, as is often the case, the fright or shock was occasioned suddenly and without warning, rendering the injured party unable to avert, or guard himself against, the effects thereof.

A further difficulty with this view is why, if the issue is one of proximate causation, and the absence of physical impact bars recovery under the *gerama* rule, there is liability for the act of holding the injured party when he is frightened. Surely this adds nothing, and does not supply the missing link to proximate causation or substitute for direct physical impact. It is interesting that the issue has generally escaped notice by the commentators, who all assume, without articulating the basis therefor, and without further analysis, that the element of holding or touching supplies the necessary predicate for imposition of liability.[36]

---

would be in the position of an actual tortfeasor, and not merely by virtue of the *garmi* rule, since sound is efficacious in causing damage, as reflected in the *sugya* [bKidushin 24b]." For more on his view, see section 3c below.

35 See Rashi, Kidushin 24b s.v. *shani adam*: "The injured party is consciously [voluntarily?] frightened because he pays attention to the scary sound that comes suddenly." For further discussion of this view, see A. Sheinfeld, *Torts* (Hebrew), (Jerusalem: 1991), 272, n. 4. And see n. 44 below.

36 See the works cited in n. 28 above. See also Kirschenbaum, n. 14 above, vol. 2, 139, who puts the matter thus:

> The exemption from the laws of man holds true as long as the frightener maintained no physical contact with his victim; he yelled at him from the back and made him deaf, or frightened him in the dark and caused him to faint. In such cases the damage is still regarded as indirect. Where, however, his act was accompanied by physical contact with his victim (e.g., he seized his victim, yelled into his ear, and rendered him deaf thereby; or pushed him violently, or seized him by his clothes as he startled him and caused him to faint, fall and sustain an injury), the tortfeasor is liable according to the laws of man and his victim may sue him in court.

A second approach is that of Maharshal, to the effect that the basis for the rule of non-liability for fright is as stated in the discussion in bBaba Kama 91a, namely, that the Rabbis, in making the requisite assessment, determined as a matter of law that the act complained of could not reasonably have caused the injury or damage.[37] Maharshal reasons that in the final analysis, we do accept as law the rule that

---

This is a difficult distinction to accept. In the first place, in my opinion, the contact required for the imposition of liability does not rise to the level of the very physical acts described by Kirschenbaum, particularly on the view of Maimonides, discussed below at n. 48. Furthermore, the argument proves too much, since if causing one to faint gives rise to liability in one instance, where there is contact, why is there not the same result where the fainting and its untoward consequences resulted from shock alone, with no attendant physical contact? But cf. Rashi on Baba Kama 56a s.v. *hamavit,* who asserts that there is no liability for fright, "because he perpetrated no physical act on his body." The implication is that the perpetration of some physical act, such as holding or touching, will give rise to liability. Quaere? Compare Annotation, "Right to recover for emotional disturbance or its physical consequences in the absence of impact or other actionable wrong," 64 ALR2d 100, 128 (1959). In connection with the proposition that many of the cases denying recovery for the physical consequences of mental distress have predicated that result on the grounds that such physical consequences are too remote, or not a foreseeable result of the wrongful act, the author adds: "If this reasoning is followed, it is difficult to see why recovery should be allowed merely because there was a contemporaneous physical impact, at least unless it was also required that the emotional distress be directly consequent upon, and not merely coincident with, that impact" (ibid., n. 11).

However, it is clear that from early times, the common law permitted recovery where the impact did not cause the emotional distress, but preceded it. Thus, where the defendant's negligence frightens the plaintiff, and that fright causes the plaintiff to react, for instance, by jumping for his life, he may recover for the emotional distress, as well as for any physical injuries sustained. See *Jones v. Boyle*, text at and n. 111 below; *Piadd*, n. 1 above, sec. 3.01[1], 117. See also 64 A.L.R.2d, 142–143.

37 Maharshal, n. 7 above. Compare Bohlen, n. 130 below, 146, which sets forth the following as one of the theories denying imposition of liability for mere emotional disturbance: "Such injury is too delicate a matter for the scales of justice to weigh."

It should be noted that the Rabbis construed what could be seen as an issue of fact, namely, whether a causal connection could be established between the act and injury, as a conclusive presumption that it could not be so established. Cf. Report of the New York State Law Revision Commission,

assessment is necessary to establish tort liability, the final conclusion of the discussion in Baba Kama, as noted above.[38] As such, the supposition first rejected by the Talmud, namely, that the rule of non-liability in the case of fright is predicated upon the requirement of assessment and the conclusive presumption that the requisite causal connection between the act and injury or damage cannot be established, is correct. It follows that the basis for non-liability in the case of fright does not flow from the proposition that the victim injured himself, but rather from a conclusive presumption of inability to prove causal connection under the circumstances.[39]

---

Study Relating to Liability for Injuries Resulting From Fright or Shock, n. 106 below, 44. In discussing the issue of remoteness as a bar to recovery for the consequences of emotional distress, *Toms v. Toronto R.W. Co.*, 22 *Ont. L.R.* 204 (Ct. of Appeals, 1910) is quoted:

> The vice of the decision [*Victorian Railways Commissioners v. Coultas*, see Appendix, text at n. 98 below] appears to be in treating as a question of law that which appears to be essentially one of fact, to be determined, like other questions of fact, upon competent evidence, namely, what are the natural and reasonable consequences, such as ordinarily flow from such acts as that of the defendants?

38 See text above between notes 18 and 19.

39 Maharshal assumes that on the conclusion of the *sugya*, there will be no liability for fright when the injury is indirect, as when the wall opposite the eye or ear is struck, and blindness or deafness results, even where the injured party is being held, based on the conclusive presumption that there is no possibility of proving a causal connection. This, of course, eliminates the logical inconsistency in the rule of non-liability to some extent, but not completely. Maharshal still maintains that in the case of one who blew into another's ear, liability would be imposed if he was held, but not otherwise. In addition, Maharshal, like the *Tosafot* on Baba Kama 91a s.v. *lo*, is troubled by recourse to the concept that the slave frightened himself as a defense. Both reason that if liability is established even in cases of indirect injury, as through a loud noise on the wall, causing deafness or blindness, then why need the baraita have fashioned a hypothetical of liability where he was struck on the eye or ear, as distinguished from non-liability when struck opposite his ear, when it could have more easily distinguished cases of liability from non-liability simply by reference to whether or not the slave was held? On the basis of this question, the *Tosafot* assert that the ground for the rule of non-liability is not that the slave frightened himself, but rather, divine decree, following Tosefta Baba Kama 9:26, discussed above in the text near n. 26. Maharshal,

This is a rather neat solution, were it not for the fact, pointed out by one commentator, that this result contradicts the discussion in Kidushin, which accepted the view of Rav Ashi, echoed by the anonymous redactor in Baba Kama, that the basis for non-liability is the view that the victim injured himself.[40] Moreover, as the commentator points out, this approach would lead to the conclusion that the discussion in Kidushin was consistent only with the preliminary assumptions of the discussion in Baba Kama, and not with its conclusion, a not unheard-of situation, but one that nevertheless warrants inquiry.[41]

A third approach is that taken by R. Meir Halevi,[42] to the effect that liability is predicated on the inability of the person to have escaped injury, for instance, where the injured party could not have turned his head aside to avoid being injured, as he was being held. If the injury could not have been averted, there is liability, even absent physical contact. But, if not held, the injured party is negligent for not having escaped by running away, or otherwise averting the injury, for example, by turning his head away from the sound.[43] But where the tortfeasor

---

on the basis of that same question, and applying the approach of the *Tosafot* without explicitly mentioning them, similarly concludes that the basis for non-liability is not that the slave frightened himself. However, he diverges from the *Tosafot*, concluding that the basis for non-liability is the conclusive presumption of inability to make the requisite assessment.

40 See R. Joseph David Zintzheim (1745–1812), *Yad David*, Baba Kama, 148–149.

41 R. Zintzheim rejects this possibility, though he concedes that Maharshal may have so reconciled the two *sugyot*.

42 R. Meir Halevi Abulafia (Rama), (1170–1244).

43 Quoted by R. Bezalel Ashkenazi, *Shita Mekubetzet*, Baba Kama, 277. (No reference to jKilayim 8:2 is explicitly made by Rama, but it can be presumed that he was aware of the passage. See Weiss Halivni, *Mekorot Umsorot*, Moed, 81, n. 9, "the text [of the Jerusalem Talmud] was known to them [the medieval rabbis], but the knowledge thereof was not complete." If so, it may have supplied the basis for his view.) See R. Menahem b. Solomon Meiri, *Beit Habehira*, Baba Kama, Schlesinger ed., 171.

R. Abraham b. David of Posquieres (Ravad), (1125–1198), states:

> 'If he struck him opposite his eye, there is no liability under the law of man': why is there no liability under the law of man; we know that sound is efficacious [in causing injury or damage] as we see from the case of … a horse that neighed and a donkey that brayed and broke vessels in the house [bKidushin 24b], where liability is imposed.

acted directly upon the body of the injured party, liability is imposed, "even if he could have saved himself, and he failed so to do."[44] This approach is also suggested by a contemporary scholar, Saul Lieberman,[45] who grounds his view in jKilayim 8:2.

The fourth approach, to which I now turn, is that of Maimonides.

---

> So why is there no liability in this case? Is the reason that assessment is required, and it is impossible to assess the impact of the sound that strikes him, or that the we are certain that the sound in question was inadequate to have caused the blindness or deafness? No. The reason is that the injured person contributed to the negligence. The proof of this conclusion is that we see that when he held him and made a loud noise in his ear, liability is imposed.
>
> (*Hidushei Haravad*, Baba Kama, Atlas ed., 223)

From the comments of Ravad, it is clear that he views contributory negligence as the basis for the rule of non-liability. He assumes, without any explanation, that if the injured party was held, he no longer contributes to the negligence, in line with the view of Rashi, cited in n. 35 above, and Rama, that being held prevented escape. But Atlas, loc cit. n. 47, points out that another version of Ravad's view is found in *Shita Meubetzet*, a version on which he did indeed agree that the basis for the rule of non-liability was that assessment was necessary, and it was conclusively presumed impossible to make the necessary assessment, or that the Rabbis presumed that, in at least some circumstances, it was conclusively determined that the injury could not have been caused by the sound. If this version is accepted, Ravad's view accords with that of Maharshal. It appears, however, that *Shita Mekubetzet* brings only a truncated account of Ravad's view, and the accurate account of it is that preserved in *Hidushei Haravad*.

Maharshal, without referring to Ravad, appears to accept the very construction of the *sugya* that Ravad rejects. Quaere: Did he know of Ravad's view?

44 *Shita Mekubetzet* quotes Rama as stating: "All that which we have said previously relates to acts of indirect causation (*gerama*). But where he [the tortfeasor] acted directly upon the body of the injured person, although the latter could have rescued himself, and refrained from so doing, the former is liable." For more on the Rama's view, see Albeck, n. 28 above, 48–50; Sheinfeld, n. 35 above, 272, n. 4. Citing R. Abramsky, Sheinfeld distinguishes between the views of Rashi and Rama. R. Abramsky asserts, in *Hazon Yehezkel*, Hidushim, Nezikin 6:5 (6:16 in the Lieberman ed.), that on Rashi's view, there is no liability for fright in the absence of physical impact, even if the injured party could not have escaped, while on the view of R. Meir, there is.

45 *Tosefta Kifshuta*, Nezikin, 107–108.

## b Codes

Maimonides was the first to provide a detailed code of the entire corpus of Jewish law. It might have been expected that Maimonides, who adopted a broad view of causation,[46] might have also allowed his jurisprudential genius to adopt rules of broadened liability in the area of recovery for emotional distress. However, in this area, with one possible exception, he felt bound by the classical texts, denying recovery, except in limited circumstances. He was followed in so ruling by the other great codifiers, as will be seen.

Maimonides rules that there is no recovery for fright and shock in the absence of contact of some sort, without specifying the basis for this rule. This, of course, lends a measure of ambiguity to his ruling.

> One who frightens his neighbor, even if he became ill from the fear, is not liable under human law, but is liable under the law of heaven. But that is only where he did not touch (*naga*) him, but merely shouted out behind him, or scared him in the dark,[47] and the like. And so if he shouted in his ear and deafened him, there is no liability under the law of man, but there is liability under the law of heaven. If he held him (*ahazo*) and blew into his ear and deafened him, or he touched him and pushed him as he frightened him, or held his garment and the like, he is obligated to pay compensation.[48]

However, it is with respect to the requirement of impact or contact that Maimonides may have intended a degree of creativity. Thus, although it was universally asserted in the classical texts, discussed above, that the only exception to the rule of non-liability was where the victim was held (*ahaz*), Maimonides appears to be the first to rule that

46 See Haut, "Causation in Jewish tort law — part II," n. 4 above.

47 Cf. *Brown v. Craven*, 175 Ill. 401 (1898), discussed by Bohlen, n. 130 below, 156. In that case, the plaintiff's back was turned when the defendant entered the room with rubber snowshoes on and spoke sharply to her, as a consequence of which she was frightened and became ill. It was held that she could not recover, since it could not have been anticipated that any injury would result. The court added: "Terror or fright, even if it results in nervous shock which constitutes a physical injury, does not create a liability" (420). It would appear that this comment by the court is an apt restatement in modern times of the non-liability rule as formulated by Maimonides long ago.

48 *Code*, Laws concerning Wounding and Damaging 2:7.

any touching was a predicate for liability. In this connection he uses the term "touched" (*naga*), rather than the phrase used in the classical literature, "held" (*ahaz*).

If this change in terminology is anything more than mere literary usage,[49] then we can say that Maimonides was the first to articulate the rule, adopted in modern times, that any touching, howsoever minimal, was sufficient to turn a act that does not generate liability into one from which liability flows.[50]

Inasmuch as the rule is presented in the context of rules dealing with the measure of damages, and not in the sections dealing with causation, or with the requirement of assessment in cases of tort liability,[51] it would appear that Maimonides treated this area as independent of the latter. The question of the precise basis for his ruling nevertheless persists. It is, of course, possible that he saw the matter as purely technical, and consistent with the general approach of Jewish law, on which an act is required for tort liability to be imposed, and thus ruled, like Rashi,[52] that without impact, no act is present in the case of fright and shock.

It is also possible that Maimonides, following and applying the approach of the Tosefta,[53] took the position that recovery was denied under a divine decree of the Torah (*gzeirat hakatuv*). If so, further attempts to elucidate the basis for his rulings in this area are meaningless.

The implication is that on his view this area of law is unique, in that there is no liability for fright and shock, since the tortfeasor has committed no wrongful act. The term tortfeasor, in fact, is simply inapplicable, and absent some act involving physical contact between the injured party and himself, he is not liable. On this approach, the rule of non-liability in cases of fright and shock, in the absence of physical

49 That it may be nothing more than a literary usage may be manifested in the last sentence in the ruling, in which Maimonides appears to utilize the terms interchangeably. If this is so, he may not have intended any innovation whatsoever.

50 See Bohlen's critique of this position, n. 130 below, 146. Commenting upon the concept of remoteness as a predicate for denying recovery, he states: "It is enough to say of this that it is difficult to see why a result which is so remote that a man is not responsible for it if it alone occurs, can become a proper subject of compensation by the same person, because he has actually caused some other harm to the plaintiff."

51 See n. 7 above.

52 See n. 35 above.

53 See text at nn. 26–27 above.

impact, could be a species of what is known to the common law as *damnum absque injuria*, injuries for which the law furnishes no redress.[54] A leading text defines it thus:

> Where no act of the defendant proximately caused the injuries suffered by the plaintiff, the plaintiff's case is illustrative of the ancient phrase '*damnum absque injuria*' — an injury to the person for which the law furnishes no redress."[55]

This approach is consistent with the views of some contemporary rabbinical authorities who predicate tort liability upon commission of an act. Hence, in circumstances where no physical act has been performed directly upon the person of the victim, as in cases of fright and shock, there is no liability.[56]

54 The ruling immediately preceding the ruling in question supports the claim that the absence of liability is by virtue of *damnum absque injuria*. It deals with inconsequential damage. Maimonides rules that physical damages of any nature and however minimal are compensable, even extending to a hair-sized loss of the victim's skin, "since the skin will not return, but a scab will result" (*Code*, Laws concerning Wounding and Damaging 2:6). It thus appears that on his view any damage, where physically inflicted, is compensable as an injury. But damage not physically inflicted, such as illness resulting from fright and shock, does not constitute injury and is not compensable.

55 79 N.Y. Jur. 2d section 3 (1989). See also John Salmond, *Jurisprudence* (7th ed.), (London: 1924), 388:

> The second heading of *damnum sine injuria* includes all those cases in which, although real harm is done to the community, yet, owing to its triviality, or to the difficulty of proof, or to any other reason, it is considered inexpedient to attempt its prevention by the law. The mischief is of such a nature that the legal remedy would be worse than the disease.

56 See Gustmann, n. 7 above, 5, for an excellent discussion of this area of Jewish tort law. He articulates the view that under Jewish tort law, there is no recovery unless the term "tortfeasor," which he terms *shem mazik*, is properly applied to the actor. It signifies that there will be no liability upon the actor, despite his having caused monetary loss, "if the act was not itself tortious" (p. 14).

In this manner he explains many instances where liability is denied, although loss ensues, including cases where there was no breach by the actor of a pre-existing duty, as well as cases where an object was damaged and its value reduced solely from the point of view of ritual law, and not

In connection with the issue of the necessity of assessment for the purpose of establishing tort ability, Maimonides rules:

> Just as we assess for purposes of the criminal law, so too do we assess for the purpose of tort liability. One who struck another with a small rock, which was insufficient to have caused injury, or struck him with a small piece of wood, and caused an injury, which is not of the type that the object is appropriate to have caused, is not liable, for it is written 'with a stone or fist'[57] — an object that is appropriate to have caused the injury. Therefore, it is necessary that the witnesses be aware of the nature of the object utilized for the injury. And that object is brought to court, so that assessment and judgment may be made upon it. And if the object got lost and the tortfeasor asserted that it was inadequate to have caused the claimed injury, and that it was a species of unavoidable accident, and the injured party asserts to the contrary, the latter may swear an oath and collect, as I shall explain hereinafter.[58]

The later medieval codes have generally followed Maimonides' formulation in both areas.

In his monumental *Tur*, R. Jacob b. Asher[59] rules as follows with respect to the requirement of assessment:

> And when the court judges the tortfeasor, it is necessary to assess the item used to inflict the injury; and the place on the injured person's body struck; if the instrument was adequate to have caused the injury at the

---

from a civil law perspective. Although he does not refer to the question of emotional distress, his approach is applicable to this area as well. He writes:

> However, it is possible that a person could injure another, even intentionally, or his ox could injure him, or other types of injury, meeting all the conditions of tort liability imposed by the Torah except for the requirement of *shem mazik*, and there would be no liability, for the Torah did not obligate any persons to make payment for tort liability, except those meeting the criterion of *shem mazik*.
>
> (p. 8)

On the application of this principle concerning objects injured, damaged, or lowered in value solely from the point of view of ritual law, see Gustmann,15–17. For further discussion of non-liability in these instances, see "Causation — part II," n. 4 above, n. 233; R. Levi Y. Helperin, *Action and its Causation* (Hebrew), (Jerusalem: 1978), 232–235.

57 Exodus 21:18, "when men quarrel and one strikes the other with a stone or fist, and he does not die, but has to take to his bed."

58 See n. 7 above.

59 R. Jacob b. Asher (1270–1340).

> place of the injury, then the tortfeasor is liable; but if not, if the instrument was not adequate to have effected the injury, or at the particular place struck, there is no liability. ... therefore the witnesses must know the nature of the instrument used to effect the injury, and it is brought to court and assessed accordingly.[60]

As to liability for fright and shock, he rules:

> One who frightens another, although he becomes ill from the fear, is not liable by the laws of man, but is liable by the laws of heaven. But that rule applies if he did not touch him, as where he shouted behind him, or scared him in the dark and the like. And if he screeched into his ear and deafened him, he is not liable by the laws of man, but by the laws of heaven. If he held him as he screeched into his ear, and deafened him, or if he touched him and frightened him,[61] as he frightened him, or if he held his garments, he is obligated to pay damages.[62]

Of interest is the fact that R. Jacob b. Asher had previously classified this rule in the category of rules relating to the absence of liability for injuries indirectly caused (*gerama*).[63] It would therefore appear that,

60 *Tur*, HM 420:19.

61 The Hebrew term used is *hifhido* — frightened him. But a variant given in the text in parentheses, *hadafo*, meaning 'pushed him,' is more consistent with the phrase "as he frightened him," which follows.

62 Ibid. 420:22. But see R. Moses Isserles (1525–1572), *Darkhei Moshe*, commenting on *Tur* ad loc., which follows the view of R. Mordecai b. Hillel Hakohen (1240–1298) in his *Mordekhai*, bBaba Kama 91a, sec. 95, "If he held him and blew into his ear and deafened him, he is liable, for the deafness was caused not by the fright, but by the sound. And the same rule applies if he held him and struck the adjacent wall and deafened him — liability follows."

R. Joseph Haim b. Elijah al Hakham (1835–1909), *Responsa Rav Pealim* on YD, II:35, questions the *Mordekhai*'s ruling that even if one only struck the adjacent wall, he is nevertheless liable if he held the injured party. He asks: since, were he not held, there would be no liability by virtue of the *gerama* rule, why is the situation different if he was held? He answers: "But for the fact that he was being held, he would not have been deafened by the sound of the wall's being struck, for by virtue of the fact that he was held and placed in proximity to the sound, he was injured. Thus, the holding is considered an act committed directly on his person. And even if it was another person altogether who struck the wall, he would nevertheless be liable for holding him, for thus he brought him into proximity with the sound of the striking, and it is as if he caused the injury with his own hands." See n. 39 above, and n. 69 below.

63 *Tur*, HM 386:3.

following the view of his father, Rabbenu Asher,[64] R. Jacob adhered to the view that non-liability in the case of fright and shock follows from application of the *gerama* rule.[65]

In the equally monumental code, the *Shulhan Arukh*, R. Joseph Caro[66] also follows Maimonides' formulation. As to the need for assessment, he rules:

> 28. Just as we make an assessment for purposes of criminal liability, so too we assess for purposes of tort liability. Thus, if one struck his fellow with a small rock inadequate to have caused injury, or with a small sliver of wood, and caused a wound that the instrument used was incapable of making, there is no liability[67]; for it is written, "with a stone or a fist," an instrument adequate to have caused the injury. Therefore the witnesses must be aware of how the injury was effected, and the instrument is brought to court, so that it may be assessed and judged.
>
> 29. Iron does not need assessment, for even a small needle can effect death, and certainly cause injury; but this rule applies to something pointed, like a needle. However, if it caused injury solely by virtue of its weight, and was not pointed, then it is just like any other object, and assessment is required.[68]

As to liability for fright and shock, he rules similarly: "If he screeched into his ear and deafened him, he is not liable by the laws of man but is liable by the laws of heaven; if he held him and made a loud noise in his ear and deafened him, or if he struck him on the ear and deafened him, there is full liability."[69]

64 Rabbenu Asher b. Yehiel (1250–1327) commenting on bBaba Batra 2:17.

65 That this was also the view of Rabbenu Asher's teacher, R. Meir of Rothenburg, is reflected in the latter's *Responsa*, n. 32 above.

66 R. Joseph b. Ephraim Caro (1488–1575).

67 "For it was just the injured party's bad luck, or misfortune" — R. Joshua b. Alexander Hakohen Falk (1555–1614), *Sema*, commenting on Caro, echoing Rashi, bBaba Kama 91a s.v. *debeinyan umdena*, n. 13 above.

68 *Shulhan Arukh*, HM 420:28.

69 Ibid., 420:25. R.Y.M. Epstein, *Arukh Hashulhan*, vol. 8, commenting on *Shulhan Arukh*, HM 420:33, states:

> The explanation that if he blew into his ear and deafened him, he is liable, applies only where he held his body or his clothes, and blew into his ear. But if he did not hold him, but merely cried out near his ear and deafened him, he is liable only by the laws of heaven, for this is an instance of *gerama*, for he did not effect an act directly upon his body. However, if he held him, even if he did not blow directly into

### c Responsa

Other than as mentioned above, the need for assessment in cases of tort liability and liability for fright and shock has received little attention in the responsa literature, with one exception: R. Isaac Elhanan Spektor's extensive analysis of the subject.[70]

The case before R. Spektor involved a man who was last seen clinging to trees over a raging torrent, when he was struck in the chest by logs flowing down the churning river, and disappeared from view, never to be seen again. The issue, of course, was the status of his wife as a chained women, or *aguna*, who would be unable to remarry until it was conclusively ascertained that her husband was deceased.[71]

In a wide-ranging dissertation, in the course of which R. Spektor established her right to remarry, he touched upon our subject, discussing the requirement of assessment for purposes of establishing tort liability, and providing a conceptual basis for it. Reasoning that generally, the basis for the requirement of assessment is to establish that it is more probable than not that the injury was consequent upon the act, he considers certain cases where assessment is not required, because there is a conclusive and non-rebuttable presumption that the commission of the tort was the competent producing cause of the injury, such as

---

> his ear, but instead, struck the wall opposite his ear, and he became deaf, he is liable. For although, insofar as animals are concerned, sound is considered an act, as we see from the case of the rooster that crowed and broke a vessel, that payment is required therefor [see text at n. 21 above, I.H.] insofar as man is concerned, sound is merely an indirect act (*gerama*), for he is an intelligent being, and he frightened himself.

See text above at n. 35.

70 *Beer Yitzhak*, EH #18. See also n. 34 above. And see Aaron Rakefet-Rothkoff, "Rabbi Isaac Elhanan Spektor of Kovno: spokesman for *agunot*," *Tradition* 29 (1995), 5, which discusses the responsum in question.

71 Under Jewish law there is no presumption of death merely by virtue of prolonged absence, as is the case under other legal systems, e.g., the common law, as well as under statutory provisions. See *Butler v. Mutual Life Ins. Co. of New York*, 225 N.Y. 197, 121 N.E. 758 (1919); *Connor v. New York Life Ins. Co.*, 179 App. Div. 596, 166 N.Y.S. 985 (2nd Dep't., 1917); Estates, Powers and Trusts Law of the State of New York, sec. 2-1.7.

damage by falling into a pit:[72] "the Rabbis posited that injuries by falling into a pit are definitely fatal, since in the majority of instances, the injured party's limbs are shattered, and therefore, assessment is rendered unnecessary."[73]

On the other hand, asserts R. Spektor:

> The basic reason that assessment is required in cases of tort liability, or to establish criminal culpability, although it appears that the victim expired because of the blow of the aggressor, is that the latter should not be heard to say, 'it was an unavoidable accident, and I had no reason to believe that my act would have those consequences.' But where the act is prohibited by virtue of the fact that in the majority of cases, injury ensues, the actor cannot be heard to defend on the ground of unavoidable accident, since he should have known that the victim would, in all probability, be injured or killed.[74]

R. Spektor states further:

> But where there was a doubt as to whether the injury was such as would in all probability be caused by the act, although it is forbidden to injure another, nevertheless, since the act was not prohibited by the probability of injury, the actor can defend on the basis of unavoidable accident. Thus, the impact of probability is as follows: Although we do not follow the majority in monetary matters,[75] nevertheless, where the act was explicitly prohibited by virtue of the probability of injury, the actor can no longer assert that the injury resulted from unavoidable accident. And he is obligated to pay, since the injury resulted from his act, as we have stated above.[76]

72 See bBaba Kama 51a, "just as [a fall into] a pit is fatal at a depth of 10 *tefahim* [approximately 20–25 inches], so too any fall of that distance is fatal."

73 *Beer Yitzhak*, EH 18:2 s.v. *ledaati*.

74 Ibid. s.v. "and another proof of that which I have written."

75 See bBaba Kama 27a-b; bBaba Batra 92a-b. Majority usage, or custom, is not determinative in a given instance as to the intention of the parties to a given commercial transaction. For example, bBaba Batra 92a-b discusses the case of a buyer of an ox, who did not specify whether he sought the ox for agricultural purposes. The ox turned out to be wild and unfit for the latter purpose, though it was fit for consumption. The sale stands, despite the fact that the majority of persons purchase oxen for agricultural purposes. See my "Jewish law of warranties," n. 2 above, 116, 122; and "*Kad* and *Havit*," 13 *Jewish Law Annual* 87–100 (2000).

76 18:64 s.v. "and this is reflected in the implication of the Mishnah."

Thus according to R. Spektor, it is the probability that the injury in question will flow from the act that establishes tort liability. On this approach, therefore, in every case of fright or shock, as well as in other areas of tort liability, it is necessary for the court to engage in this analysis to determine liability.

### 4 *Conclusion: Implications for the Growth and Development of Jewish Law*

In the Appendix, I will trace the tortuous path of the common law, from the rule prohibiting recovery for emotional distress, except in cases of intentional tort, to that permitting recovery in a variety of circumstances, including cases involving external physical injury, or impact of some sort, to the view that recovery is permitted, where injury, mental or physical, is established, without any preconditions whatsoever, other than those, of course, of proximate cause and proof of injury. The survey demonstrates that the common law arrived at a view that accords with substantive justice and the needs of a modern society. It is my hope that this model can provide a paradigm for the development of Jewish law with respect to this matter.

As noted by Prof. Throckmorton:

> If A, by his negligence, brushes slightly against B, a pregnant women, and while doing her no injury by the impact, yet frightens her so badly that a nervous shock results from the fright — not from the impact — and the nervous shock causes B to have a miscarriage, it is admitted that she may recover from A for the physical pain and suffering endured by her in the shock and miscarriage. But, it is said, if A is driving negligently on the street and stops his horse within a few inches of impact with B, but frightens her just as badly as in the former case, with the resultant nervous shock and miscarriage, B may not recover from A, albeit her physical injury is just as great as before and just as much due to A's fault. **A rule of liability so highly technical, so completely without foundation in reason, is not out of place in a primitive system of jurisprudence, but is unworthy of any system based on the theory of granting redress for every substantial wrong.** (emphasis added)[77]

Throckmorton's comments are equally appropriate to Jewish law. Except for some areas of law, the rules of which are open to question,

77 A. Throckmorton, "Damages for Fright," 34 *Harv.L.R.* 260, 278 (1921).

as they are here as well as in Jewish divorce law and a few other areas,[78] it is beyond question that the Jewish legal system is one in which redress is generally sought, if not always attained, "for every substantial wrong."

We have seen that the rabbis, ancient and medieval, struggled mightily to explain the view of Jewish law in this area, denying recovery for emotional distress, even where intentionally caused, in the absence of impact or contact of some sort, and denying recovery outright where negligent, rather than intentional, activity is involved.

Jewish law has, to this point, been spared the criticism directed at the common law, by virtue of the fact that, due to the long exile, it has not, with certain exceptions at various periods, been the legal system of a politically viable society. However, with the establishment, once again, of a Jewish state, and the potential for the adoption of Jewish law, it becomes necessary, and, indeed, mandatory, for rabbinical leaders and students of Jewish law to subject it to the type of criticism that has been directed at the common law, with a view to providing a basis for its growth and development.

This article cannot explore the manner in which this process should be effected. Suffice it to say that mechanisms for change do exist within the system, whether by establishment of a Sanhedrin, or by means of rabbinical decrees or enactments, by the Chief Rabbinate and others, which I have called for elsewhere. I am well aware that the common law is essentially a human system of law, having its roots in human concepts of truth, justice and equity, unlike Jewish law, which to a great extent derives its binding authority and force from the divine will, ensconced in the Torah. Nevertheless, the Rabbis arrogated to themselves the right and power to modify even the Torah and the divine will, as it were, as and where necessary. "The Torah is not in heaven," declared R. Joshua,[79] quoting Deuteronomy 30:12, in opposing a heavenly voice that announced that the law was contrary to a position he held. And indeed, it is left to the rabbinical authorities to administer, legislate and adjudicate the law.

In my opinion, the rabbinical authorities, ancient and medieval, were great lawyers, men of jurisprudential genius. They labored mightily to explain and interpret their legal system, which sustained them, and were, I believe, motivated by the same considerations that

78 See n. 2 above.

79 bBaba Metzia 59b.

moved English and American common law judges to formulate and modify rules and principles of general application.

In *Battalla v. State*,[80] the Court of Appeals abolished the rule precluding recovery for injuries, physical or mental, incurred by fright negligently induced, pointing out that of the grounds for denying recovery discussed by the trial court in an earlier case,[81] the only one that could be sustained was that of public policy — the avoidance of feigned injuries and a resultant flood of litigation. The Court also noted that these policy consideration were grounded in the perceived difficulty of proof as to the nature of the injuries.

I would suggest that the approach of Jewish law in this area may have been predicated on precisely these elements. The Rabbis may, similarly, have been concerned about the potential for flooding the courts with spurious claims and difficult-to-prove cases. This is evidenced by the fact that in the Talmud, the issue of recovery for fright and shock is raised in the context of discussing whether assessment is necessary for purposes of tort liability, that is, whether an objective or a subjective standard is to be applied for the determination of compensable injury. The former would, of course, be more effective in weeding out spurious claims.

The Court of Appeals of New York in *Battalla* rejected those policy considerations and, in broadening the ambit of liability, stated: "We act in the finest common law tradition when we adapt and alter decisional law to produce common sense justice. *** Legislative action there could, of course, be. But we abdicate our own function, in a field peculiarly nonstatutory, when we refuse to reconsider an old and unsatisfactory court-made rule."[82]

The Rabbis were aware, as are modern jurists, that once rules prohibiting recovery are relaxed and the ambit of recovery broadened, it is necessary to start drawing lines.[83] As it avoids the need to draw

80 *Battalla v. State*, 10 N.Y.2d 237, 240–242, 219 N.Y.S.2d 34, 36–37, 176 N.E.2d 729 (1961). For further discussion, see text at n. 134 below.

81 *Mitchell v. Rochester Ry. Co.*, 4 Misc. 575, 25 N.Y.S. 24 (Sup. Ct., Monroe Co., 1893).

82 10 N.Y.2d 239, 219 N.Y.S 2d 36, 176 N.E.2d 730, quoting *Woods v. Lancet*, 303 N.Y. 349, 355, 102 N.E. 691, 694, 27 A.L.R.2d 1250.

83 See Prosser, n. 5 above, 891. In discussing the advisability of enlarging yet further the ambit of recovery for fright and shock to innocent bystanders, who were strangers to the injured person (see text at and nn.144–146 below), he states: "**It is again a question of drawing the line**. There seems

lines and make subtle distinctions, a system that precludes liability in a wide range of circumstances is easier to administer, and simplifies adjudication.

Nevertheless, in any system of law that seeks to redress wrongs, mechanisms for change and development from within — and hence, the need to draw lines — are unavoidable, when the judges or society at large recognize that a wrong requiring redress has been effected. It is in this context that the statement of the Court of Appeals in *Battalla*, quoted above, becomes applicable to Jewish law, insofar as adherence to precedent is concerned, for no better reason than that it does constitute a precedent. It is true that, having embarked on a course of creating remedies for wrongs, the courts are required to apply jurisprudential and policy concerns in drawing lines. Common law courts have faced this challenge, and courts administering Jewish law must do so as well.

This area of law affords insight into the growth and development of law generally, which could well serve as a model for Jewish law, in this, as in other areas, since despite twists and turns, the common law is still in the throes of expansion, raising the question of where this expansion of legal redress is to end. While this is a legitimate concern, I nonetheless submit that those upholding the validity and sanctity of Jewish law should follow the path of courageous judges of common law courts, who have not hesitated to overrule their own decisions, even only a few years later, when convinced of the error of the earlier decisions.[84]

I have elsewhere written of the need to overrule decisions, even of Torah giants, when this is mandated by contemporary social conditions and the needs of substantive justice, particularly where respected minority views can be marshaled in support of the innovation or

---

to be no absolute necessity for limiting recovery to near relatives of the person attacked, since an innocent bystander who is frightened out of her wits by a murder committed before her eyes may suffer an equally serious and genuine shock." (emphasis added)

84 See, e.g., the decision by the Appellate Division of the Fourth Department in *Hartford Insurance Co. v. Halt*, 646 N.Y.S.2d 589 (1996), in which the majority overruled its own decision to the contrary, rendered in 1989, partly on the basis of legal analysis, partly on the basis of authorities to the contrary from most jurisdictions in the United States. See Mr. Justice Callahan's strenuous dissent, applying the principle that however wrong it may seem to the present observer, a precedent, if based on a reasoned and painstaking analysis, is entitled to initial respect. Quaere?

change.[85] It ill behooves us to neglect the ethical considerations underlying the need for the growth and development of Jewish law, when such considerations are an integral part of the decision-making process of common law judges, professors and lawyers.

### *Appendix: The Common Law to the End of the Twentieth Century*

The common law, unlike Roman Law, and like Jewish law, manifested great reluctance to "accept the interest of peace of mind as entitled to dependent legal protection, even as against intentional invasions."[86] Roman law had no such compunction, as one scholar pointed out:

> It may therefore be noted as a curious fact that damages for mental suffering which our courts find so difficult, and frequently impossible, to estimate, were the rule in the tort of *iniuriae* at Roman law. The attitude of not a few American courts, which have deliberately denied redress in these cases because of the assumed difficulty in determining the money value of mental distress, would have been incomprehensible to the Roman magistrate.[87]

At an early date, the common law had already permitted the recovery of damages for emotional distress, where such was incident to another recognized claim. Thus, in the early case of *I. de S. et ux. v. W. de S.*,[88] it was held that the plaintiff, the proprietress of a tavern, could recover damages for fright, where an irate would-be customer threw a hatchet at her, missing, but frightening her. In so holding, the court determined that an assault had been committed, and recovery of damages was permitted.[89]

85 See works cited in n. 2 above.
86 Prosser and Keeton, n. 5 above, sec. 12.
87 M. Radin, "Fundamental concepts of the Roman law," 12 *Cal. L. Rev.* 481, 486–487 (1923–1924). See also Lyman P. Wilson, "The New York rule as to nervous shock," 11 *Cornell Law Quarterly* 512 (1926).
88 Y.B. Lib. Assis. f. 99, pl.60 (1348).
89 See Fowler V. Harper and Mary Coate McNeely, "A re-examination of the basis for liability for emotional distress," *Wisconsin L.R.*, 426–427 (1938):

> If the actor intentionally created the threat of fear or apprehension, or if he actually sought to inflict direct physical injury upon the other, the common law has for centuries allowed a recovery for the emotional disturbance under the formula of assault.

This decision was followed by other decisions permitting recovery for mental distress, where it resulted as an incident of wrongful acts, intentionally committed.[90] These damages came to be known as "parasitic

---

See *Piadd*, n. 1 above, Fright-5, where the author states:

> Ever since the famous 1348 case of *I. de S. et ux. v. W. de S.*, in which a tavern keeper's wife successfully eluded the hatchet of an irate customer, courts have struggled to recognize mental tranquility (or, as more frequently stated, the right to freedom from emotional distress) as an interest worthy of legal protection.

The case is found in the old English reports in the original French of that period.

A rough translation, supplied by Prof. Joseph Songolowsky, follows:

> In a claim for *trespass vi et armis*, it was argued that the defendant was not guilty. As a result of investigation, it appeared that the defendant came to the tavern of the plaintiff to purchase something. However, the door of the tavern was closed, and he struck the door with the hatchet in his hand. Thereupon the woman put her head out the window and the defendant struck a blow with the hatchet, but did not touch her. The defendant argued that he was not liable because he did not harm her. Held, that he is liable in damages for the assault.

90 See *Tomes v. Painter*, 12 East, 675 (King's Bench, 1810–1811). In this case, the defendant, sitting in the same room as the plaintiff, jumped up from his seat with his fist clenched as if to strike the plaintiff, but was pulled back to his seat by another before he was within reach of the plaintiff. Recovery of damages was permitted on the grounds that "clenching his fist at the plaintiff was an assault and an act of personal offence." See too *Morton v. Shopee*, 3 Car. & P. 373, 172 English Reports 462 (Nisi Prius, 1828). For an early American case, see *Lewis v. Hoover*, Supreme Court of Indiana, 1834, 407–408:

> This [an assault] is called an unlawful setting upon one's person, and is an inchoate violence for which the party assaulted may have redress by an action of *trespass vi et armis*, and shall recover damages as a compensation, although no actual suffering or injury is proved. The damages are assessed not for mere corporal injury or pecuniary loss, but for the malicious and insulting conduct of the defendant.

See also *Warmelink v. Tissue*, 257 Mich. 228, 214 N.W. 203 (1932); *Preiser v. Wielandt*, 48 App. Div. 569, 62 N.Y.S. 890 (2nd Dept., 1900).

damages" attached to a recognized tort,[91] and hence, recovery was sometimes,[92] but not always,[93] permitted.

In time, the intentional infliction of emotional distress took on the character of a separate cause of action, and recovery was permitted in a great variety of situations.[94]

It was not until the middle of the nineteenth century that a common law judge, Lord Wensleydale, dealt with this issue in the context of an action for defamation, and stated by way of dictum:

> Mental pain or anxiety the law cannot value, and does not pretend to redress, when the unlawful act complained of causes that alone; though where a material damage occurs and is connected with it, it is impossible a jury, in estimating it, should altogether overlook the feelings of the party interested.[95]

91 Prosser and Keeton, n. 5 above, 57.

92 Ibid. See *Wilkinson v. Downton*, 2 Q.B. 57 (1897), where recovery was allowed for violent nervous shock sustained when the defendant, by way of a practical joke, falsely advised plaintiff that her husband had met with a serious accident whereby both his legs were broken; *Preiser v. Weilandt*, n. 90 above, in which an ill tenant, forcibly evicted from her premises, suffered miscarriage as the result thereof and died. For further discussion of *Wilkinson*, see n. 115 below.

93 See, e.g., *Huxley v. Berg and others*, 1 Stark 97, 71 English Reports 413 (King's Bench, 1815). In an action of trespass for breaking and entering, consequential injury to the wife, resulting from terror, was admissible **only** for the purpose of showing how outrageous and violent the breaking was, but not as a substantive ground of damage. The wife had apparently taken ill as a result of her fright, and died soon after. See too *Nelson v. Crawford*, 81 N.W. 335 (Sup. Ct., Mich. 1899).

94 For excellent discussion of the development of this area of law see Prosser and Keeton, n. 5 above, *Piadd*, n. 1 above, sec. 2. See David Crump, "Evaluating independent torts based upon 'intentional' or 'negligent' infliction of emotional distress: how can we keep the baby from dissolving in the bath water?" 34 *Ariz L. Rev.* 441 (1992), for a discussion of the growth of the rule permitting recovery of damages for emotional harm from being incidental to a tort such as trespass, to an independent tort, and the policy considerations underlying this development. See too Prosser, n. 5 above. For further discussion of the old English case, see *St. Elizabeth Hospital v. Garrard*, 730 S.W. 649 (Sup. Ct., Texas, 1987). In its modern form, this tort consists of four elements under the formulation of the Restatement (Second) of Torts (1965), sec. 46. These are: the defendant engages in extreme and outrageous conduct (1), which is committed intentionally or recklessly (2), which causes (3) severe emotional distress (4). For discussion of the Restatement view, see Crump, 448–451. For recent application of these rules by the courts of New York, see *Howell v. New York Post Company*, 81 N.Y.2d 115, 596 N.Y.S.2d 350, 612 N.E.2d 699 (1993); *Vasilopoulos v. Romano*, 645 N.Y.S.2d 501 (2nd Dep't., 1996); *Rocco v. Town of Smithtown*, 645 N.Y.S. 2d 187 (4th Dep't., 1996).

95 *Lynch v. Knight*, IX H.L.C., 576, 598, 11 English Reports 854, 863 (1861).

The view was expressed early on that with respect to an action for fright and shock, "merely mental pain unaccompanied by any injury to the person, cannot sustain an action of this kind."[96] In these circumstances, there was no liability, not because the damages were too remote, but rather, because of the inability to prove them.[97]

The next development in the common law was that even where physical consequences, such as deafness, blindness or miscarriage, ensued from the fright suffered, there could be no recovery unless the injury sustained was from without, as distinguished from within, the body of the injured person. In other words, there was required to be an outward, physical manifestation of an injury of some sort before recovery would be permitted for the physical consequences of fright and shock. This approach appeared most arbitrary to other courts, and was resoundingly rejected by many, though not all.

In the case of *Victorian Railways Commissioners v. Coultas*,[98] the defendant railway was sued for the negligence of its employee in permitting the plaintiffs' horse and buggy to go through the toll gate when a train was approaching, with the result that the buggy narrowly missed being struck by the train. A suit was instituted for injuries resulting from the fright of being placed in imminent peril of death. The plaintiffs claimed that the wife-plaintiff had, by reason of the fright, sustained severe nervous shock, with physical injuries resulting, including delicate health, impaired memory and impaired eyesight. However, these injuries benefitted her not at all, in the absence of physical impact of some sort between the train and the buggy, or externally-sustained physical injuries.

The Privy Council dismissed the case on two grounds. The first was that "damages arising from mere sudden terror, unaccompanied by any actual physical injury, but occasioning a nervous or mental shock, cannot under such circumstances, their Lordships think, be considered a consequence, which, in the ordinary course of things, would flow from the negligence of the gatekeeper."[99] In so holding, the court

96 *Dulieu v. White and Sons*, 2 K.B. 669, 673 (1901), citing Beven, *Negligence Law*, 2nd ed., 77. See *Huxley v. Berg*, n. 93 above; *A.T. & S.F., Railroad Co. v. McGinnis*, 46 Kan. 109 (1891).

97 *Dulieu*, ibid. The court quotes Frederick Pollock, *The Law of Torts*, 6th ed., 51: "Fear ... taken alone, falls far short of being actual damage, not because it is a remote or unlikely consequence, but because it can be proved and measured only by physical effects."

98 P.C. 1888, 13 App. Cas. 222.

99 Ibid., 225.

disregarded the physical consequences of the emotional distress where no external and contemporary physical impact or injury occurred. The court relied on the older English case of *The Notting Hill*,[100] and applied the rule that "the damages must be the natural and reasonable result of the defendants' act; such a consequence as in the ordinary course of things would flow from the act."[101]

The attitude of the common law was identical to that expressed by the halakhic authorities, discussed above,[102] who predicated the absence of liability on the lack of proximate cause between the act and the claimed injuries; the injuries being viewed as too remote for the imposition of liability.

However, the court in the *Victorian Railways* case also appealed to the interest of public policy to avert liability, and concluded that to permit liability in the presented circumstances would open a Pandora's box[103] of fraudulent litigation, and would result in "a wide field opened for imaginary claims."[104] The ramifications of this case, decided in the closing decade of the nineteenth century, are still being felt in common law jurisdictions. The case introduced into the common law principles remarkably parallel to those long embedded in Jewish law.

This approach was rejected in *Dulieu v. White*[105] by the King's Bench, which was not bound by the decision of the Privy Council in the *Victorian Railways* case.[106] The case involved an action for injuries that resulted when defendant's horse and wagon were negligently driven into the bar tended by plaintiff in her husband's public house, frightening her and causing shock and other physical injuries, including miscarriage. The court, while following the rule that physical injury was required as a predicate for recovery for fright and shock,[107] held that injury need not be the result of contemporaneous impact, but it was sufficient

100 9 P.D.105 (1884).

101 N. 98 above, 225.

102 See section 3a above.

103 For an eloquent refutation of this argument, see n. 141 below.

104 N. 98 above, 226.

105 N. 96 above.

106 N. 98 above. On difficulties that persisted for courts in other parts of the British Commonwealth, still bound by the *Victorian Railways* decision, see William M. Prosser, *The Law of Torts*, 4th ed. (1971) sec. 54, 330, n. 63; Report of the New York State Law Revision Commission, Study Relating to Liability for Injuries Resulting from Fright or Shock, 1936, Legislative Doc. No. 65(E), 14–17.

107 See n. 97 above.

if the physical injuries were the consequence of the fright and shock.[108] The court added a condition with implications for liability with respect to innocent bystanders who witness an accident involving others, and sustain injuries resulting from fright and shock.[109] It stated: "the shock, where it operates through the mind, must be a shock which arises from a reasonable fear of immediate personal injury to oneself," adding, "A has, I conceive, no legal duty not to shock B's nerves by the exhibition of negligence towards C, or towards the property of B or C."[110]

The court also relied on the old English case of *Jones v. Boyle*,[111] which was decided by the same court that decided the *Huxley* case, discussed above.[112] In the *Jones* case, the issue presented was whether the plaintiff was reasonably apprehensive for his own safety when he jumped from a coach to avert what could be perceived as imminent injury, and broke his leg, though the coach did not actually overturn. The court ruled that if the jury found that he acted reasonably, they could find for the plaintiff. In this case, of course, the outward physical injury was apparent, although there was no actual impact of the instrument that occasioned the harm — the coach — on the plaintiff. Nevertheless, liability followed.

As we have seen, at least with respect to intentional torts, Jewish law was, in the past, far in advance of the common law. Yet the common law, under the pressure of judges who would not accept precedent as binding solely because it was precedent,[113] has forged dramatically ahead of Jewish law. It is therefore illuminating to examine the parallels between these two systems.

In America, the weight of authority was, until recently, in accord with the *Victorian Railways* case.[114] In an early decision by a New York

108 N. 96 above. The court states: "If impact be not necessary, and if, as must be assumed here, the fear is proved to have naturally and directly produced physical effects, so that the ill results of the negligence which caused the fear are as measurable in damages as the same results would be if they arose from an actual impact, why should not an action for those damages lie just as well as it lies where there has been an actual impact?" (p. 675).

109 See text at nn. 144–146 below.

110 N. 96 above, 675.

111 1 Stark. 492 (1816), 71 E.R. 540 (1927). See n. 36 above for further discussion.

112 N. 93 above.

113 See text at nn. 82–83 above.

114 N. 98 above

trial court,[115] it was held that fright and shock generating internal physical injuries only, could form the basis for recovery in tort, in the absence of any physical impact. In that case, plaintiff, waiting to board the defendant's cars, sustained fright, rendering her unconscious, when one of the horse-drawn cars went out of control, and she was almost trampled by the horses. However, no portion of her body sustained any impact whatsoever. As a result, she suffered a miscarriage, and was sick for a long time. The trial court permitted recovery, distinguishing cases denying recovery, "where there is no physical injury as a result of the injury, but where the plaintiff suffered nothing but mental anguish, or 'pain of mind.' "[116]

However, in a decision that was influential throughout the United States,[117] the Court of Appeals of New York,[118] relying on the *Victorian Railways* case,[119] and other early American cases, reversed the Order of the Appellate Division, which had affirmed the trial court Order. The Court of Appeals stated that since the law was well established that there could be no recovery for "mere fright" occasioned by the negligence of another: "It is somewhat difficult to understand how a defendant would be liable for its consequences. Assuming that fright cannot form the basis of an action, it is obvious that no recovery can be had for injuries resulting therefrom."[120]

And then, in language that could well have been borrowed, or quoted from the classic Jewish texts, the court stated: "That the result

115 *Mitchell*, n. 81 above. Interestingly, the court in *Wilkinson v. Downton*, n. 92 above, relied on the decision of the New York Supreme Court in this case, which was reversed on appeal. See n. 117 below.

116 Ibid., 577.

117 See *St. Elizabeth Hosp. v. Garrard*, n. 94 above, 651, n. 2:

> Thirteen years later, the *Coultas* decision was expressly overruled in the case of *Dulieu v. White*. The *Dulieu* decision approved a cause of action for serious illness and the premature birth of plaintiff's baby resulting from distress caused by the defendant's negligence.
>
> Unfortunately, prior to its having been overruled, the *Coultas* decision was followed in *Mitchell v. Rochester Ry. Co.*, 151 N.Y. 107, 45 N.E. 354 (1896). Eventually a majority of American jurisdictions adopted the Mitchell rationale, and a number of artificial barriers were erected preventing litigants from maintaining suits to recover for mental distress, absent special circumstances.

118 *Mitchell v. Rochester Ry. Co.*, 151 N.Y. 107, 45 N.E. 354 (1896).

119 N. 98 above.

120 N. 118 above, 151 N.Y 109, 45 N.E. 354.

may be nervous disease, blindness, insanity, or even a miscarriage, in no way changes the principle. These results merely show the degree of fright or the extent of the damages."[121] The court concluded that since there could be no recovery for mere fright, there could be no recovery for injuries that are direct consequences of it.[122]

In modern times, under the influence of textbook writers and law review articles,[123] the courts have labored assiduously to overcome the effect of these older decisions, culminating in a movement to overrule them completely, thereby opening up the Pandora's box even further.

According to Prosser and Keeton, the first such effort was to determine that the common law rules denying recovery did not apply where there was physical injury involving even the slightest physical impact, however minimal.[124] They point out[125] that the courts used the following arguments in asserting non-liability for fright and shock absent physical injury or impact:

a. Mental disturbance cannot be measured in terms of money, and so cannot serve, in itself, as a basis for the action.[126]
b. Its physical consequences are too remote, and so not "proximately caused."[127]
c. There is a lack of precedent.[128]
d. A vast increase in litigation would ensue.[129]

121 N. 118 above.

122 See *Spade v. Lynn & Boston R. Co.*, 168 Mass. 285, 290, 60 Am. St. Rep. 393 (1897):

> We remain satisfied with the rule that there can be no recovery for fright, terror, alarm, anxiety, or distress of mind, if these are unaccompanied by some physical injury; and if this rule is to stand, we think it should also be held that there can be no recovery for such physical injuries as may be caused solely by such mental disturbance, where there is no injury to the person from without.

123 For articles on the progress of the law during the first half of the twentieth century, see Prosser and Keeton, n. 5 above, 55 n. 1, and for more recent articles, 360 n. 10.

124 Prosser and Keeton, n. 5 above, 363.

125 Ibid., 360.

126 Citing *Lynch v. Knight*, n. 95 above, and *Mitchell v. Rochester Railway Co.*, n. 118 above.

127 Citing *Victorian Railways*, n. 98 above; *Mitchell*; and *Catwalk v. Philadelphia Rapid Transit Co.*, 224 Pa. 13, 73 A. 4 (1909).

128 Citing *Lehman v. Brooklyn City R. Co.*, 47 Hun. 355 (2nd Dep't., 1888) and *Victorian Railways*.

129 Citing *Mitchell* and *Spade v. Lynn & Boston R. Co.*, n. 122 above.

Although they dismiss these arguments for non-liability, they acknowledge that there are troubling aspects to permitting recovery in this area, including: "(1) the problem of permitting legal redress for harm that is often temporary and relatively trivial;[130] (2) the danger that claims of mental harm will be falsified or imagined; and (3) the perceived unfairness of imposing heavy and disproportionate financial burdens upon a defendant, whose conduct was only negligent, for consequences that appear remote from the 'wrongful act.' "[131, 132] They also point out that the consequences for fright and shock are seldom very serious, unless there was some predisposing physical condition,[133] which leads directly to the issue, discussed in section 2 above, of Jewish law's requirement that injuries be assessed for purposes of tort liability.

Courts in America have thus **sometimes** striven to avoid the implications of the common law rule, which has been expressly overruled in some, but not all states; New York was one of the first states to do so. In *Battalla v. State*,[134] the Court of Appeals, the very court that was so instrumental in hamstringing the law in this area in the first place,[135] abolished the rule denying recovery. In so doing it rejected two bases

130 See the seminal article by Francis Bohlen, "Right to recover for injury resulting from negligence without impact," 50 *Amer. Law Reg.* 141, 142 (1902):

> Probably many reasons underlay this conception [of no liability]. In the first place, mental suffering was comparatively trivial in the great majority of cases, sometimes, perhaps, it was considerable, but the effort of the Common Law has been to lay down rules of general application, and not to provide for every exceptional contingency.

131 Citing *Patton v. Abbot Labs*, 386 Mass. 540, 437 N.E.2d 171, 178–181 (1982); Restatement (Second) of Torts, n. 94 above, sec. 436A, Comment b.

132 Prosser and Keeton, n. 5 above, 360.

133 Ibid., n. 13, citing I. Harvard, "Reasonable foresight of nervous shock," 19 *Mod. L. Rev.* 478 (1956). See also ibid., 363. Prosser and Keeton state that in cases of mental disturbance with physical injury, "with a cause of action established by the physical harm, 'parasitic' damages are awarded, and it is considered that there is sufficient assurance that the mental injury is not feigned."

See ibid., n. 37, as to the applicability of the thin-skulled plaintiff rule and its application to parasitic psychological injuries, citing T.A. Street, 1 *Foundations of Legal Liability* 470 (1906); *Martinez v. Teague*, 96 N.M.446, 631 P.2d 1314 (1981). Prosser and Keeton add: "The thin-skulled plaintiff rule applies to parasitic psychological injuries, so that a plaintiff with a particular susceptibility to psychological disorders may recover for her idiosyncratic emotional harm resulting from her physical injuries and the accident."

134 N. 80 above.

135 N. 118 above.

oft-invoked for the rule denying recovery: (a) the difficulty of proof as to the nature of the injuries, and (b) the potential for flooding the courts with spurious claims. In *Battalla*, a young girl was placed in a chair-lift by an employee of the defendant-state; the employee failed to secure and lock the belt intended to protect the occupant. As a result of that negligence, the girl became frightened and hysterical upon descent, with consequential injuries. The Appellate Division[136] had denied recovery under the constraint of the *Mitchell* case.[137] The Court of Appeals overruled *Mitchell*. The effect of the *Battalla* decision was immediate. As pointed out by Prosser,[138] other courts soon followed suit, abolishing the impact requirement.[139]

Well past the mid-point of the twentieth century, the contrary approach was taken by the Supreme Court of Pennsylvania in the disturbing case of *Bosley v. Andrews*.[140] Mrs. Bosley had a farm. Cows from across the road kept crossing over and eating her fruit. On one occasion, learning that the cows were coming, she went out to chase them away. However, that day, not only the cows, but a bull too, came across. The bull gave chase to Mrs. Bosley, but never reached her, as her dog started to chase the bull and the bull went after the dog. Mrs. Bosley ran away from the bull, took five steps, and fell down from a heart attack. The Supreme Court of Pennsylvania denied recovery because of the long-established rule in Pennsylvania that there can be no recovery of damages for injuries resulting from fright, or nervous shock, or mental, or emotional disturbance, or distress, unless they are

136 11 A.D.2d 613, 200 N.Y.S.2d 852 (3d Dep't., 1960).

137 N. 118 above.

138 N. 106 above, 332, nn. 83–84.

139 See *St. Elizabeth Hosp. v. Garrard*, n. 94 above, where the court reviews the law of Texas and holds that proof of physical injury is no longer necessary to recover for negligent infliction of mental anguish. It appears that the plaintiff and her husband sustained mental anguish after their stillborn daughter's body had been disposed of in an unmarked common grave, without their knowledge or consent. The court noted that the old Texas case of *Hill v. Kimball* had enunciated in 1890 the right of recovery for negligently-inflicted mental anguish. In that case, the plaintiff had suffered a miscarriage after witnessing an incident involving profanity and bloodshed. However, that court deemed improper a recovery where the plaintiff's suffering did not manifest itself physically. The latter requirement was eliminated by the court in its 1987 decision. It noted that the courts of eight jurisdictions, including Texas, had adopted the tort of negligent infliction of mental anguish in a more or less pure form, 730 S.W.2d 654, n. 6.

140 393 Pa. 161, 142 A.2d 263 (1958).

accompanied by physical injury, or physical impact.[141] As matters now stand, there are quite a number of jurisdictions in the United States which still adhere to some form of the rule requiring physical injury or impact of some sort as a condition of recovery for emotional distress.

Thus, the common law had, by the last two decades of the twentieth century, arrived at a point where in some jurisdictions there were still limitations on the right to recover for emotional distress, but in other jurisdictions there were no such limitations, insofar as the person directly frightened or shocked by the negligence of another is concerned. This reflects well on the ability of the common law to accommodate itself to modern notions of the needs of an ordered society.

And yet, the saga of the common law continues, reflecting that a legal system should — and can — never remain in a condition of stasis. Recently, the following issue has come up: is there a right to recovery where the person suffering emotional distress was merely an innocent bystander to another's negligently-inflicted physical injuries?[142]

Where the emotional distress and its consequences are not caused by any fear for the plaintiff's own safety, but, rather, by distress at witnessing some peril or harm to another person, a growing number of common law jurisdictions permit recovery in a variety of circumstances.[143] Thus, some courts have adopted an approach whereby bystanders may recover for mental distress, provided they were within the "zone of danger."[144] Other courts have adopted the approach that recovery is permitted, regardless of whether the plaintiff was in the

141 See the powerful dissenting opinion of Judge Musmanno, ibid., a jewel of judicial writing. He states that if the animal's charging horns had advanced closer and had just grazed Mrs. Bosley, without seriously harming her, she would be entitled to recover. So just because the animal merely nearly scared her to death, but did not touch her with his horns, recovery should not be denied. He also eloquently disposes of the Pandora's box argument (see text at n. 103 above) relied upon by the majority in denying recovery.

142 For early discussion of this issue, see Report of The New York State Law Revision Commission, n.106 above, 78; Prosser, n. 5 above, 889. On the need for, and difficulties in finding, limits is this area of law, see Crump, n. 94 above, 493ff.

143 See generally, Prosser and Keeton, n. 5 above 365–366; Annotation, "Right to recover damages in negligence for fear of injury to another, or shock or mental anguish at witnessing such injury," 29 ALR3d 1337 (1970); *Piadd*, n. 1 above, sec. 3.05.

144 In *Bovsun v. Sanperi*, 61 N.Y.2d 219, 473 N.Y.S.2d 357, 461 N.E.2d 843 (1984), it was held that where a defendant negligently exposes a plaintiff

"zone of danger," provided the person physically injured was a blood relative of the plaintiff.[145]

The comments of Judge Kaye in *Bovsun v. Sanperi*[146] are instructive. In dissenting from the majority decision permitting recovery in the case of an innocent bystander, she stated:

> Recovery for emotional distress from observing physical injury to another is a departure from precedent and recognition of a new duty. Because sound policy considerations supported this court's decisions consistently denying such recovery, because no reason is given for a change and because the limitations now imposed are artificial and arbitrary and must in fairness give way to far-reaching liability affecting the public generally, I respectfully dissent.

Without addressing the issue of whether Judge Kaye was correct in this particular instance, it must be noted that like assertions regarding the binding nature of past precedents and the weight of authority have been made in the past, and are still made, to block change in Jewish law as well. These issues are beyond the scope of this article, and best dealt with elsewhere.[147]

---

to an unreasonable risk of injury or death, there can be recovery for emotional distress sustained as a consequence of observing serious injury or death of a member of the plaintiff's immediate family. Of course, as always, it must be shown that the defendant's conduct was a substantial factor in bringing about such injury or death. This rule was later limited by the same court; see *Trombetta v. Conkling*, 82 N.Y.2d 549, 605 N.Y.S.2d 678, 626 N.E.2d 653 (1993), where recovery of damages for the emotional distress of an aunt who witnessed an accident in which her niece, with whom she had strong emotional bond, died, was denied.

145 See e.g. *Dillon v. Legg*, 68 Cal.2d 728, 69 Cal. Rptr. 72, 441 P.2d 912 (1968), permitting recovery for the emotional trauma caused by the defendant when the plaintiff witnessed the injury or death of a close relative, even though the plaintiff was not herself within the "zone of danger," provided that the emotional injury was reasonably foreseeable.

146 N. 144 above, 61 N.Y.2d 234, 473 N.Y.S.2d 364, 461 N.E.2d 850.

147 This article had its genesis in a lecture delivered at the Wall Street Synagogue on March 24, 1993, for which the assistance of R. Hager is gratefully acknowledged. Let me also note the contribution of members of the weekly Talmud class — especially that of Steve Prystowsky and Manny Bloom — at the firm of Lester Schwab Katz and Dwyer, whose hospitality is gratefully acknowledged. Thanks is also due Ms. Nancy Josephs, Head Librarian of the New York Law Institute, and her staff, particularly Ken Giese and Ralph Caiazzo, for research assistance. I am grateful to my mentor, R. David Weiss Halivni, for his friendship, counsel and gentle criticism. Thanks for helpful comments is also due Samuel Morell, Yakov Elman, and my wife, Rivka Haut.

*The Jewish Law Annual*, Vol. XIV

# AGENCY AND DIVORCE PROCEEDINGS: ON THE LEGAL METHODOLOGY OF MAIMONIDES' *MISHNE TORAH*

DAVID HENSHKE*

## 1 *The Nature of Divorce Proceedings according to Maimonides*

In a brief verse, the Bible describes the divorce process: "... and he writes her a bill of divorcement, and hands it to her [lit. gives it into her hand] and sends her away from his house" (Deut. 24:1).[1] Clearly, the handing over of the writ of divorce to the wife is the direct cause for the divorce. Nonetheless, there arises a substantial doubt as to the nature of this 'handing it' to her. This fundamental question can be formulated as follows: does the actual ceremony of the husband's handing the bill of divorce to the wife cause the legal effect of divorce? Or is it perhaps the case that there is no ceremony of giving per se, but the legal outcome of divorce is effected by the fact that the writ of divorce is actually found in the wife's hand? Should one relate this question to the biblical verse above, the interpretive question would be: does the phrase "hands it to her" represent the ceremony of the divorce process, or only the means of achieving the state of there being a writ of divorce in her hand, this state being that which effects the divorce? On the first view, the verse has two parts: "And he writes her a bill of divorcement" describes the means, while the phrase "hands it to her" connotes the act of divorce itself. On the latter view, the entire verse describes the means, and as a result of the bill of divorce's reaching the wife's hand, she is legally divorced, and he "sends her away from his house."

* David Henshke teaches in the Department of Talmud at Bar-Ilan University.

1 The verse's brevity stems from the fact that its intent is not to describe the divorce process in and of itself, but to prohibit one from remarrying his former wife should she have married someone else in the interim. The issue of why the institution of divorce is mentioned only parenthetically is not within the scope of this article.

This issue brings to the fore the issue of the husband's status and the wife's function in the divorce process. If the actual ceremonial handing over of the writ of divorce by the husband effects the divorce, then his role is primary. However, if it is the fact of the bill of divorce's being in the wife's hand that effects the divorce, then the husband's act of handing it to her is only a secondary condition. Although the writ of divorce must find its way into the wife's hand as a result of the husband's actions, and not those of a stranger, or of the wife, nevertheless, the husband's actions are only to further the goal of the bill of divorce's being in the wife's hand, which is what really effectuates the divorce. Likewise, the significance of the wife's receipt of the writ of divorce similarly varies. If "hands it to her" denotes a ceremonial giving on the part of the husband, then "to her [hand]" answers the question: to whom must the husband give the writ? A ceremonial giving is only meaningful when it takes place between a giver and a receiver. Without a receiver, the act of giving loses its ceremonial value. The act of giving as a ceremonial act of divorce relates to the individuals involved, and the divorce process is understood as an act of giving by the husband to the wife. The phrase "her hand" denotes the wife. However, if the giving is only a general means, and the divorce takes effect only when the writ of divorce had found its way into her hand, then "in her hand" answers the question: where must the bill of divorcement be found? The writ of divorce must be found in the wife's domain, and "in her hand" represents not her person, but her domain.

Whereas most rabbinical authorities accept the first view — in this article represented by R. Jacob Turim[2] — Maimonides apparently upheld the second. In demonstrating Maimonides' absolute commitment to this view, this article will elucidate his position on employing an agent in the divorce process, a position that has been sharply criticized since its appearance at the end of the twelfth century. The article will first elaborate on the two views set out above, and then proceed to explicate the issue of the agent in the divorce process.

2 On this issue, R. Jacob b. R. Asher (Rosh), author of the *Turim*, follows his predecessors and their accepted opinions. His position will not be discussed in and of itself, but only as a counter-view to Maimonides' position. Hence, there is no need to trace his sources and how they developed.

Maimonides opens chapter 2 of the *Code*'s Laws concerning Divorce as follows:

> The verse in the Torah "and he writes her a bill of divorcement, and hands it to her" [lit., gives it into her hand] includes both one who writes it in his own handwriting and one who tells another to write for him. It also includes one who himself hands it to her and one who tells another to hand it to her. The reason for the statement "and he writes" is to teach that she may be divorced only with a writ. [The reason for] "And he hands" [is to teach] that she should not take it herself.[3]

This formulation clearly states that both "he writes" and "he hands" are not acts that must be carried out only by the husband. There is no positive value in his writing the writ of divorce or his handing it to her. Certainly he must hand it to her — but that is only so that she will not take it herself. Maimonides formulated the laws of divorce proceedings at the beginning of chapter 1 of his Laws concerning Divorce accordingly. His formulation contrasts sharply with that of the *Turim* (EH 120):

| Maimonides | *Turim* |
|---|---|
| A woman may only be divorced by a writ **that reaches her**. | A woman may only be divorced by a writ, as it is written, "and he writes her a bill of divorcement, and hands it ..."; ... he should write ... that he is he is releasing her ... **and place it in her hand**. |

Maimonides emphasized that the sole requirement for divorce is that the writ of divorce reach the wife, while the issue of how it gets to her is secondary. The law that the husband or his agent must give her the writ of divorce only appears in the Laws concerning Divorce later on, as the tenth and last essential element of the "ten elements mandated by the Bible as essential for divorce." However, the author of the *Turim* had a different opinion. Although he opened his Laws concerning Divorce by copying Maimonides' formulation, when he came to the words "that reaches her," he deleted them. Moreover, in lieu of this deleted phrase, the *Turim* listed the handing over of the writ of divorce as central to the divorce proceedings.

3 This homily appears in *Midrash Tannaim*, ed. R. D.Z. Hoffman, 154, but its source is the *Midrash Hagadol Ledvarim* (Jerusalem: 1973), 540, which had in turn copied it from Maimonides' works. A source for this homily from the period of the Sages has yet to be discovered.

This conflict concerning the part played by the husband's handing over of the writ of divorce is reflected elsewhere in their respective formulations (*Code*, Laws concerning Divorce 1:12; *Turim*, EH 138):

| Maimonides | *Turim* |
|---|---|
| If a writ of divorce was lying on the ground, and he said to her, 'Pick up your writ of divorce from the ground' and she picked it up … it is not a [valid] divorce, as it is written "and hands it to her," implying **that she should not take it herself**, and here neither he nor his agent handed it to her. | "And hands it to her" — the handing over by the husband … must be actually from his hand or the hand of his agent.… How so? [If] he said to her, 'Pick up your writ of divorce from the ground,' it is meaningless … since he did not help her to take it. |

According to Maimonides, the essential implication of "hands it to her," is that the wife must not take it herself. What invalidates the divorce when she picks up the writ is not that the husband has not handed it to her, but rather, the fact that the wife has taken it by herself, as emphasized at the beginning of chapter 2, quoted above. This follows from Maimonides' position that the husband's giving of the writ of divorce is only a means, and there is no requirement in and of itself for him to hand it to her. If the husband had even partially handed it to her, as is clear from the continuation of Maimonides' formulation ("if he bent his body or arm toward her until she wrested the bill of divorce from him"), then her taking it is no longer her act alone, and the divorce is valid. In contrast, according to the *Turim*, in a case where he says 'pick up your writ,' the act is meaningless, as the essential ceremony of the divorce proceeding — the husband's handing it over to her — is missing.

Indeed, R. Vidal of Tolosa, author of the *Magid Mishne*, had already noted the singularity of Maimonides' position concerning divorce proceedings. Nonetheless, commentators who were faithful to the generally accepted view had difficulty with R. Vidal's explanation. In Laws concerning Divorce 9:2, Maimonides determined the law of a husband who says to his wife: 'This is your bill of divorce, but you will not be divorced until thirty days have passed' — after the thirty days, the divorce is valid. However, in Laws concerning Sales 2:9, Maimonides had stated, regarding one who says to his colleague, 'Pull [as an act of acquisition] this cow, but it will not become yours until thirty days have passed,' that his colleague does not acquire it even after the thirty days have passed. In the *Magid Mishne*, R. Vidal resolved this apparent contradiction:

> The reason for this [difference] is: The means of acquiring the cow is by pulling it (*meshikha*), and after thirty days that action has ended (*kalta meshikhato*). Hence, if he did not say 'from now,' it is meaningless. However, in the [case of the] writ of divorce, she is divorced by the writ, and the writ still exists on the thirtieth day.

In his *Kesef Mishne* commentary on Maimonides' *Code*, R. Joseph Caro questions this solution:

> With a writ of divorce she is only divorced through the husband's handing it to the wife, and after thirty days that action has also ended, just as in the case of the cow, the action of pulling is no longer going on.

Nevertheless, it is clear that the author of the *Magid Mishne* understood Maimonides' position as it is defined here: the divorce is not valid due to the means of its execution — the act of handing it to her — as an acquisition is validated by the means of its acquisition — pulling an object. The divorce is valid by virtue of the fact that the writ of divorce is found within the woman's domain, and that writ is indeed found in her domain after thirty days.[4]

These contrasting views are especially prominent in another significant disagreement between Maimonides and R. Jacob Turim — one that touches upon the subject of the agent. What is the law concerning a husband who sent an agent to bring the writ of divorce to his wife, and before the agent fulfilled his mission, the husband became mentally ill?[5] In Maimonides' opinion, although the preferred course of action is to wait for the husband to recover, should the agent hand the bill of divorce to the wife, the divorce is biblically mandated to be valid

4 See all the *Aharonim* noted in the index of the Frankel ed. of the *Code*. Having difficulty with the position taken in the *Magid Mishne*, they explained it in different ways.

5 Maimonides translated the talmudic description "he was gripped by a *kardiakas*" (mGitin 7:1) on the basis of I Samuel 16:14. R. A.I. Karelitz, *Hazon Ish* (Bnei Brak: 1959) on the *Code* ad loc. already pointed out that one need not conclude from Maimonides' position on *kardiakas* that the same applies to one who is totally insane.

(Laws concerning Divorce 2:15).[6] In contrast, the *Turim* maintains that from a biblical perspective the divorce is worthless.[7] For the most part, post-medieval authorities (*Aharonim*) explain this disagreement as pertaining to the very nature of an agent: is the agent considered the extended arm of the principal, so that, legally speaking, all the agent's acts are 'transferred' to the principal? Or does, perhaps, the concept of agent signify that the principal has transferred all his power to the agent, so that the latter performs his activities independently of his principal? Those who accept the second view will declare the agent's activities to be valid even if the principal is no longer mentally sound, since from the moment the agent was granted power to represent his principal, he acts independently. Those who accept the first position see the agent as deriving his power from his principal continuously, and subsequently invalidate the acts of the agent from the moment they can no longer be ascribed to his principal, as when the principal is no longer mentally balanced.[8] Notwithstanding that this formulation is logically sound for explaining such a disagreement in the realm of acquisitions, it is difficult to extend it to other areas of Jewish law where the institution of agency is utilized. For example, with respect to observance of many of the commandments, one may use an agent, and the agent's performance of the commandment discharges the principal's obligation to fulfil the commandment himself. In such cases it is difficult to apply the above explanation, for in the realm of observance

6 The author of the *Hazon Ish* (n. 5 above) did not accept this opinion, and suggested emending the text of the *Code* so that Maimonides does not make this statement. This is untenable not only because all textual evidence supports the present text, but this very position was advanced by R. Abraham of Montpellier in his commentary on bKidushin 78b (printed in the Vilna edition of the Talmud erroneously under the name *Tosafot Ri Hazaken*). Hence, there is no point in emending the Maimonidean text, as in any case one would have to explain R. Abraham's position. Moreover, R. Abraham of Montpellier is famous for his dependence on Maimonidean positions; see the introduction of M. Blau to his editions of R. Abraham of Montpellier on tractates Jebamot, Nedarim and Nazir (NY: 1962) and Suka (NY: 1978). Apparently, here too Maimonides was his source, and R. Abraham had the same Maimonidean text we do.

7 *Turim*, 121. The disagreement also extends to the writing of the writ of divorce, and not just its delivery to the wife. However, though related, that issue is distinct from the question discussed here.

8 See the list of sources in N. Rakover, *The Jewish Law of Agency in Legal Proceedings* (Hebrew), (Jerusalem: 1972), 16, n. 17.

of commandments, there are no legal powers to transfer to the agent. Clearly, the obligation to fulfill the commandment cannot be transferred to another person. Hence, the institution of agency, as explained, is not appropriate in this context. In ritual matters one must simply view the agent as representing the principal and carrying out actions on his behalf. Thus, if it is to be applicable, the above explanation for the controversy between Maimonides and the *Turim* would have to distinguish between different types of agency for different areas of Jewish law. This, however, is without sufficient basis in the sources, for the institution of agency is understood in the same way in all areas of Jewish law.[9]

Thus, it would appear logical not to explain this local disagreement in the realm of divorce as part of a general controversy concerning the nature of agency, but to attribute it to disagreement over the status of the husband's handing of the writ of divorce to the agent. On the *Turim*'s view, namely, that the ceremony of handing over the writ of divorce to the wife is the essential act of divorce, and the agent's handing over the writ of divorce to the wife is considered tantamount to the husband's, then in the case where the husband is mentally unfit, the actual handing over becomes meaningless. However, on Maimonides' view, namely, that the actual handing over of the writ of divorce is not the primary factor in the divorce proceedings, but rather, the divorce is effectuated by the writ of divorce finding its way into the wife's hand through the actions of the husband or his agent, the fact that the writ of divorce is in her possession accomplishes the divorce. There is thus no essential difficulty with a divorce where the husband becomes mentally unbalanced, as long as the writ of divorce was written and the agent appointed while the husband was of sound mind. The agent's role is not to make it possible for his handing over of the writ of divorce to be ascribed to his principal. His role is to ensure that the writ of divorce reaches her hand, and his accomplishment of this task must be by virtue of the husband's legal capacity to act, and not that of a stranger. Since the writ of divorce did indeed reach the wife through

9 See Rakover, ibid., 19. For the purposes of this essay, the laws of agents and partners are found in Maimonides's *Code*, Book of Acquisition (for the most part agents are utilized in monetary matters). Nevertheless, in 2:1–2, Maimonides addresses the laws of agents "in the entire Torah." See also S. Albeck, *Principles of Talmudic Private Law* (Hebrew), (Jerusalem: 1994), 203.

a duly appointed agent, it reached her person, from her husband, as prescribed by biblical law.

This explanation allows one to see that Maimonides' definition of the divorce proceedings influenced his understanding of the agent's role in delivering the writ of divorce. A closer analysis of Maimonides' understanding of the institution of agency in divorce proceedings is thus essential.

## 2 *The Nature of the Agent for Purposes of Fetching*

In Jewish law, there are two types of agents in divorce proceedings. One is the agent for purposes of receiving, appointed by the wife; upon his receipt of the bill of divorce from the husband, the divorce takes effect, with the result that the wife is divorced — just as she is when she herself receives it. The other type is an agent appointed by the husband to convey and deliver the writ of divorce, and hand it to the wife. As soon as she receives it, she is divorced — just as she is when the husband himself hands it to her.[10] However, as Nachmanides noted, there was a disagreement among the early medieval authorities (*Rishonim*) as to whether a third type of agent existed — an agent to fetch the writ of divorce:

> R. Hananel and Rashi [lit., the son of Isaac] are of the opinion that a wife cannot appoint an agent to fetch the writ of divorce, only to receive it, as can be inferred from their commentaries on the chapter [of tractate bBaba Metzia], "He who hires professionals."[11] And R. Moses the Spaniard [Maimonides] wrote that a wife could appoint an agent either to receive the writ of divorce or to fetch it. And I have no way to determine the law, although Maimonides' opinion appears logical, and the simple explanation of the talmudic passage proves it accordingly, and I need not go on at length. And in the *Halakhot Gedolot*[12] it is written concerning the wife: "and she also appoints an agent to deliver it."[13]

10 This article deals with the Maimonidean position only. On the development of the laws of agency in divorce in the Rabbinic literature, see, e.g., N. Aminoah, "Origins and earliest development of talmudic divorce by proxy" (Hebrew), *Dinei Israel* 5 (1974), 189ff.

11 This refers to bBaba Metzia 76a. The commentary of R. Hananel ad loc. has not been preserved, and the quotation in the Domb edition of R. Hananel on bBaba Metzia 76a (Jerusalem: 1988) is taken from this passage in Nachmanides. Rashi on bBaba Metzia 76a (s.v. *have li giti*) does indeed state that a woman cannot appoint an agent for the purpose of fetching.

12 *Halakhot Gedolot*, Laws of Divorce (Jerusalem: 1980), 173.

13 *Hidushei Haramban Legitin*, ed. M. Herschler et al. (Jerusalem: 1995), 355.

From Nachmanides' comment, it appears that this controversy cannot be resolved on the basis of the sources, which can be explained in accordance with either position,[14] but logic, reason and sound explication must determine its solution. Moreover, according to Nachmanides, although the Maimonidean position has some basis in the Geonic literature, the Geonim did not delineate the subject in an unequivocal fashion.[15] As is the case regarding many other issues, Maimonides did not arrive at his position *ex nihilo*, but recast ambiguous and partially-expressed views with definitive formulations within a comprehensive and consistent structure. Thus, the agent appointed by the wife to fetch a writ of divorce first appears as a completely developed legal institution only in Maimonides' legal works, and thus warrants further analysis. In his *Commentary on the Mishnah*, Gitin 2:5, Maimonides wrote:

> Know that the agents in divorce proceedings are of three types: The first is he who delivers the writ of divorce and states: 'it was written before me and signed before me,' and this [type of agent] is but a conveying agent (*shaliah holakha*).
>
> The second is someone to whom the husband gives the writ of divorce, and says to him, 'Deliver this writ of divorce to my wife,' or, one whom **the wife sent to fetch the writ of divorce**, and the husband handed the writ of divorce to him and said to him, 'Deliver it to her' — **both are the same**. This writ of divorce must also have its signatures confirmed, then given to her, and with it, she is divorced, after it is confirmed, as we have explained. This agent is also called a conveying agent (*shaliah holakha*).
>
> The third is one whom the wife appointed as an agent to receive the writ of divorce for her, and whose hand becomes like hers, and she is divorced as soon as the writ of divorce reaches her agent's hand, and this [agent] is called a receiving agent (*shaliah kabala*).

14 B. Lifshitz, "Additional remarks to the Geonic version of the sugya *'have li giti,'*" *Tarbiz*, 48 (1979), 358–362, links the development of the different variants of the relevant texts and commentaries on bGitin to this question of whether or not a wife has the power to appoint an agent for the purpose of fetching. This question will be taken up in sec. 3.

15 As to the position of the *Halakhot Gedolot*, one could argue that the agent for the purpose of fetching is appointed afterwards by the husband as a conveying agent, and derives his power from the husband, see n. 17 below. This is explicitly stated by a Gaon in a responsum quoted in the *Itur* (R. Meir Yona ed.), Shlishut Get, 47b, concerning a wife who had appointed an agent to bring the writ: "Delivery proceeds from the power of the husband, and it is as if the husband himself had appointed him." However, it is impossible to suggest this explanation for the Maimonidean position; see below.

This tripartite classification of agents is not primarily concerned with the very nature of the agent in divorce proceedings, but rather with the obligation to certify the writ of divorce before it is handed to the wife, which is the subject of the Mishnah in question: the first agent must say 'it was written before me and signed before me'; the second agent, who receives a already written-up writ of divorce, cannot attest to how it was written, and so his delivery can only be made after the writ of divorce has been certified, that is, after it has been certified that the witnesses were legitimate. The third agent, whose receipt of the writ of divorce effects the divorce, is not required to provide any further certification.[16] As to the nature of the agent's legal status, the first two types are identical ("This agent is also called a conveying agent"). Nevertheless, according to Maimonides, it is clear that there are two types of agents who deliver the writ of divorce (*shaliah holakha*): either an agent appointed by the husband to convey the writ of divorce, or, an agent appointed by the wife to fetch it. It appears that although both types of agent are categorized as "conveying" agents, they are nonetheless distinct. The agent who fetches the writ of divorce does not act on behalf of the husband, or by the power of his appointment, but derives his legal power from the wife. If not, what purpose is there to his appointment by the wife — he would only be the husband's regular conveying agent, and nothing more![17] Although, in his description of the agent for the purpose of fetching, Maimonides states that the husband instructed him, 'Deliver it to her,' it is clear that this is not needed in order to grant the agent any legal power, but rather, to signify that

16 Cf. Rashi, Gitin 2a s.v. *tzarikh*; the commentary of Ran on Alfasi, Vilna ed., ad loc. s.v. *vekatav; Otzar Mefarshei Hatalmud Legitin* (Jerusalem: 1997), near nn. 17–23.

17 Indeed, on some opinions, an agent for the purpose of fetching is only effective because he has also been appointed by the husband as a conveying agent. To explain the distinctive nature of this type of agent, those who uphold this position explain that its advantage is that there is no need for an explicit appointment by the husband, as is generally required in the case of a conveying agent. See Rashbash, *Responsa*, #266; *Taz, SA*, EH 140:2. This explanation cannot be utilized in the case of the Maimonidean position, however, since the formulation in the *Code*, as cited below in sec. 3, leaves no doubt that the husband is not involved at all in the appointment of an agent for the purpose of fetching, and that such an agent's legal powers are derived solely from the wife. See below, especially the quotation from the Laws concerning Divorce, 6:11–12.

the intent is divorce. Had the husband not said, 'Deliver it to her,' it may well have been the case that the husband, not having as yet completely made up his mind to divorce his wife, handed it to the agent for safekeeping. Thus, the certification of the writ of divorce is the connecting theme in the treatment in the *Commentary on the Mishnah*.[18]

The *Code* classifies agents in the context of divorce proceedings on the basis of their essential role (and not on the basis of their role in attesting that the writ was 'written before me and signed before me'); it is thus important to compare the two texts. In the *Code*, Laws concerning Divorce 6:1–5, Maimonides writes:

> The agent appointed by the wife to receive her writ of divorce from her husband is called the receiving agent. As soon as the writ of divorce reaches his hand,[19] she is divorced, just as if it had reached her hand. And he must be appointed in front of two witnesses .... The husband has no authority to appoint a receiving agent for his wife, but he can appoint an agent to deliver the writ of divorce to his wife,[20] and this is called a conveying agent.
>
> Likewise, the wife may send an agent to fetch her writ[21] of divorce to her from her husband, and this is called an agent for the purpose of fetching.

18 S.Y. Freidman, *Talmud Arukh, BT Bava Mezi'a VI; Critical Edition with Comprehensive Commentary* (Jerusalem: 1991), 50, did not note this connection. While he maintains that on the Maimonidean position, an agent for the purpose of fetching is appointed through the power of the husband, he does not explain what is distinct about this; see the previous note. It certainly does not explain the position Maimonides takes in the *Code*, where the agent for the purpose of fetching has no connection at all to the husband.

19 According to the Frankel (1977), Kafih (1988), and Rabinovitch (1997) editions of the *Code*, based on mss. Standard editions read: "the hand of her agent."

20 Thus in standard editions and the Frankel ed., based on some mss. In first printings and Yemenite mss (and thence to the Kafih ed.) the text reads: "But he hands the writ of divorce to an agent to deliver the writ of divorce to his wife." An almost identical version, based on a Yemenite ms (Oxford 594), appears in the Rabinovitch ed., as well as in other mss listed in the Frankel ed. On this version, which appears to be the original, the appointment of the agent by the husband is not noted, just the handing over of the writ to the agent. The essence of the conveying agent, to be explained below (sec. 3), fits this version perfectly.

21 Thus in all mss and the editions listed in n. 19. In standard editions: a writ.

> The appointment of a conveying agent or an agent for fetching does not require witnesses. The wife is not divorced with a writ of divorce sent by the husband or brought by an agent for the purpose of fetching until it reaches her [own] hand. Wherever in matters of divorce the term 'an agent' is mentioned, without further clarification, it refers to a conveying agent or an agent for fetching.

In the *Code,* then, it also appears that the conveying agent and the agent for the purpose of fetching belong to the same basic class, whereas the receiving agent is an independent category. Furthermore, the classification is arranged according to the essence of each agent's role; hence, Maimonides did not combine them. The agent for the purpose of fetching is referred to as such, and not as a conveying agent, and the husband's words to the wife's agent ('Deliver it to her') are not recorded, for this statement is only needed to confirm that a divorce proceeding is indeed underway. Essentially, however, the agent for the purpose of fetching, which is the focus of the treatment in the *Code,* is dependent only on appointment by the wife.

At this point, a significant objection to Maimonides's position was voiced by R. Nissim (Ran):

> This is astonishing! If the wife told the agent to fetch her the writ of divorce from her husband, and he went to the husband, who said to him, 'Deliver it to her' — it is certainly valid, for the husband has made him into his agent. But should the husband say that he does not want him as his agent at all[22] — how will she be divorced, for she has not received the writ of divorce, not from her husband, and not from his agent!?[23]

Although Ran wrote his critique without attributing it to anyone, he was really expressing, in an interrogative form, what had already been formulated in a declarative manner by R. Pinhas Halevi, the older

22 Here, the intent is that the husband does not want this person as **his** agent, but does not object to his being the wife's agent; he does, however, intend that the divorce be effective. Were he opposed to any involvement of this person as an agent, he could have so stipulated, to prevent such involvement. Indeed, in the source for Ran's thesis, the position taken by R. Pinhas Halevi (see n. 24 below), the formulation is: "And if the husband explicitly said, '**Here is the writ of divorce**, but I do not want you to be my agent at all.'"

23 Ran on Alfasi, bGitin 62b, Vilna ed., 28a.

brother of R. Aharon Halevi (Reah).[24] R. Pinhas disagreed with Maimonides, and declared that in a case in which the agent had been appointed by the wife to bring the writ of divorce, the divorce was invalid for the aforementioned reason. And indeed, the argument is clear: an agent appointed by the wife to fetch the writ of divorce has not been appointed to receive it for her. In fact, with respect to the matter of receiving it on her behalf, the agent has no legal status at all, for if he did, the wife would be divorced immediately upon his receipt of the writ of divorce, that is, he would be a receiving agent. Thus, the role of an agent for the purpose of fetching is such that only when the wife herself receives the bill of divorce will the divorce take effect. However, in such a case, where the wife's receipt of the writ of divorce is from someone who is neither the husband nor his agent, there is no valid divorce. Ran himself attempted to solve this problem:

> And it appears to me that perhaps, since the rule is that one's agent is like oneself, it is similar [to a case where] she received it, but has stipulated that she does not want the divorce to take effect until the writ of divorce has reached her [hand].

The concept of a stipulation had already arisen in R. Pinhas' critique, but he had employed it to negate the idea of an agent for the purpose of fetching: a receiving agent is valid even when the divorce, due to some stipulation, will take effect at a later date. The writ of divorce has reached someone who essentially has the capacity to render the divorce effective upon its receipt, and thus the scriptural demand, "and hands it to her," has been fulfilled. However, the agent for the purpose of fetching was not appointed to receive the writ of divorce, and at no time is his receipt of the writ sufficient for the divorce to be effective. Thus, if such an agent for the purpose of fetching is employed, the wife's receipt of the writ of divorce, which alone ensures a proper divorce, will not be accomplished through delivery

24 The commentary *Attributed to the Ritba*, Gitin 62b, ed. E. Lichtenstein (Jerusalem: 1981) has been identified by its editor as authored by R. Crescas Vidal, a disciple of Reah. The quotation was taken from an inscription ascribing it to: "Our Master, in the name of his brother, the scholar, R. Pinhas Halevi." On R. Pinhas, see Y.S. Spiegel, "Rabbi Pinhas Halevi and his *Azharot Leshabat Lifnei Rosh Hashana*" (Hebrew), in *Rabbi Y. Nissim Memorial Volume* (Hebrew), vol. 5 (Jerusalem: 1985), 71ff.

from her husband or his agent, and thus a proper delivery of the divorce is lacking.

When Ran attempted to resolve the matter, he adopted the concept of stipulation, adapting it to answer the questions posed by R. Pinhas. Essentially, an agent for the purpose of fetching is really an agent to receive it — it is just that the wife has added a stipulation suspending the legal effect of the divorce until the bill of divorce reaches her person. Nevertheless, this solution is fraught with difficulty, as was already noted by post-medieval authorities.[25] Only the husband can add a stipulation to the divorce, but a wife, who can be divorced without her consent, has no power to suspend the legal effect of the divorce once the writ of divorce has reached her. Her only power is in appointing the agent. Thus if the appointment of an agent is valid with respect to receiving the writ of divorce, then from the moment the agent receives it, she no longer has any power to suspend the legal effect of the divorce. Moreover, such a stipulation would be classified as "making a stipulation to overrule what is written in the Torah," and thus null and void, with the result that the acts of the agent would be effective. And should the very appointment of the agent be deemed incomplete, and the agent's receipt of the writ not deemed tantamount to the wife's receipt of the bill of divorce, then the question raised concerning the Maimonidean position arises anew: the wife's receipt of the writ of divorce is meaningless, since it did not come from the husband or his agent. Moreover, on Maimonides' view, the appointment of a receiving agent must be made before two witnesses, in contrast to the appointment of a conveying agent, which does not require any witnesses at all. Thus, it is clear that an agent for the purpose of fetching is unlike a receiving agent, for Maimonides explicitly stated that an agent for the purpose of fetching could also be appointed without witnesses.

To answer these questions, the *Aharonim* accepted the reasoning underlying Ran's solution. Essentially, an agent for the purpose of fetching is similar to a receiving agent, but one should differentiate between the two distinct stages in the divorce process, each defined in the Torah by a separate term. The phrase "And hands it to her [lit., gives it into her hand]," which is written in the Bible (Deut. 24:1), involves two separate laws: (1) the husband's handing over of the writ of divorce to his

25 See for example R. E. Alfandari, *Mikhtav Mieliyahu*, 6:4 (Constantinople: 1723), fol. 77, col. 2; R. M. Sokolovsky, *Imrei Moshe* (Petah Tikva: 1953), 20, end of letter 10.

wife must be executed, but he need not hand it to her alone; and (2) for the divorce to take effect, the wife must receive it "into her hand."[26] When is the "and hands it" requirement deemed to have been fulfilled? And what does "into her [hand]" add? In answering these questions, various approaches have been adopted in the writings of the *Aharonim*,[27] the dominant approach being the following:

> "Into her hand" is stated with a legal-monetary meaning — the wife must acquire the writ of divorce and become its owner in order to be divorced. However, to fulfill the condition of "and hands it," it is sufficient to hand it to her domain, even if she does not acquire it, and she lacks actual ownership of the writ of divorce. Accordingly, when an agent for the purpose of fetching receives it, the condition "and hands it," has been fulfilled, for he is the wife's agent, and the writ has been given to her through the agent's receiving it. Nevertheless, for the divorce to take effect, the writ of divorce must be found in her hand or possession alone; that is, the wife must acquire it. This power of acquisition she has not granted to her agent. When the writ of divorce reaches the wife, or her agent, who has been granted power to acquire it for her, then the divorce becomes effective. Thus, the agent for the purpose of fetching is a partial agent for receiving it. His task is to receive the writ of divorce in fulfilment of the requirement "and hands it;" while the law still requires the wife's receipt of it to fulfill the requirement of "into her hand."

However, this explanation is problematic for two reasons, one having to do with the theory itself, and the other, with the question of whether it can been anchored in Maimonidean texts. Concerning the

26 See, for example, two of the *Aharonim: Or Sameiah* on Maimonides, *Code*, Laws concerning Divorce 6:8 s.v. *uma; Even Haazel* on *Code*, Laws concerning Divorce 6:4.

27 The following view is found, for example, in *Imrei Moshe* and *Even Haazel* (nn. 25–26 above). For a different view, one that suggests that the agent for fetching receives the writ of divorce for the wife, see e.g., R. Isaac Bekhor David, *Divrei Emet*, kuntres 11 (divorce), 52 (Constantinople: 1760), 133d, but his presentation is not completely clear. For a clear formulation, see R. S. Fischer, *Beit Yishai* (Jerusalem: 1987), 65. The novel ruling in the *Pnei Yehoshua* on bGitin 9b, that the husband cannot retract the divorce once he has handed over the writ to the agent for the purpose of fetching, is probably based upon this theory. However, there is no basis for the theory in the words of Maimonides. Maimonides' comparison of, and reiterated equation of, the agents for conveying and for fetching, seems to undermine this view: in both types of agency the husband can retract until the writ of divorce has reached his wife.

theory itself, many *Rishonim* and *Aharonim* have already determined that for divorce to take effect the wife need not acquire the writ of divorce and become its owner from a monetary perspective.[28] There is no coerced acquisition on the part of someone who would acquire an object, but in divorce proceedings a wife becomes divorced even against her will. The Torah only demanded the physical presence of the writ of divorce in the domain of the wife — even if, legally-speaking, she does not own it. Thus, if the domain of an agent for the purpose of fetching is considered the wife's domain vis-à-vis the "and hands it" condition, nothing, it would appear, need delay the legal effect of the divorce until the writ of divorce reaches her hand.

Furthermore, even if one were to explicate the difference between "and hands it" and "into her [hand]" otherwise, this would still not yield the description of an agent for the purpose of fetching in the Maimonidean formulation. As mentioned above, Maimonides views the agent for the purpose of fetching as parallel to the conveying agent, the only difference being which party designated him an agent — the conveying agent is appointed by the husband, whereas the agent for the purpose of fetching is appointed by the wife. Nonetheless, both agents function in the same way. Thus, on Maimonides' description, an agent for the purpose of fetching is not a partial receiving agent, whose task is to receive the writ of divorce (though the divorce will be completed upon the wife's actual receipt of the writ of divorce into her hand). An agent for the purpose of fetching is precisely what the name implies: his task is to fetch the writ of divorce to the wife, just as the task of a conveying agent is to convey the bill of divorce. Just as the latter represents the husband in transferring the writ of divorce from one domain to the other, so the former represents the wife in the very same transfer from one domain to the other, while receipt of the writ of divorce is a different matter altogether.

Thus, Maimonides' position still calls for explanation, in any event. If the wife's agent is 'like' her, why is she not divorced as soon as the writ of divorce reaches the agent, as is the case regarding receiving agents? And if he is not, then she has not received the writ of divorce from her husband or his agent.

28 See for example, Rashi on bEruvin 92b s.v. *eina megureshet*: "For a woman does not have to acquire the writ of divorce." And see the *Ketzot Hahoshen*, 200:5, and the literature cited in the *Tabaat Hahoshen* ad loc.

### 3 *Conveying and Fetching the Writ of Divorce — Methods of Transfer*

At the end of the first section, it was suggested that if the husband's presentation of the writ of divorce is the essence of the act of divorce, it would follow that the consignment of the writ to the conveying agent is valid, based on the principle that one's agent is like oneself. Thus, the agent's delivery is tantamount to the husband's. To be more precise, the conveying agent is really an agent for handing over the writ. However, should the handing over of the writ of divorce be viewed as only preparing the way for divorce, and the divorce itself viewed as effected by the writ of divorce's being in the wife's domain, then there would be no role for an agent for handing over the writ, and in reality, such an agent would be but a conveying agent. On this conception, there is no need for the ceremony of the husband's handing the writ of divorce to his wife, and the divorce takes effect by the mere presence, as a result of actions on the part of the husband or his agent, of the writ of divorce in the wife's domain. The requirement that an agent hand over the writ of divorce is only rooted in the necessity of the writ's reaching the wife through the legal power of the husband, and not that of someone else. By appointing a conveying agent, the writ of divorce has been transferred to the wife through the legal power of the husband, since the agent operates by virtue of that power. The conveying agent exists only to ensure that the transfer of the writ of divorce from husband to wife is indeed accomplished, and no foreign element is involved.

Accordingly, there is no longer any difficulty with regard to the status of an agent for the purpose of fetching. He is not a partial receiving agent, but an agent whose role is solely to take the writ of divorce and bring it to the wife. The difficulty arose from the conception that the actual handing over of the writ of divorce by the husband to the wife is what effects the divorce, and the fact that such an agent's receipt of the writ of divorce is unlike the wife's (since she is not divorced immediately upon his receiving it). Since the handing over is done neither by the husband nor by his agent, the element of the husband's handing it into her hand is lacking; how, then, can the wife be divorced?

However, on the Maimonidean view, the act of divorce is essentially the presence of the writ of divorce in the wife's domain, and the husband's handing it over is only a means of transferring the writ of divorce from him to her domain. This process is only valid when accomplished without involving any foreign elements, but the transfer itself is purely technical, and not a formal ceremony. Thus the agents for conveying and fetching are carrying out a single process, but in opposite directions, as their names imply.[29] By means of these agents, the writ of divorce is transferred from the husband to the wife without the involvement of any parties foreign to the matter. By means of the conveying agent appointed by the husband, or the agent for the purpose of fetching appointed by the wife, the writ of divorce arrives in a proper manner, from husband to wife, without any outside interference, for the agents of transmission between them have been legally appointed. These agents are only appointed to transfer the writ of divorce from one place to the other. Thus, the conveying agent's delivery of the writ of divorce does not constitute a ceremony of handing over the writ, for the husband's handing over of the writ of divorce is only a technical transfer of the writ. Likewise, the acceptance of the writ by the agent for the purpose of fetching is not considered acceptance on the part of the woman, for he has only been empowered to transfer it.

On this account, the significance of the agents for conveying and for fetching is not that they enable attribution of the agent's deed to his principal. The handing over of the writ by the conveying agent is not to be seen as tantamount to the husband's, nor its receipt by the agent for fetching as tantamount to the wife's. The significance of agency here is that resort to an agent ensures that there are no foreign elements involved in the transfer of the writ of divorce from husband to wife, and that all interaction between them takes places through agents who represent them. The actions of the agents are only acts of liaison, that need not be attributed to husband or wife. Nevertheless, it should be stressed that although the actions of the agents need not be attributed to their principals, their value in this context derives from the fact that they are agents according to all the laws of agency. Only the principle "one's agent is like onself" serves to eliminate their status as foreign and independent, thereby making it possible for the writ of divorce to be considered to have been transferred from husband to wife as dictated

29 For another example of this phenomenon, see the description of the waving of the two breads and the Pentecost offerings in mMenahot 5:6: "And he places his two hands under them and thrusts his hand outwards (*holakha*) and brings them inwards (*havaa*), raises them and lowers them," and many other similar sources. The Hebrew terms used here are the very terms that designate the two types of agents in the divorce context.

by Jewish law. Were there no agency here, then the writ of divorce would reach the wife through the agency of a foreign element, and would be invalid.

On this basis, the Maimonidean position can be further elucidated. Some talmudic passages[30] deal with an agent of the wife who misrepresents himself before the husband. Two problems arise. Does the husband rely upon the agent's declaration? Does the agent, through his misrepresentation, invalidate his appointment? A number of positions that determined the law to be applied were suggested by early medieval authorities,[31] but this article focuses only on the Maimonidean position, as formulated in Laws concerning Divorce 6:11–12:

> [In a case] where the wife's agent came to take[32] the writ of divorce from the husband and said to him: 'I am a receiving agent,' and the husband replied to him: 'Here is, for you (*heilakh*),[33] this writ of divorce, just as she said' — This implies 'I am not canceling her appointment [of you] as an agent,[34] rather, whether you have been appointed as a receiving agent or as a conveying[35] agent, your status remains as she said.' If, when he brings the writ, she says to him: 'I only appointed you to be an agent for the purpose of fetching,' she is not divorced even if the writ of divorce[36] reached her hand. For the agent has voided her appointment, in effect having told the husband, 'I was never appointed as an agent for the purpose of fetching for her.'

30 bGitin 62b–63a and the parallel passage in bBaba Metzia 76a-b; jGitin 6:1 (47d).
31 See Friedman (n. 18 above), 44–55.
32 Thus in the editions listed above, n. 19, according to mss; in standard editions, "to receive." Since in reality he was not appointed to receive, the version in the mss is certainly preferable.
33 Thus in the Frankel and Kafih eds., on the basis of some textual evidence; the Rabinovitch ed., based on other textual evidence, is almost identical, but reads *he lekha*, the meaning of which is the same as that of the contraction *heilakh* (see below, n. 37). However, standard editions read "Deliver" (*holekh*), which appears to be a scribal error, for the husband did not appoint him as a conveying agent, but his appointment was as "she said."
34 Thus according to mss. Standard editions read "your appointment as an agent."
35 Thus in the Frankel and Rabinovitch eds.; standard editions and the Kafih ed. read: "fetching." It is already clear that according to Maimonides, the two are essentially the same, and the terms can be interchanged. See the quotation from the *Commentary on the Mishnah* in sec. 2 above.
36 According to editions based upon mss versions; in standard editions the phrase "the writ of divorce" is omitted.

> If the agent said to the husband, 'I am an agent for the purpose of fetching,' and the husband replied to him, 'Here it is for you, as she said'; and [then] the agent brings the writ of divorce, and she says to him, 'I appointed you as a receiving agent,' she is divorced as soon as the writ of divorce reaches her hand.[37] For the agent has not voided her appointment, but merely diminished it, since she said, '[I appointed you] a receiving agent,' while he had said to the husband, '[I was appointed] only an agent for the purpose of fetching.'

From Maimonides' words, it is clear that the husband's reliance on the agent's statement is irrelevant, for the husband is not involved at all in the appointment of the wife's agent. This is in accordance with his position that the wife has the power to appoint two types of agents, and not just a receiving agent.[38] One can only analyze the agent's deeds and their intent: did his words cancel the wife's appointment, or is it sustained? Note that where the agent changed his mandate from that of receipt to that of bringing, Maimonides states that this does not cancel the original agency, but just diminishes it, and hence the wife is divorced once the writ reaches her hand. R. Meir Simha Hakohen of Dvinsk, in his *Or Sameiah*, interpreted this in line with the explanation of Ran and his circle, namely, that agency for the purpose of fetching is but partial agency for receiving. S.Y. Friedman[39] has already noted, however, that if so, the first case is incomprehensible. In this case, the agent changed his status from agent for fetching, as appointed by the wife, to self-declared agent for receiving. The agent has completed the fetching, which is tantamount to partial receipt of the writ, and changed his mandate to 'complete' receipt of the writ. Thus, he has not "voided her appointment," but added to it; why then is she not divorced when she receives the writ of divorce? Why should changing his mandate from "fetching" to "receiving" void the agent's powers and invalidate

37 According to all editions based on mss, and likewise in early printings. However, standard printed editions read "deliver," which is a scribal error; see n. 33 above.

38 This account best fits Maimonides' version of the passages in bGitin and bBaba Metzia (based on Geonic versions of the text), according to which the issue of "does he rely on his words or hers?" is not discussed in relation to the agency of divorce at all; see Lifshitz (n. 14 above), 357ff. The commentators on the *Code* were not familiar with that version, and thus had difficulty explaining the Maimonidean position in view of the talmudic passages.

39 N. 18 above, 48–49.

the divorce, if changing the mandate from "receiving" to "fetching" does not do this? Why is the divorce valid when he cancelled the receiving agency and was never appointed to fetch the writ of divorce?[40]

It would thus appear that the above explication provides a satisfactory clarification of Maimonides' position. Both the fetching and conveying agents merely connect the husband and wife. The role of the agent is not to enable his deeds to be attributed to his principal, but his value is in the fact that as an agent, he is not a foreign element in the divorce transaction. Thus, an agent for the purpose of fetching who does not take upon himself the task of fetching the writ of divorce, and is only ready to receive it, is ineffective. He was not empowered to receive the writ, and himself voided his appointment to fetch the writ, and thus can no longer serve in that capacity as the wife's agent. Upon receipt of the writ, he terminated his role as an agent by canceling his mandate, and the wife has not received the writ through her agent or her husband's. In contrast, a receiving agent who voided his appointment to receive it, but took it upon himself to bring the writ to the wife, retains his status as an agent. The wife had appointed him as a receiving agent, and since he voided this mandate to receive the writ on her behalf, that mandate remains unfulfilled, and his appointment as an agent still stands. Moreover, he has not resigned from his status as her agent, for he has taken it upon himself to bring her the writ of divorce in the capacity as agent for the purpose of fetching, and as such is considered to be like his principal. Thus, although the act of fetching cannot be attributed to the wife, for she did not send him as such, there is really no need for such attribution. The whole point of the agency is that as an agent for the wife, his foreignness is negated. This remains the case, both from his perspective and from hers, and thus the divorce is valid. The wife received her writ of divorce from her husband through someone who connects them to each other and is not a foreign element, but her agent.

## 4 *Receiving Agent for a Minor Girl — Maimonides' Account*

In contrast to an agent for the purpose of fetching, the Sages never argued over the existence of the receiving agent. Nevertheless, it

40 Friedman, 49–52, views the agent for the purpose of fetching as really the husband's agent, and attempts to solve the problems arising from the Maimonidean position accordingly. Nevertheless, as explained in sec. 2 above, it is just too difficult to attribute such a view to Maimonides.

appears that the nature and essence of this agent, as set out by Maimonides, is clarified by the explication of divorce proceedings that has been suggested in this article. In Laws concerning Divorce 6:9, Maimonides writes:

> A minor girl may not appoint a receiving agent, although her courtyard acquires the writ of divorce for her just as it does for an adult woman, because the appointment of a receiving agent requires witnesses, and no testimony may be given concerning the acts of a minor, because his mind is not completely formed.

The law that a minor cannot appoint a receiving agent is not doubted, its source being mGitin 6:3. However, the reason offered by Maimonides is surprising, as noted by Rabad in his critical comment on the passage.

> Abraham said: This reason lacks cogency [lit., both taste and smell]. But it is derived from the ["also" in the] verse "You also shall [set apart] (*tarimu gam atem*)" (Num. 18:28), to include your agents. Just as you are of sound mind, so should your agent be of sound mind. Consequently, both the principal and the agent must be of sound mind.

Rabad refers to two difficulties: both the reason offered by Maimonides, and, that which he omits to mention. Concerning the latter, the Mishnah itself provided the reason: "A minor cannot appoint an agent." Thus, the inability of a minor to appoint an agent is not the result of any specific requirement that there be witnesses to the appointment of a receiving agent, but a result of the minor's lacking the general ability to appoint agents. Not only is the reason mentioned by the Mishnah, but Maimonides himself adopts this reason in his Laws concerning Agents and Partners 2:2:

> Those not of sound mind, including the deaf-mute, one who is mentally disabled, and minors, cannot act as an agent or appoint an agent. It makes no difference whether the minor involved is male or female.

Considering that Maimonides essentially accepted Rabad's critique, his formulation in the Laws concerning Divorce is astonishing. Why does he put forward a different reason? Not only is there no apparent need for this novel reason, but its implications for Jewish law are strange: if the problem is only with a receiving agent, as the formulation in the Laws concerning Divorce seems to indicate, then the implication is that an agent for the purpose of fetching can be appointed by a minor wife, since this appointment, as noted above, does not require witnesses. This conclusion contradicts Maimonides' formulation in the Laws concerning Agents and Partners, which states that a minor wife cannot appoint any type of agent, since she is not of sound (that is, adult) mind.[41]

With regard to the difficulty raised by the fact that this explicit Mishnah appears to uphold the reason adduced by Rabad, and not that adduced by Maimonides, the commentary of an early medieval commentator is illuminating: "'A minor wife who said, "Accept for me my writ of divorce" — it is not valid until she receives it into her hand' (mGitin 6:3) — commentary: since a minor does not appoint an agent."[42] Lichtenstein concluded that this commentator's text of the Mishnah did not contain the reason found in most texts, and thus had to add it as commentary.[43] Accordingly, Lichtenstein suggested that Maimonides had before him a similar version of the Mishnah, and therefore suggested a different reason. This argument can be strengthened by analyzing the language of the Mishnah: "A minor girl who said, 'Accept for me my writ of divorce' — it is not valid until she receives it into her hand; therefore, if the husband wants to retract, he may retract, for a minor does not appoint an agent." The reason provided at the end of the sentence is misplaced, as it does not explain the preceding phrase ("if the husband wants to retract, he may retract"), but refers to the beginning of the sentence. Consequently, it could be argued that the reason offered in the Mishnah is a later addition, perhaps

41 It is difficult to be satisfied with the comments found in the *Magid Mishne* ad loc. in response to Rabad's critical comment: "Since it makes no difference to the essential law, I will not expound upon it." If Maimonides' explanation in the Laws concerning Divorce determines the law, it certainly makes a difference with respect to other types of agency as well; cf. *Lehem Mishne*, ad loc.

42 Recently published by E. Lichtenstein from a manuscript in his *Hidushim Miktav Yad* (Jerusalem: 1981). In his introduction, 13–14, the editor concludes that this volume belongs to the genre of compilations that present rabbinical commentaries by many authors (*shita mekubetzet*), but are essentially based on the work of R. Meir Abulafia (Rama) and Rashba. The same opinion is held by R. A. Shoshana, who printed the same work in his *Hidushei Harama Veshitot Kadmonim Al Masekhet Gitin* (Jerusalem: 1985), 12–27.

43 In n. 269.

a marginal note that was eventually interpolated, albeit in the incorrect place, into the Mishnaic text proper.

Unfortunately, however, in all manuscript versions of the Mishnah, including Maimonides' own version of the Mishnaic text, there is no textual evidence to support the claim that the text was missing the phrase in question.[44] It is, therefore, more logical to assume that Maimonides left out the Mishnaic reason on the strength of the reason he himself put forward. It follows that he had a source for his reason, either in the writings of the Sages or in the Geonic writings, a source we would do well to search for.[45]

However, the essential difficulty is the inner contradiction within Maimonides' writings. Since Maimonides admits to the fact that minors cannot appoint agents at all, due to their being of unsound mind, why did he require a special reason for a receiving agent? Later rabbinical authorities were hard pressed to resolve this inner contradiction.[46] It is very difficult to comprehend why Maimonides did not cite the simple reason provided by the Mishnah, unless we can explain

44 The *Halakhot Gedolot* (n. 12 above), 176, reads: "A minor girl does not appoint an agent"; and see the variants that read: "a minor boy." Nevertheless, the implications of the formulation "minor girl" are no different: an agent cannot be appointed because the child is a minor and does not have the power to appoint an agent, in contrast to the explanation offered by Maimonides. In all other versions of the Mishnah, the reason offered is similar to that found in the printed edition.

45 The author of the *Migdal Oz* ad loc. quotes the Mishnah in Gitin and the passage in bKidushin 44b, and comments: "Behold, your eyes see that Maimonides' reason is explicit in mGitin and the passage in Kidushin! And open your eyes, too, to see the wisdom of Maimonides, who saw the future, for a time will come and scholars will not be able to discover the reason for Maimonides' ruling. And thus he expounded at length on the reason found in tractate Kidushin … to discover its source … and this is explicit and set out directly in the Talmud." As is generally the case regarding the *Migdal Oz*, his words are astonishing, for in the passage in Kidushin, there is no conjecture that agency might be efficacious for a minor, as a courtyard would be. The only idea discussed (and rejected) is that a young daughter of 12 is considered part of the courtyard of her father, and therefore **cannot** appoint an agent. Some have suggested that Maimonides' source was bBaba Kama 112b, which states that testifying about a minor is like testifying when a litigant is absent. However, the issue addressed by this source is that one cannot testify on matters pertaining to a minor, and not a minor's competence to appoint an agent, discussed in our Mishnah, mGitin 6:3. Cf. *Code*, Laws concerning Sales 29:9.

46 See the index in the Frankel ed., ad loc.

why he brought the reason he did in its stead. It is vital, therefore, to account for the reason put forward by Maimonides. And indeed, Maimonides was not satisfied with providing his reason, but includes within his words an explanation of the very need to account for the fact that a minor cannot appoint an agent: "A minor girl may not appoint a receiving agent, **though her courtyard acquires the writ of divorce for her just as it does for an adult woman** ...." Yet this account is not readily comprehensible — how is the matter of agency related to that of a courtyard? She certainly has the legal standing for acquisition through a courtyard, since a minor can hold legal ownership; but appointing an agent is a legal process a minor is incapable of executing. The author of the *Magid Mishne* explained that a courtyard procures property for its owner on the basis of the principle of agency, and thus Maimonides had to explain why agency and a courtyard's power of acquisition are not equivalent here. Nevertheless, later rabbinical authorities noted that although the Talmud (bBaba Metzia 10b) suggested that the courtyard's power of acquisition is based on the principle of agency, Maimonides himself rejected this basis for a courtyard's power of acquisition, and opted for the alternative suggested in the Talmud: acquisition by a minor girl's courtyard is based upon the principle that it is an extension of her hand.[47] Both the reason offered by Maimonides, and his rationale for providing it, remain difficult to understand.

## 5 *The Singularity of the Receiving Agent according to Maimonides*

In sec. 3 above, the roles of the agents for conveying and for fetching were described against the background of the status of the act of handing over

47 *Code*, Laws concerning Robbery and Lost Property 17:10. Maimonides explained that with regard to a woman, her courtyard's power to acquire something for her is derived from "her hand," while the courtyard of a man is derived from his agent. Consequently, a minor girl has a courtyard, just as she has a hand, while a minor boy does not have a courtyard to acquire objects, just as he cannot appoint an agent. Thus, it is clear that agency of a minor girl has nothing to do with a courtyard. Rav Ashi's formulation (bBaba Metzia 12a) that the effectiveness of courtyard in such acquisition is derived from "her hand," and is no less than that of an agent, does not add anything that would solve the problem. A courtyard will be no less effective than an agent, but one cannot infer the reverse — that an agent will be no less effective than a courtyard. Cf. the *Aharonim* in the index mentioned in the previous note.

the writ of divorce within the divorce proceedings. Since this disagreement has implications for the nature of the wife's receipt of the writ of divorce, it is logical to assume that the role of the receiving agent can be understood in different ways. If the essence of the divorce proceedings is the ceremony of the handing over of the writ of divorce by the husband to his wife, then the role of the receiving agent is readily grasped. Since the wife's person must receive the writ of divorce, and her agent represents her person, then his receipt of it is tantamount to her receipt. On the other hand, if the essential element in divorce is the fact that the writ of divorce is in her hand or domain, the use of a receiving agent necessitates further explication. The wife's agent is tantamount to the wife, and can represent her person, but we do not find that an agent is transformed into a representative of the courtyard and the domain of his principal. What use is it for a receiving agent who represents the legal person of the wife to procure the writ of divorce if that writ does not reach **her domain**?

At this point, we need not be surprised to find two approaches to the question of the essence of the receiving agent, represented by the *Turim* and Maimonides. The *Turim* summarizes the laws of the wife's domain, in the context of the laws of divorce, in sec. 139, while he brings the laws of the receiving agent, along with the laws of the conveying agent and agent for purposes of fetching, in sec. 140. All agents are thus considered to be agents in the classic sense of the term — as legally representing their principal. Just as the actions of a conveying agent are viewed as tantamount to the husband's handing over the writ of divorce, so too receipt of the writ of divorce by the receiving agent is tantamount to its receipt by the wife — one's agent is like oneself.

However, at the beginning of chapter 5 of his Laws concerning Divorce, Maimonides formulates the law as follows:

> The Torah's statement, "and hands it to her," means only that the writ of divorce should reach[48] her.[49] It makes no difference whether it reaches her hand or her lap or her courtyard or **her agent whose hand she had made**

48 On the significance of the phrase "should reach" used here by Maimonides, see above, sec. 1.

49 Some of the textual versions have "her hand"; see the list of variants in the Frankel ed. However, in the Oxford ms (above, n. 20) the language is more expansive: "The intention of the scriptural verse is not that the writ of divorce should reach her hand, but that it should reach her." In the Rabinovitch ed., based on this ms, this version was copied as the text, but no comment or explanation was added. Apparently, this is not an original

> **the equivalent of her own hand** — it is all the same ... and when the writ of divorce reaches her domain, she is divorced.

Maimonides thus explicitly states that the receiving agent does not function as an agent in the classic sense, representing his principal, but rather is included in her courtyard and domain.[50] Therefore, the appointment of a receiving agent is not like any appointment of an agent to represent the principal's legal person, but must fall under the concept of "she made his hand like hers." The appointment of a receiving agent has an element not present in the cases of the other agents: the wife enlarges her domain through the agent's good offices, and his "hand" is considered tantamount to the courtyard and domain of the wife. Handing over the writ of divorce to a receiving agent is not an act that relates to the legal person of the wife. Just as placing the writ of divorce in the wife's courtyard effects the divorce, since the writ has reached her domain, though it has not reached her person, so too handing over the writ of divorce to her receiving agent is equivalent to placing it in her domain, for she has made his hand like her own. Maimonides had already hinted at this in his Laws concerning Divorce 1:3:

> "And hands it to her" teaches that she is not divorced until the writ of divorce is delivered[51] to her [hand], or to the hand of her agent, **which is the same as her hand**, or to her courtyard, **all of which are regarded as equivalent to her hand**.

---

version of the text, but a synthesis of the above versions. The implications of this version are that her **hand** is **not to receive the writ, and instead, she, i.e., her person**, must receive the writ. However, from the continuation, it is clear that this reference to her person is only an **elaboration of** the concept of "her hand." On this version of the text, Maimonides should have written: 'The intention of the scriptural verse is not that the writ of divorce should reach her hand **only**, but that it should reach her.'

50 R. Joshua Benveniste, *Sdei Yehoshua Layerushalmi* (Constantinople: 1749), on mGitin 6:2, wrote that a receiving agent is derived from "her hand." The author of the *Ketzot Hahoshen* (244:3) questioned this, since bKidushin 41a derived a receiving agent from the biblical verse "and he shall send her," which teaches agency in general, and not from "her hand." Nevertheless, Maimonides himself explicitly held the view expounded by R. Benveniste. However, R. D. Friedman, *Piskei Halakhot Im Biur Yad David*, I (Warsaw: 1898), 121c, already noted that the passage in bGitin 21a explicitly mentions the possibility that the receiving agent can be derived from "her hand," and could have served as Maimonides' source.

51 Note the passive voice in Maimonides's formulation: "until the writ of divorce is delivered to" and not 'until he delivers the writ of divorce.' This is in accord with his position as presented here.

Two points are being made here. First, the role of the receiving agent is based on the concept of a courtyard or domain, and not on the agent's being the legal representative of his principal by virtue of the laws of agency. Thus, he is not just an agent, but acts as her "hand." In his description of the conveying agent (in Laws concerning Divorce 1:1), Maimonides did not state that he is like his principal's hand, for the conveying agent is like all other agents in Jewish law: he represents the legal person of his principal, but is not considered tantamount to his courtyard.[52]

Accordingly, the problem raised in the last section concerning Maimonides' formulation that a minor wife cannot appoint a receiving agent, can now be solved. First, he himself explained the problem as follows: "A minor girl may not appoint a receiving agent, **though her courtyard acquires the writ of divorce for her just as it does for an adult woman**." Maimonides is, in effect, stating that were a receiving agent like all other agents, certainly a minor girl could not appoint such an agent, as stated in the second chapter of the Laws concerning Agents, for a minor does not have the legal power to appoint such an agent to act on his or her behalf. However, a receiving agent does not act on the basis of agency, by representing the legal person of his employer, but acts on the basis of the principle that he is considered part of the domain and courtyard of the wife. His appointment actually expands the wife's domain to legally encompass the agent's hand. With regard to a courtyard, there is no difference between a minor girl and an adult woman, since both may own a courtyard. Hence, it might have been thought that a minor wife could appoint a receiving agent, as he is considered part of her courtyard. Consequently, Maimonides offered a reason this was not so: "because the appointment of a receiving agent requires witnesses, and no testimony may be given concerning the acts of a minor, because his mind is not completely formed." A minor possesses sufficient sound mind for acquisitions made through a courtyard, but since the particular recourse to the courtyard here (that is, to serve as the minor wife's 'agent') is for purposes of divorce, it requires witnesses, as is the case in other aspects of the divorce proceedings.

52 See also the *Commentary on the Mishnah*, Gitin 2:5 quoted above in sec. 2: "whom the wife appointed as an agent to receive the writ of divorce for her, and whose hand becomes like hers." This description is presented after that of the conveying agent, where the explanatory phrase "whose hand becomes like hers" is not used.

Since a witnessed appointment calls for the "completely formed" mind necessary for legal proceedings, a minor is unable to make such an appointment.

The unique reason offered by Maimonides to explain the role of a receiving agent appointed by a minor wife stems from his general position that the essence of a receiving agent is that he is part of the wife's hand, domain and courtyard.[53] This in turn reflects a basic thesis held by Maimonides as to the nature of the divorce proceedings. The fact that the writ of divorce is found in her hand or domain, and not the ceremony of the husband's handing over the writ of divorce to the wife, effectuates the legal result — divorce.

If this article has succeeded in providing a correct understanding of various aspects of the Maimonidean position on the subject of the different types of agency in the context of divorce, then the formulation of his impressive legal position may be said to be characterized by its unity, harmony and coherence. As is the case with respect to other legal questions, it is possible to identify the Maimonidean sources — a few here, a few there. Maimonides' achievement was to utilize these fragmentary sources as a foundation for his formulations, giving them coherence and comprehensiveness.

53 B.Z. Benedikt, *Maimonides' Strict Reliance on the Talmud* (Hebrew), (Jerusalem: 1985), 55ff., viewed this rationale as an example of a stratum of reasons offered by Maimonides in the *Code* where his legal formulations were rather casual, though in another stratum he determined the law with scrupulous care. The present article maintains that, on the contrary, it exemplifies exacting meticulousness of formulation. And see my articles, "The basis of Maimonides' concept of halakha," *Shenaton Hamishpat Haivri* 20 (1995–1997), 107, n. 15; "The reasons for the halakha presented by Maimonides in his *Mishne Torah*" (Hebrew), *Maimonidean Sudies* 4 (2000), 45–80.

*The Jewish Law Annual*, Vol. XIV

# HALAKHA AND *METZIUT* (REALIA) IN MEDIEVAL ASHKENAZ: SURVEYING THE PARAMETERS AND DEFINING THE LIMITS

EPHRAIM KANARFOGEL*

## I

Even a cursory perusal of the literature of the *rishonim* brings the reader face to face with the ways in which medieval halakhists dealt with social realia that appeared, prima facie, to conflict with talmudic law. On the very first page of tractate Avoda Zara, for example, *Tosafot* poses a brief but weighty question. In light of the clear Mishnaic (and talmudic) restrictions enunciated in regard to doing business with idolaters on the days preceding their holidays or religious observances (and certainly on these days themselves), how is it that Jews do business with Christians on Christian holy days as a matter of course? Or, to put it more precisely, upon what authority does the Jewish community rely?[1]

*Tosafot* and other parallel Ashkenazic rabbinic texts[2] suggest a series of explanations, which can be broken down into two basic categories or approaches. One approach maintains that societal conditions or attitudes had changed since the talmudic period (for example, Christians are not genuine or dedicated idolaters; refusal to do business with the Christians would generate unmitigated enmity). Moreover,

* E. Billi Ivry Professor of Jewish History, and Chair, Rebecca Ivry Department of Jewish Studies, Stern College for Women/Yeshiva University. An earlier version of this study was presented at the tenth annual conference of the Yeshiva University Orthodox Forum (New York, 1998).

1 "על מה סמכו העולם לשאת ולתת ביום איד העבודת כוכבים עמהם" *Tosafot*, Avoda Zara 2a s.v. *asur laset velatet imahem*, and *Tosafot R. Elhanan*, ed. David Frankel (Husiatyn: 1901), ad loc.

2 See, e.g., *Sefer Or Zarua*, part 4, Piskei Avoda Zara, secs. 95–102; *Sefer Raban*, sec. 288 (at the beginning of Avoda Zara); R. Barukh b. Isaac, *Sefer Hateruma*, Hilkhot Akum, sec. 134; and cf. *Hidushei Talmidei Rabeinu Yona Al Masekhet Avoda Zara*, ed. H. Zarkowsky (NY: 1995), 2–4. *Sefer Hateruma*, sec. 134, was partially censored; see Israel Ta-Shma, *Ritual, Custom and Reality in Franco-Germany, 1000–1350* (Hebrew), (Jerusalem: 1996), 245, n. 17.

accommodation for these types of changes was anticipated and provided for by the Talmud itself, allowing ample justification for the prevailing Ashkenazic practices.

A second approach, espoused in this case (and in other instances as well) by Rabbenu Tam, suggests that the underlying Mishnaic and other rabbinic texts in question can be (re-)interpreted in a way that obviates the problem entirely. According to Rabbenu Tam, the primary concern of the Mishnah and its attendant texts was to ensure that Jews did not provide idolaters with animals or materials that could then be offered in idolatrous service (מידי דתקרובת). *Tosafot* asserts that for Rabbenu Tam, even if Christianity and Christian worship are judged to be forms of idolatry, the only thing that can be considered an offering is money. Only if a Jew were to lend or give a Christian money, without interest, would a problem arise. All other business exchanges and transactions were permitted, without any restriction. As *Tosafot* concludes, "there is no reason to wonder, according to the approach of Rabbenu Tam, at the common Jewish practice of doing business with Christians, even on Christian holy days" (ולפי פר"ת אין לתמוה על מנהג העולם).[3]

Significant attention was focused on the interplay between realia (*metziut*) and halakha in Ashkenaz by a series of Israeli scholars writing in the mid-1950s and early 1960s, including Shalom Albeck,[4] E.E. Urbach,[5] Haim Hillel Ben-Sasson,[6] and Jacob Katz.[7] Almost all the cases investigated and treated by these scholars were in the realm of economic or monetary law,[8] and involved interactions with non-Jews.

3 Ri's son R. Elhanan (a grand-nephew of Rabbenu Tam) maintains (see above, n. 1) that even monies given to Christian clergymen (collection offerings) were not being given principally for idolatry itself, but for the personal benefit of these individuals.

4 "Rabbenu Tam's attitude to the problems of his time" (Hebrew), *Zion* 19 (1954), 104–141.

5 *The Tosafists* (Hebrew) (Jerusalem: 1955), esp. 55–80 (1980 ed., 1:60–93).

6 In his review of Urbach's *The Tosafists*, entitled "Torah leadership" (Hebrew), *Behinot Bebikoret Hasifrut* 9 (1956): 46–49.

7 *Exclusiveness and Tolerance* (Oxford: 1961), esp. chs. 3–5. Cf. idem, *Halakha and Kabbala* (Hebrew), (Jerusalem: 1986), 2–3, 344–346.

8 Albeck, "Rabbenu Tam's attitude," n. 4 above, 105, raises the possibility that Rabbenu Tam's position on counting a minor as the tenth person in a *minyan* was related to the small size of the northern French communities, but he then acknowledges that this factor may not have been decisive. Cf. I. Ta-Shma, "By the power of the Holy Name — the history of a forgotten custom" (Hebrew), *Sefer Bar Ilan* 26–27 (1995), 389–399.

They considered questions such as the following: how did the communities of medieval Ashkenaz, which had extensive and vital business dealings with Christians, square their practices and interactions with talmudic passages that restricted the ability of a Jew to accept the oath of a non-Jew, and restricted, for related reasons, the types of commodities that could be bought or sold? How did Jews, whose involvement in money-lending became more entrenched and pervasive as the Tosafist period progressed, justify this in light of talmudic *sugyot* that appeared to look down on any form of interest-bearing or usurious loans, including those between Jews and non-Jews? How did Jews involved in viticulture deal with the unavoidable (and often necessary) presence and activity of non-Jews during various phases of the production process, which could easily render the wine unfit both for consumption by Jews, and as a source of livelihood and profit?

The ability of halakhists to deal effectively with these types of societal situations and economic realities might be viewed simply as a partial or modified *pikuah nefesh* argument. If Jews had to be involved in certain professions in order to survive, it was necessary that they be given the means to do so. This goal is most easily achieved when the immediate prohibitions are fundamentally rabbinic in nature, and where talmudic law itself appears to make provisions for economic exigencies.[9] *Tosafot* argues, for example, that the high levels of taxation imposed by kings and other noblemen or feudal rulers render all economic initiatives extremely vital for one's livelihood (לפי שיש עלינו מס מלך ושרים והכל כדי חיינו). Thus, lending money to non-Jews at interest need not be curtailed in any way, despite the rabbinic notion (expressed by R. Nahman in the name of R. Huna) that usurious transactions with non-Jews may have a corrupting effect on the Jewish lender. The Talmud itself maintains that this possible effect is not to be taken into consideration if the Jew's livelihood is in jeopardy.[10] Similarly, Rabbenu Tam, who permitted one Jew to lend money to another at interest by using a non-Jew as a middleman (so that the first Jew was actually lending to the non-Jew, who in turn became the lender to the second Jew), made the following statement in support of

9 Any changes in realia whose impact was measured in purely economic terms could also be addressed more easily, utilizing the principle of "valid confiscation by a rabbinical court" (*hefker beit din hefker*).

10 See *Tosafot*, Baba Metzia 70b s.v. *tashikh lo sagi delav hakhi*; *Sefer Or Zarua*, part 3, Piskei Baba Metzia, secs. 207–208; and *Tosafot*, Kidushin (below, n. 17).

his view: "It appears to me to be completely permitted, and indeed a meritorious act that provides sustenance for Jews, to have the borrower transfer the pawns to a non-Jew who will then interact with the lender. This is not a subterfuge but is perfectly legal. ... In order that all know that this is completely permitted, I have expressed myself on this matter at length."[11]

And yet, Rabbenu Tam's formulation points in a direction other than pure economic survival. Rabbenu Tam stresses the fact that his ruling renders the practice completely permitted (*heter gamur*). His answer is not couched as a concession to financial exigencies or other temporal realities.[12] Rabbenu Tam also upholds, in strong terms, the rights or prerogatives of the individual in other situations that are essentially economic but which have wider implications, such as the power of the majority in matters of communal government, and the applicability or scope of the *herem hayishuv* (ban on settlement) in his day.[13]

Moreover, Rabbenu Tam and other Tosafists dealt with issues of social concern related to ritual practices and customs with no economic implications. In a pioneering study, Jacob Katz traced the solutions proposed by Ashkenazic halakhists to justify the widespread custom (prevalent throughout medieval Europe, as it had been already in the Geonic period) of praying the evening service before the stars came out, which appears to run counter to talmudic law. Katz demonstrates that unlike Geonic, Spanish and Provencal halakhists, who tended to maintain that the correct procedure was to pray after the stars had come out, and did not try in a meaningful way to justify the practice of their communities, Tosafists, including Raban, Rabbenu Tam and Ri, offered interpretations and constructions that defended the existing

11 "*Venire beeinai heter gamur umitzva min hamuvhar latet mihya livnei brit shemutar lalove velamalve sheyiten halove hamashkonot leyad goy ... ki ein ze haarama ela din gamur ... lemaan daat kol adam shehu heter gamur heerakhti badavar.*" See *Sefer Or Zarua*, sec. 202, and *Responsa Maharam Rothenburg* (Prague ed.), #796.

12 Note too the phrase in R. Tam's *Sefer Hayashar* (Helek Hasheeilot Utshuvot), ed. Shraga Rosenthal (Berlin: 1898), 131: "We may not invent reasons, but must proceed only on the basis of law" (*veein lanu levadot taamim ela al pi hahalakha*).

13 See Urbach, n. 5 above, 1980 ed., 1:91; and my "The development and diffusion of unanimous agreement in medieval Ashkenaz" in I. Twersky and J. Harris (eds.), *Studies in Medieval Jewish History and Literature* III (Cambridge, MA: 2000), 21–44.

custom as authentic and accurate. Indeed, Rashi himself had already provided a measure of justification for this custom. It should be noted that the justifications suggested by the various Tosafists differ, with Rabbenu Tam, once again, offering the most innovative approach.[14]

This case further demonstrates that the Tosafists who resolved possible conflicts between *metziut* and halakha were not simply trying to extricate the people of their day from difficult societal and economic situations. Also at stake for the Tosafists in this instance, and in most of the situations described above, was the fact that established Ashkenazic custom, which pre-dated the twelfth century and reflected the practices of a bona fide "holy community" (*kehila kedosha*), appeared to be at odds with the corpus of the Oral Law. Both Rabbenu Gershom and Rashi were aware of certain discrepancies, and occasionally offered their own solutions. It fell to the Tosafists of the twelfth century, however, and to their students, to not only systematically reconcile divergent talmudic and rabbinic sources, but also to reconcile these sources with accepted contemporary usage.[15]

Interestingly, Tosafists offered justifications and resolutions even in instances where the precise origins of the customs and practices in question were not indicated, suggesting that veneration of pre-Crusade customs was not predicated solely on any specific approbation given them by earlier rabbinic scholars. The nature and dedication of the Ashkenazic community itself, both before the First Crusade and after, played a role in the positions taken by its halakhic leaders. Jacob Katz has suggested that lay members of the medieval Ashkenazic community

14 See J. Katz, "Alterations in the time of the evening service: an example of the interrelationship between religious custom, halakha, and the social background" (Hebrew) *Zion* 35 (1970), 35–60 (also in *Halakha and Kabbala*, n. 7 above, 175–200). In his *Goy Shel Shabat* (Jerusalem: 1984), 43–56 [also available in English translation], Katz outlines the accepted (permissive) practices with regard to the services non-Jewish servants could perform in Jewish homes on the Sabbath. In this instance, there was a difference between northern French and German customs within Ashkenaz. See also Ta-Shma, n. 2 above, 149–167. For additional examples of halakhic adjustments due to realia in ritual and other non-economic contexts in medieval Ashkenaz, see Eric Zimmer, *Society and its Customs* (Hebrew), (Jerusalem: 1996), 163–167; E. Kanarfogel, "The *'aliyah* of 'three hundred rabbis' in 1211: Tosafist attitudes toward settling in the land of Israel," *JQR* 76 (1986), 191–215; idem, "Rabbinic authority and the right to open an academy in medieval Ashkenaz," *Michael* 12 (1991), 233–250; and see n. 8 above.

15 See Katz 1961, n. 7 above, 28–29.

can be characterized by both a strong "ritual instinct," an intuitive ability to avoid overstepping the boundaries of Jewish law, and a high degree of fealty to their rabbinic authorities (*kefifa lasamkhut*), that is, by a strong likelihood that they would follow what was prescribed by their rabbinic decisors.[16]

These tendencies were less prevalent, however, in non-Ashkenazic societies of the Middle Ages, which helps explain the differing profiles adopted by Ashkenazic and non-Ashkenazic *rishonim* in dealing with social and human concerns in the application of halakha. As the case of the time for the evening service indicates, Spanish and Provencal halakhists, and their Geonic predecessors, did not generally manifest a desire to find solutions to conflicts between *metziut* and halakha, as did the Tosafists.[17] In underscoring (and accounting for) this difference, Haym Soloveitchik has written:

> They [the scholars of Provence and Spain] never imagined that contemporary conduct was informative of talmudic law, that the deeds of the common folk were revelatory of Divine intent. The Franco-German community in its state of intense religiosity saw the word of God as being, as it were, incarnated in two forms: first, in the canonized literature (i.e., the Talmud); second, in the life of its people.[18]

## II

Israel Ta-Shma has recently compared and contrasted the views of modern scholars on the string of lenient rulings offered by Ashkenazic

16 See Katz 1984, n. 14 above, 173–183, and see also Zimmer, n. 14 above, 232–233. Katz's approach assumes that the practices in question were never undertaken for dishonorable reasons, thereby minimizing any differences between practices adopted, initially, by rabbinic figures, and those of laymen. Cf. my "Rabbinic attitudes toward nonobservance in the medieval period," in Jacob Schacter (ed.), *Jewish Tradition and the Non-Traditional Jew* (Montvale, NJ: 1992), 30–35.

17 This is largely true even for those Spanish and Provencal *rishonim* who are considered students of the Tosafists. See, e.g., my "Rabbinic attitudes," ibid., 17, n. 43, 33; and see n. 18 below. Cf. *Tosafot*, bKidushin 41a s.v. *asur laadam; Mordekhai*, Ketubot, sec. 179; Maimonides, *Code*, Laws concerning Marriage 3:19; and Ta-Shma, n. 2 above, 151–160, 241–253.

18 H. Soloveitchik, "Religious law and change: the medieval Ashkenazic example," *AJS Review* 12 (1987), 211–212, 221, and see also idem, *Pawnbroking: A Study in the Inter-Relationship Between Halakha, Economic Activity and Communal Self-Image* (Hebrew), (Jerusalem: 1985), 111–112, 119.

halakhists, and by Rabbenu Tam in particular, in situations of social need that were occasioned by changes or developments in the realia of their day.[19] Ta-Shma groups the views into two broader classes. The first includes solutions (proposed by Urbach, Albeck and Ben-Sasson) that attempt to identify Rabbenu Tam's intentions in his lenient rulings (that is, to ascertain how much weight, if any, should be given to societal needs, economic realities and the like), in light of his insistence (against the claims of R. Meshulam of Melun and others) that entrenched ritual customs and popular religious practices ought not be modified or streamlined, even when there was some halakhic basis for doing so.[20]

The second class, represented principally by Jacob Katz, stresses that Rabbenu Tam and the Tosafists were not the initiators of the lenient rulings and changes. Rather, the Ashkenazic community as a whole gradually accepted certain customs and usages over a period of time. The primary role of the Tosafists was to ratify those changes that were acceptable within traditional bounds, and to rule out any violations. As such, the focus was not so much on the broad halakhic tendencies or sensitivities of Rabbenu Tam and his colleagues, but rather on the nature of the community and the direction in which it was moving.

This is also the approach taken by Haym Soloveitchik, who maintains that it was the self-image of the medieval Ashkenazic community that allowed it to adopt practices and customs that appeared, prima

19 "Halakha and reality — the Tosafist experience," in Gilbert Dahan et al. (eds.), *Rashi et la culture juive en France du Nord au moyen age* (Paris: 1997), 315–329. This article is essentially an English translation, and partial re-working, of the third and fourth sections of the opening chapter of Ta-Shma 1996, n. 2 above, 19–35.

20 See above, nn. 4–6. According to Urbach, where vexing economic problems were involved, Rabbenu Tam sought to find lenient solutions, even as he wished to preserve the more stringent practices in other areas of Jewish law and ritual where such problems did not arise. It is therefore impossible to speak only of lenient tendencies with regard to Rabbenu Tam. Albeck maintains that Rabbenu Tam purposely pursued lenient rulings as a matter of common patterns of logical thinking, as well as the sense of justice prevalent in his day. Ben-Sasson argues, on the other hand, that while Rabbenu Tam understood that his lenient rulings would impact favorably on the people, he arrived at the interpretations that led to these conclusions without any pre-conceived notions or agenda. Rabbenu Tam believed that his interpretations and novellae *(hidushim)* penetrated the core of the meaning of the talmudic text, bringing the beneficent intentions of the Talmud to the fore.

facie, to conflict with talmudic law. The Ashkenazic community, due to a strong sense of its own religiosity, was confident that there were ultimately no disparities between its practices and Jewish law, and its halakhists were committed to aligning the law with accepted practice and tradition.[21]

Ta-Shma himself favors an approach that lies somewhere between the two categories just described. Employing interpretational models found among jurists in Pavia during the eleventh and twelfth centuries, as analyzed in the work of Charles Radding, Ta-Shma contrasts the methodology of pre-Crusade talmudic scholarship with Tosafist methodology. Pre-Crusade scholarship is characterized by extreme attention to linguistic and grammatical details and questions, and a desire to interpret texts according to their own narrow conceptions. The Tosafists, on the other hand, like the later Pavian jurists, were able to be more flexible in their interpretation of talmudic texts, and to examine the meanings of individual laws against more general legal conceptions.[22] The Tosafists' ability to address issues of *metziut* and halakha, and the lenient rulings that emerged, were not the result of a commitment on their part to resolve halakhic dilemmas along the lines of some particular pattern. Rather, these developments resulted from a new interpretive direction that elevated dialectic and harmonizing casuistry to a central position. In addition to their impact on direct textual interpretation, these methodologies opened new avenues and possibilities with regard to the interface between interpretation and practical application.

The wide range of views we have encountered in discussing various aspects of *metziut* and halakha in medieval Ashkenaz is ample evidence of the subtleties and complexities that pervade this subject. Indeed, as the first section of our study has shown, it is difficult to completely separate the various approaches described by Ta-Shma. Nevertheless, we have sketched the basic parameters involved, and outlined the theories that modern scholarship has put forward to

21 See Soloveitchik 1987, n. 18 above, 205–221. Ta-Shma 1996, n. 2 above, does not discuss Soloveitchik's view, though he mentions (p. 35, n. 22) that he is publishing a critique of it in a forthcoming study. See his, "The attitude of German halakhists to Aggadic sources: suicide and the killing of others as *kidush hashem*" (Hebrew) in Y.T. Assis et al. (eds.), *Facing the Cross* (Hebrew), (Jerusalem: 2000), 150–157.

22 Cf. my *Jewish Education and Society in the High Middle Ages* (Detroit: 1992), 69–74.

explain some rather interesting halakhic developments in medieval European Jewish society.

In the remainder of this study, I would like to move beyond these established parameters and discuss two additional questions. First, is there any evidence for stringent tendencies with regard to halakha and realia (מציאות והלכה לחומרא) in medieval Ashkenaz? That is, do Tosafists and other Ashkenazic halakhists accept and justify popular practices that appear to be more stringent than talmudic law, and if so, what strategies do they employ in so acting? The case for this part of the discussion will be the Ashkenazic responses to challenges of martyrdom (*kidush hashem*), which often entailed suicide or even the killing of others in the face of persecution, actions not easily countenanced by talmudic law.[23] Second, given the evidence for medieval Ashkenazic halakhists who, in light of various societal concerns, suggested or ratified customs and practices that appeared, at first blush, to diverge from talmudic law, do we find similar attitudes in cases involving more narrow human concerns or dilemmas? To address this question, a series of rulings by the Tosafist R. Tuvyah b. Elijah of Vienne[24] will be examined.

## III

A number of recent studies have reopened and refocused the question of how Ashkenazic Jewry justified the responses of suicide and the killing of family members in the face of severe persecution by Christians. In the perceived absence of bona fide halakhic discussion of these matters, two overarching theories have emerged. One proposes that the Ashkenazic community, with its high degree of piety and religious fervor, and the self-image these attitudes engendered, extended the parameters of the precept of *kidush hashem* to include not only voluntary martyrdom, but also suicide and the killing of others. To express

23 See Maimonides, *Code*, Laws concerning the Fundamental Principles of the Torah 5:1–5, and below, n. 42. Cf. Ta-Shma 1996, n. 2 above, 201–215, for the sustained stringency in medieval Ashkenaz concerning the status of the first-born offspring of a non-kosher animal in the Diaspora (*bekhor beheima tmeia behutz laaretz*).

24 Vienne is located in central eastern France, and is considered part of *Tzarfat*. It should not be confused with the Austrian city of Vienna. R. Tuvyah was a contemporary and close colleague of R. Yehiel of Paris. See Urbach 1980, n. 5 above, 1:486–492, and below, n. 93.

this development another way, the actions of Ashkenazic martyrs were considered, by their community, to represent Divine intent. These actions were therefore not only fully justified, but even worthy of emulation.[25]

A second view argues that Ashkenazic Jewry accepted as halakhic dicta the various models and guidelines for responses in situations of *kidush hashem* that are found in Midrashic and Aggadic literature. Although a number of medieval authorities did not consider Aggadic literature to be an appropriate source for halakhic practice,[26] it is possible to demonstrate that there were Ashkenazic rabbinic scholars who looked to the corpus of talmudic Aggada as an authentic legal source.[27] To be sure, instances of suicide in the name of *kidush hashem* can be documented more easily than situations involving the killing of others.[28] Interestingly, two pieces of manuscript evidence suggest that R. Judah Hehasid, among other Pietists, considered the ending of one's life through suicide to be a valid form of expiation of sin in certain circumstances.[29]

25 See Soloveitchik 1987, n. 18 above.

26 See, e.g., *Encyclopedia Talmudit* (Hebrew), v.1 (Jerusalem: 1973), 132; Menahem Elon, *Jewish Law* (Hebrew), (Jerusalem: 1988), 1:85–86.

27 See Avraham Grossman, "The origins of *kidush hashem* in early Ashkenaz" (Hebrew) in I. Gafni and A. Ravitzky (eds.), *The Sanctity of Life and Martyrdom* (Hebrew), (Jerusalem: 1993), 99–130; Ta-Shma, n. 21 above. In a paper presented recently at Tel Aviv University, Ta-Shma made this point with respect to a responsum of Ri regarding an informer that is preserved in Rabad's *Temim Deiim* (Warsaw: 1897), sec. 203.

28 Cf. Louis Rabinowitz, "The Massada martyrs according to the halakhah," *Tradition* 11 (1970): 31–37; idem, "The zealots' sucide at Massada" (Hebrew), *Sinai* 55 (1964), 329–332; R. Shlomo Goren, "The bravery at Massada in light of the halakha" (Hebrew), *Mahanayim* 87 (1964), 7–12; M.S. Neriah, "Suicide: the heroes of Massada in light of the halakha" (Hebrew), *Or Hamizrah* 8 (1961), 8–12.

29 See ms Bodl. 682, fol. 370r, and cf. Shlomo Spitzer, "Responsa of R. Judah the Pious on matters of repentance" (Hebrew), *Memorial Volume for R. Samuel Baruch Verner* (Hebrew), J. Buksbaum (ed.), (Jerusalem: 1996), 202; Simcha Emanuel in Avraham David (ed.), *From the Archives of the Institute for Microfilmed Manuscripts* (Hebrew), (Jerusalem: 1995), 105; and Ta-Shma 2000, n. 21 above. See also ms Paris (Bibliotheque Nationale) 1408, fol. 31 (sec. 88), and cf. Ephraim Kupfer, "A contribution to the chronicles of the family of R. Moses b. Yom-Tov 'the Noble' of London" (Hebrew), *Tarbiz* 40 (1971): 384–387; Urbach, n. 5. above, 2:498–499; Grossman, n. 27 above, 126–127; and idem, *The Early Sages of France* (Hebrew), (Jerusalem: 1995), 503–504. On suicide as a form of expiation of sin, see also R. Jacob Reischer, *Responsa Shevut Yaakov*, 2:111; idem, *Iyun Yaakov* on bKidushin 81b s.v. *salik veka yativ begave*; and Hida, *Birkei Yosef*, YD 345:2.

To properly assess the role of rabbinic decisors in this regard, we must consider several Tosafist formulations that have not, to my mind, received sufficient attention or analysis. Although these formulations address different aspects of martyrdom, what is common to them, and to their authors, suggests that at least some members of the rabbinic leadership of Ashkenaz did attempt to relate to these issues in conventional halakhic terms. These rabbinic scholars may well have been primarily interested in justifying the actions of their predecessors during the First Crusade and in similar contexts, but their formulations reflect more than self-image or the amassing of Aggadic texts.

Rabbenu Tam offers a cryptic justification of suicide in the face of conversionary efforts, a justification predicated on the effectiveness of torture. Rabbenu Tam was commenting on the talmudic passage describing the harsh death of R. Hanina (Hanania) b. Tradyon during the Hadrianic persecutions.[30] R. Hanina was tied up and set on fire, tufts of wool that had been soaked in water having been placed near his heart to prolong his fiery death. When his students asked R. Hanina why he did not open his mouth and allow the flames to end his life more quickly, he responded that Jewish law prohibits suicide even in this situation — "Better that the One who gave life should take it, but a person should not harm himself (*veal yahbol hu beatzmo*)."

The comment of Rabbenu Tam reads: "Rabbenu Tam stated that when a person harms [and kills] himself (דחובל והורג את עצמו) because he is fearful that non-Jews may compel him to transgress the Torah through torture or blows or a cruel death that he will not be able to withstand, he fulfills a religious precept when he harms himself (מצוה לחבול בעצמו)."[31] This ruling proposes that in a case unlike that of R. Hanina b. Tradyon, who was headed toward certain (albeit slow) death, if a Jew is concerned that a Gentile will resort to torture or other harsh physical means to compel him to violate cardinal sins (such as

30 bAvoda Zara 18a.

31 *"Omer rabeinu tam deheikhi dehovel vehoreg et atzmo mihamat shemityare shelo yahfuhu goyim al yedei yisurim umakot umita raa yoter laavor al divrei tora veyira shelo yukhal laamod bahem — mitzva lahbol beatzmo."* See *Tosafot*, Avoda Zara 18a s.v. *veal yahbol hu beazmo. Tosafot R. Elhanan* (see above, nn. 1, 3) attributes this ruling simply to R. Jacob. More significantly, in *Tosafot R. Elhanan*, the passage concludes with the phrase "he is **permitted** to harm himself (מותר לחבול בעצמו)." On the use of Aggada as a source for halakhic practice in the thought of Rabbenu Tam, see *Sefer Hayashar*, n. 12 above, 81, 85.

idolatry or adultery, which must be avoided even on pain of death), and the Jew is fearful he will be unable to maintain his convictions in face of the impending onslaught, he is permitted to take his own life (in advance, as it were) to avoid being compelled to commit any of these cardinal sins.

Rabbenu Tam's apparent extension of the talmudic passage to cover a situation different than that faced by R. Hanina b. Tradyon is fairly common in Tosafist methodology.[32] Nonetheless, *Tosafot R. Elhanan* considers the talmudic proof-text adduced by Rabbenu Tam in support of his ruling to be somewhat lacking. The proof-text[33] is the account of how 400 young men and women (*yeladim*) who had been taken captive in order to be violated ( נשבו לקלון ), cast themselves into the sea to avoid the illicit acts that would be demanded of them.[34] *Tosafot R. Elhanan* notes that in this case, the young people had no other way to avoid committing the illicit acts, as they were being held captive. This is not necessarily so, however, in the situation addressed by Rabbenu Tam. *Tosafot R. Elhanan* goes on to ratify Rabbenu Tam's ruling despite the distinction raised. At the same time, the weight or authority of this ruling is characterized as logical inference (*svara*), suggesting to some that Rabbenu Tam considered the permissibility of suicide in the face of persecution to be axiomatic, even in the absence of any firm talmudic proof-texts.[35]

And yet, two other elements of Rabbenu Tam's formulation, which have not been discussed by modern scholars, suggest that Rabbenu Tam proceeded with an eye to maintaining the standard halakhic character (and weight) of his ruling. Variant *Tosafot* texts cite an additional source, a passage in Genesis Rabbah, in support of R. Tam's view. The Midrash views King Saul's plan to kill himself rather than to allow

32 See, e.g., Urbach, n. 5 above, 2:676–680, 734–744.

33 bGitin 57b.

34 A parallel passage in Lamentations Rabbah, Buber ed. (Vilna: 1899), 81 on the verse "For these things I weep" (Lam. 1:13), characterizes this incident and its participants as follows: "Vespasian filled three ships with men and women from the finest families of Jerusalem, to participate in mortifying acts" (*aspasianus … mile shalosh sfinot anashim venashim migdolei yerushalayim lehaamidan lekalon beromi*). On the nature of the acts that were being demanded, see R. Elijah Joseph Rivlin, *Ohalei Yosef* (Jerusalem: 1868), 1b–2a.

35 See Soloveitchik 1987, n. 18 above, 210, n. 8, and Robert Chazan, *European Jewry and the First Crusade* (Berkeley: 1987), 156–157.

himself to be captured by the Philistines as a proper act.[36] This act is seen by the *Tosafot* texts as another example of permissible suicide, in that its goal is *kidush hashem*.[37]

Nonetheless, using the case of Saul to justify suicide in face of persecution has several palpable weaknesses. First, did Saul wish to kill himself to avoid being tortured by the Philistines into committing illicit acts, or did he do so to avoid the desecration of the Name of Heaven (*hilul hashem*) that would occur were a king of Israel captured and degraded by his enemies in front of his subjects? The latter purpose would provide less of a justification for the common Jew facing religious persecution. In addition, as other medieval Ashkenazic texts note, there is a dissenting rabbinic view that holds that King Saul acted inappropriately in seeking to end his life.[38] A close analysis of the *Tosafot* texts that cite the Midrash Rabbah passage about Saul shows that Rabbenu Tam himself never offered this passage as proof for his ruling,[39] thereby avoiding the difficulties just described.

Moreover, the core of Rabbenu Tam's formulation reflects an additional talmudic construct, on which it appears to have been based. The notion that torture may cause a Jew to succumb to an idolater's demands and commit idolatry (in the standard *Tosafot* Avoda Zara text, "lest the idolaters cause him to transgress through torture that he cannot withstand

36 See Midrash Rabbah 34 (on Gen. 9:5, "And even your blood of your lives will I require; at the hand of every beast will I require it" (*veakh et dimkhem lenafshoteikhem edrosh miyad kol haya edrashenu*)): "'Even' (*akh*) — to include one who strangles [kills] himself. Does this also include [King] Saul? No, this is excluded by 'even.' Does this include Hanania, Mishael and Azaria? No, this is excluded by 'even'" (*akh lehavi et hahonek* [*et*] *atzmo yakhol keshaul talmud lomar akh yakhol kehanania mishael veazaria talmud lomar akh*). See also Midrash Shmuel, parasha 24 (Lev. Rabbah, parasha 26:7).

37 See *Tosafot Harash Mishanz* (R. Samson of Sens) on Avoda Zara 18a (in *Shitat Hakadmonim Al Masekhet Avoda Zara*, ed. M.Y. Blau [NY: 1969], 65); *Gilyonei Hatosafot* cited in *Hidushei Haritva Lemasekhet Avoda Zara*, ad loc.; and *Tosafot Hakhmei Anglia Al Masekhet Avoda Zara*, ed. S. Sofer (Jerusalem: 1971), 151. See also R. Isaac of Corbeil, *Sefer Mitzvot Katan*, commandment 3; and R. Abraham b. Azriel, *Arugat Habosem*, ed. E.E. Urbach (Jerusalem: 1939), 1:222.

38 See *Sefer Orhot Haim Lerabi Aharon Hakohen Milunel*, part 2, vol. 1, ed. Moses Schlesinger (Berlin: 1899), 26 (sec. 4, the law of loving and fearing the Almighty); *Tosafot Hashalem*, ed. Jacob Gellis (Jerusalem: 1982), 262; and Chazan, n. 35 above, 155–156.

39 See above, n. 37.

" (פן יעבירום עובדי כוכבים עבירה כגון ע"י יסורין שלא יוכל לעמוד בהם) is more than a personal observation by Rabbenu Tam about human nature and potential. The Talmud records the Amora Rav's statement that had Hanania, Mishael and Azaria been beaten, they would have bowed to King Nebuchadnezzar's idol (אלמלי נגדוה לחנניה מישאל ועזריה [הוו] פלחו לצלמא) and would not have sanctified God's Name by jumping or being pushed into the fire, as recorded in the Book of Daniel.[40]

This talmudic formulation was certainly known to Rabbenu Tam. Rabbenu Tam offers his own analysis of it when he interprets a talmudic passage earlier in tractate Avoda Zara, fifteen folio pages before, but in the same chapter as, the story of R. Hanina b. Tradyon's death.[41] The case of Hanania, Mishael and Azaria, as understood by Rav and supported by the talmudic *sugya* in Ketubot, unequivocally testifies to the power of torture in situations of *kidush hashem*, and places it in a halakhic framework. Although the story of Hanania, Mishael and Azaria is anecdotal, rather than a reflection of talmudic legal theory per se, the fact that this story is found in the biblical corpus gives it much greater weight in the halakhic context than the purely Aggadic rendition of the fate of the 400 young people. Indeed, Maimonides too supports his conception of *kidush hashem* (which was markedly different from that of his Ashkenazic contemporaries in that he did not recognize voluntary martyrdom of any kind) by citing Hanania, Mishael and Azaria as role-models who were prepared, appropriately, to give up their lives rather than submit to forced idol-worship.[42]

A possible difficulty with this analysis is that Rabbenu Tam does not mention the case of Hanania, Mishael and Azaria explicitly, even as he enunciates and employs its underlying principle. To be sure, a *Tosafot*

40 See bKetubot 33a–33b.

41 See below, n. 48.

42 See *Code*, Laws concerning the Fundamental Principles of the Torah 5:4; idem, *Book of Precepts*, positive commandment 9; *Igrot Harambam*, ed. Y. Shilat (Jerusalem: 1987), 1:41 (*Igeret Hashmad*), and cf. 1:24 (*Igeret Teiman*), and below, n. 46. Hanania, Mishael and Azaria are also assigned a significant role in the Crusade Chronicles. See, e.g., Chazan, n. 35 above, 117–121, 162–163, 220–221; Ivan Marcus, "From politics to martyrdom," *Prooftexts* 2 (1982), 45. See also the Aramaic liturgical poem about Hanania, Mishael and Azaria, and commentary thereon, in *Mahzor Vitry*, ed. S. Hurwitz (reprinted Jerusalem: 1969), 320–323, 337–338, and cf. Ta-Shma, "The commentary to the Aramaic *piyutim* included in the *Mahzor Vitry*" (Hebrew), *Kiryat Sefer* 57 (1982), 701–705.

text in Gitin that is clearly parallel to the Rabbenu Tam passage does cite the case of Hanania, Mishael and Azaria.[43] *Tosafot* Gitin opens with the position of R. Hanania b. Tradyon, which appears to contradict the response of the 400 young people (he did not commit suicide; they did). The *Tosafot* text resolves the apparent contradiction by maintaining that, "here [in Gitin, in the case of youngsters], they were fearful of the torture (*yereiim hayu miyisurin*), as demonstrated [by the *sugya*] in Ketubot that Hanania, Mishael and Azaria would have bowed to the *tzelem* had they been struck." In the case of the young people, they were susceptible to being beaten and tortured as a means of coercion rather than simply killed if they resisted. They had not been captured in order to be killed; they were taken in order to be violated. In *Tosafot Gitin*, then, the case of Hanania, Mishael and Azaria is being used precisely as intimated in the formulation attributed to Rabbenu Tam in *Tosafot* Avoda Zara. But *Tosafot* Gitin does not mention the name of Rabbenu Tam.[44]

43 See *Tosafot* Gitin 57b s.v. *kaftzu kulan*. See also *Tosafot Harosh* ad loc., and ms Parma (Palatina) 325, fol. 198v.

44 R. Alexander Suslin Hakohen of Frankfurt (d.1349), in his *Sefer Aguda* on Gitin ad loc. (ed. E. Brizel, 73), attributes the *Tosafot Gitin* passage to R. Isaac of Dampierre (Ri):

פר"י הא דאמר' בע"א מוטב שיטלנה מי שנתנה ואל יחבול הוא בעצמו הכא יראים מיסורים כדאמרינן אלמלא נגדו וכו'.

The *Sefer Aguda* version concludes with the observation that "from here is a proof for those who kill themselves and their beloved children at the time of persecution" (*umikan semakh leotan shehorgin et atzmam veet beneihem bar minan beshaat gzeirot*). Ri was undoubtedly aware of R. Tam's position, as suggested, also, by its inclusion in *Tosafot R. Elhanan* and *Tosafot Shanz* on Avoda Zara. See above, nn. 31, 37, and R. H.J.D. Azoulay (Hida), *Responsa Haim Shaal*, #46, but cf. *Tosafot* Baba Kama 91b s.v. *ela hai tana; Yam Shel Shlomo*, Baba Kama 8:59; and Soloveitchik, n. 35 above. The standard *Tosafot* Gitin are of French origin; see Urbach, n. 5 above, 2:633–634. The *Tosafot*'s comment in Gitin is also similar to one in Avoda Zara re the precision of its proofs; see text above at n. 39.

An anonymous Tosafist biblical compilation adduces a passage in Midrash Rabbah that construes the actions of Hanania, Mishael and Azaria as an allowance for an individual who is afraid he will be unable to withstand presssure to commit suicide; see nn. 36, 38 above, and n. 59 below.

Nonetheless, there are two ways to explain the fact that Rabbenu Tam does not refer explicitly to Hanania, Mishael and Azaria in *Tosafot* Avoda Zara. First, there is another talmudic passage, in bBaba Metzia 86a, which openly presumes the coercive powers of torture, and is interpreted in this manner by Rashi. The Talmud describes how Rabbah bar Nahmani, while being pursued by tax officers, stopped to help an innkeeper in need. Rabbah later asked the innkeeper not to disclose to the authorities that he had seen Rabbah. In his gratitude to Rabbah, the innkeeper stated that "if they threaten me with death, I will not reveal your presence. But if they torture me [in the Aramaic of the Talmud, *"vei negidei menagdin li,"* which Rashi interprets in Hebrew as *"veim yisruni"*], I will be forced to reveal the information." This suggests that the effects of torture were readily known or assumed by the Talmud and its best-known interpreter. As such, the possible effects of torture, which the Talmud itself regards as self-evident, do not require additional proof.[45]

There may also be a more subtle reason why Rabbenu Tam was content to refer only to the concept that informed the actions of Hanania, Mishael and Azaria, without mentioning them by name.

45 R. Eliezer of Metz, a leading student of Rabbenu Tam, is cited in *Shita Mekubetzet* on Ketubot 33b s.v. *uvakuntresin katuv*, as holding the unusual view that one must give up only his life *al kidush hashem* (as per the literal reading of the biblical phrase, "with all your soul" (*bekhol nafshekha*). Torture (*yisurim*) is so harsh, however, that there is never an obligation to submit to it. This is the meaning of the talmudic passage — Hanania and the others would have submitted in the face of torture (beatings). Rabbenu Tam apparently responded to R. Eliezer's claim with the description of what was done to R. Akiva, "they raked his skin with combs of iron and he did not submit" (*shesarku et besaro bemasreikot shel barzel velo palah*). R. Akiva endured both torture and death in the name of *kidush hashem* (and see also *Tosafot* Ketubot, n. 47 below). For R. Eliezer of Metz, the type of torture perpetrated on R. Akiva contributed directly to his impending death. Any form of sustained torture, such or lashes and beatings administered over a period of time (*hakaa sheein la kitzba*), need not be endured in the name of *kidush hashem*. The *Shita Mekubetzet* passage ultimately rejects the view of R. Eliezer, in favor of that of Rabbenu Tam. Cf. *Hidushei Haritva Lemasekhet Ketubot*, ed. M. Goldstein (Jerusalem: 1982), 281; *Tosafot Rid Al Masekhet Avoda Zara*, ed. N. Zaks (Jerusalem: 1979), 5–7, n. 24; *Responsa Maharik*, #24 s.v. *asher taan*; R. Elijah Joseph Rivlin, *Ohalei Yosef*, fols. 24a–25b; Ta-Shma, "Aspects of heroism in the halakha" (Hebrew), *Mahanayim* 87 (1964), 74–75; Edward Peters, *Torture*, NY: 1985, 40–73; n. 57 below.

There are talmudic *sugyot* which suggest that Hanania, Mishael and Azaria were acting *lifnim mishurat hadin*, doing more than what was obligatory according to the letter of the law.[46] In light of these *sugyot*, Rabbenu Tam interprets the *tzelem* to which they were being forced to bow down by Nebuchadnezzar as a representation of the ruler rather than an actual object of idolatry. Hanania, Mishael and Azaria were committing a voluntary act of *kidush hashem* for something that was not technically idolatry. In accordance with this view, Rabbenu Tam interprets Rav's statement that had Hanania, Mishael and Azaria been tortured they would have succumbed to the pressure and bowed to the *tzelem*, to mean that since torture can be more painful than death, they would not have acted *lifnim mishurat hadin* in the face of torture, but would have bowed down to it, since the *tzelem* was not really an idol in any event.[47]

On this interpretation, the power of torture, as indicated by the case of Hanania, Mishael and Azaria, is still presupposed. But the case itself could not be cited to justify suicide at a time of persecution, where actual idolatry was at stake, because the situations were not the same. Nonetheless, the key element for Rabbenu Tam in *Tosafot* Avoda Zara is the power of torture, which might cause simple Jews to succumb and commit cardinal sins, just as it would have persuaded the exceptionally righteous and steadfast Hanania, Mishael and Azaria to waver, at their own level, in a *lifnim mishurat hadin* context.[48]

46 See bPesahim 53b: "What caused Hanania, Mishael and Azaria to give themselves to the fiery furnace as a santification of the Name?" This implies that their response was not mandatory. See also bSanhedrin 93a, "And now I grasped just the one bough (*sinsan ehad*) of Hanania, Mishael and Azaria"; and cf. bTaanit 18b, "Hanania, Mishael and Azaria were totally righteous and were worthy that a miracle should have been done for them."

47 See *Tosafot* Avoda Zara 3a s.v. *shelo histahavu latzelem; Tosafot* Pesahim 53b s.v. *ma rau hanania mishael vaazaria; Tosafot* Ketubot 33b s.v. *ilmale nigduhu; Tosafot Harashba Mishanz Al Masekhet Ketubot*, ed. Abraham Liss (Jerusalem: 1973), 62; *Sanhedrei Gedola*, v. 6 (Likutei Tosafot Shanz), ed. Y. Lifshitz (Jerusalem: 1974), 242 (sec. 289). Cf. *Hidushei Harashba Lemasekhet Ketubot*, ed. Moshe Hershler (Jerusalem: 1973), 102, citing Midrash Hazita (Song of Songs Rabbah), 7:8; and *Hidushei Haramban Lemasekhet Ketubot*, ed. Ezra Chwat (Jerusalem: 1990), 148.

48 *Nimukei Yosef*, Sanhedrin, ch. 8 at the end, writes that Hanania, Mishael and Azaria represent a paradigm (at least for devoted religious leaders) for giving up one's life for *kidush hashem*, even in situations where there is no obligation to do so: "But if a leading figure who is pious and Heaven-fearing

This explanation yields another important point. Had Rabbenu Tam wished to adduce an explicit, air-tight proof-text for suicide, he could have interpreted the *lifnim mishurat hadin* aspect of the case of Hanania, Mishael and Azaria as R. Isaac of Dampierre (Ri) did. According to Ri, genuine idolatry (*avoda zara*) was at stake (the *tzelem* was an actual figure of an idol and not merely a representation of the ruler), but Hanania, Mishael and Azaria could have escaped at some earlier point (as Daniel did). It was their decision to remain and to prepare themselves to die *al kidush hashem* that was beyond the letter of the law.[49]

Due to other considerations of talmudic exegesis, however, Rabbenu Tam preferred his approach.[50] Thus, even as Rabbenu Tam (in *Tosafot* Avoda Zara) sought to justify the actions of those who committed suicide, he did so according to his usual high standards of talmudic interpretation, relying on the acknowledged power of torture (*yisurim*) that emerges from the case of Hanania, Mishael and Azaria (and is presumed in other *sugyot* as well), while being careful to preserve what was unique about their act by not mentioning them by

---

sees that his generation is loose, he is permitted to sanctify the Name and give himself [to death] even over a simple precept, so that the people will see and will learn to fear the Name and to love Him with all their hearts (*aval im hu adam gadol vehasid yire shamayim veroe shehador parutz hakha reshai lekadesh hashem velimsor atzmo afilu al mitzva kala kedei sheyiru haam veyilmedu leyira et hashem leahavo bekhol libam vehainu deamrinan ma rau hanania mishael veazaria shehepilu et atzmam lekavshan haesh*)."

The approach of *Nimukei Yosef* can also shed light on the Maimonidean perspective on the actions of Hanania, Mishael and Azaria (above, n. 42). See Ta-Shma, "Giving up one's life out of devotion in Jewish law" (Hebrew), *Mahanayim* 41 (1960): 101–105; Efrat Yakovson, "Premeditated suicide" (Hebrew), *Michlol* 1 (1991): 53–54.

49 For Ri's interpretation, see *Tosafot* Pesahim 53b s.v. *ma rau*. See also *Sanhedrei Gedola*, n. 47 above, 241 (sec. 288); *Arugat Habosem*, n. 37 above; and cf. above, n. 44. For the interpretation of R. Meir, father of Rabbenu Tam, see also *Sefer Hayashar* (Helek Hahidushim), sec. 354, and *Tosafot Rashba Mishanz Al Masekhet Pesahim*, ed. M.Y. From (Jerusalem: 1956): 139.

50 For example, the *sugya* in Avoda Zara 3a compares Hanania, Mishael and Azaria (among other righteous figures) with Abraham. Abraham is credited with not committing idolatry (and allowing himself to be thrown by Nimrod into the furnace rather than so acting), while Hanania, Mishael and Azaria are credited with not bowing to the *tzelem*. This comparison clearly suggests that actual idolatry was not at stake in their case (as it was for Abraham).

name. Rabbenu Tam did not manipulate talmudic texts to serve his purpose when he sought to justify contemporary practices. Rather, he achieved his aim through incisive interpretation.[51]

## IV

Ritva on Avoda Zara 18a, citing an otherwise unidentified marginal note or text in *Gilyonei Hatosafot*, indicates that those who killed their children and other family members at times of religious persecution, to prevent them from being compelled to convert to Christianity, did so, in part, on the basis of Rabbenu Tam's formulation. Although the coercive power of torture would certainly be applicable to children and other dependents, Rabbenu Tam himself never discussed the killing of others *al kidush hashem*. Indeed, there are virtually no medieval halakhic sources that discuss this type of action. Ritva notes unnamed "great scholars of France" (*gdolei tzorfat*) who ruled that it was permissible, but their rulings are not extant.

One of the only extant rabbinic statements of justification for killing others is a formulation attributed by R. Moses of Zurich to the leading German Tosafist of the late twelfth and early thirteenth centuries, R. Eliezer b. Joel Halevi (Rabia): "Those holy martyrs, who slaughtered themselves and their children when put to the test, because they did not want to rely on themselves [as the Rabbis said, do not trust yourself [not to sin] until the day of your death], and they were afraid lest they desecrate the Name of Heaven due to the pressure of compulsion, have all earned a share in the world to come, and are considered completely holy."[52] The fact that this ruling is found, however, in R. Moses of Zurich's fourteenth-century commentary on R. Isaac of Corbeil's *Sefer Mizvot Katan* (*Semak* of Zurich) raises questions

51 Cf. above, n. 20, and text at n. 22, and my "Unanimity, majority and communal government in Ashkenaz during the High Middle Ages," *PAAJR* 58 (1992), 79–106.

52 *Sefer Semak Mitzurikh*, ed. Y. Har Shoshanim, v.1 (Jerusalem: 1973), 57–58, cited by A. Grossman, n. 27 above, 115–116.

ואותם הקדושים ששחטו את עצמם וזרעם כשבאו לידי נסיון מפני שלא רצו לסמוך על דעתם דאמרו רבותינו אל תאמין בעצמך עד יום מותך והיו יראים שעל ידי אונס יהא שם שמים מחולל על ידם .כולם יש להם חלק לעולם הבא וקדושים גמורים הם.

Rabia is referred to in this text by the name of his work, *Avi Haezri*.

about its authenticity, or at least about its attribution to Rabia.[53] Even if there are no other texts of its kind, confirming the attribution of this text to Rabia would give it great significance.

Recent manuscript research has revealed that this formulation by Rabia also appears in the work of a northern French Tosafist from the mid-thirteenth century, composed within one generation of Rabia. R. Abraham b. Ephraim (a student of the Tosafist R. Tuvyah of Vienne) authored a halakhic work, based on R. Moses of Coucy's *Sefer Mizvot Gadol*, entitled *Sefer Simanei Taryag Mitzvot*.[54] In discussing the precept of *kidush hashem*, R. Abraham reproduces the Rabia passage. It should be noted that *Semak* of Zurich cites a number of comments from the *Sefer Simanei Taryag Mitzvot*, and it is likely that the Rabia text reached the *Semak* of Zurich from R. Abraham's work.[55]

To be sure, R. Meir of Rothenburg, in his understated yet poignant responsum in defense of a Jew who had killed his family in anticipation of conversionary efforts during a pogrom in Koblenz, only to have his own life spared, does not cite the formulation of Rabia.[56] This would not be the only instance, however, in which a later Tosafist was unaware of a predecessor's formulation, even a momentous ruling such as that under discussion. Indeed, Maharam does not mention the formulation of Rabbenu Tam, discussed above, either, even as he presents elements of common material. R. Meir bases his defense, for the most part, on the imperative of not casting aspersions on (the positions

53 The very existence of the phenomenon indicates that there were Ashkenazic rabbinic leaders who approved, at least tacitly, of killing others at a time of religious persecution. On the other hand, unnamed as well as otherwise unknown rabbis are mentioned as holding that such actions are prohibited. See *Tosafot Hashalem*, n. 38 above, and Soloveitchik, n. 35 above.

54 See ms Paris 392 (Ashkenaz, 1271), fol. 5r; ms Paris 1408 (Ashkenaz, fourteenth century), fol. 175v. This passage was transcribed, as part of a larger selection, by Abraham Havazelet, "R. Abraham b. Ephraim's *Sefer Simanei Mitzvot*" (Hebrew), in David Lau (ed.), *R. Isaac Yedidya Frankel Memorial Volume* (Hebrew), (Jerusalem: 1992), 290–291. A later manuscript cluster omits the reference to *Avi Haezri*. For a description of the manuscripts and their interrelationship, see Havazelet's introduction to his transcription, 286–287. On the provenance and dating of this work, see also Ivor Wolfson. "The Parma colophon of Abraham b. Ephraim's *Book of Precepts*," *Journal of Jewish Studies* 12 (1970), 39–40.

55 See Havazelet, ibid., 285, and cf. n. 60 below.

56 See R. Meir of Rothenburg, *Teshuvot, Pesakim Uminhagim*, ed. Y.Z. Kahana, v. 2 (Jerusalem: 1960), 54, sec. 59.

espoused by) predecessors (*hotzaat laaz al harishonim*), a principle that carried a degree of halakhic valence in twelfth and thirteenth-century Ashkenaz.[57] Since earlier Ashkenazic scholars of great stature (*gedolim*) killed their children in the face of persecution, for Maharam to intimate that the Jew of Koblenz acted inappropriately in any way would cast aspersions on the actions of these venerable earlier figures.[58]

Although R. Meir of Rothenburg does not mention the ruling of Rabia, a gloss by the Tosafist R. Peretz b. Elijah of Corbeil (a contemporary of Maharam) on the discussion of the precept of *kidush hashem* in *Sefer Mitzvot Katan*, cites an abbreviated version of the Rabia passage verbatim (albeit without attribution). This gloss provides additional evidence that this ruling was not unfamiliar in thirteenth-century Ashkenaz.[59]

57 On the reasoning behind the reponsum of Maharam, cf. David Berger, *The Jewish-Christian Debate in the High Middle Ages* (Philadelphia: 1979), 25–26; Chazan, n. 35 above, 156–158; and Soloveitchik 1987, n. 18 above, 208–209. Like Rabbenu Tam, R. Meir of Rothenburg considers the situation of Hanania, Mishael and Azaria evidence that sustained torture (*yisurin sheein lahen kitzva*) is worse than death, and may cause one to succumb to idolatry. See *Responsa Maharam*, ed. Prague, #39, 938, and n. 45 above. Interestingly, Maharam held that martyrs feel no pain at the time of their death, see #517; and see David Tamar in *Kiryat Sefer* 33 (1948), 376; and my *'Peering Through the Lattices': Mystical, Magical and Pietistic Dimensions in the Tosafist Period* (Detroit: 2000), 123–124. For another example of Maharam's (initial) unawareness of an important position held by Rabbenu Tam, see his responsum #941 (at the end).

58 See Eliav Shochetman, "The concern for *la'az 'al ha-Rishonim* as a consideration in determining the halakha" (Hebrew), *Sefer Bar Ilan* 18–19 (1981), 170–195, and *Responsa R. Haim Or Zarua*, #167.

59 See *Hagahot Rabeinu Peretz Lesefer Mitzvot Katan*, commandment 3 (gloss 5): "Those holy people who slaughtered themselves and did not rely on themselves are completely holy, as can be proven from [King] Saul. And one cannot raise a question from [the case of] R. Hanina b. Tradyon, who did not open his mouth, etc., since he knew that the Name of Heaven would not be defiled by him"

ואותם הקדושים ששחטו עצמם שלא סמכו דעתם לעמוד בנסיון קדושים גמורים הם וראיה משאול.ואין להקשות מר' חנינא בן תרדיון שלא רצה לפתוח פיו וכו' שיודע היה בעצמו שלא יתחלל שמים על ידו

(On R. Peretz's view, akin to that of R. Meir of Rothenburg, that martyrs feel no pain, see Kanarfogel, n. 57 above, 124.) See also the *Orhot Haim* and *Tosafot Hashalem*, cited above, n. 38, which present an (anonymous) justification for the killing of others from the Hanania, Mishael and Azaria, and King Saul, cases. The subsequent objection recorded in these texts discounts both cases, although the rejection of the possible proof from King Saul is more strongly worded. Cf. Soloveitchik, n. 35 above.

A further look at the Rabia passage, and its placement in *Sefer Simanei Taryag Mitzvot*, is in order. Following his initial statement about the permissibility of killing others at a time of persecution if their ability to withstand torture is uncertain, Rabia supports his view by citing the case of the 400 young people in Gitin, and the scriptural derivation found in the Midrash Rabbah to justify suicide in the face of torture, without mentioning the specific case of King Saul.[60] Rabia also cautions that one should not question these actions on the basis of the case of R. Hanina b. Tradyon, who did not take his own life, because R. Hanina knew that there was no chance that he would be untied and then coerced into committing an act of desecration of the Name of Heaven. The *Semak* of Zurich version of the Rabia passage mentions an additional justification for killing the young children, not found in *Sefer Simanei Taryag Mitzvot*. Just as in the case of a stubborn and rebellious son (*ben sorer umore*), where the Torah allowed for the disobedient son to be put to death, so that he would die innocently rather than be allowed to accrue the collection of grave sins he almost inevitably would were he to live, it was appropriate to kill these young children now as innocents, since we are fearful that if they were forcibly converted, they would then live the rest of their lives as Christians.

Leaving aside the unusual *ben sorer umore* analogue (whose appearance only in the derivative *Semak* of Zurich version suggests that it was not part of Rabia's original formulation), there is an obvious similarity between the Rabia passage and the formulation of Rabbenu Tam discussed above. The Aggadic proof-texts are the same, or rather, selectively limited in the same way. Rabia also presumes the terrible impact of torture: "they were afraid that they would be compelled to desecrate the Name of Heaven" ( יראים שעל ידי אונס יהא שם שמים מחולל על ידם ), adding the rabbinic aphorism "do not trust yourself until the day of your death" (*al taamin beatzmekha ad yom motkha*) found in Ethics of the

60 The reference to Saul is omitted only by the earliest manuscripts of the *Simanei Taryag Mitzvot* text, which attach the scriptural derivation found in Midrash Rabbah to "the case that we have mentioned" (*kemaase sheamarnu*). See Havazelet, n. 54 above, 290 n. 32, and n. 54 above. As will be discussed below, the antecedent case in *Simanei Taryag Mitzvot* (also referred to by Midrash Rabbah; see n. 36 above) is that of Hanania, Mishael and Azaria. Saul's name is included, however, in the later *Hagahot R. Peretz* and *Semak Mitzurikh* versions. The only other significant difference between the *Sefer Simanei Taryag Mitzvot* and *Semak Mitzurikh* passages concerns the reference to *ben sorer umore*; see below.

Fathers (mAvot 2:4) and cited in bBerakhot 29a. Even more noteworthy, however, is the way R. Abraham b. Ephraim inserts the Rabia passage into his work.

In discussing the precept of *kidush hashem*, R. Abraham begins, as is his wont, with a paraphrase of this precept as it appears in *Sefer Mitzvot Gadol*.[61] R. Abraham concludes his paraphrase of the *Semag* with the notion that a person who is prepared to meet his death as a martyr should not do so relying on the possibility that a Divinely ordained miracle will spare him at the last moment: "When one gives himself [to martyrdom], he should not rely on a miracle's occurring, for anyone who relies on a miracle will not have a miracle performed for him (וכשמוסר עצמו, לא יהא סומך על הנס, שכל הסומך על הנס אין עושין לו נס)." This point is supported by a passage from Sifra[62] which asserts, based on verses in the third chapter of the Book of Daniel,[63] that Hanania, Mishael and Azaria were careful to demonstrate their readiness to give up their lives without any expectation of a miraculous intervention.

R. Abraham then cites the Rabia passage: "And those holy martyrs, who slaughtered themselves and their children… (ואותם הקדושים ששחטו את עצמם וזרעם וכו')." In the manuscripts of *Sefer Simanei Taryag Mitzvot*, this passage is not set off from the preceding one, and it begins with a conjunction ואותם. The juxtaposition of the *Semag* and Rabia passages by R. Abraham (also found in the *Semak* of Zurich version)[64] yields the following line of argument. The behavior of Hanania, Mishael and Azaria serves as a paradigm for the behavior of other Jewish martyrs. Hanania, Mishael and Azaria were prepared to accept their fate without relying on miracles, as must all martyrs. Other

61 See *Semag*, positive commandment 5, and cf. Havazelet, n. 54 above, 282.

62 Sifra, ed. I.H. Weiss (NY: 1946), fol. 99b (Emor), on Leviticus 22:32: "Do not defile My Holy Name, and sanctify Me in the midst of the children of Israel"; cf. bShabat 32a; bTaanit 20b; and above, n. 46.

63 Daniel 3:17–18: "If our God whom we serve, is able to deliver us, He will deliver us from the fiery furnace and out of your hand, O king. But if not, be it known to you, O king, that we will not serve your gods nor worship the golden image which you have set up."

64 In *Semak Mitzurikh*, the *Semak* text (commandment 6) concludes with the notion that one who is prepared to give his life for the sanctification of the Name of Heaven may not do so with the expectation that a miracle will occur. The *Semak Mitzurikh* gloss (sec. 19) cites the proof from Hanania, Mishael and Azaria, and then continues with the defense of those martyrs (*kedoshim*) who killed themselves and their children for the sanctification of the Name of Heaven.

Jews in situations of *kidush hashem* were likewise to be commended for accepting their fate, and, lest they falter, not relying on themselves to resist the various forms of compulsion and coercion that could be employed. The possibility of wavering (or of being co-opted against their will) would be especially true for children. It appears that R. Abraham b. Ephraim, like Rabbenu Tam, wished to utilize the biblical example of Hanania, Mishael and Azaria to buttress his halakhic position in support of martyrdom.[65]

Similarly, his juxtaposition of "do not rely on a miracle" (לא יהא סומך על הנס) from his paraphrase of *Semag*, and "they did not want to rely on themselves" (שלא רצו לסמוך על דעתן) from the Rabia passage, is not merely a literary device. The pairing of these texts suggests that knowing one's limitations when faced with death, especially when confronted by coercive forces (אונס), is a talmudic or rabbinic imperative. Whether this was Rabia's view as well, or only that of R. Abraham b. Ephraim, cannot be determined with absolute certainty.

In sum, Tosafists in northern France and Germany during the high Middle Ages endeavored to present well-based halakhic support for the actions of the martyrs. They chose their proof-texts carefully, adducing similar arguments and avoiding the more speculative Aggadic material, while highlighting the response of Hanania, Mishael and Azaria, just as did Maimonides. These carefully crafted Tosafist formulations demonstrate the existence of a measure of halakhic justification by leading rabbinic scholars for the phenomenon of medieval Ashkenazic martyrdom, in addition to any considerations of devotion or piety.[66]

## V

The following ruling by R. Tuvyah of Vienne, issued in a widely-discussed case of domestic law, is recorded in *Sefer Simanei Taryag Mitzvot*, the halakhic compendium of his student R. Abraham b. Ephraim:

> There was an incident in which a woman gave her son to [the care of] a nursemaid. A very stringent oath that has no means of being renounced was administered to the nursemaid, enjoining her from stopping to nurse

65 See also n. 60 above.

66 Cf. Israel Yuval, "Vengeance and damnation, blood and defamation: from Jewish martyrdom to blood libel accusations" (Hebrew), *Zion* 58 (1993), 66–75, and Abraham Gross, "On the Ashkenazi syndrome of Jewish martyrdom in Portugal in 1497" (Hebrew), *Tarbiz* 64 (1995), 96–97, n. 34.

> the child until 24 months [had passed]. Following this [binding oath], the mother married a *kohen* named R. Jacob Sevara of Cracow in Poland, who was a great scholar with vast knowledge of the Talmud. The greatest scholars of the generation challenged his position and almost wished to place a ban on him. They sent responsa [supporting their position] far to the west and to the south, and his [R. Jacob's] words reached my teacher R. Tuvyah. My teacher ruled that since it is clear that the nursemaid will not back out [quit] because of the very severe oath, he should not be compelled to divorce her. And even if he has not yet married her, he may do so without any impediment, as the Talmud [in a chapter of tractate Ketubot] relates that Rav Nahman allowed the house of the Exilarch to act thus, because once they give their children to a nursemaid, she would never quit. And the matter requires further study.[67]

There are no remnants of the exchange of letters referred to in this passage. A responsum by R. Isaac b. Moses *Or Zarua* is preserved, in which R. Isaac sides with the view of the rabbinic majority against the position held by R. Jacob Hakohen Sevara of Cracow (and R. Tuvyah of Vienne). Neither a binding oath — nor even a sizable security bond (*eravon gadol*) — can guarantee that the nursemaid will remain at her post (and not depart at some point in order to marry or for some other personal reason). The material in *Sefer Or Zarua* indicates that R. Moses b. Hisdai (Taku) of Regensburg, and other scholars of the region, also ruled against R. Jacob, as did an unnamed northern French scholar (*gaon ehad migeonei tzorfat*), who concluded that "there are no grounds to permit" the arrangement suggested by R. Jacob.[68]

According to the Talmud, a nursing widow may not remarry within twenty four months of the birth of her child, because this may cause her to stop nursing the child (which is not in the child's best

67 Ms Vatican 176, fols. 50v–51r; Moscow 1, fol. 22v; ms Parma 813, fol. 43r:

> מעשה הָיה באישה שנתנה בנה למינקת על דעת רבים בשבועה דאורייתא, שבועה חמורה שאין בה התרה, שלא תחזור בה מלהניק הבן עד כ"ד חודש. ואח"כ נישאת האם לכהן אחד ושמו הרב יעקב סברו מקרקו היושב בפולנייא, חכם גדול ובקי בכל התלמוד. ונחלקו עליו גדולי הדור וכמעט ורצו להרחיקו. ושלח תשובות לקצווי ים ודרום. והגיעו דבריו עד מורי הר' טוביה. והורה מורי מאחר דפשיטא לן דלא תיהדר מתוך חומר השבועה אין קופין אותו להוציא. ואפי' אם לא כנס יכנוס לכתחילה, כדאמרי' בפרק אף על פי רב נחמן שרא לבי ריש גלותא משום דכי יהבי בנייהו למינקת לא הדר להו. וצ"ע.

For other versions and citations of this passage, see Ta-Shma, "On the history of Polish Jewry in the twelfth and thirteenth centuries" (Hebrew), *Zion* 53 (1988), 353.

68 See *Sefer Or Zarua*, part. 1, Responsa, sec. 740, and Ta-Shma, ibid., 354–355. Ta-Shma suggests that rabbinic reports and discussion of this incident were subject to internal censorship. He maintains that the incident occurred between 1225 and 1234, while Urbach dates the incident to 1245.

interests). Although there is a Tannaitic dispute as to how long she must wait, with some advocating a shorter period of time, both Rav and Samuel agree to the twenty-four month waiting period.[69]

Rashi explains more precisely the concern for the child that mandates the waiting period. If the woman is allowed to remarry, she may become pregnant, which will, in turn, force her to wean the first child. Since the new husband is not the father of the first child, there is concern lest the husband refuse to provide his wife's child with the (additional) milk and eggs that are necessary for his nutrition if he can no longer nurse.[70] The Talmud maintains that even if the mother gave the child to a nursemaid, or if she had already weaned him, she may not remarry before the twenty-four month period ends. As Rashi explains, these provisions are a precaution to prevent the mother from purposely weaning the child in order to be able to remarry.[71] The Babylonian Talmud suggests that perhaps they must be adhered to even if the first child dies, lest a mother be tempted to kill her child in order to remarry. Although the Babylonian Talmud rejects this last possibility as extreme (and this is the view codified by Maimonides),[72] the parallel passage in the Jerusalem Talmud retains the restriction, even where the first child has died.

---

See R. Abraham b. Azriel, n. 37 above, v. 4, 120–121. R. Meir of Rothenburg was also among those who ruled strongly against the position of R. Jacob, although perhaps not at the time of the incident itself. (The *Mordekhai*, Jebamot, sec. 19, records the ruling from northern France as a responsum of Ri the Elder; see also *Beit Yosef*, EH 13 s.v. *afilu im gemala hanaar*. This attribution is problematic, however, in light of the dating of the incident, and the other rabbinic figures involved.)

69 A passage in a responsum of R. Moses Halawa (who studied with Rashba, ca. 1310; see *Responsa of Maharam Halawa*, ed. Moshe Hershler [Jerusalem: 1987], 146), suggests that R. Yehiel of Paris was the source of R. Tuvyah of Vienne's lenient ruling (*veani amarti ki harav tuvia z"l hora beshem harav yehiel z"l sheim tishava shevua hamura* …). According to this version, however, the oath was to be taken (somewhat implausibly) by the mother herself, to "guarantee" that she would continue to nurse her son in any event. Cf. Ta-Shma, n. 67 above, 354, n. 25; and n. 73 below. See bKetubot 60a-b, and bJebamot 43a.

70 See Rashi, bKetubot 60b s.v. *ad esrim vearbaa hodesh*. Maimonides (*Code*, Laws concerning Divorce 11:25), explains that the pregnancy may affect the quality of the mother's milk, and her second husband may not take the appropriate (medical/financial) steps to improve the quality of the milk.

71 Rashi, bKetubot 60b s.v. *bigzeirotav*, and s.v. *gemalato asur*.

72 Laws concerning Divorce 11:27.

Nevertheless, a handful of later Sefardic decisors suggested the possibility of leniency. The Talmud records that R. Nahman permitted members of the household of the Exilarch to retain a nursemaid for a nursing child whose father had died (thereby allowing its mother to remarry). According to R. Nahman, it may be assumed that the nursemaid would not relinquish her position at any time, due to her fear of (the prestige and power of) the Exilarch. Since the child is assured its proper nutrition, the mother may remarry. Similarly, the remarriage of the nursing mother should be permitted whenever it is possible to guarantee and to ensure that the hired nursemaid will not shirk her responsibilities.[73]

This appears to have been the reasoning of R. Tuvyah of Vienne (and R. Jacob of Cracow as well), and indeed, R. Tuvyah's ruling may have been the impetus for the Sefardic decisors.[74] If the nursemaid were to submit to a very strong, biblically ordained oath (*shvua min hatora*), which would bind her to her responsibility and position, R. Tuvyah felt that this would more than suffice to prevent her from backing out: "It is clear to us that she could not quit due to the severity of the oath" (*pshita lan delo tihadar mihomer hashvua*). On the other hand, the Tosafists and other Ashkenazic halakhists who rejected R. Tuvyah's position stressed that any comparison to the house of the Exilarch was inaccurate and unacceptable. The power and influence of the Exilarch was unique, and widely known to all.

In maintaining their unyielding position, it is possible that the Ashkenazic halakhists were influenced by the Jerusalem Talmud, which allowed no leniency of any kind in this matter, even in the case where the child had died.[75] It is also possible that the Ashkenazic halakhists, who displayed remarkable sensitivity to the physical and emotional needs of infants and children generally, felt that it was necessary to protect the child in this case by favoring a more stringent

73 For references to these Sefardic decisors, see *Magid Mishne*, Laws concerning Divorce, 11:26; *Responsa Rashba*, 1:723; *Responsa Ran*, #58; and *Beit Yosef*, EH 13 s.v. *afilu im nishbea leadam gadol*. Rabbenu Yona, Rashba and other Spanish *rishonim* specifically reject this view. Both Rif and Rambam omit any reference to the case of the Exilarch, suggesting that they too did not consider it a viable model for others. See also R. Menahem Hameiri, *Beit Habehira*, Ketubot, ad loc.

74 See *Responsa Rosh*, 53:1–2; *Responsa Ran*, #12; and the preceding note.

75 Cf. Urbach, n. 5 above, 2:704–712; Ta-Shma, *Early Franco-German Ritual and Custom* (Hebrew), (Jerusalem: 1992), 61–85; and Grossman, n. 29 above, 384–386, 428–430.

interpretation.[76] To paraphrase a popular rabbinic aphorism, they were not being overly harsh in terms of the mother, but rather, acting as advocates on behalf of the child.

In any event, the more conservative approach to this case is certainly well grounded in talmudic law and interpretation. R. Tuvyah's intuitive extension or extrapolation, "it is clear to us" (*pshita lan*), ostensibly based on the case of the house of the Exilarch, is more speculative. And yet, R. Tuvyah not only rules that the second husband could not be compelled to divorce the mother if they had already married, he insists that they may marry without any hesitation.[77] The comment, "And the matter requires further study" (*vetzarikh iyun*) that follows R. Tuvyah's ruling was added by his student R. Abraham b. Ephraim, who was undoubtedly aware of the fact that his teacher's view was very much in the minority.[78]

R. Tuvyah's approach is to identify a human response or concern as a significant factor in resolving a halakhic dilemma. Another instance where R. Tuvyah evinces this approach is in regard to oaths taken by inveterate gamblers. Such individuals sometimes took oaths promising that they would stop gambling, as a deterrent. A gambler often found, however, that he could not keep his oath, and asked for a rabbinic release from it. A passage in the Jerusalem Talmud proscribes release from an oath where the one who had taken the oath could, were he released, resume a sinful activity, even something prohibited only according to rabbinic law.[79]

Rashba ruled, on the basis of the Jerusalem Talmud, that vows made by gamblers should not be nullified: "We do not respond to him, because gambling is sinful, and we cannot nullify a vow that will allow him to transgress [once again] (*veein nizkakin lo sheshok hu aveira veein*

76 See my "Attitudes toward childhood and children in medieval Jewish society," in David Blumenthal (ed.), *Approaches to Judaism in Medieval Times*, v. 2 (Chico, CA: 1985), 1–34, and Ta-Shma, "Children of medieval German Jewry: a perspective on Aries from Jewish sources," *Studies in Medieval and Renaissance Studies* 12 (1991), 269–270.

77 To be sure, the specific case of R. Jacob Hakohen of Cracow had an additional measure of urgency to it. In a situation where the second husband was a non-*kohen*, even were he compelled to divorce the mother, he could remarry her after the twenty-four month period (assuming, of course, that she married no one else in the interim). In this case, however, R. Jacob, as a *kohen*, could not divorce and remarry her.

78 See Urbach, n. 5 above, 1:191.

79 jNedarim 5:4. Cf. *Tosafot*, Gitin 35b s.v. *kasavar*.

*metirin lo neder laavor*)."[80] This was also the position of a number of early Tosafists, including Rabbenu Tam and R. Isaac b. Asher Halevi of Speyer.[81] R. Tuvyah of Vienne and his northern French Tosafist colleague, R. Samuel of Evreux, were the first to take a different direction. According to R. Tuvyah, "Now, in this era, the vow [of abstention from gambling] should be nullified, for it is a virtually involuntary act, since they cannot control themselves."[82] Similarly, R. Samuel asserted that, "If it is certain that [the gambler] will not be able to restrain himself and will violate his oath, it is better to release him from it."[83] Here again, R. Tuvyah (and R. Samuel of Evreux) rendered a lenient halakhic decision that demonstrated great sensitivity to human responses and needs.[84]

Several other formulations by R. Tuvyah reflect his sensitivity to personal issues and concerns as a crucial factor in determining halakhic practice. R. Tuvyah is cited by R. Meir of Rothenburg as criticizing those who would not touch their menstruant wives during an illness (so as to render them assistance): "Those who are careful not to touch their menstruant wives when they are sick, are acting out of foolish piety (חסידות של שטות)."[85] R. Meir also appears to have cited R. Tuvyah as advocating a position which he endorsed, namely, that a woman

80 See Rashba, *Responsa*, 1:755, 3:305, 7:4; *Responsa Rashba attributed to Nachmanides*, #252. Cf. Rosh, *Responsa*, 12:5–6; *Responsa Zikhron Yehuda*, #71; Ran, *Responsa*, #51.

81 See *Mordekhai*, Gitin, sec. 374, Shevuot, secs. 756, 787 (glosses); ms Paris BN 1408, fol. 68r (*upasak rabeinu tam deein lehatir neder shel mishak*); *Beit Yosef*, YD 228 (fol. 147a); Kanarfogel, n. 16 above, 29, n. 75.

82 See *Mordekhai*, Shevuot, sec. 787:

דעתה בזה"ז יש להתיר נדר של קוביא כי כמו שגגה היא כי אינם יכולים להתאפק ולמשול ברוחם

Cf. Rashba, *Responsa*, 7:537; *Responsa Rashba attributed to Nachmanides*, #281; *Shiltei Hagiborim* on *Mordekhai*, Shevuot, sec. 756, n. 1; *Nimukei Yosef Al Masekhet Gitin* (35b), ed. Moses Stern (Jerusalem: 1963), 88 (in the name of Ritva); *Responsa Mahari Bruna*, #125; and *Responsa Rema*, ed. Asher Siev (Jerusalem: 1971), 440 (#103).

83 See *Sefer Orhot Hayim*, n. 38 above, part 2, v. 3, 495, and cf. Leo Landman, "Jewish attitudes toward gambling: the professional and compulsive gambler," *JQR* 57 (1967), 302.

84 R. Samuel's formulation is couched in the language of "better they sin inadvertently than deliberately" (*mutav sheyihiyu shogegin veal yihiyu mezidin*). In R. Tuvyah's case, there is the barest whisper of this principle (*ki kmo shagega hi*).

85 See *Shiltei Hagiborim* on *Mordekhai*, Shabat, sec. 238, para. 5, who notes dissenting opinions as well. See also Urbach, n. 5 above, 1:488 n. 37; and *Darkhei Moshe*, YD 195:6. The lenient ruling issued by R. Tuvyah for drinking

should not be designated as the *sandak*, the person selected to hold the baby during a circumcision, since this would require her presence in the main section of the synagogue, which might in turn lead to inappropriate distractions and behavior there.[86]

In one instance where R. Tuvyah ruled on the basis of social constraints, he refers to an earlier Tosafist: "I heard from R. Tuvyah, in the name of Riva, that any foods which young men (*bahurim*) take from one another [from Purim eve until the next evening], even without permission, on account of the Purim celebration, are not considered stolen and cannot be adjudicated, provided they do not overstep the guidelines of the seven good men of the city (*shiva tuvei hair*)."[87] There are several Tosafists who are referred to as Riva. It is likely that Riva in this case denotes R. Isaac b. Abraham of Dampierre (referred to more often as Ritzba), whose funeral was attended by R. Tuvyah.[88] In any event, both Riva and R. Tuvyah were comfortable rendering their ruling in light of prevailing social norms, without explicit talmudic support.

A final example brings us full circle in our discussion of R. Tuvyah's rulings. The Tosafists argued over whether a non-Jew was allowed to warm the central living quarters of a home (the so-called *beit hahoref*, lit., winter house)[89] by tending to the hearth on the Sabbath.[90] Several twelfth-century northern French Tosafists already permitted this to be done by a non-Jewish maidservant if she herself was cold, and also

---

wine or water after the four cups at the Passover Seder may also be relevant in this regard. See Urbach, 1:490, n. 47, and cf. *Hagahot Maimuniot*, Laws concerning Leavened and Unleavened Bread 8:10 [כ, מ]; *Peirush Harosh*, Pesahim 118a (sec. 33); *Beit Yosef*, OH 481 s.v. *katav adoni avi*.

86 See R. Samson b. Tzadok, *Sefer Tashbetz*, sec. 357; *Sefer Minhagim Devei Maharam Mirotenburg*, ed. Israel Elfenbein (NY: 1938), 80; Kahana, n. 56 above, 49 (secs. 155–156); and Daniel Sperber, *Minhagei Yisrael*, v. 1 (Jerusalem: 1989), 64–65.

87 See *Responsa Trumat Hadeshen*, #110 (based on *Sefer Mordekhai Hakatzar*), and Urbach, n. 5 above, 1:487, n. 35.

88 See Urbach, 1:271, and cf. Henri Gross, *Gallia Judaica* (Paris: 1897), 193. (Note that the early German Tosafist Riva (R. Isaac b. Asher Halevi) was among those who held, against R. Tuvyah, that gamblers' vows could not be nullified; see n. 81 above.)

89 On this structure, see Mordechai Breuer, "Toward the investigation of the typology of western *yeshivot* in the Middle Ages" (Hebrew), in E. Etkes and Y. Salmon (eds.), *Studies in the History of Jewish Society in the Middle Ages and in the Early Modern Period* (Hebrew), (Jerusalem: 1980), 51–52.

90 See n. 14 above.

because of the principle that "all can be rendered ill by exposure to the cold" (*hakol holim etzel kor vetzina*).[91] This leniency was not accepted, however, by German rabbinic authorities, due perhaps in part to differences in climate, in addition to other halakhic concerns. The following account was related by a son of R. Isaac b. Meir of Dura. R. Isaac was, as the text indicates, a student of R. Tuvyah of Vienne:

> I heard from my father and teacher, R. Isaac, that when he studied Torah with R. Tuvyah in France, and R. Yehiel came there, he [R. Yehiel] saw that many important students were studying with R. Tuvyah. And the [non-Jewish] nursemaid was sitting near the fire with R. Tuvyah's son. Then our teacher R. Tuvyah said to R. Yehiel: see how many good things this child does for us. The fire has been made for him, and we can warm ourselves by virtue of him. R. Yehiel responded, but perhaps [the nursemaid] will increase the size of the fire on their account [which is prohibited]. There were many German students there, and they said that if so, it should nonetheless be permitted for them to warm themselves in the winter rooms of their home on the Sabbath, when the maidservant has warmed the room for a young child. R. Yehiel asked how their winter rooms were warmed. They responded that the heat required for one person is no different from that required for many people. R. Yehiel answered and said, if so, I would have warmed myself in such a room were I there ...[92]

The halakhic principle behind R. Tuvyah's lenient ruling is that if the lingering cold can cause illness (even if not severe), involving a non-Jew (*amira laakum*) may be permitted. What is most interesting and suggestive about R. Tuvyah's ruling, however, is that he based it solely on the presence of his (or any) child. He was not prepared to allow the room to be heated by the non-Jew simply because the cold might prove to be detrimental to the occupants in general. Rather, the cold would certainly pose a problem for an infant or child, and it was the responsibility of the maidservant to see to the child's well-being.

R. Yehiel of Paris was still troubled by the fact that the maid might add extra wood, or expend additional effort in fanning the fire, on

91 See the sources in Ta-Shma, n. 2 above, 163–164.

92 Ms Cambridge Add. 377, fol. 114r (in the margin). See also Urbach, n. 5 above, 1:487, and Ta-Shma, ibid., 165.

שמעתי מאבא מרי הרב ר' יצחק שי', כשלמד תורה לפני מורי הר"ר טוביה בצרפת, ובא לשם הר' יחיאל מפריש וראה שהיו יושבים אצלו הרבה תלמידים חשובים, והמינקת ישבה נגד האור עם בנו של ר' טוביה.ואז אמר מורינו הר' טוביה לר' יחיאל: תראה כמה טובות עושה לנו זה הנער שהאש נעשה בשבילו ואנו מחחמין בזכותו.והשיב לו ר' יחיאל, שמא ירבה בשבילם.והיו שם הרבה תלמידים אשכנזיים, ואמרו, אם כן מותר להחם בבתי חורף שלנו בשבת שהחמה השפחה בשביל התינוק.ושאל הר' יחיאל היאך מחממין את בתי החורף שלהם.והשיבו לו בשביל אחד צריכה [חימום] כמו בשביל הרבה בני אדם.וענה ואמר להם הר' יחיאל, אם כן אני בעצמי הייתי מחמם בו אילו הייתי שם...

behalf of other Jews in the room who were not young children. Nevertheless, both he and R. Tuvyah's German students accepted R. Tuvyah's premise that any heating done for the infant was permissible. Thus, for a structure where the heat, once adjusted, would remain at a constant temperature no matter how many people were in the room, which was apparently the case in certain German homes, R. Yehiel would agree fully with R. Tuvyah.[93]

R. Tuvyah based his leniency on a usual occurrence in, and typical need of, the Jewish household, again reflecting his tendency to focus on human concerns and responses. Since the nursemaid was expected to tend to the child's needs, she could also tend to the fire, regardless of whether others benefitted as well. Although we would expect every halakhic decisor to be aware of the facts of a situation before him, R. Tuvyah's ability to formulate halakhic categories and issue lenient rulings, and rather unique ones at that, based in no small measure on his assessment of human concerns and proclivities, is noteworthy. It should also be noted that R. Tuvyah cannot be characterized as a lenient decisor overall. A comparison of his positions with those of R. Moses of Coucy in the areas of permitted and prohibited substances and practices (*isur veheter*), such as *taam lifgam*, the nullification of leaven before Passover and the baking of matza, and the laws of mourning (a comparison facilitated by R. Abraham b. Ephraim's *Sefer Simanei Taryag Mitzvot*), shows R. Tuvyah to be stricter than *Semag* in his rulings on these matters.[94]

To be sure, R. Tuvyah's methods were not widely copied in medieval Ashkenaz, as far as we can tell.[95] Nevertheless, it is reasonable to suggest that at least some of the approaches to halakha and *metziut* in Ashkenaz discussed above, with regard to widespread social needs and societal issues, impacted on the halakhic methodology of R. Tuvyah of Vienne as well, or perhaps evolved from a common mindset.[96]

93 Note the convergence of the views of R. Tuvyah and R. Yehiel mentioned in n. 68 above. Like R. Tuvyah (above, n. 85), R. Yehiel was also outspoken in regard to customs or practices he considered frivolous (*minhagei shtut*). See, e.g., *Hagahot R. Peretz Lesefer Mitzvot Katan*, 93:4 (where R. Samuel of Evreux concurs); *Beit Yosef*, OH 553, s.v. *veyesh osrim* (where R. Samuel of Evreux disagrees). Cf. Urbach, n. 5 above, 1:459, 463–464; and n. 20 above.

94 See Urbach, n. 5 above, 1:490.

95 Cf. *Hagahot Maimuniot*, Laws concerning Prayer, 8:4[6], and *Sefer Mitzvot Katan*, commandment 11, with regard to constituting a quorum for but one person who has not yet prayed. See also Eleazar of Worms, *Sefer Rokeiah*, sec. 320.

96 Differences between the rabbinic scholars of northern France and Germany on some of the larger issues of halakha and realia can occasionally be discerned. See above, nn. 3, 8, 14, 68–69, 85, 88, 93.

*The Jewish Law Annual*, Vol. XIV

# *ONAA* AND THE OPERATION OF THE MODERN MARKETPLACE

AARON LEVINE*

One of the Torah's central tenets for the marketplace is the prohibition against price fraud: "When you make a sale to your fellow or when you buy from the hand of your fellow, do not victimize one another" (Lev. 25:14). The interdict against price fraud is commonly referred to in the talmudic literature as the prohibition against *onaa* (price fraud). Our purpose here will be to propose a rationale for the prohibition against *onaa*. This rationale will serve as a guidepost to the workings of *onaa* in the modern marketplace with respect to such matters as a differentiated product market, discount pricing, and the pricing policy of a convenience store. In developing our rationale for the prohibition against *onaa*, we will encounter sources in the talmudic literature that provide insight into the workings of the marketplace that anticipate by many hundreds of years explicit discussions of these matters by economic theorists.

**The Law of *Onaa*** The most fundamental point regarding the law of *onaa* is that *onaa* is a form of theft.[1] The law of *onaa* prohibits an individual from concluding a transaction at a price that is more favorable to himself than some reference price.[2]

The Sages identified three degrees of *onaa*. Depending on how far the price of the subject transaction departs from the reference price, the injured party may have recourse to void or adjust the transaction. Provided the price discrepancy is assessed to be within the margin of

* Samson and Halina Bitensky Professor of Economics, Yeshiva University.

1 bBaba Metzia 61a; R. Jacob b. Asher (Germany, 1270–1343), *Tur*, HM 227:1; R. Joshua b. Alexander Hakohen Falk, *Sema*, HM 227 n. 1.

2 Baraita, bBaba Metzia 51a; R. Isaac b. Jacob Alfasi (Algeria, 1012–1103), *Rif*, ad loc.; Maimonides (Egypt, 1135–1204), *Code*, Laws concerning Sales 12:1; R. Asher b. Jehiel (Germany, 1250–1327), *Rosh*, bBaba Metzia 4:17; *Tur*, HM 227:1; R. Joseph Caro (Israel, 1488–1575), *Shulhan Arukh* (henceforth *SA*), HM 227:1; R. Jehiel Michel Epstein (Belarus, 1829–1908), *Arukh Hashulhan* (henceforth *AH*), HM 227:1.

error,[3] the plaintiff's right to void the transaction is recognized when the difference between the sale price and the reference price is more than one-sixth.[4] We shall refer to this level of violation as first-degree *onaa*. The plaintiff's rights here consist only of the right to cancel the transaction at hand, but do not extend to the right to keep the transaction intact and make a price reduction on the basis of the *onaa* involved.[5]

Second-degree *onaa* occurs when the differential is exactly one-sixth. In such a case, neither of the parties may subsequently void the transaction on account of the price discrepancy. The plaintiff is, however, entitled to full restitution of the amount involved.[6]

Finally, third-degree *onaa* occurs when the sale price differs from the reference price by less than one-sixth. Here, the transaction not only remains binding, but in addition, the complainant has no legal claim to the price differential.[7]

**The Rationale for the Prohibition Against *Onaa*** In searching for a rationale for the prohibition of *onaa*, the basic point that must be

3 bBaba Batra 78a and Rashi, R. Solomon b. Isaac (Franco-Germany, 1040–1105) ad loc.; *Rif* ad loc.; *Code*, Laws concerning Sales 27:5; *Rosh*, Baba Batra 5:7; *Tur*, HM 220:5; *SA*, HM 220:8; *AH*, HM 220:7.

4 bBaba Metzia 50b; *Rif* ad loc.; *Code*, ibid.; *Rosh*, Baba Metzia 4:15; *Tur*, HM 227:6; *SA*, HM 227:4; *AH*, HM 227:3.

5 *Code*, ibid.; *SA*, HM 227:4 and *Sema* ad loc., n. 6. Expressing a minority opinion in this matter is R. Jonah b. Abraham Gerondi (Spain, ca. 1200–1263). In his view, as long as the plaintiff does not uphold the transaction, the offender, too, is given the prerogative of voiding it. The offender's rights in this matter proceed from the magnitude of the price discrimination involved. Since the concluded price diverged more than one-sixth from the market norm, the offender may insist that the original transaction be treated as an agreement consummated in error (*mekah taut*). Once the transaction is, however, upheld by the plaintiff, the offender loses his right to void the sale. Denying the offender **full** nullification rights here follows from the fact that the offender enjoys no such rights when his offence consists of the less severe violation of contracting for a sale price involving second-degree *onaa*. Conferring **full** nullification rights on him when his offence is graver seems counter to the canons of equity. (R. Jonah b. Abraham Gerondi, quoted in *Tur*, HM 227:6, *Rema*, and *AH*, HM 227:4; *Rosh*, Baba Batra 5:14, rules in accordance with R. Jonah).

6 bBaba Metzia 50b; *Rif* ad loc.; *Code*, Laws concerning Sales 2:2; *Rosh*, Baba Batra 4:15; *Tur*, HM 227:3; *SA*, HM 227:2; *AH*, HM 227.

7 bBaba Metzia 50b; *Rif* ad loc.; *Rosh* loc. cit.; *Tur* loc. cit.; *SA*, HM 227:2; *AH*, HM 227:6.

clarified is the reference price used in adjudicating cases of *onaa*. Examination of R. Asher b. Jehiel's treatment of third-degree *onaa* clearly shows that this reference price is the objective market value of the goods at issue.

Noting the absence of any provision for legal redress in cases of third-degree *onaa*, R. Asher speculates whether it might be permissible, in the first instance, to contract into third-degree *onaa*. Pivotal to resolving this question, in R. Asher's view, is the definition of market price. Is market price to be understood as a single value, or is it to be defined as the range of deviations of less than one-sixth from the price of the disputed transaction? Adopting the latter view leads to the conclusion that third-degree *onaa* is not fraud at all. Adopting the former, however, leads to the conclusion that knowledge of the market norm prohibits either party from contracting into a price agreement that is even slightly more favorable to himself than the norm. The absence of legal redress for third-degree *onaa* would then be explained by the presumption that when the degree of *onaa* involved is relatively minor, the plaintiff waives his claim to restitution. This presumption follows from our inability to fix the value of the article sold. While some experts would insist that *onaa* took place, others would just as vehemently deny it. Because the experts are divided as to whether *onaa* occurred, and, if it did, to what degree, we can safely presume that the victim of this possible price fraud waives his rights to restitution.

Though offering no definitive resolution of the above dilemma, R. Asher urged the following guideline for third-degree *onaa*. Cognizant of the prevailing norm, an individual should not contract into a price agreement that is even slightly more favorable to himself than this norm. On the other hand, if an individual falls victim to third-degree *onaa*, he should accept his loss graciously and express no complaint.[8]

What can be extrapolated from R. Asher's analysis is that the validity of a claim of *onaa* is always based on the assessment of experts. Because experts are divided in a case of third-degree *onaa* as to whether price fraud took place, the *onaa* claim is unrecoverable. But, in first- and second-degree *onaa*, expert testimony establishes clearly that the price differed from what experts regard as the objective value of the goods in question.

The proposition that the reference price in a claim of *onaa* should be identified with what experts regard the objective value of the goods

8 *Rosh*, Baba Batra 4:20.

to be can also be seen by examining the time limitation the halakha sets for lodging a claim of *onaa*. Let us examine this criterion as it applies to both the buyer and the seller.

When the buyer is the one who lodges the claim of *onaa*, his claim is not allowed beyond the time he would need to show the article in question to a merchant or relative, to evaluate whether the price charged was fair.[9] While the Mishnah is silent on the amount of time this criterion translates into, it certainly amounts to less than a day.[10] Failure to lodge a claim beyond this period creates a presumption that plaintiff waives his rights in the matter.[11]

Because the seller is no longer in possession of the article he sold and is therefore not in a position to show what he sold to a fellow merchant, the time the seller is allotted to lodge an *onaa* claim of underpayment extends until such time as he comes into possession of a similar item and does not lodge an immediate claim of *onaa* against the first customer. If the item in question is a standardized product, so that the seller can easily ascertain its market price, the seller forfeits his claim of *onaa* unless he lodges the claim immediately.[12]

Whether applied to plaintiff buyer or plaintiff seller, the time limitation the Sages adopted with respect to lodging a claim of *onaa* shows that the reference price in an *onaa* proceeding is the market value of the goods in question as determined by experts.

The proposition that the reference price is none other than the market price of the goods can further be seen by an examination of instances where the claim of *onaa* is not recognized. We will examine

9 mBaba Metzia 4:3; *Rif* ad loc.; *Code*, Laws concerning Sales 12:5; *Rosh*, Baba Batra 4:15; *Tur*, HM 227:15; *SA*, HM 227:7; *AH*, HM 227:8.

10 The amount of time needed to show the article at hand to a merchant or relative can be inferred by an examination of R. Tafron's minority position. In opposition to the majority view, R. Tarfon (mBaba Metzia 4:3) ruled that unless the price discrepancy reached one-third, the offender need not return the amount involved. When the merchants of Lod heard the ruling of R. Tarfon, they rejoiced. But when R. Tarfon told them that the time limitation to lodge a claim of *onaa* extended an entire day, they reacted to his ruling by saying, "Let R. Tarfon leave us alone in our place," and went back to the words of the Sages. The disappointment the merchants of Lod voiced with R. Tarfon's one-day time limit shows that the Sages took the position that the plaintiff had **under one day** to lodge a complaint.

11 Rashi, bBaba Metzia 49a.

12 bBaba Metzia 50b; *Rif* ad loc.; *Code*, Laws concerning Sales 12:6; *Tur*, HM 227:10; *SA*, HM 227:8; *AH*, HM 227:1.

two cases, one known as *nose beemuna* (lit., selling on trust), and the second involving the purchase of some personal effect from a householder.

The circumstance *nose beemuna* refers to is a matter of dispute in the *Rishonic* literature.[13] One understanding of *nose beemuna* that is widely recorded in the talmudic literature as well as in the Codes includes the following elements: A vendor (S) divulges to a prospective buyer (B) both his cost price and his proposed profit margin. Should B agree to these terms and consummate the transaction with a *kinyan* (symbolic act), a subsequent finding that the price S charged involved *onaa* does not allow B to modify the original transaction in any manner.[14] Agreeing to allow S a specified profit margin demonstrates a lack of concern, on the part of the buyer, with the objective value of the commodity. Since realization of the agreed-upon profit rate requires the sale to be concluded at the stipulated price, subsequent claims of *onaa* are denied.[15] What the *nose beemuna* shows is that ordinarily the intent of S and B is to trade the article at hand based on its objective market value. Consequently, concluding a transaction on terms that diverge from the market value of the item at hand creates the possibility of modifying and even annulling the original transaction.

Let us now consider the second case. If B buys personal effects such as jewelry and household implements from a householder (H), and it is subsequently determined, based on the article's fair market value, that the purchase entailed an overcharge, B's claim of *onaa* is not honored.[16] Some authorities extend the householder's immunity even to claims of first-degree *onaa*,[17] while others limit the householder's exemption to second-degree claims.[18]

The privileged status of the householder here proceeds from the presumption that anyone dealing with him realizes that he would not

13 For a discussion of the various views, see Berachyahu Lifshitz, *Asmakhta — Obligation and Acquisition in Jewish Law* (Hebrew), (Jerusalem: 1989), 172–176.

14 *Code*, Laws concerning Sales 13:5, *Tur*, HM 227:27; *SA*, HM 227:27; *AH*, HM 227:28. For a slightly variant recording of this law, see R. Israel Krems (mid. 14th c.), *Hagahot Asheri*, Baba Metzia 4:17.

15 *AH*, HM 227:28.

16 R. Hisda, bBaba Batra 51a; *Rif* ad loc.; *Code*, Laws concerning Sales13:2; *Rosh*, Baba Batra 4:16; *Tur*, HM 227:23; *AH*, HM 227:24.

17 R. Joseph ibn Habiba (Spain, 15th c.), *Nimukei Yosef*, *Rif*, bBaba Metzia 51a; *SA*, HM 227:24.

18 *Shita Mekubetzet*, bBaba Metzia 51a; "some authorities" quoted in *SA*, loc. cit.

dispose of his personal effects unless he could sell them above market price.[19] The Sages extended their exemption to the householder without qualification (*lo pelug*). Hence even if the householder was known to be pressed for cash at the time he sold his personal effects, he nonetheless qualifies for the *onaa* exemption. Alternatively, selling one's own personal effects is regarded as degrading. Hence, even when pressed for cash, the householder, as a means of saving face, would hold out for more than the market price.[20]

What the householder exemption shows is that ordinarily, the intent of S and B is to trade the article in question based on its objective market value.

The basis of the *onaa* claim requires further clarification. There are several ways to rationalize overturning a transaction or modifying its terms on the basis of the availability of a better opportunity for the plaintiff when the deal was entered into. One possibility is that the claim is essentially a plea of **ignorance** of market conditions by the plaintiff: had he been aware of the better opportunity, he would have availed himself of it. On this understanding, the plaintiff claiming *onaa* is protesting that for him, the transaction at hand entailed an **actual** loss in the form of a foregone opportunity. Economists call the loss of this foregone opportunity an opportunity cost. Since the halakha does not expect a market participant to conduct transactions in the marketplace with perfect knowledge, the claim of *onaa* is legitimate. Absent this presumption of ignorance, the claim would be thrown out.

The above approach must, however, be rejected. Certainly, the plaintiff's awareness of the market norm at the time he entered into the transaction at hand does not **automatically** vitiate a subsequent claim of *onaa*. The Talmud at bBaba Metzia 51a specifically deals with such a case, whose particulars are as follows: S was selling a parcel of silk ribbons for six *zuz*. B knew that they were worth only five and was convinced that he could bargain down the price to five and a half. But concluding the transaction at five and a half would reduce the *onaa* involved to third-degree and he would have no recourse to recover the one-half *zuz* overpayment. Instead, B decided against bargaining with S and paid S his asking price of *six zuz*. Immediately upon completing the deal, B informed S that he was launching a claim of second-degree *onaa* against him. Making such a declaration immediately after the deal

19 *Code*, loc. cit.; *Tur*, loc. cit.; *SA*, loc. cit.

20 *Responsa Rosh*, quoted in *Tur*, HM 227:34; *AH*, loc. cit.

was concluded indicates that B was aware of the *onaa* all along. Nonetheless, B does not lose his *onaa* rights, as his conduct manifested a strategy to first secure possession of the ribbons and only then launch a claim of *onaa*. B's conduct clearly shows that he did not waive his rights in this matter.[21]

Another possible rationale for the claim is that the halakha regards the objective market value of the article at hand as its "fair value." What *onaa* does is therefore to **define** the competitive norm. Market participants are **entitled** to trade the article on the basis of its competitive norm. Unless the plaintiff conducts himself in a manner demonstrating that he has waived his rights in the matter, his claim of *onaa* remains intact.

21 *Rema*, SA, HM 227:7. In presenting the case where B **knowingly** enters into an *onaa* transaction, R. Moses Isserles (Poland, ca. 1525–1572) mentions no caveats and makes no reference whatsoever to the silk ribbons case. Taking note of this, R. Joshua b. Alexander Hakohen Falk (Poland, 1555–1614) reads into the Rema's remarks that B's claim of *onaa* remains valid even if it is a first-degree claim and B cannot provide a good excuse for why he entered into the transaction in the first place (*Sema, SA*, HM 227 n. 18). Sharply disputing R. Falk's contention, R. Jacob Moses Lorberbaum (Poland, 1760–1832), *Netivot Hamishpat, SA*, HM 227 n. 4, contends that the claim of *onaa* is valid only when it is second-degree. R. Lorberbaum contends that this is also position of R. David b. Samuel Halevi (Poland, 1586–1667) in *Turei Zahav* on Rema ad loc.; R. Jehiel Michel Epstein, *AH*, HM 227:9, concurs.

R. Joel Sirkes (Poland, 1561–1640), in *Bah* on *Tur*, HM 227 n. 9, understands the silk ribbons case as referring to the instance where B did not conclude the deal until he had first, in the presence of witnesses, declared his intention to launch a claim of second-degree *onaa* against S. Here, B's conduct clearly demonstrates that he does not waive his *onaa* rights in the matter. Ordinarily, the time limitation of *bekhdei sheyare letagar* is set for lodging the *onaa* complaint. This time limit, according to R. Sirkes, does not apply to the case at hand. By communicating his intent to lodge a complaint of *onaa* **before** he entered into the transaction, B has clearly shown that he does not waive his rights in the matter and should therefore be given an indefinite period to lodge his complaint. Taking issue with R. Isserles, R. Sirkes denies B's claim of *onaa* when it is evident that B knew beforehand that the asking price entailed *onaa*, but went through with the deal anyway. Here, B's claim is denied even though he can provide a solid excuse for going through with the transaction knowing it entailed *onaa*. R. Aryeh Loeb Hakohen Heller (Poland, 1745–1813), in *Ketzot Hahoshen, SA*, HM 227 n. 5, defends *Rema* and disagrees with *Bah*.

Now, if the halakha held market participants to a responsibility to engage in market research before striking a deal, a claim of *onaa* would have no basis. The implication to be drawn from making the competitive norm an **entitlement** of traders is hence that to a certain degree, the halakha **releases** market participants from the responsibility to engage in market research. Deliberately transacting to one's advantage at an *onaa* price hence exploits the ignorance of the other party to the deal, and deprives that person of his entitlement. To be sure, the halakha does not legitimize the **mindless** consumer. Consider that where the price discrepancy goes beyond the margin of error, the *onaa* claim is not honored. This shows that the halakha fully expects market participants to have at least an approximate notion of market conditions when striking a deal. What, then, are we to make of a transaction concluded on price terms that exceed reasonable misjudgment of value? The only plausible interpretation is that the underlying intention of the parties involved was not to trade the article at hand, but rather to use the transaction as a **vehicle** to effect a voluntary gift transfer.[22]

Support for the latter formulation of the *onaa* claim is found in the fact that the halakha regards *onaa* as a form of theft. Now, if the claim of *onaa* is no more than the plaintiff's protest that the transaction at hand caused him to incur an **actual** opportunity cost, the issue before us is whether the original transaction was entered into by error (*mekah taut*) and should either be cancelled or adjusted. Calling the offence involved a form of theft indicates that defendant's *onaa* has violated the plaintiff's legitimate right to trade the commodity at hand on the basis of its competitive norm.

**First-Degree *Onaa*** One of the puzzles of the law of *onaa* is why the Sages found it necessary to establish the category of first-degree *onaa*. Would it not suffice to declare that *onaa* amounting to one-sixth or more calls for the differential to be returned to the victim?

Perhaps the key here is that the Sages desired to impose a stiffer penalty on the offender when the degree of *onaa* exceeds one-sixth. In a different context, Meir Brachfeld points out that the seller (S) always has a strong need for liquidity. From the perspective of S, keeping **only** the "fair market" value of the purchasing price he received is a penalty far preferable to facing cancellation of the transaction. Accordingly, empowering the buyer with the right to cancel the transaction when

22 bBaba Batra 78a and Rashi ad loc.; *Rif* ad loc.; *Code*, Laws concerning Sales 27:5; *Rosh*, bBaba Batra 5:7; *Tur*, HM 220:5; *SA*, HM 220:8; *AH*, HM 220:7.

the degree of *onaa* exceeds one-sixth **penalizes** the seller more than merely calling for him to return the differential.[23] Brachfeld's observation works well to explain the separate category of first-degree *onaa* when the buyer (B) is the defrauded party. But first-degree *onaa* also pertains to the case where S is defrauded. Now if the idea is to impose a stiffer penalty on the offender when his offence rises to first-degree *onaa*, why should S be more disadvantaged when the offence against him is first-degree than when it is only second-degree? In the latter case, S is entitled to the differential. Why, then, should S lose the right to retain the differential when the offence against him is graver, namely, first-degree *onaa*?

The opportunity-cost rationale of the law of *onaa* provides us with an understanding of why the Sages established a separate category of first-degree *onaa*. The key here is that calling for the offender to simply return the price differential does not always restore to the plaintiff the market opportunity that was reasonably accessible to him at the time he entered into the disputed transaction. Examination of the Jerusalem Talmud's treatment of first-degree *onaa* will bear this out. The specific issue the Jerusalem Talmud addresses is why the **buyer** (B) has the right to overturn the transaction when the degree of *onaa* exceeds one-sixth. Several opinions on this matter are recorded:

1. B's right to overturn first-degree *onaa*, according to R. Zeira, is based on the argument that this approach works best to quiet the ridicule directed at B for demonstrating naivete in commercial matters.[24]
2. Another approach is offered by an anonymous authority: credibility is given to B's contention that his original intention was to purchase an expensive item that would confer status on him. Because the item at hand turns out not to be a status symbol, but merely an ordinary item that is terribly overpriced, calling for the price differential to be returned effectively frustrates B's original intention of obtaining a high-status item. To enable B to realize his original objective, the first-degree *onaa* transaction must be voided.[25]

23 Meir Brachfeld, "The Mishna of *onaa* (overcharging) in the light of economic theory," in M. Koppel and E. Merzbach (eds.) *Higayon* 4 (Jerusalem: 1997), 80, 85.

24 jBaba Batra 13b.

25 Jerusalem Talmud, loc. cit. See, however, R. Johanan's opinion.

R. Zeira's rationale can easily be framed in opportunity cost terms. Specifically, if the law gives B only the right to a cash refund of the differential, B keeps the item purchased. Whenever B has the item with him, people are reminded of his foolishness in overpaying to such a degree. By extension, if S was victimized by first-degree *onaa* and the remedy was to entitle S only to a cash refund for the differential, B's retaining the purchased item would similarly serve as a reminder of S's folly. Restoring to S or B the opportunity that was reasonably available to them when they entered into the moot transaction requires us to do no less than empower the victim to remove the item of purchase from B's possession. Such action serves to minimize the possible ridicule the victim would have suffered on account of the item's being in B's possession.

The anonymous opinion expressed in the Jerusalem Talmud can also be framed in opportunity cost terms. Specifically, if the remedy for first-degree *onaa* is only a monetary adjustment, B can rightfully claim that the remedy does not restore to him the opportunity that was reasonably available to him at the time he entered into the moot transaction. Credence would be given to B's claim that the relatively high price S charged him meant that he was purportedly getting a "status" item for his money. But since the same item sold at a lower price elsewhere in the marketplace, the item was not, in fact, a status item. Conferring on B only the right to claim the differential leaves him stuck with the item and defeats his original intention of acquiring a high-status item.

The same opportunity cost logic can explain why the transaction is overturned when S is victimized by first-degree *onaa*. This is so because entitling S only to a price adjustment, even when the *onaa* involved was first-degree, sends the false message that *S* invites hard-nosed bargaining from his customers and is amenable to making his wares available at a deep discount. Aiming to minimize this sort of harm to the parties' reputations, the Sages call for first-degree *onaa* to be voided, rather than requiring only a return of the price differential.

The Jerusalem Talmud's analysis of first-degree *onaa* gives us insight into why first and second-degree *onaa* were not merged into a single category. The plaintiff's contention that the remedy of awarding him an adjustment in price does not fully capture the opportunity cost he suffered by entering into the transaction strains credulity as the price difference involved gets smaller and smaller. Accordingly, the Sages established a cutoff point for the remedy of nullification of the original transaction: it ceases to be available when the price difference is exactly one-sixth. At that point, the plaintiff is entitled only to a price adjustment.

***Onaa* and the Reference Price** Further refinement is needed in defining the reference price in a claim of *onaa*. Consider that the product's market may consist of many sellers along with a variety of prices for the same item. In the opinion of R. Meir Arik (Poland, 1855–ca. 1925), the reference price for the purpose of adjudicating the claim of *onaa* should be identified as the price the majority of the sellers are charging.[26] But how should we define majority? Do we look at the price the majority of the sellers are charging, with no regard to the proportion of the total market they cater to? Or should, perhaps, the per unit price that corresponds to the majority of the sales volume be regarded as the reference price?[27]

Resolution of this issue, I believe, revolves around how we formulate the reference price in a claim of *onaa*. Should the reference price be defined as the **best estimate** of the market value of the item at hand? Or should we define the reference price as the price that was **reasonably accessible** to the plaintiff at the time he entered into the disputed transaction? If we take the former tack, the reference price should be set at the per unit price associated with the majority of the sales volume, as this would be the best measure of the market value of the item. But if we define the reference price in terms of accessibility, the price the majority of outlets charge should provide the appropriate measure.

Both of the above approaches apparently find support in the rabbinical literature. This can be seen from an analysis of the case where each seller in a particular market charges a different price for the same item. This is called the "unknown price" (*shaar sheeino yadua*) case. The talmudic milk and wool markets, according to R. Joseph Caro, fall into this category. The salient feature of these ancient markets was that each seller sold individual customers different quantities at different prices. (We note parenthetically that from the perspective of economic theory, the economic condition R. Caro describes is an anomaly. Self-interest would be expected to drive consumers to engage in comparative shopping. Aggressive market research of this sort would quickly bring about price convergence in this market.) Since the market price here is not readily ascertainable, a claim of *onaa* is not honored in these

26 R. Meir Arik, *Responsa Imrei Yosher* 2:154.

27 For a discussion of this point, see R. Judah Itach (Israel, contemporary), *Netiv Yosher*, 6 n. 14.

markets.[28] Disputing this ruling, R. Moses Isserles and others aver that even though each seller charges a different price, the market price is nevertheless ascertainable through **estimation**, and hence the claim of *onaa* should stand.[29]

The above dispute seems to revolve around how we define the reference price with respect to the claim of *onaa*. In the opinion of R. Isserles, the reference price is defined as the **best estimate** of the market value of the item at hand. Notwithstanding that each seller is selling different quantities of the same item at different prices, experts can use a weighted average and arrive at a market value for the item. In the opinion of R. Caro, however, the reference price should be defined as the price we may presume to have been reasonably accessible to the plaintiff at the time he entered into the disputed transaction. If each seller in a particular market is selling different quantities of the same item at different prices, there is no **single price** that we can point to as the price reasonably available to the plaintiff at the time the transaction was entered into. To the contrary, since each seller was selling the item at hand at a different price, no price was more accessible to the plaintiff than the actual price he ended up paying. The claim of *onaa* must therefore be dismissed.

At this juncture, we should take note that the claim of *onaa* is valid only when it is based on a **reference price** that existed under the same market conditions as prevailed when the overpayment or underpayment was made. If the defendant insists that the reference price reflects changed market conditions, the burden of proof is on the plaintiff to demonstrate that the market conditions did not change.[30]

**R. Asher B. Jehiel and Economic Theory** Before we apply the law of *onaa* to the modern marketplace, let us take note of the economic theory and insights into the workings of the marketplace nascent in Rosh's discussion of third-degree *onaa*.

We begin by considering a notion from modern economics, the notion that whenever an exchange is entirely voluntary, there must be a net gain for both parties. To illustrate: Suppose A accepts two pounds of strawberries from B in exchange for giving B four of his economics

28 R. Joseph Caro, *Beit Yosef*, *Tur*, HM 209.

29 R. Moses Isserles, *Darkhei Moshe*, *Tur*, HM 209:1; *Bah*, *Tur*, HM 209:1; R. Shabbetai b. Meir Hakohen, (Poland, 1621–1662), *Siftei Kohen*, *SA*, HM 209 n. 1.

30 *Rema*, *SA*, HM 227:9.

textbooks. To be sure, the exchange does nothing to change the total quantity of the two goods available between them. But assuredly, the exchange increases the **total utility** available to each. Specifically, if A did not subjectively value the two pounds of strawberries **more** than the four economics texts he gives up, he would not have agreed to the exchange. Similarly, if B did not value the four economics textbooks **more** than the two pounds of strawberries he is giving up, he would not have agreed to the trade. What is true for a barter deal is equally true for an ordinary marketplace exchange effected by means of the medium of exchange. What this means is that if A gives up $10 to buy three pounds of strawberries, we must conclude that **A values the three pounds of strawberries more than the $10 he gave up to obtain them**. The difference between the maximum price the consumer would pay rather than do without the goods in question, and the actual price he pays to obtain the goods, is called "consumer surplus." Every marketplace transaction perforce entails a measure of consumer surplus for the consumer. Provided the exchange at hand is voluntary and entails no misrepresentation, this will hold true even if other sellers are charging less for the item and complainant is aware of the price discrepancy. We take note that formal discussions of the concept of consumer surplus do not appear in the literature until the writings of Jules Dupuit in 1844.[31]

Recall that in his first approach to explaining third-degree *onaa*, Rosh defines market price not as a particular value but rather as **a range of values that diverge less than one-sixth from the better market opportunity the plaintiff identifies.** Rosh defends his position by invoking both demand- and supply-side considerations. One can easily read the modern economic concept of consumer surplus into Rosh's presentation of the demand side of his argument. At the core of Rosh's speculating that third-degree *onaa* **might** be permissible in the first instance is the consumer surplus concept. Given that every instance of voluntary exchange entails a certain measure of consumer surplus for the consumer, the buyer's contention that the transaction shortchanged him is dismissed when the comparison price differs by less than one-sixth of the price of the disputed transaction.

Reinforcing the judgment that the price paid by the consumer in a third-degree *onaa* transaction is subjectively equivalent to the market

31 See Mark Blaug, *Economic Theory in Retrospect*, 4th ed. (Cambridge: 1985), 319.

price is the consideration that the law of *onaa* generally operates only within the framework of a competitive marketplace, and not in a monopoly market.[32] Consider that a competitive marketplace works to lower an article's price from what it would have been had it been sold under monopoly conditions. Because consumer surplus is inversely related to price, third-degree *onaa* in a competitive marketplace affords the consumer more consumer surplus than would have been the case had the consumer bought the same goods from a monopolist. The judgment that the third-degree *onaa* transaction does not shortchange the buyer is thus credible.

The consumer surplus argument has its limitations, however. Consider that a **lower price** was available to the consumer at the time he entered into the disputed transaction. Arguing that the consumer realized **subjective equivalence** at the **higher price** he actually paid is hence reasonable only when the price discrepancy amounts to a relatively small amount. This small amount was defined by the Sages as a price difference of less than one-sixth.

Let us now move to Rosh's supply-side argument. Here, again, his argument can be couched in modern terms. To be sure, the vendor can always sell his wares at the market price. But the vendor cannot expect to sell out his supply **instantaneously**. Instead, he must be patient and can only accomplish this over the lifetime of the goods' normal inventory cycle. If the vendor desires to liquidate his inventory faster than the normal inventory cycle, he can do so only by slashing his price to below market price. What drives the vendor to act in this way is either a personal liquidity need not related to business; a belief that the **market price will soon drop sharply**, or a desire to liquidate his current inventory and acquire merchandise that affords the prospect of even greater profit. Because it is economically rational and even profitable at times for the vendor to **knowingly** sell below market price, the vendor's complaint that he was shortchanged is dismissed when only third-degree *onaa* is involved.

The inventory cycle argument has its limitations. Its appeal wears thinner and thinner as the difference between the transaction price and the alternative price widens. The Sages, therefore, established a cutoff point for this argument. Accordingly, once the price difference rises to exactly one-sixth, the argument is no longer accepted.

32 See text at nn. 61–69.

We now turn to consideration of how the law of *onaa* applies to the modern marketplace. The issues we will deal with include: 1) identification of the reference price; 2) spatial and temporal separation of the marketplace; 3) cost differences; 4) competitive price-cutting and discount price policies; and 5) monopoly pricing.

**Defining the Marketplace** Rosh's discussion of third-degree *onaa*, noted above, provides a good starting point for achieving greater precision in identifying the reference price to adjudicate the *onaa* claim. Preliminarily, let us note that talmudic decisors generally follow Rosh's second rationale for third-degree *onaa*.[33] Recall that on this rationale the complaint is dismissed on the basis of the presumed disagreement among experts as to whether *onaa* took place at all.

Commenting on the Rosh's view, R. Jehiel Michel Epstein points out that this disagreement among experts is only comprehensible when the product market involved is heterogeneous in nature. However, when the product market is homogeneous or standardized, the alternative opportunity the plaintiff identifies is clearly a better one. Experts would agree on this, so it is unreasonable to presume that the plaintiff waives his right to an adjustment.

Given agreement among experts, the presumption that the plaintiff waives his rights in a case of third-degree *onaa* is invalid when the product market is standardized. This observation leads R. Epstein to propose that third-degree *onaa* is inoperative in the case of a standardized product market. Accordingly, if the price difference is one-sixth or less, the plaintiff is entitled to recover the difference, even if it amounts to an inconsequential amount.[34]

Another implication of R. Asher's analysis of third-degree *onaa* is a narrow definition of what constitutes a product market. This narrowness follows from the fact that division among experts as to whether price fraud took place is only possible when the products being compared have offsetting advantages and disadvantages. Within this framework, when the difference in price is less than one-sixth, the plaintiff presumably waives his claim to the differential. If the difference in price is one-sixth or more, the trade-off involved no longer justifies the presumption of waiver. Differences among experts would not,

33 *Code*, Laws concerning Sales 13:3; Ramban (Nahmanides), (Spain, 1194–1270), on Leviticus 25:14; *Tur*, HM 227:4; *SA*, HM 227:2.

34 *AH*, HM 227:27.

however, be expected to emerge when the product in question contains all the features of competing products, and in addition has some distinctive characteristic. Differentiation here clearly separates the product from the competition and confers upon the seller an element of monopoly status. Monopoly status, in turn, vitiates the *onaa* claim.

Let us illustrate this point. Suppose B lodges a claim of *onaa* against a showroom furniture store on the grounds that an identical piece of furniture was available at a lower price in a catalog furniture store. The *onaa* claim is invalid. Since the showroom store offers differentiation, in the form of product display, its product is traded in a market **separate** from that of the product in the catalog store. The pricing policy of the latter establishment is therefore irrelevant in assessing the merits of a claim of *onaa* against the showroom store.

The principle of marketplace separation should also apply to a supermarket and grocery store located in the same neighborhood. Consider that the supermarket carries every item that the grocery store has and in addition carries a large variety of items that are not on the shelves of the grocery store. Because the supermarket offers **one-stop shopping** (complementarities of consumption), experts would agree that the supermarket provides a service **superior** to that provided by the grocery store, and is therefore not in the same marketplace as the grocery. Consequently, a claim of *onaa* lodged against a supermarket on the basis that an item it carries is cheaper in the grocery store is denied.

It might be argued that within the context of the modern product world, no competing products are identical. Differentiation today has advanced well beyond the level of the physical properties of the product to include such factors as proximity to the consumer, convenience of hours, complementarities of consumption, product display and service level. All market purchases involve some trade-off of offsetting advantages and disadvantages, and the law of *onaa* should be viewed within the framework of this modern product market. Relating this argument for defining a product market broadly to the furniture market example yields the proposition that the showroom and catalog stores should indeed be lumped together in a single product market. While the showroom store offers differentiation in the form of product display, the catalog store may offer the convenience of proximity to the consumer.

But the argument is not entirely valid. Differentiation works to erode the distinctiveness of a competing brand only when a basis exists for presuming that consumers value the differentiation involved.

Pointing in this direction is the determining role R. Asher assigns to the agreement or disagreement of experts in adjudicating cases of *onaa*. Clearly, cost differences among sellers play no **direct** role in adjudicating *onaa* cases. What does matter is the legitimacy of the assumption that consumers are willing to spend **extra money** for the differentiation involved. Following this line of thinking, proximity to the consumer would not be regarded as an offsetting advantage for the catalog store in the furniture market. Since the furniture market is not a local, neighborhood market, proximity of the seller to the consumer cannot be said to generate a presumption that consumers are willing to spend extra money to acquire this advantage. With respect to the consumer nondurable market, consumers may regard proximity, within limits, especially in the inclement weather season, as an advantage to which they attach price significance. Scientific surveys could prove very helpful in determining which aspects of differentiation consumers are willing to pay extra money to acquire. Such information would naturally add a measure of refinement to the preceding analysis.

One aspect of differentiation that consumers undoubtedly value is convenience of hours. In this regard, suppose A needs a remedy for a migraine headache when only one outlet that sells this item is open. Notwithstanding that this item is usually sold in a competitive marketplace, A's impatience, in the form of an immediate and perhaps desperate need, confers monopoly status on the outlet that has this item available when A's migraine strikes. Recognition that there is a market demand for various staple products at odd hours has spawned the emergence of neighborhood convenience stores open twenty-four hours a day. If the claim of *onaa* is conceptualized as the right of a market participant to trade at the price that was reasonably accessible to him at the time he entered into the disputed transaction, there should be no problem for the convenience store to charge whatever the market will bear during the time window it enjoys monopoly status. Under a dual pricing system, the operation of a convenience store would fall into two separate marketplaces. In regular business hours, when competing businesses are open, the pricing of the convenience store would be subject to *onaa*. But after-hours, the convenience store would be free to charge whatever the market would bear, as it enjoys monopoly status for that portion of the day. This dual price arrangement would, however, prove very unsatisfactory from the standpoint of the goal of maximizing profits. Consumers would quickly realize that the way to beat after-hours exploitation would be to stockpile goods when alternative outlets were available. Any shift in market demand from after-hours to regular hours would add to the pool of customers shared by all the outlets. In short shrift the convenience stores would end up catering in the odd hours **only** to the imprudent consumer who failed to stockpile. Profit maximization policy for a convenience store would hence lead it to charge a uniform price regardless of the time of day people shop there. But to recover its higher costs, compared to those of its rivals, the convenience store would set its uniform price higher. Does this policy not violate the law of *onaa*? No, provided it charges the **same** price per item over the entire twenty-four hour stretch, the differential the convenience store charges can be viewed as a premium for giving the consumer access to the item at the same price over an entire twenty-four hour period. Because its rivals make the item available only during ordinary business hours, the convenience store offers differentiation in the form of **continuous** access to the product. Because the convenience store is not likely to go out of business suddenly, there is assurance that the item at hand will be available in the after-hours at the regular-hours price for a reasonable time horizon. Consider that the viability of the convenience store hinges on its ability to charge a higher price than regular-hours rivals in order to recover its differential costs in running the store on a twenty-four hour basis. By maintaining a uniform pricing policy throughout the day, the convenience store is essentially telling the consumer that it will not provide an item at a relatively low and predictable price in the off hours unless it charges that price during regular business hours as well, even though that price will be higher than the price rival sellers will be charging for that item. Consumer reaction to a uniform pricing policy presents the classical setting for free rider conduct. Why don't consumers steadfastly avoid patronizing the convenience store during regular hours and limit their patronage to the time periods when no other alternatives are available? The viability of the convenience store demonstrates that the free rider motive is not rampant enough to knock the convenience store out of the marketplace. Accordingly, a claim of *onaa* lodged against a convenience store re an item purchased during regular business hours is dismissed on the grounds that the consumer was well aware of the differential, but paid it willingly either because he accepted the overcharge as the necessary price for ensuring the item would be available at the same price after-hours, or because of some other advantage. If we assume that the uniform pricing policy clearly communicates the above message to the marketplace, anyone who patronizes the convenience store during regular business hours **accepts** the higher charge as the price he must pay to ensure that the item at hand will also be available to him for purchase whenever he has a need to buy it after-hours. Let us not lose sight of the critical importance of the **uniform pricing policy** that allows the convenience store to charge above competing stores and not violate the prohibition against *onaa*. What the consumer gets for the premium price is no more than a **good faith assurance** that the convenience store will be around to serve him at a predictable and reasonable price in the odd hours, should he need its services. This differentiation is parallel to the assurance a firm offers that in the event a customer is dissatisfied with her purchase, the store will buy it back. If no rival offers a returns policy, the returns policy offered by store A amounts to a differentiation that sets A apart, and, other things being equal, allows it to charge a higher price for its product without violating the prohibition against *onaa*.

**Spatial and Temporal Separation of the Marketplace** In connection with the law that governs the liquidation procedure for property dedicated to the Sanctuary, the rule states that the sale of such property for the benefit of the Sanctuary must be conducted both in the locale (*mekomo*) where the dedication was made and in the time period (*shato*) when it was made (*ein lehekdesh ela mekomo veshato*).[35] The *mekomo veshato* rule, according to Nahmanides[36] and Ritva,[37] applies not only to the Sanctuary but to monetary matters generally. R. Abraham David Wahrmann explicitly posits the *mekomo veshato* rule in connection with the law of *onaa*.[38]

While the *mekomo veshato* rule finds application to both the adjudication of *onaa* cases and as a rule for liquidating property dedicated to the Sanctuary, the meaning of this rule appears to me to differ in the two contexts.

Let us first take up the rule as it relates to the Sanctuary. One instance where the rule applies is the following scenario: A vows the value of his pearl to the Sanctuary. Now suppose the place where A made the vow was a village. Because there is little demand for pearls in a village, seeking a buyer there will not fetch much of a price for

35 mArakhin 6:5.

36 Nahmanides, bKidushin 12a.

37 R. Yom Tov Ishbili (Spain, ca. 1250–1330), bKidushin 12a.

38 R. Abraham David Wahrmann (Ukraine, ca. 1771–1840), *Kesef Hakdoshim*, *SA*, HM 227:9.

the pearl. For the purpose of maximizing the Sanctuary's gain, may the treasurer of the Sanctuary demand of the consecrator that he bring the pearl to the city marketplace, where there is a brisk demand for pearls, and liquidate the jewel there? No. The consecrator is ordered to liquidate the pearl in the locale where he made his vow. Similarly, suppose the vow consisted of the value of one's cow. Here again, the cow is liquidated on the day the vow was made, and we do not wait for the market day, even though selling the cow on the market day will fetch a much higher price.[39] The rationale the Talmud offers for this procedure is the verse: "And he shall give the valuation on that day" (Lev. 27:23). The phrase "on that day" is taken to convey that the Sanctuary should acquire the value of the property **without delay**. This implies that the Sanctuary's claim to the value of what was consecrated is limited to both the locale where the vow was made and the time period when the vow was made.[40] In his commentary on the Mishnah, Maimonides first rationalizes the *mekomo veshato* rule by invoking Leviticus 27:23. He then goes on to say that despite the best of intentions, efforts taken to add value for the Sanctuary may very well bring in less. Accordingly, delay for the purpose of enhancing the Sanctuary's gain is not allowed.[41]

It follows from the above analysis that the *mekomo veshato* rule as it pertains to the Sanctuary is nothing more than a liquidation procedure. The rule as formulated for the Sanctuary would not, however, apply in adjudicating a claim of *onaa*. To illustrate, suppose S sells his pearl to B in a small village, getting a relatively low price for it. S subsequently lodges a claim of *onaa* against B on the grounds of the higher price of pearls in the nearby city marketplace. Should we invoke the *mekomo veshato* rule and deny S's claim? No. Consider that if anyone in the village wanted to sell a pearl, normal practice would not be to seek a buyer among fellow villagers, but instead to travel to the nearest city where a **pearl marketplace** is in actual operation. Because the claim of *onaa* is the right of a market participant to transact at the market price of the item in question, S's claim should stand. Similarly, because it is common practice for anyone in the village who wants to sell his cow to put it up for sale **on the market day**, the price the cow would have

39 mArakhin 6:5.

40 bArakhin 24a.

41 Maimonides, *Commentary on the Mishnah*, mArakhin 6:5.

fetched had S waited for the next market day should be the relevant reference price for adjudicating a claim of *onaa* in this case.

Recall that the claim of *onaa* is denied when the transaction price in relation to the market price was beyond the margin of error. Let us conceptualize *mekomo veshato* for cases of *onaa* as a guide for identifying the relevant marketplace, using a case recorded in the Codes to illustrate our point. S, who is known to be pressed for cash, sells an item he owns for less than its market price. If the price S agreed to, in relation to the market price, was beyond the margin of error, S's claim of *onaa* is denied, as S is assumed to have agreed to the below-market price on account of his immediate and pressing need for cash.[42] Suppose the item was a pearl and the owner lived in a village. Instead of traveling to the city market to sell his pearl, S sought out a buyer in the village. In assessing whether the price S **accepted** was beyond the range of error, should the reference price be what the pearl could have fetched in the village, or should it be what the pearl could have fetched in the city marketplace? Proceeding from the above formulation of *mekomo veshato* for *onaa*, the reference price should be the city pearl market. To be sure, S can certainly **liquidate** his pearl in his local village, but one who wants to **sell** pearls **ordinarily** takes the trouble to travel to an **organized marketplace for pearls**, and will therefore put them up for sale in a city marketplace. Hence, the appropriate reference price to determine whether the transaction at hand was concluded at a price beyond the margin of error is the price of the pearl in the city marketplace.

At this juncture let us note that the Talmud also discusses the reference price notion in connection with the forward contract. Entering into a forward contract may violate the rabbinical extension of the prohibition against interest payments, called *avak ribit* (lit., the dust of interest). This obtains when the market price of the commodity involved, say, grain, has not yet been established, and in addition, the seller is not in possession of the grain he desires to sell. Under these conditions, it is prohibited for S to contract to provide grain to B at a set price over a period of time. The concern here is that over the term of the contact the market price of grain may rise. Because the contract calls for a set price over the term of the contract, a rising market price for grain over this period of time decidedly benefits B. But S also benefits from this arrangement, as he has **advance** use of B's money

42 *Responsa Rosh*, klal 102, §7; quoted in *Tur*, HM 227:1; *SA*, HM 227:9; *AH*, HM 227:12.

before he delivers the grain to B. The benefit of advance use of B's money obtains even if it turns out that the market price of grain rises over the period of the contract. Given the above benefit for S, the Sages view B's advance payment as a disguised loan and the future delivery of the grain, during a period when the market price is rising, as entailing a premium above the value of the sum B gave S in advance of the deliveries.[43]

One way to remedy the *avak ribit* problem inherent in a forward contract of the type described is for S to wait until the market price for grain is set and then contract to deliver grain to B at that price over an extended period of time. Here, even though S is not in possession of grain at the moment he strikes his deal with B, the deal does not violate the *avak ribit* law. This remedy is called *yatza hashar* (lit., the price has gone out).[44] The rationale here is that once the market price for grain has been established, S has the ability to buy the quantity of grain he committed himself to deliver to B. Since S is capable of buying and delivering the grain to B at the price he stipulated to B, B's payment is no longer viewed as a disguised loan, and S's deliveries are no longer viewed as premium installment payments for the loan.[45] For this remedy to make any sense, the reference market price that S sets for his contract with B must have some **stability**. Without the element of stability, S would not have the requisite time to buy up in the marketplace the order he promised to deliver to B at the price he set.[46] In identifying the market price that is sufficiently stable to remedy the *avak ribit* problem in forward contracts, the Talmud speaks of three possibilities. One possibility is the market price established in the small provincial towns in close proximity to the harvest.[47] This price, according to R. Abraham Danzig (Prague, 1748–1820), has stability for only a few days.[48] Another choice for the reference price is the price established in the central cities.[49] This price first goes into effect sometime after the harvest, but once established, has stability for two or three months.[50]

43 mBaba Metzia 5:7.

44 mBaba Metzia 5:7; *Rif* ad loc.; *Code*, Laws concerning Creditor and Debtor 9:1; *Rosh*, Baba Metzia 5:60; *Tur*, YD 175:1; *SA*, YD 175:1.

45 bBaba Metzia 72b; *Rosh*, ibid.; *Tur*, ibid.; *SA*, ibid.

46 See *Divrei Soferim* 175:3.

47 bBaba Metzia 72b.

48 R. Abraham Danzig, *Hokhmat Adam*, 141:1.

49 bBaba Metzia 72b.

50 *Rif*, quoted in Shita Mekubetzet ad loc.

Finally, there is a price that is stable even longer than the central market price, and this is the price that is established at big granaries and shippers.[51] The market price codifiers of Jewish law generally adopt as the appropriate price for remedying the *avak ribit* problem of the forward contract is the central city price.[52]

Let us now relate the above discussion regarding forward contracts to the law of *onaa*. In adjudicating *onaa* disputes, what is the appropriate reference price to adopt? Addressing this issue, Efraim Kleiman proposes that it should be:

> The shortest of all short-run market [prices] — the one obtaining at the particular locality and particular moment at which the transaction concerned was effected. Such a price has little to be said for it on either equity or efficiency grounds. The ethics of the *onaa* rule applied not to the price itself, but to the withholding of information about it.[53]

In evaluating Kleiman's thesis, there can be no doubt that the *mekomo veshato* rule supports his contention that for adjudicating claims of *onaa*, the reference price should take on a **short-run** character. But the reference price for *onaa* should certainly not be equated with the market price established for dedications made to the Sanctuary. It is in connection with the liquidation procedure established for dedications made to the Sanctuary that Kleiman's phrase — "shortest of all short-run market [prices]" — is very apt. This is so because in figuring out what one owes the Sanctuary as a result of dedicating a particular item, the **on the spot liquidation value of the item** is mandated. But in adjudicating claims of *onaa*, the reference price is either the **market value** of the item at hand, or alternatively, the price that was **reasonably accessible** to plaintiff at the time he entered into the disputed transaction. Within the framework of either of these measures, the reference price in the *onaa* dispute is not the liquidation value the item has on the spot, but rather its value on the marketplace where people in the plaintiff's locale ordinarily go to trade this item.

51 bBaba Metzia 72b.

52 *Rif*, on the interpretation of *Beit Yosef*, *Tur*, YD 175; *Rosh*, Baba Metzia 5:60; *SA*, YD 175:1. However, R. Jacob b. Asher (*Tur*, loc. cit.) and R. Moses Isserles (*SA*, loc. cit.) regard the price of the small provincial towns as the appropriate price to use in structuring forward contracts.

53 E. Kleiman, "'Just price' in the talmudic literature," *History of Political Economy* 19 (1987), 39.

Setting the price the item sells for in the marketplace the plaintiff ordinarily turns to when he seeks to trade in that type of item as the reference price in an *onaa* proceeding makes a definite statement regarding what a "fair price" is. I therefore dispute Kleiman's contention that *onaa* has nothing to contribute vis-a-vis equity.

Similarly, I dispute Kleiman's claim that *onaa* has little to recommend it with respect to efficiency. Let me begin by saying that I take it as a given that in Jewish society people strive to achieve integrity of reputation, and avoid actions that will brand them as untrustworthy and crooked. Recall that Jewish law regards *onaa* as a form of theft. Because engaging in *onaa* calls into question the integrity of the violator, a market participant would be driven to avoid jeopardizing his reputation by searching the marketplace more intensely to keep from entering into a fraudulent deal that would later be challenged. Such increased marketplace investigation by all market participants drives the marketplace closer to prices that more accurately reflect the opportunity cost of the various goods and services. Hence, the law of *onaa* does indeed promote economic efficiency.

**Cost Differences** Suppose A faces higher costs than rival B, for example, in the form of higher rent and/or higher taxes, and these differentially higher costs are well known to the public. Do A's well-known higher costs give him free rein to charge a higher price than B? Addressing this issue, a contemporary decisor in Jerusalem feels that A's higher costs justify a higher price, and B is not required to inform his customer that the item at hand is available at a lower price elsewhere in the marketplace.[54] Disputing this view, R. Jacob Isaiah Blau (Israel, b. 1929) contends that differentially higher costs, even if well understood by the public, do not per se license the high-cost seller to charge a higher price.[55]

If *onaa* is conceptualized as an opportunity cost claim, the circumstance that the defendant operates under differentially higher costs should not be a mitigating factor in adjudicating the case. R. Blau's position thus finds support in the opportunity cost rationale for the *onaa* claim.

Consider a variation of the above case. Suppose it is well known that S operates under differentially higher costs and also **charges**

54 Anonymous authority, quoted in *Mamon Kasher* (Jerusalem: 1982), 90.
55 R. Jacob Isaiah Blau, *Pithei Hoshen*, Laws of Theft and Fraud, 299.

**higher prices** than competing firms in the same market. If B enters into a transaction with S, both parties presumably know that the trade entails *onaa*. Is B's claim of *onaa* recognized? The silk ribbons case discussed earlier is relevant here. Recall that the salient feature of the case was the presumption that the complainant was aware at the time he concluded his transaction that it entailed *onaa*. The complainant's claim of *onaa* stands, according to R. Isserles, only because consummating the transaction provides the best strategy for keeping the article and also recovering the differential. As will be recalled, this strategy makes sense only when the *onaa* involved is second-degree. R. Isserles's line of reasoning leads to the general principle that whenever we are reasonably certain that the complainant was aware of the *onaa* at the time he entered into his transaction, he forfeits any subsequent claim, on the grounds that his original silence constituted a waiver of his rights in the matter. What follows is that if S's differentially higher costs and higher prices are well known to the public, paying him a higher price for merchandise that is cheaper elsewhere in the same *onaa* marketplace should generally be taken as a waiver by B of his *onaa* rights.

**Competitive Price Cutting** Within the framework of the marketplace, **deliberate** price cutting is an ordinary occurrence. Does the law of *onaa* require a rival to match a competitor's price cut? Relevant to this issue, which has many variations, are the following talmudic texts:

> [R. Judah says] He may not lower the price of his goods below the market price. But the Sages say: He is remembered for good.[56]
>
> What is the Sages' reason? Because he lowers the market price (*mirvah letara*).[57]

Halakha takes the view of the Sages as normative.[58] But the commentators differ as to how far the price-cutting privilege goes.

One school of thought, led by R. Meir b. Isaac Eisenstadt (Poland, 1670–1744), understands the price-cutter (A) of the Mishnah to be a retail grain dealer. A's price-cutting is legitimate, according to R. Eisenstadt and others, only because it results in the reduction of the market price of an essential commodity, i.e., grain.[59] Rashi, commenting on the

56 mBaba Metzia 4:12.

57 bBaba Metzia 60a–60b.

58 *Code*, Laws concerning Sales 18:4; *Tur, SA*, and *AH*, HM 228:18.

59 R. Meir b. Isaac Eisenstadt, *Panim Meirot* 1:78; *AH*, loc. cit.; R. Judah Loeb Graubart (Russian Poland, 1862–1937), *Havalim Baneimim* 2:113.

Mishnah, describes the scenario whereby this result obtains: A's price-cutting makes hoarders of grain believe that the market price of grain is on the way down. This leads them to dump their supplies on the market, causing the market price of grain to go down.[60] Suppose the commodity in question was not grain but beer. Here, avers R. Eisenstadt, A's price-cutting will assuredly not set into motion market forces that will push down the market price of grain. This is all the truer in situations where the economy operates under government price controls. When A's price-cutting will not set into motion market forces that will push down the price of grain, this conduct is regarded as an unfair competitive tactic.[61]

Sharply disputing this view, R. Solomon Kluger (Ukraine, 1785–1869) avers that the Sages legitimize price-cutting even when it does not set into motion market forces that will drive down the price of grain. Moreover, the tactic is legitimate even when the conduct does not force rival sellers to match the price cut. A close reading of Rashi's remarks referred to earlier clearly demonstrates that his scenario involving a retail grain dealer is offered only as representing a circumstance where the Sages would heap praise on the price-cutter. But price-cutting is fundamentally a legitimate competitive tactic, even when it has no effect on either lowering the price of grain or lowering the price rival sellers charge for the commodity in question.[62]

It follows from R. Solomon Kluger's interpretation of the Sages' view that under certain conditions the halakha would have no objection to a non-uniform price structure for a particular commodity. This occurs when aggregate demand exceeds aggregate supply at the lower price the price-cutter A sets. Here, the effect of the price cut is merely to redistribute aggregate demand in favor of A, but not to force rival sellers to match the price cut.

On the foregoing scenario, A should lose any right to lodge a claim of *onaa*. This is so because **deliberate** price cutting communicates a desire on the part of A to gain customers at the **expense** of the higher-priced rivals. Moreover, when the price cut is communicated in advertisements, validation of A's claim of *onaa* amounts to nothing less than approval of a deceptive advertising technique.

60 Rashi, mBaba Metzia 60b.
61 *Panim Meirot, AH,* loc. cit.
62 R. Solomon Kluger, *Hokhmat Shlomo, SA,* HM 228:18.

If a deliberate price-cutter's claim of *onaa* is invalid, rival sellers should be under no obligation to inform customers of the lower-priced opportunity A is offering. This is so because the law of fair competition requires rival sellers only to **tolerate** A's price cut, but does not go so far as to require them, effectively, to **send customers** to him.

Another way to arrive at the same conclusion is to analyze the issue at hand from the perspective of the consumer (B). Does B, who bought the item from the high-priced seller, have a claim of *onaa* against him? Consider that the claim of *onaa* is the right to obtain the item in question at the **market price.** Does the discount price the low-priced seller charges represent the market price? No. Since the market will bear a higher price, the low-priced seller is clearly driven by an **investment motive.** This motive could consist of a desire to acquire a reputation for low prices in order to boost sales volume in the future. Alternatively, the motive could be to attract customers to the store in the hope that they will also buy other items that are not on sale. An extreme version of this technique is called the "loss leader stratagem." Because the market will bear a higher price than the price the low-priced seller charges, the differential is nothing but a **gift** the lower-priced seller offers customers in the hope of realizing a **return on this gift** now or in the future. Given the investment rationale behind the low-priced seller's price, other sellers should bear no obligation whatsoever to follow suit and match his price. The customer's claim of *onaa* on the grounds of the **discount price** of the same item in another store should therefore be dismissed outright.

The above argument should apparently be limited to the instance where the low-priced seller somehow communicates that his price is a **discount price.** Suppose, however, that one of a whole group of sellers takes the lead in reducing the item's price, without communicating to his customers that the new, lower, price is a **sale price.** Recall R. Meir Arik's proposition that the price the majority of sellers charge in a particular marketplace determines the reference price for adjudicating claims of *onaa* in that marketplace. It follows from this view that B's claim of *onaa* against a high-priced seller S will be dismissed when S's price was equal to the price the majority of the sellers were charging. This judgment should hold whether or not the low-priced seller **officially** called his price a discount price. The rationale here is that B's entitlement extends only to trading the item at its market price. Since the majority of that item's sales volume traded at the price S charged, B presumably realized market value with his purchase, and hence his claim of *onaa* is dismissed. Alternatively, B is entitled to trade the item at the price that was reasonably accessible to him in the marketplace for that item. Since S's price conformed to the practice of the majority of the relevant sellers at the time B entered into his transaction with S, the transaction must be deemed a fair trade, and there is no basis for either modifying or cancelling it.

Let us consider a variation of the above case. Suppose domestic textile manufacturers are all charging the same price for a particular broadloom. A law that is enacted unexpectedly lifts all tariffs from imported broadloom. S breaks away from the pack and lowers his price, while all the other sellers remain at the old price. Within this new price structure for the industry, B makes a purchase from one of the high-priced sellers, H. Is B's claim of *onaa* against H valid? Consider that competitive conditions clearly intensified for domestic producers of textiles when the import duty was lifted. Because market conditions have changed **decidedly** and the price is on the way down, S's lower price should not be viewed as a discount price, but rather, as the price that reflects **the new realities** of the marketplace. Accordingly, B's claim of *onaa* against H on the basis of S's lower price should be valid, notwithstanding that H's price conformed to the general industry standard for the moment.

One final point. A claim of *onaa* must be based on the market conditions at the time the plaintiff entered into the disputed transaction. Should the plaintiff maintain that the reference price he invokes reflected market conditions at time he entered into the disputed transaction, but the defendant insists that the more favorable price the plaintiff invokes reflects market conditions for the period after the transaction took place, the burden of proof rests with the party who claims that market conditions were the same at the time of the transaction and thereafter.[63] This is so because market price is always presumed to be in a state of flux.[64]

**Monopoly** The halakha's treatment of a complaint of *onaa* lodged against a monopolistic seller can be derived from this discussion in bBaba Metzia 58b: "R. Judah b. Batera [mid 1st c.] said: The sale of horse, sword and buckler on [the field of] battle are not subject to *onaa*, because one's very life is dependent upon them."

63 *Rema*, *SA*, HM 227:9.

64 R. Mordekhai b. Hillel Hakohen (Germany, 1240–1298), *Mordekhai*, Ketubot 7:206, quoted in *Rema*, loc. cit.

The battlefield case entails a monopoly vendor situation. Consider that while the commercial market for horses and weapons is normally subject to a competitive norm, the marketplace for these articles completely collapses within the framework of the battlefield. The economic environment that prevails within such a war zone effectively precludes the emergence of a "competitive" price for these articles. Resource mobility and knowledge of market alternatives are conspicuously absent here, as the movement of market participants is severely restricted. With economic activity characteristically unorganized and sporadic, the market for these articles becomes minutely fragmented. Within this framework, the individual bargain between a buyer and seller determines price.

Given the breakdown of the marketplace in the battlefield case, the vendee's claim of *onaa* should be rejected on the simple grounds that he had no alternatives at the time he entered into the trade. But R. Judah does not let this explanation suffice, and instead invokes his rationale that the vendee got a fair deal because his very life was dependent on the trade. Why the **no alternative** rationale does suffice here can be explained by the fact that the battlefield case is not a typical **voluntary** exchange. Only in a genuine voluntary exchange case is it reasonable to presume that the transaction is predicated on mutual gain. This is not the case here. Because of his desperate situation, the vendee is for all intents and purposes **coerced** into buying what he needs to survive the battle. It is for this reason that R. Judah invokes his rationale that it was a "fair deal" because the vendee's very life was dependent on the trade. Because the trade extricates the vendee from a life-threatening situation, the presumption that the trade entailed "mutual advantage" is valid for this case as well.

Talmudic decisors dispute whether R. Judah b. Batera's ruling represents mainstream talmudic thought. R. Hai b. Sherira of Pumbedita (939–1038)[65] and R. Isaac b. Jacob Alfasi[66] rule that R. Judah b. Batera's opinion represents a minority view and should therefore be rejected. R. Hananel b. Hushiel, an eleventh-century North African decisor, however, rules in accordance with R. Judah b. Batera.[67]

65 R. Hai b. Sherira, *Ketab-al Shira wa-al*, translated into Hebrew by R. Isaac al Bargelone, *Sefer Hamikah Vehamimkar* (Venice: 1602).

66 Rif ad loc.

67 *Rabbenu Hananel* ad loc.

The acceptability of R. Judah b. Batera's opinion, according to R. Moses Hakohen of Lunel, a thirteenth-century decisor, hinges upon the validity of assimilating his battlefield case to the fugitive-ferryman case discussed in bBaba Kama 115a. Here, the Talmud relates that if an absconding criminal agreed to pay a ferryman an above-market price to provide him with conveyance across a river, he is entitled to recoup from the ferryman the differential involved.[68]

The point of similarity between the two cases is obviously that in both instances the buyer's interest in the product involved is price-inelastic: he would agree to pay any price the seller insists on. In the ferryman-fugitive case, since the conveyance averts the fugitive's imminent capture, the transaction can be regarded as entailing mutual advantage. Nonetheless, were he not a fugitive, this same individual's demand for the conveyance would properly be described as price-elastic, and he would presumably not value the service above market price. With his price-inelastic demand reflecting transitory subjective value, the fugitive is entitled to recoup from the ferryman any amount above the competitive norm. Similarly, absent the war setting, the vendee would presumably decline to pay the asking price for the implements of war.

Though R. Moses Hakohen cites no reason why this assimilation should be rejected, what distinguishes the two cases is market structure. Whereas a competitive norm exists for the services of the ferryman at the time the fugitive strikes up his bargain, **no competitive norm** exists at the time an individual buys implements of war in a battlefield situation. What follows clearly from the approach that accepts the analogy between the fugitive-ferryman case and the battlefield case is the general principle that exercise of monopoly power, when the relevant aggregate demand schedule is perfectly inelastic, is ethically immoral.

It can be inferred from the fugitive-ferryman cases that there would be no moral objection for a monopolist to sell his output at whatever the market will bear when the relevant demand is price elastic. The following Mishnah (mKetubot 13:7) supports this contention:

> If someone (A) went overseas, and the path to his field was lost — Admon says: he may go by the shortest path. The Sages, however, say: He must buy a path [even] for one hundred *mane*, or fly in the air.

68 R. Moses Hakohen of Lunel, quoted in *Shita Mekubetzet* ad loc.

In its elucidation of this Mishnah, the Talmud narrows the dispute between Admon and the Sages, proposing that there are cases where the disputants agree. In the instance where the surrounding fields are owned by different people, Admon agrees with the Sages that A has no right to a path, as each neighbor can keep him out and claim "your path is not located in my field." Accordingly, each neighbor can refuse to sell A a path unless he agrees to pay the price demanded. In the instance where all the surrounding properties are owned by a single individual (S), the Sages are in agreement with Admon that S must yield to A the right to the shortest path. The dispute between Admon and the Sages deals with the circumstance where S presently owns all the surrounding properties, but before A's path was lost, all the fields had different owners. Here, Admon requires S to yield to A the shortest path. Disputing Admon, the Sages permit S to exert leverage over A and tell him, 'Either agree to the price I demand or I will prevail over the previous owners to take back the fields and you will have to deal with each owner separately and end up paying a higher price for the path than the price I demand of you now.'[69] Talmudic codifiers follow the view of the Sages.[70]

What the above Mishnah regarding the sale of a path shows is that when the buyer's very life does not depend on successfully acquiring the article at hand, it is not morally objectionable for the monopolist seller to exercise leverage so as to maximize his gain.

The morality of monopoly pricing is treated in the rabbinical literature. R. Meir Eisenstadt, for instance, validated the practice of auctioning to the highest bidder the privilege of performing a public ceremonial function.[71] The case R. Eisenstadt deals with is akin to monopoly pricing, since the ceremonial honor put up for sale is unavailable elsewhere. With no reference price to turn to, competitive bidding among the auction participants determines value.

Other instances where there is no reference price to turn to include the auctioning of a rare painting to the highest bidder, the sale of a patent right, and the sale of a building that has "site value."[72] In all

69 bKetubot 109b.

70 *Code*, Laws concerning Pleading 15:11; *Tur, SA, AH*: HM 148:1.

71 R. Meir Eisenstadt, *Panim Meirot* 11:25; see R. Ezra Basri, *Dinei Mamonot* (Jerusalem: 1976), vol. 2, 172.

72 Real estate transactions are not subject to the full scope of *onaa* regulation. This exclusion proceeds from exegetical interpretation of the biblical source of *onaa*, "And if thou sell aught unto thy neighbor or acquire of thy

these instances the vendee's need for the item at hand cannot be categorized as desperate. Economic theory would deem the demand in these cases decidedly elastic. Accordingly, there should be no ethical objection for the seller to exploit the market for whatever price it will bear. Support for this contention can be drawn from the case involving the case of the path.

One caveat should, however, be noted regarding the regulation of monopoly pricing in Jewish law. In talmudic times the Sages enacted an ordinance to restrict the profit margins of vendors dealing in essential commodities to twenty percent. Elsewhere[73] we discussed the particulars of this ordinance. Our finding was that in enacting this regulation, the Sages did not intend to interfere with the natural forces of supply and demand. Instead, vendors of foodstuffs were permitted to sell at the market price. The practical significance of the ordinance was to prohibit sellers from collusively restricting supply for the purpose of raising their profit margin above the twenty-percent level. Included in the edict was a prohibition preventing monopolists from **artificially** raising market price by holding back supply.

**Conclusion** In this final section, our objective is to summarize this paper with respect to what the notion of *onaa* has to say about equity and efficiency in the marketplace.

Our thesis has been that *onaa* is the **entitlement** of a market participant to trade the article in question at its objective market value.

---

neighbor's hand" (Lev. 25:14) — something that is acquired (by being passed) from hand to hand (is subject to *onaa* regulation), thus excluding land, which is not movable (see bBaba Metzia 56b). Nahmanides (commentary ad loc.) points out that insofar as a biblical interdict against *onaa* is mentioned explicitly in connection with real estate transactions, the exemption above must be taken to refer exclusively to the restitution procedure normally provided for in cases of *onaa*. Hence, real estate transactions are subject to the prohibition against *onaa*, though not to its prescribed restitution procedure.

What follows as a corollary from our analysis of the ethics of monopoly pricing is that the interdict is violated only when the real estate transaction involved an authentic opportunity cost; i.e., property with the same general characteristics was available in the marketplace at a price above or below the transaction price. No moral issue, however, arises regarding the price differential attributed to "site" value.

73 Aaron Levine, *Economic Public Policy and Jewish Law* (Hoboken, NJ: 1993), 27–32.

This makes *onaa* essentially an opportunity cost claim. What the opportunity cost notion translates into, on a practical level, is apparently a matter of dispute. One way to look at the matter is to conceptualize *onaa* as the right of a market participant to trade the article in question on the basis of its objective market value. Alternatively, *onaa* can be viewed as the right to trade the article in question at the price that was reasonably accessible to the plaintiff at the time he entered into the deal.

Because *onaa* is not a claim of ignorance of market conditions, but rather a **right** to trade the article in question at its market norm, the presumption that the plaintiff was aware of the better marketplace opportunity when he entered into the disputed transaction does not automatically invalidate his claim of *onaa*. If the plaintiff can come up with a credible reason why he **knowingly** went through with the deal, he retains his *onaa* rights until such time as he signals that he waives his rights in the matter.

The plaintiff is not given license, in putting forth his claim that a better opportunity was available to him, to point to **any** reference price he can find. Rather, the reference price is limited both spatially and temporally: it is limited to the marketplace to which people in the plaintiff's position would ordinarily turn to conduct the transaction at hand.

Another limitation on the plaintiff regarding the reference price he brings up in his claim is that it must be a market price and not a discount price. Consider that the claim of *onaa* is the right to obtain the item at hand at **the market price**. Does the discount price the low-priced seller charges represent the market price? No. Since the market will bear a higher price, the low-priced seller is clearly driven by an **investment motive**. This motive could be the desire to acquire a reputation for low prices in order to boost sales volume in the future. Alternatively, the motive could be to attract customers to the store in the hope that they also buy items that are not on sale. Because the market will bear a higher price than the price the low-priced seller charges, the differential is nothing but a **gift** the lower-priced seller offers customers in the hope of realizing a **return on this gift then or in the future**. Given the investment rationale behind the low-priced seller's price, other sellers have no obligation whatsoever to follow suit and match the price. The claim of *onaa* based on the **discount price** of the same item in another store should therefore be dismissed.

The reference price for the purpose of adjudicating the *onaa* claim is usually calculated by noting the price the majority of the sellers charge in the relevant marketplace. An exception to this rule obtains when a particular seller S initiates a price cut below the industry norm, in response to an event that clearly changed the market conditions. S's lower price should not be seen as a discount price, but as a new market price, reflecting the new marketplace realities.

The law of *onaa* also tells us that a marketplace transaction is fair only if it was entered into on a voluntary basis. In a voluntary transaction both parties gain, or else the transaction would not be taking place. What should be made of the case where the life of a buyer (D) depends on acquiring some article, and he agrees in advance to pay more than its ordinary price? Is this also a voluntary transaction? The answer is somewhat mixed. If only D's situation is desperate, and the ordinary price prevails for everyone else, D is regarded as being exploited, and is therefore entitled not to hand over to the seller the extra payment he promised. Instead, D can claim that he was just mocking S when he made his promise to pay the exorbitant amount. But suppose everyone shares D's desperate need for the items in question. Here, the ethics of charging whatever the marketplace will bear is a matter of dispute. The prototypical case is the sale of implements of war on the battlefield, discussed in bBaba Metzia 58b.

Let us now turn to the issue of whether the law of *onaa* fosters efficient pricing in the marketplace. We take it that an efficient price is a price that reflects the true opportunity cost associated with acquiring the goods at hand. Recall that Jewish law regards *onaa* as a form of theft. I also take it as a given that in Jewish society people seek a reputation of integrity, and avoid actions that will brand them as untrustworthy and crooked. Because an infraction of the law of *onaa* calls into question the integrity of the violator, a market participant would be driven to avoid jeopardizing his reputation by searching the marketplace further so as to avoid entering into a deal that would later be challenged. More intensive marketplace investigation by all market participants thus drives the marketplace closer to prices that more accurately reflect the opportunity cost of the various goods and services. Hence, the law of *onaa* promotes economic efficiency.[74]

74 This paper was delivered at the Conference on Biblical Economics, The Hebrew University, Jerusalem, Israel, June 7, 2000.

# REVIEW ARTICLE

# SOME RECENT WORK ON LOGIC, MATHEMATICS AND HALAKHA

EPHRAIM NISSAN*

Michael Chernick, *Gezerah Shavah; its Various Forms in Midrashic and Talmudic Sources* (Hebrew), Lod, Israel: Haberman Institute for Literary Research, 1994.

Michael Chernik's dense Hebrew book in octavo presents work that constitutes nothing less than a breakthrough, and a necessary first step toward formalization of that eminently elusive exegetical criterion, *gzeira shava*, one of the canonic thirteen criteria of exegesis. *Gzeira shava* is, to simplify somewhat, a word-comparison device — it applies in cases where an 'equivalent' term is found by identifying the same wording in different textual contexts in the Torah. While productive in the Aggadic domain, *gzeira shava* is quite problematic in the legal domain; so much so, indeed, that it was 'neutralized' fairly early on by the Sages. As it would allow sweeping analogies where they are not warranted, it is unsuitable in the halakhic domain if not relegated to an ornamental role, for *de jure condendo*. The restriction of the device's applicability evolved to the point where *gzeira shava* could only be invoked in support of an extant justification for a norm. Already in the Jerusalem Talmud it was relegated to the role of a literary embellishment. The gradual narrowing of the scope of its application, as instantiated in the talmudic literature, is meticulously analyzed in Chernick's book. Chernick first delimits the range of his data, "consider[ing] only those Midrashic expositions explicitly called gezerah shavah in the tannaitic midrashim as bona fide examples." *Gzeira shava* is

> not the result of whim.... [these inferences] are governed by formal rules that prevent comparison of every similar word from the Torah for legal or aggadic purposes.... The basic formal rule for 'plain' gezerah shavah is that its source is a word or phrase repeated only twice in the Pentateuch. The 'mufne' gezerah shavah's formal requirements are less rigid, but generally require the appearance of comparable words in a single

* School of Computing and Mathematical Sciences, University of Greenwich, London. An expert on computational linguistics, he also writes on legal applications of computing, and on philological aspects of Rabbinic texts.

> Pentateuchal pericope or in a single Pentateuchal legal framework. The word must also be syntactically or logically extraneous.... There are word-comparison expositions that the Tannaim did not call gezerah shavah.

Chernick's abstract states that *gzeira shava* expositions "may not be purely logical like kal va-homer expositions." Were we to try to reduce *gzeira shava* to logic, how would we accomplish this? Chernick's book is a good place to start, but we must resign ourselves to the fact that for the time being, we simply do not know how to go about it.

Let me clarify this assessment, which may raise eyebrows in view of my opening sentence. The book is a breakthrough in research on *gzeira shava* in general. While not itself mathematically oriented, it is a must for those logicists who, seeking to formalize the canonic criteria of exegesis, are likely to be stymied by *gzeira shava*, finding it more than just a stumbling block, but rather, a giant barrier akin to the Aggadic beast (*reem*) David the shepherd encountered in the wilderness.[1] How is one to go about (sur)mounting it? And, once one has, one might well be as sorry as David was. In an email exchange on the feasibility of formalizing some of the thirteen principles of exegesis, Tel-Aviv University's Ron Shapira suggested: "*Gzeira shava* seems to me to be too hard a challenge to tackle. Its underlying logic is presumably one of symmetry. In order to understand *gzeira shava* one has to define equivalence classes, describe transformations, perhaps demonstrate that there is a group of symmetries involved, etc. I can't imagine doing all this against the foul backdrop of context dependence."[2] Armed with this insight, reading Chernick's book should be the next step, as a result of which the reader may be relieved to discover that "the foul backdrop of context dependence," while remaining formidable, is somewhat less unwieldy that it would otherwise appear. Chernick's classification of the occurrences of *gzeira shava* enables the more ambitious of his readers to reduce the forest into what seem to be more manageable groves of trees.

*Higayon — Studies in Rabbinic Logic* (Hebrew, with English summaries; some articles in English), 1–4 (1989–1997). Aluma, at the Center for Jewish Public Policy, Jerusalem. Order c/o M. Koppel and E. Merzbach, Dept. of Mathematics, Bar-Ilan University, Ramat Gan, Israel.

The journal under review, a forum whose contributors come mainly, but not exclusively, from the ranks of mathematicians, but whose

1 Yalkut Shimoni, Psalms, para. 688.
2 E-mail correspondence, 1997.

intended audience is broader (hence the journal's accessible style), highlights the discipline's contribution to the understanding of rabbinical law and philosophy. The journal publishes papers that either reconstruct a mathematical concept ascribable to an authority of old, or reinterpret a topic from rabbinical sources according to some present-day mathematical insight. The interconnections between logic and both philosophy and lawmaking form a pervasive, rich-textured mesh underlying Jewish, Western and Muslim cultures, and predate the emergence of the kind of discourse whose present-day state we are concerned with in this review. The ancient connections between what we are used to viewing as separate disciplines created a transcultural common ground for the intellectual elites in the Hellenistic and Roman world, including scholars and literati during the Jewish Second Commonwealth, the Tannaitic period, and later years. Saul Lieberman (1898–1983) provided a cogent picture of this interaction in his *Greek and Hellenism in Jewish Palestine* (1984). In the words of Mark Riley, "Mathematicians, geometers, and others in what we would call (anachronistically) the scientific specialties were almost certainly considered part of the literary world — or more precisely, as possible participants in literary discussion."[3]

Late antiquity witnessed the codification of the Mishnah and Gemara and, *lehavdil*, of Justinian's *Corpus Juris Civilis*. In medieval Paris, scholasticism, seeking a harmonistic interpretation of Roman law, was nurtured at the Sorbonne. And until the dominant society set out to burn the Talmud and drive the Jews from France, the Tosafists of Franco-Germany — so vividly portrayed by the late Ephraim Elimelech Urbach in his *Baalei Hatosafot*[4] — applied a standard set of logical criteria to show that the talmudic teachings constitute a harmonic whole, however vast. Likewise, the connections between logic and lawmaking find expression in Islamic law, in ways that call to mind, but are by no means identical with, the thirteen criteria of halakhic exegesis.[5]

3 Mark Riley, "Theoretical and practical astrology: Ptolemy and his colleagues," *Transactions of the American Philological Association* 117 (1987), 235–256, p. 251. Riley's focus was astrologers, who, he claims, were perceived as falling into the same category as the Greek sophists. The Jewish astrology of antiquity is the subject of a forthcoming book by Meir Bar-Ilan; like Jewish magic and Jewish numerology (not to be identified with Gematria), it was part of a Jewish culture of which rabbinical literature was but a part, which is not to say that the rabbis would not have been adept at the other aspects of the culture.

4 *The Tosaphists: Their History, Writings and Methods* (Hebrew), (Jerusalem: 1955).

5 See, e.g., M.A.Kh. Omar, "Reasoning in Islamic law: part one," *Arab Law Quarterly* 12 (1997), 148–196.

In *Higayon* 3, "Halachic generalization," by Azriel Rosenfeld, a renowned computer scientist, shows how generalization impacts several of the thirteen canonic *midot* of Jewish exegesis. Analogical inference in halakhic reasoning, in terms of the *midot*, is often contrasted to the more restrictive deductive reasoning of medieval scholasticism, with its emphasis on syllogistic constructions with two premises and a conclusion. For a noted twentieth-century rabbinical thinker, R. David Cohen, 'the Nazir,' the import of analogy is momentous, even cosmic, rather than merely legal or Aggadic. Dov Schwartz, in *Higayon* 2, relates how the Nazir ascribes messianic significance to determining the rules of analogy, not just in the kind of exegetical contexts in which the thirteen *midot* are traditionally applied, but in a broad spectrum of sources, from the Prophets to mysticism.

The latest issue of *Higayon*, no. 4, includes two papers in English ("*Rov* and probability" by Yaakov Werblowsky, and "Forms of a-fortiori argument" by Avi Sion), and twelve in Hebrew. Several address uncertainty and majority. For example, Leib Moscovitz discerns a divergence between the Babylonian Talmud and the Jerusalem Talmud with regard to situations where members of a minority are present within the majority (*rov*), as, for instance, when, in a set of objects of a given halakhic status, an item of a different status is found. In the Babylonian Talmud, the ruling is usually according to the majority, whereas it appears that for the Tannaim and Amoraim of Eretz Yisrael, the strict ruling is to apply, due to uncertainty.

Ely Merzbach and Nechemia Taylor's "Lottery in the world of prayer" deals with the halakhic distinction between an as-yet-undetermined outcome, and a result that is determined but unknown, especially with regard to the permissibility of prayer for a desired result. What is the status of a lottery based on computer calculations that are not really random, but pseudo-random? Meir Brachfeld examines the rule of overcharging (*onaa*) from mBaba Metzia 4:3 in light of economic theory and commercial reality. Geometry is the subject of a paper by Boaz Tsaban and David Garber, who analyze all talmudic discussions of circles and disks.[6]

Greek treatises on circles and spheres translated from the Arabic are mentioned in Gad Freudenthal's paper, "Les sciences dans les

6 Cf. their paper in *Higayon* 3, which is followed by Shimon Bollag's overview of talmudic and halakhic treatments of the numeric value of $\pi$, also discussed in N. Rabinovitch, "An Archimedian tract of Immanuel Tov-Elem," *Historia Mathematica* 1 (1974), 13–27.

communautés juives medievales de Provence."[7] Freudenthal (p. 88) also remarks on a twentieth-century controversy on *Mishnat Hamidot*: in 1933, Solomon Gandz claimed this was "the first Hebrew geometry," dating it around 150 CE, but in 1959, its indebtedness to Arabic —, and thus much later — sources was proven by Gad Ben-Ami Sarfatti, the acclaimed linguist and historian of mathematics.[8] Freudenthal (ibid., 127) also attempts to infer a cultural interpretation of apostate Abner of Burgos' declared life-long desire to find a way to square the circle.[9] The volume *Mone Mispar*, a practical, didactically-lucid mathematical treatise by R. Saadia Chouraqui in beautifully terse Hebrew, written in Tlemcen, Algeria in 1691 — for a modern edition of which we are indebted to Sarfatti, who edited, annotated and wrote an introduction to it[10] — among other things applies geometry to questions of ritual law, and thus would have been relevant to Bollag's paper. R. Chouraqui's treatment of the squaring of the circle is followed by an analysis of how to calculate the volume of water in a cylindrical *mikve* (ritual bath), and in the few concluding lines he explains that if it is elliptical (or oval), it suffices to make the calculations as though it is a circle with the lesser diameter, since their purpose is merely to check whether there is enough water; if it is triangular, he suggests carrying out the calculations for the circle inscribed inside the triangle. However, Chouraqui's focus in that section is not mathematics per se, but fulfilment of the ritual requirements.

In *Higayon 4*, Hayim Herman, Aben Khvoles and Alex Klein apply differential equations to a Midrash concerning water in a *mikve*. Naftali Tucker applies logic to an Aggadic metaphor, the Midrashim on the Sabbath as a bride. Measuring distance, in Jewish law, may involve physical distance, or the time needed to traverse it. Daniel Felsenstein shows that, according to one interpretation of the beheaded heifer (*egla arufa*) rule associated with unsolved murders (a corpse having been found in the countryside), distance from the nearest town, which incurs duties in this context, "is measured using a composite index comprised

7 *Revue des etudes juives* (REJ) 152 (1993), 29–136, pages 88, 64, 72.

8 Sarfatti's work on the history of Jewish mathematics is exemplified by his *Mathematical Terminology in the Hebrew Scientific Literature of the Middle Ages* (Hebrew), (Jerusalem: 1968).

9 See too Freudenthal's "Science in the medieval Jewish culture of southern France," *History of Science* 33 (1995), 23–58.

10 Ramat Gan: 1973.

of both physical distance and city size; this leads to a simple gravity-type solution." In *Higayon 2*, Ely Merzbach and Boris Singer, who also address the beheaded heifer rule, solve the problem of which town is closest to the place where the corpse was found using a Dirichlet tessellation of a map into areas associated with towns. Sheldon Epstein, Yonah Wilamovsky and Bernard Dickman treat the laws of cities of refuge as a facility location problem of mathematical optimization: how to locate the said towns so as to allow inadvertent manslayers "optimal opportunity to safely arrive at a place of refuge." While "minimax simply attempts to minimize the furthest distance that anyone will be forced to travel" (p. 12), other methods take into account the distribution of the population (of potential eligible manslayers) by giving an advantage to those furthest away from the facility.

In *Higayon* 3, Netanel Leibowitz offers a discussion of, and an algebraic solution for, the different ways halakhic authorities interpreted the calculation of the liability for damage caused by two oxen goring each other. Ariel Assaf applies utility theory from economics to the mishnaic rule used by courts to evaluate the current value of a *ketuba*, construing it as a case of expected future income under uncertainty. Daniel Gutenmacher discusses responsa by R. Solomon ibn Adret (Rashba) on majority rule in communal government. Moshe Koppel addresses the emergence of formal rules of legal exegesis (possibly starting with Hillel and Shammai), in contrast to earlier, apparently less formal methods of interpreting the Oral Law. Koppel suggests — not in terms of formal rules, but in terms of the connectionism paradigm from computing and computational neuroscience, thereby projecting a debate from artificial intelligence, Koppel's own area of research, onto the halakhic context — an analogy with the cognitive processes of first-language learning.[11] Also in *Higayon* 3, the present reviewer (Ephraim Nissan) introduces a device from discrete mathematics (applying formal grammars to sets) for representing the procedure the Mishnah prescribes for solving the problem that arose when paschal lambs ran away and could not be distinguished from each other. Once the lambs are intermingled, the groups of people (*havurot*) who were to eat them cannot partake of the meat of any of the lambs without either

11 Koppel has further elaborated his ideas in English in *Meta-Halakhah: Logic, Intuition and the Unfolding of Jewish Law* (Northville, NJ: 1997), reviewed by Robert Klapper in *Tradition* 33 (1999), 70–80, and by Isaac Chavel in *Tora u-Madda Journal* 8 (1998–1999), 318–326.

ascertaining whether a certain lamb is indeed the lamb on the basis of which the group was constituted, or, failing that (which we can assume), applying the Mishnah's provisions by which the groups are to stipulate with each other that their boundaries are to be redrawn. The paper draws upon artificial intelligence and notions from discrete mathematics in formalizing the Mishnah's solution.

Intermingling of babies rather than lambs, obviously with different halakhic effects, is a problem dealt with in another paper in the same issue, by Merzbach and Reuven Miller, who develop a probabilistic analysis. (Combinatorics is involved in the model for the intermingled lambs. Moshe Koppel, in *Higayon* 2, discusses a combinatoric theorem in tractate Kinim concerning a law governing pigeon offerings by women who have given birth.) Of general interest in the area of halakhic methodology and classification are the papers in *Higayon* 3 by R. Shlomo Zalman Havlin, on Maimonides' categories of Oral Law, and Alex Klein, on questions posed by the Amora R. Yeremya.

In *Higayon* 2, Michael Avraham proposes an algebraic model of *kal vahomer*, whereas Meir Brachfeld, in the following article, proposes a logical model of *kal vahomer* that is an abstraction of the interpretation of *kal vahomer* given in *Halikhot Olam*, 4:3. On the spectrum of opinions about the thirteen exegetical *midot*, Avraham's algebraic model is at the opposite end from that which claims that halakhic reasoning must abide by classical logic. In a sense, Avraham "frees" from the demands of logic even the one exegetical principle, *kal vahomer*, that is, on the face of it, consonant with them. He presents a table that defines operations for determining the result in various classes of arguments where this principle is instantiated. Also in *Higayon* 3, Yerachmiel Brody advocates the adoption of a formal notation for talmudic argumentation. This is a recommendation that Avi Sion, too, makes for the yeshiva curriculum, in the volume to which I now turn.

Avi Sion, *Judaic Logic: a Formal Analysis of Biblical, Talmudic And Rabbinic Logic*, Geneva: Editions Slatkine, 1997.

To Sion, a major problem with the otherwise quite close fit between logic and halakhic thinking is that the way halakhists do logic tends to focus on the concrete, with no concessions to abstract calculations that would, if carried out in the fashion mathematicians are used to, endow halakhic decision making with a neatness that meets logicians' standards.

Historians of science used to criticize past practices, but this is now considered reprehensible 'Whiggery' by current practitioners of the discipline, who thus paradoxically practice what they critique; in any event, this 'teach-formal-logic-in-the-yeshiva: formulas are so neat' argument calls to mind the nineteenth century French physicist who was reduced to inactivity and despair by a stroke ascribed to his efforts to carry out calculations by rote, with no shortcuts and no fancy mathematics, out of disdain for, or lack of skill in, the mathematical techniques that would have made them easier. Today, interdisciplinary convergences are in vogue. Though some reproach much of current philosophy for an abstractness said to belong in pure mathematics, it is becoming increasingly apparent that the convergence of legal philosophy and mathematical logic is conducive to practical developments at the forefront of legal computing.

The application of formal notation and calculation to Jewish law is advocated by Brody in *Higayon* 3 (see above) and Sion, in the book being reviewed. But in other fields of legal argumentation, too, the use of formalization is an emerging trend, e.g., in the investigation of facts and in legal proofs, for which computer tools are being developed (an area the present reviewer is active in). Sion brings as epigraphs, at the beginning of his book, two of Maimonides' statements on logic about which Freudenthal has much to say (see the review below).

Sion's book can be followed and understood by non-logicians; the non-specialist will find the introduction to logic in chapters 1 and 4 useful. While staying within the boundaries of Orthodoxy, it scrutinizes the logical validity of arguments and inferences in the sources in light of mathematical logic. The chapters I found most compelling, at least if taken on their own terms, are those in which there is a sustained logical thrust, with the author developing formal arguments. Yet the work is also disarmingly personal. Sion is not keen on addressing any factors in the halakhic decision-making process other than logic and inference, despite the fact that it has long been acknowledged that there is more to lawmaking than logic. This is not a book about law, legal sociohistory (like works that, for example, compare the two Talmuds), philology, narratology (like works that explore reasoning in the Aggadic Midrash), or ethics, though the latter seems to be an underlying goal. *Judaic Logic* does not limit itself to the Rabbinic sources; it covers logic as displayed in several biblical verses as well. Chapter 2, "Adductive logic in the Torah," where "adduction" is the confirmation or rejection of hypotheses, develops an engaging discussion from two passages in Deuteronomy (13:2–4; 18:21–22) on how to tell a true from a false prophet.[12] Section 2.4 is on the compatibility of logic and mysticism; this reviewer, however, is left pondering whether the semiotics of the Spheres (*sfirot*) is really falsifiable on astronomical grounds. Might it not be an autonomous space of expression? Think of the universe defined by the design of a computer interface — can the definition of a language be false? Sion's paper in *Higayon* 4 is a shorter version of the important third chapter of his book, where he classifies the different kinds of a fortiori argument prior to illustrating a fortiori argument in the sources. Chapter 4 ("*Kal Vahomer*") starts by showing how even in contemporary encyclopedias of philosophy there are misapprehensions about a fortiori arguments as well as about the nature of syllogistic constructions (p. 46), known to be notoriously deceptive. (On formal models of *kal vahomer* see also the above review of *Higayon*, especially no. 2.)

To capture *kal vahomer* logic, so central to rabbinical argumentation, in his book Sion "painstakingly analyze[d] a dozen concrete biblical and talmudic examples, trying out a great many symbolic representations, until [he] discerned all the factors involved in them" (p. 48). According to Sion, emphasis on the *kal vahomer* argument serves to illustrate his claim regarding "the independence of Judaic logic" (p. 50). Early examples of a fortiori arguments analyzed in chapter 4 include rhetorical questions in the Torah, such as Numbers 12:14, Exodus 6:12, Genesis 44:8, and Deuteronomy 31:27. Sion reformulates them in terms of a major premise, a minor premise, and a conclusion, and teaches the reader how to analyze other occurrences (p. 54). Turning to rabbinical *kal vahomer*, in sec. 4.3 he discusses the *dayo* principle, as opposed to proportionate inference: as though Miriam was liable for more than seven days, as stated for lesser circumstances. Section 4.5 tests Sion's formalization on rabbinical formulations of *kal vahomer*, such as Ramhal's, as well as on recent formulations such as that of Chavel. Chapter 5 returns to biblical a fortiori arguments, examining the wording of occurrences signaling them, e.g., *hen ... veeikh ...*; *hen/hinei ...* (*ve*) *af ki ...* (he returns to them again, providing a yet deeper analysis, in chapter 6), as well as their distribution in the various books of the Bible; then turns to later sources. Chapter 14, "On the concept of *mitzvah*," could be a fruitful starting point for further elaboration in terms of the burgeoning field of the logics of obligation (deontic logic) and agency. Chapter 7, not

12 On Nachmanides' distinction between 'sign' and 'wonder,' p. 25, Sion might have also considered Dan Ben-Amos's paper, "*Niphla'ot ve-Nissim*" (English), *Fabula* 35 (1994), 20–49.

devoted to logic, originates in an essay on faith (cf. chapter 14), truthfulness, ideals and one-upmanship. Chapter 8 considers the epistemology of interpreting the sources in general, as well as induction in the logic of *davka* (contingent) and *lav-davka* (indefinite) particulars, *kushia* and *teirutz* (logic problem solving). Chapter 9, on inference, elucidation, and harmonization, introduces the heart of the book: chapters 10–12, on the thirteen exegetical *midot*. These make for dense, demanding reading, and on occasion point to what Sion considers logically weak reasoning: "whatever it is, it is not a teaching of pure logic" (p. 171).

Sion acknowledges the loop of tradition making, co-opting successive layers of authorities. "It is not in heaven — *lo bashamayim hi*" arguably empowers human decisors, freeing them from the test of mathematical perfection (see p. 219 in the Epilogue, and chapter 15). That Sion on occasion detects, in the body or processes of halakhic thought, instances of what he, by the standards of mathematical logic, considers questionable inference, is not alarming with respect to the value of the extant record from the Orthodox perspective. For Orthodoxy, as opposed to the Conservative stance, recognizes, as does Sion, the cumulative principle, by which the historical record of the halakha is not invalidated by the emergence of conditions differing from those that constitute a premise of some ruling. Sion, too, sees a way out, recourse to which allows even a logically invalid conclusion to be validated by replacing a faulty premise with one that is sound; however, he does point out the existence of the problem.

Gad Freudenthal, "Science in the medieval Jewish culture of southern France," *History of Science 33 (1995), 23–58.*

Gad Freudenthal, "The study of mathematics as 'a great religious secret' in the fourteenth century: Abraham b. Solomon's commentary on the beginning of Euclid's *Elements*. An annotated critical edition" (Hebrew), in A. Ravitzky (ed.), *Joseph Baruch Sermoneta Memorial Volume, Jerusalem Studies in Jewish Thought 14 (1998), 129–158.*

Gad Freudenthal, of the Institut d'Histoire des Sciences of the CNRS in Paris, is a leading scholar in the history of medieval science, Jewish science in particular. Of his numerous papers, the two selected for review here are of more general interest than the volumes reviewed above. To be sure, aside from the Tosafists, medieval Jewish philosophy embraced logic, most conspicuously in Maimonides' brand of Aristotelianism.

(Medieval Hebrew works on philosophical logic are the subject of: S. Rosenberg's "Logic and Ontology in Jewish Philosophy in the 14th Century" (Hebrew).[13]) In contrast to the Tosafists, Maimonides, who among other things was a logician, made it quite explicit (e.g., when discussing views on individual Providence in the *Guide for the Perplexed*) that he was adopting a paradigm of debate shared with foreign schools of thought. Freudenthal (1998, p. 105), in quoting Maimonides on logic, cautions us (as does Sion's epigraph) that even in Maimonides, there is an ambivalent attitude toward the value of the sciences per se; in his *Eight Chapters*, for example, Maimonides holds that mathematics is (only) a propaedeutic to theology. The study of medicine could not be undertaken, in the Middle Ages, without first studying logic (p. 107). One of Maimonides' early works was on logic proper (pp. 62–63). Aristotle's teachings on logic, as epitomized in Averroes' Arabic writings, were translated into Hebrew in Provence in 1288 and again in 1329, and were printed in 1559 (pp. 64–65).

Over the centuries, several Jewish thinkers have also been mathematicians. Medieval Provence produced the exceptional Levi b. Gershom, Ralbag or Gersonides (1288–1344). As a scientist, he is among the fathers of trigonometry; he also was an original, though, alas, uninfluential writer on logic in his *Book of Correct Syllogism*.[14] Maimonides, in *Guide for the Perplexed*, I:73, and Shem Tov ibn Falaquera (1225–ca. 1295), in his commentary on the *Guide*, *More Hamore* (*Guide to the Guide*), discussed, as part of an argument to demonstrate how reason transcends the perceptible, the mathematical concept of an asymptote (i.e., the straight line that some curves, e.g., a parabola, increasingly approach but never touch). This apparently prompted the translation and original authorship of works in Hebrew on asymptotes and conic sections in the Middle Ages.[15]

The typical situation, however, was that even when the scientific disciplines were tolerated and cultivated (e.g., by the Gaon of Vilna, who

13 PhD dissertation, The Hebrew University, 1973.

14 See Charles H. Manekin's *The Logic of Gersonides: A Translation of the Sefer ha-Heqqesh ha-Yashar*, New Synthese Historical Library 40 (Dordrecht: 1992). See too Manekin's "Modal logic in Gersonides," *Iyyun* 42 (1993), 347–382. Also see Gad Freudenthal, ed., *Studies on Gersonides: A Fourteenth-Century Jewish Philosopher-Scientist* (Leiden: 1992).

15 See Freudenthal 1993, n. 7 above, 58, 72–73, 116–117; cf. Freudenthal, "Maimonides' *Guide for the Perplexed* and the transmission of the mathematical tract '*On Two Asymptotic Lines*' in the Arabic, Latin and Hebrew medieval traditions," *Vivarium* 26 (1988), 113ff.

took a keen interest in the sciences), the kind of interdisciplinary endeavors we are witnessing today, with valuable contributions being made to both the secular disciplines and Jewish leaning, were not, generally speaking, undertaken. And when a secular discipline did get the attention of scholars, it was not acknowledged to be valuable, not just as ancillary to things holy, but in its own right. Mathematics, to the extent that it was cultivated, was undervalued. A related point is made by Freudenthal in the *Sermoneta Memorial Volume* paper, where he presents the fourteenth-century treatise on Euclid by Abraham b. Solomon Yarhi, along with an interpretative essay. This treatise, Freudenthal points out immediately, was an exception in Jewish scholarship, in that it advocated the study of mathematics for its own sake, rather than as a propaedeutic to the study of metaphysics. Freudenthal tentatively proposes (p. 140) that the reason the treatise does not invoke the authority of Maimonides is that while Maimonides did indeed advocate the study of mathematics, his justification was the propaedeutic role of mathematics, an attitude contrary to that of Yarhi. Freudenthal then remarks (p. 141):

> Elsewhere I raised the question of how it came to pass that, notwithstanding the intensive involvement of Jews in mathematics during the Middle Ages, no prominent mathematicians arose in their midst (apart from Gersonides). The answer I proposed is that the very motives that led Jews to take an interest in mathematics also prevented them from making this involvement a goal in and of itself. On the one hand, there were some who studied mathematics for its practical value, especially since it was a necessary prerequisite for astronomy.... On the other hand, there were those who studied mathematics as it was an integral part of the Aristotelian-Maimonidean curriculum, which culminated in the study of metaphysics.... The philosophy that Abraham b. Solomon sought to develop might well have led adherents to make mathematical investigation a lifetime endeavor.

Freudenthal draws a comparison with the rise of modern science in the seventeenth century, where a major factor was that in the religious and cultural climate of Protestant Europe at the time, knowledge of the natural sciences was considered a means to spiritual redemption. It is telling, in a sense, that during the present-day boom in science and technology, and renewal of the Jewish people and Jewish studies — a Renaissance of general as well as Jewish studies — a significant encounter between the two is at last taking place.

# THE CONTROVERSIES OF THE SAGES OF POLAND IN THE SIXTEENTH CENTURY: A CHAPTER IN THE HISTORY OF JEWISH LAW, ITS GENERAL RULES AND METHODS OF DECISION-MAKING

MEIR RAFFELD*

This essay will present a number of attempts to solve a historical riddle, the first traces of which are found in cryptic notes. The entire matter is related to the scholars and cultural life of the Jews of Poland during the sixteenth century, and constitutes an interesting chapter in the history of Jewish law at that time.

The incident is cryptically referred to in a few lines found in a responsum sent by R. Solomon Luria (Maharshal, ca. 1510–Lublin, 1574) to his kinsman, R. Moses Isserles (Rema, Cracow, 1520–1572)[1]:

> Because of my many sins, and as the result of the rebellion of my students, who have rebelled and transgressed against me; and they rely upon the strength of the Elder and his son the Gaon, may God preserve them. They have removed me from my quarters and have damaged my body and the health of my mind. ... should turn their hearts of stone and cruelty to hearts of flesh, or give me strength and courage to save my soul and the souls of my worthy students from them. And even when I was in the land of my enemies and under their control, the Lord, may He be blessed, did not detest or loathe [me], nor break the covenant with me. And He increased my jurisdiction, [granting me] proper disciples from all four corners of the world, and they are like thorns in [my enemies'] eyes ... .[2]

The following paragraphs will summarize the main views of nineteenth century and present day scholars regarding the identity of

* Dr. Raffeld is a Senior Lecturer at Bar-Ilan University, where he teaches in the Talmud Department.

1 On Maharshal, see M. Raffeld, *Maharshal and the Yam Shel Shlomo* (Hebrew), (Ramat Gan: 1971), 23–70, henceforth *Maharshal*. On Rema, see A. Siev, *Rabbi Moses Isserles–Rema* (Hebrew), (NY: 1972), henceforth Siev, *Rema*.

2 *Responsa Maharshal* (Jerusalem: 1993), #15, 55–56. All page references will be to this edition, as it is based on the first printing of the *Responsa* (Lublin: 1575). Where necessary I have corrected errors on the basis of the Lublin edition.

"the Elder and his son the Gaon" and the nature of the controversy.[3] S.I. Fein[4] identified the protagonists as R. Meir Katzenelenbogen of Padua and his son R. Samuel Judah, apparently based upon Maharshal's responsum #6, p. 21 [= Rema, responsum #18, p. 116]: "Concerning the halakhic decision issued by the Elder, filled with wisdom, my relative, R. Meir of Padua and his son the Gaon, who have taken the place of their father in Torah and piety, our Rabbi Judah, may God preserve him."[5] Although the terms match perfectly, it is difficult to suppose that Maharshal was referring to a controversy between the rabbis of Poland and Italy. The content of the complaint clearly indicates that those involved in the controversy had actually met one another in venues and study halls near each other, as attested by the language of the responsum.[6]

Most scholars have identified "the Elder and his son" as R. Shalom Shachna (Rashash) and his son R. Israel, known as the Wise Men of Lublin. The former was the official Chief Rabbi, and also head of the yeshiva. Rashash employed distinctive methods of halakhic determination and a singular methodology for Talmud study.[7] However, scholars disagree as to the explanation of the controversy.

H. Graetz suggested that the main issue was Maharshal's personality: as a 'man of truth,' he disliked the *pilpul* and hairsplitting that

3 For a summary, see my "The halakha follows the later Sages" (Hebrew), *Sidra* 8 (1992), 137, n. 45, henceforth *Halakha*. And see A. Reiner, "The yeshivas of Poland and Ashkenaz during the sixteenth and seventeenth centuries — historical developments" (Hebrew), in Y. Bartel, C. Turniansky, E. Mendelson (eds.), *Studies in Jewish Culture in Honor of Chone Shmeruk*, (Jerusalem: 1993), 54, n. 72, henceforth Reiner.

4 *Kiryat Neemana* (Vilna: 1860), 56.

5 *Responsa Rema*, ed. A. Siev (Jerusalem: 1971).

6 See Siev, Introduction to *Responsa Rema*, 34–35. Note that Siev cites only the last part of Maharshal's responsum: "And they were not careful to respect the Elder and his son" (p. 24). The designations are identical only in this quotation, which is in the body of the responsum, and clarifies the connection made by Fein concerning the rabbis Meir and his son Samuel Judah of Padua. See A. Siev, ed. *Responsa Mahari Mintz, Responsa Maharam Mipadua* (NY: 1995), 325–366.

7 See the following studies: M.S. Lew, *The Jews of Poland* (London: 1944), 23; N. Shemen, *Lublin: City of Torah, Rabbinism and Piety* (Yiddish), (Toronto: 1951), 42–46; M. Balaban, *The House of Israel in Poland* (Hebrew), vol. 1 (Jerusalem: 1948), 28; T. Preshel, "R. Shalom Shachna of Lublin" (Hebrew), *Sinai* (100), 1987, 682–700, henceforth Preshel. Preshel's article contains a wealth of information on Rashash.

characterized those who were jealous of him.[8] Apparently, Graetz's thesis stems from projection of his own personal opinions to past halakhic authorities and their methodologies of study and decision making, and is not based on analyzing the works of Maharshal and his contemporaries. Another scholar, R.N.N. Rabbinovicz, author of *Dikdukei Sofrim*, approached the subject with caution and pedantry:

> And that which I had stated, that there had been a controversy between R. M. Shachna [Rashash] [and Maharshal], I did not find explicitly. But in my opinion, if they loved each other, then R. Shachna would not have accepted into his academy those students who had abandoned Maharshal, nor would Maharshal have been bound by the rabbinical authority of those students. However, he was under the rabbinical authority of Rashash, because he was the head of the court. And I stated that both were in charge of the yeshiva in Lublin, from his statement "even when I was in the land of my enemies," and so on. Apparently he had been advised to leave Lublin and establish himself in a different city, for someone shamed in one city should go to another city, and we find that in 1554 Maharshal settled in the community of Ostraha.[9]

The formulation found in Maharshal's complaint, and the description of his paying homage to the Elder identified as Rashash, directed Rabbinovicz to a further hypothesis:

> And I surmise that at that time there had been a controversy between Maharshal and R. M. Shachna, for each ran a yeshiva in Lublin, and the students wanted *pilpul* and hairsplitting. Thus, they deserted Maharshal and flocked to R. Shachna [and his son R. Judah], the disciple of R. Jacob Pollack, the Master of *hilukim*, as Maharshal mentioned in the responsum he sent to Rema (#16).

Certainly, part of Rabbinovicz's interpretation of this incident is derived from Maharshal's own responsum. Nevertheless, it remains only a hypothesis, since there is no concrete proof that Maharshal was

8 See *Graetz, History of the Jews* (German), trans. S.P. Rabinovitch (Warsaw: 1899), vol. 7, 30. Graetz did not explicitly identify the "Elder and his son" as referring to Rashash, but this was suggested by Rabinovitch (p. 30, n. 5). Nevertheless, Reiner, n. 3 above, is correct that from the description given by Graetz, he can be viewed as the first to identify the parties in question as Rashash and his son.

9 *Essay on the Printing of the Talmud* (Hebrew), ed. A.M. Habermann (Jerusalem: 1952), 62–63, n. 5, quoting *Responsa Maharshal*, #8.

living in Lublin at the same time that Rashash served as head of the yeshiva.[10] Likewise, the assumption that *pilpul* and hairsplitting were prevalent only in Rashash's academy, and this is what caused the students who "rebelled and transgressed" to abandon one academy for the competing one, has no basis in the sources.[11]

A different view would link the controversy to an essential argument over different methods of *pilpul*. There is a tradition cited in David Ganz's historical study that describes the creation of the *pilpul hahilukim* by R. Jacob Pollack.[12] Some scholars have uncritically accepted this tradition, while others have partially or totally rejected it.[13]

10 On the other hand, one should not be surprised that Maharshal (Rema, responsum #61, 284) and other scholars like Rema (# 85, 352–353) dealt with questions concerning Lublin and the famous fairs held there. Perhaps these issues arose at the time Rashash served as rabbi of the region. See also S. Nissenbaum, *On the History of the Jews of Lublin* (Hebrew), (Lublin: 1900), 5; Shemen, n. 7 above, 35–36.

11 See also S. Assaf, "A contribution to the biography of Rabbi Solomon Luria" (Hebrew), *Louis Ginzburg Jubilee Volume*, (NY: 1946), 47, who suggested that the main cause of the controversy was an essential difference between the scholars' methods of study. A similar suggestion was made by M. Breuer, "The Ashkenazic Yeshiva toward the Close of the Middle Ages" (Hebrew), (PhD diss., Hebrew University of Jerusalem, 1966), 115; C. Tchernowitz-Rav Zair, *History of the Jewish Codes* (Hebrew), (NY: 1948), vol. III, 88. This is incorrect for the simple reason that Maharshal himself employed the *pilpul* method, while Rashash had recourse to textual criticism, see Raffeld, *Maharshal* (n. 1 above), 256, 302. Rashash's textual criticism is found in a work by R. Benjamin of Pozna in Oxford Bodleian mss 507–708, 512–513 (film nos. 19068–9, 19073–4 in the Institute for Microfilmed Hebrew Manuscripts at the Jewish National and University Library, Jerusalem).

12 *Tzemah David*, ed. M Breuer (Jerusalem: 1983), 138.

13 See the following sources: Breuer, n. 12 above, 77 ff. [= idem., "The rise of *pilpul* and *hilukim* in the yeshivas of Franco-Germany" (Hebrew), *Memory Volume for Rabbi J.J. Weinberg* (Hebrew), (Jerusalem, 1970), 241ff.]; I. Ta-Shma, "*Tosafot Gornisch*," *Sinai*, 68 (1971), 135, n. 5; P.H. Wetstein, "R. Jacob Pollack and study by way of *hilukim*" (Hebrew), *Hashiloah* 5 (1899), 536–543; I. Ta-Shma, "New material on 'Tosafot Gornisch'" (Hebrew), *Alei Sefer* 2 (1976), 87; Y. Dinari, The *Rabbis of Germany and Austria at the Close of the Middle Ages* (Hebrew), (Jerusalem: 1984), 108, n. 185. See also D. Assaf, *Poland* (Hebrew), (Tel-Aviv: 1990), Units 5–6, 63–66. On the tradition reported in Ganz, see Reiner, n. 3 above, 47–53. Note that although Ganz flourished close to the time of R. Jacob Pollack, he himself was uncertain of this tradition and formulated his report cautiously: "And some say."

H.Z. Dimitrovsky accepted Ganz's report, giving it a new interpretation related to the present issue. Essentially, he argues, there was a controversy between those who supported the novel method of *hilukim* that was transmitted by R. Jacob Pollack to his disciple Rashash, and those who were partisans of the classical *pilpul* method that Maharshal attempted to impart to his disciples.

From the content of Maharshal's bitter complaint, it is clear that the student rebellion was caused by the different study methodologies in place at the two academies. Some students left Maharshal's academy for the rival academy, a move that distressed Maharshal. The rebellion and exodus of these students can only be explained, it is argued, on the premise that the rival academy had an alternate type of *pipul* unknown in Maharshal's school. The new *pipul* was characterized by its novelty, keenness and clarity, and it attracted Maharshal's senior pupils.[14] This was the principal difference between the two academies, and Maharshal considered the approach utilized by the rival academy invalid.

There are a number of arguments against this account. First and foremost, Maharshal's complaint was not against a system of study that was similar in methodology to his own.[15] It appears to be the result of long-standing tension over a matter of principle that had caused a rift between Maharshal and the Elder and his son. Moreover, they, in contrast to Maharshal, were mighty men whose lofty status had caused his yeshiva to decline and his students to desert him.

Recently, Reiner discussed this question and suggested some new and interesting approaches which combine tradition, law and pedagogy:

> "The Elder and his son" have been identified as Shalom Shachna and his son Israel of Lublin, an unnecessary and unproven identification, although one that is quite possible. For our purposes, before an identification of the personalities can be made, it should be noted that the expression "Elder" was encased in quotation marks. It would appear that Maharshal meant to

14 H.Z. Dimitrovsky, "On the pilpulistic method" (Hebrew), *Salo W. Baron Jubilee Volume* (Jerusalem: 1975), 115–116.

15 See Reiner, n. 3 above, 55. See also the remarks in Preshel, n. 7 above, 690, describing Maharshal's esteem for R. Jacob Pollack, the mentor of Rashash: "The greatest of his generation, R. Jacob Pollack." Moreover, he once stated: "Since the Gaon emended it, it must not be a text" (responsum #48). Clearly, he respected the innovator of *hilukim* — the new *pilpul*. This has all been summarized in my *Maharshal*, n. 1 above, 280–282.

> indicate that he was engaged in a controversy with an academy at whose head stood the "Elder," and hence, with the pedagogic and legal tradition of this academy, which benefitted from the stature of its proponent. If indeed Shalom Shachna and his son are referred to, then Maharshal views himself, together with his academy, as engaged in a controversy with an academy associated with a [different] tradition, one that viewed R. Jacob Pollack as the first among Polish scholars, R. Shalom Shachna as continuing his methodology, and R. Shachna's disciple, Rema, a relative of Maharshal and the addressee of the letter in which the incident was recorded, as the person who was passing it on.... The nature of the controversy and their transgressions is unclear, and cannot be derived from the text.... Apparently, Maharshal's bitterness did not stem from theoretical debate concerning learning methodologies.... He does not demand an apology from "the Elder and his son," but from the disciples, whose desertion he viewed as rebellious and criminal. The subject of this paragraph is his students' flight, and not the power of the Elder; it is the decline of Maharshal's academy, and not the rise of a different academy. The personality of his rival is a marginal aspect of Maharshal's complaint; "the strength of the Elder and his son," is an expression employed to indicate their power in Torah, and not the offices they held.[16]

One cannot deny the logic of Reiner's approach. It does not contradict any text under discussion, and explains a number of features of these texts. More sources can be marshaled to confirm the thesis that the subject of the reference by Maharshal in the letter to Rema was the outcome of a controversy between Maharshal and Rashash. *Yam Shel Shlomo* (henceforth *YSS*) and the responsa of both Maharshal and Rema contain references to legal and halakhic controversies and tensions.

1. In *YSS*, Jebamot 14:3, concerning divorce by someone insane, Marharshal wrote:

> Indeed, in those provinces in which the bans of R. Gershom against coercion in divorce and polygamy are valid, there is no solution, but he must

16 Reiner, n. 3 above, 54–56. His explanation is part of his general explication of the controversy over pedagogic methodologies in Poland and Germany during this period. It should be noted that in the halakha and literature on Ashkenazic customs just prior to this period, the term "Elder" had a number of meanings, including sage, and a unique status. See, for example, the introduction by R. Joseph Hostit to *Leket Yosher*, I, 3, where he refers to his mentor, R. Isserlein, as "the Gaon, the Elder Isserlein"; see also ibid., p. 48. Likewise, R. Meir Halevi of Ehrfurt was so called in *Pesakim Ukhtavim Lemahari*, #81 (Jerusalem: 1981), 357. Also see *YSS*, Baba Kama 10:13 and n. 19 below. Nevertheless, the term "elder" may simply connote old age.

> provide food and clothing for her until Heaven seals it for them. In my day, there was an similar incident with a young rabbi whose wife went insane, and after a number years he turned to me and other rabbis to permit him to divorce her and marry another. And I did not want to agree with their view. Nevertheless, I did not dispute them, for I had no colleague to force my own truth as the law .... R. Gershom, the Light of the Exile, did not issue his ban in order to forestall bringing children into the world .... After a number of years I searched the Rabia, and found that many great rabbis had already actually prohibited it, and this is the essence of the law. See also the text of responsum #65 by my grandfather, R. Isaac, which is in the possession of my uncle who is proficient in Torah, R. Isaac, may God preserve him, and my copy was burnt because of our many iniquities.[17]

From the report, it appears he was involved in a controversy with his mentors concerning an important and well-known question that cut across different sectors of Ashkenazic Jewry: did the famous ban of R. Gershom, which prohibited a man from divorcing his wife against her will, also apply in cases where the husband would effectively be unable to fulfill the commandment to procreate? And which rabbis were referred to in the phrase "other rabbis"? A partial but significant list is found in the testimony of R. Joel Sirkes: "Indeed, I received [the tradition] from R. Shachna of blessed memory, that he actually permitted someone to marry another [while still married to a first wife]. In a case where there is still a need to fulfill the commandment to be fruitful and multiply, R. Gershom's regulation never applied at all. Thus wrote the rabbis of Frankfurt in a lengthy responsum permitting it, and all the sages of Germany and Russia agreed with them."[18]

17 The words of the Rabia were transcribed by Maharshal in his responsum #65. In this responsum, Maharshal also stated: "What is clear in your eyes, that he can divorce her forcibly when she has gone insane, is not my view." The case is described at length in the responsum. Maharshal's opinion requires further clarification; see *YSS*, Jebamot 6:32, 39. See also *Responsa Bah Yeshanot*, #93. R.M. Stration, *Selected Writings* (Hebrew), (Jerusalem: 1969), 180–181, also discusses this. In an article forthcoming in *Sidra*, "Problems in Jewish marital law in the Polish rabbinical literature in the sixteenth and seventeenth centuries" (Hebrew), I analyze the attitude to R. Gershom's ban on the part of the sages of Poland of that time; see too E. Westreich, "Grounds for Permitting a Man to Marry Bigamously in Jewish Law" (Hebrew), (PhD diss., Hebrew University of Jerusalem, 1990), 251–259.

18 *Responsa Bah Yeshanot*, #93.

We can surmise that the debate between Maharshal and R. Shalom Shachna and his supporters was direct ("turned to me and other rabbis"), and Maharshal's stance opposing the resolute opinion of R. Shalom Shachna caused the continuing controversy between them. During the debate, Maharshal may have been aided by a responsum (no longer extant) by his grandfather, R. Isaac Klover, which hints at a confrontation between different academies, as Reiner suggested.

2. Responsum #135 by R. Meir b. Gedalya (Maharam) of Lublin records an extraordinary incident unlike any in the rabbinic literature:

> As I recall from my youth, during the days of the Gaon R. Shachna, of blessed memory, there was a wicked rascal, and this rabbi permitted his eyes to be poked out and his tongue cut out. After this punishment was executed, he converted and married a Christian, and brought into the world foreign children, and he and his sons caused evil to Israel throughout their lives.

It is unclear whether the incident took place during R. Meir's childhood, or he heard about it while he was young.[19] In any case, Maharshal's reaction is known:

> In my opinion, the law to be put into practice is to judge any tale-bearer who is a detriment to the public ... and who acts thus [as follows]: to destroy [such a person] with one's hands and have no mercy upon him. Not, however, to put out his eyes and cut out his tongue, but to destroy the evil from among us. On the contrary, one should be wary, and it is almost certain, that the person will be more obstreperous, and will convert in order to avenge himself, and make up fictitious libels against Israel. And so I have seen in my day, and a great disaster would have befallen Israel, were it not for the great mercy and loving-kindness of God.[20]

The implication is clearly that Maharshal disagreed with the legal decision by R. Shalom Shachna, though he did not invoke his name. This may have been the initial clash that triggered all the later controversies between them. However, one must admit that Maharshal may have been just recording the negative results of the incident, and had not actually participated in it.[21]

19 See Y. Rosenthal, *Studies and Texts* (Hebrew), (Jerusalem: 1967), 482, n. 11; J. Elbaum, *Openness and Insularity* (Hebrew), (Jerusalem: 1990), 19–20.

20 *YSS*, Jebamot 10:20.

21 See Preshel, n. 7 above, 687, n. 25. One should be aware of R. Shalom Shachna's aggressiveness in legal and communal affairs. The minutes (*pinkas*) of the Council of the Four Lands contains the following document

A singular event was the legal decision by R. Shalom Shachna that gifts sent by the groom to the bride before consummation of the marriage (*nisuin*) should be considered an act of marriage. During the talmudic era, the Sages were undecided regarding the acceptance of

---

from April 23, 1540: "A complaint was brought before us by our subject, the Jewish community, i.e., the Cracowians, Poznanians, and the Lvovians, concerning one Rabbi Shachna in the city of Lublin, which is under your jurisdiction. He is in the habit of arousing at this time [the time of the Lublin fair] many controversies and rows, to disturb our subjects, the other Jews, in their livelihoods and businesses, to oppress them with irregular bans, and customs that contradict their religion" (*Acta Congressus Generalis Judaeorum Regni Poloniae* [*Pinkas Vaad Arba Aratzot*], ed. I. Halperin, (Jerusalem: 1990), 300). It is unclear whether the complaint stemmed from internal economic motives, or from some legal controversy. In any case, it reflects R. Shalom Shachna's aggressive decisiveness regarding matters of Jewish law. Also pertinent is the following. In *YSS, Baba Kama* 10:13, Maharshal addressed the laws of someone who has been placed under a ban. Within his legal ruling, we find the following: "And they may… not circumcise his son or bury his dead. …" Nevertheless, there are things one cannot do: "God forbid to evict his sons from the study hall or the yeshiva. And once, a great scholar, the elder of his generation, and a decider of Jewish law, wrote to me that I should remove my sons, who had been placed under a ban, from the yeshiva, and I totally ignored him." If the "elder" mentioned here is Rashash, who was quick to impose bans, this may add a new facet to the controversy. Moreover, consider the following homiletic explanation attributed to Rashash, which appears to manifest the aggressive approach he favored, and reflects the demands he made of his audience:

> I heard the following explanation in the name of R. Shachna, of blessed memory: The reason why one should not remove his phylacteries in front of his mentor is actually the law that any activity performed by a slave for his master, a disciple does for his mentor. And we also say that if he is in a place where he is unknown, and he is not wearing the phylacteries worn on the head, and is wary lest people say that he is a slave [who is exempt from wearing phylacteries], then he does not put on his mentor's shoes nor remove them, as is recorded in the *Tur*, YD 242. Consequently, he said that it is forbidden to remove one's phylacteries in front of his mentor, for he is thereby removing the yoke of servitude from himself, for his mentor is in that case forbidden to utilize his service in front of someone who does not know him. This I heard. [*Mitzvat Tfilin Mibaal Hashela Hakadosh* (Jerusalem: 1977), 26, quoted in Preshel, n. 7 above, 795].

gift's from the groom by the bride: did these gifts from the bridegroom constitute an act of betrothal (*kidushin*), as did giving a ring, or raise the suspicion that this was his intention? Were the betrothal to be voided, would a writ of divorce be required to completely free the bride? In Franco-German communities prior to the period of R. Israel Isserlein in the fifteenth century, there was no unified, accepted practice. Thus, R. Isserlein decided that: "In our day, it is not customary to betroth before the actual consummation of the marriage, and thus it is clear that in our regions, one who sends gifts must later betroth."[22] His opinion that there is no need to suspect that gifts were intended as an act of betrothal became the prevailing practice in Germany. In contrast, Rashash ruled that one should be wary of betrothal, and he put this decision into practice. His decision was probably based upon the custom of the city of Posen that he had witnessed in his youth. He authored two responsa on the subject, which were published in Cracow in 1540. From all contemporary sources, it is clear that all the other sages of that generation disagreed with him.[23]

This issue of the bridegroom's gifts is also found in the writings of Maharshal, including responsum #21 and *YSS*, Kidushin 2:17–19. In these sources, Maharshal does not refer directly to Rashash's decision, but decisively sides with the traditional German stance based on acceptance of R. Isserlein's opinion. Moreover, Preshel's suggestion

---

This source is clear, and the idea is quoted at length in *Shela*, Hulin, *Ner Mitzva* (Josefov: 1879), vol. II, 3b, and in the Bah on *Tur*, OH 38:7, in the name of Rashash. Notwithstanding the various explanations suggested to explain this statement, it is clear that this scholar affirms the total subjugation of disciple to mentor, and maintains that no exemption of students from this subjugation can be contemplated. Perhaps this describes the social mores in Rashash's yeshiva. However, this homily is problematic in that it is also attributed to Maharshal by his disciple, R. Joshua Falk Katz, author of the *Perisha* (*Tur* 38:8), as noted by Preshel, 696. Moreover, the passage where it is quoted in the name of Maharshal, concludes with the words "and thus he is rebellious against his mentor," indicating that the same is likely applicable to Maharshal's mode of mentoring as well.

22 *Responsa Terumat Hadeshen*, #207.

23 On the German practice, see Dinari, n. 13 above, 111–112. More generally, see A.H. Freimann, *Betrothal and Marriage in the Post-Talmudic Period* (Hebrew), (Jerusalem: 1965), 208–210, and Preshel, n. 7 above, 683–685. For an expansive explanation, see Siev's introduction to *Responsa Rema*, n. 5 above, 54–56. And see also Rema's responsum #30, nn. 37–38.

that the following quotation was directed against Rashash is quite logical:

> And some of the rabbis have recently been stringent on the issue of gifts. How can the Master permit this?! For they pursue this stringent decision for their own benefit and that of their scribes.... Their apologies that their stringency is not against religion are lies, vanities, and hot air, for why should they bring it about that daughters of Israel will be unfit to marry a priest [since a divorced woman cannot marry a *kohen*] .... According to the strict letter of the law, I need not expound at length on this issue. However, in that place, where such an incident took place, the sages refused to take a stance to permit the woman [to marry another], since others claim that a marriage was performed, until I came with a signed and sealed pamphlet [permitting it] (*YSS*, Kidushin 2:19 = responsum #21).

However, one should note that these words were written after the twelfth of Shevat, 1559, that is, after Rashash had passed away on the New Moon of Kislev, 1558 (Rema, responsum #25). There is no way of determining if there was a direct controversy between Maharshal and Rashash about this or not. However, a responsum by one of the disciples of Maharshal, R. Benjamin Aharon Salnik, may shed light upon this question:

> And I saw that the great rabbi, R. Shachna of blessed memory, wrote a responsum in which his severity regarding such a case was quite extreme. I feel that I cannot quote all his words within my words here, for although this rabbi was a very great scholar, he relied on his greatness, and chose a new interpretation for explaining the passage in bKidushin. Based upon this interpretation, he decided to be stringent, but we have no use for new interpretations. We rely upon Rashi's commentary, and the *Tosafot*, and other early compilations that [we have] before us. And all my mentors and other great rabbis of the generation were disciples of the above-mentioned Gaon, and not one of them took his words into consideration.[24]

24 *Responsa Masat Binyamin* (Vilna: 1894), #16, 18b. This was quoted by Dimitrovsky, n. 14 above, 125–126. See his n. 73, where he deduced that Maharshal had been a student of Rashash for at least a short duration. This is chronologically possible, and if so, then we can surmise that the controversy between them began during Maharshal's youth, which sheds light on the breadth and intensity of the controversy. Siev, n. 5 above, 182, end of n. 102, and in the introduction, 56, mentions the responsum in *Masat Binyamin*, and is astonished that this scholar did not mention the opinions of Maharshal and Rema. This is incorrect, for Maharshal is quoted on p. 17b,

R. Benjamin's description of R. Shachna, his character, and his novel methodology and interpretations, certainly contains enough material to suggest a controversy between R. Shachna and his contemporaries. The phrase "all my mentors" probably refers to Maharshal and Rema, the latter disagreeing with his mentor (Rashash) on the issue of gifts. Moreover, the phrase "and not one of them took his words into consideration" appears to describe a direct confrontation between the protagonists in this debate. This debate over the bridegroom's gifts is connected to the other debates between Maharshal and Rashash.

In his responsa (#12–16), Rema described a lengthy controversy involving a libelous charge of adultery concerning a wife in Prague. The case was brought before Rema's rabbinical court in Cracrow, and it was agreed that R. Isaac b. Bezalel of Ludmir would be among the judges.

Other scholars dealt with this complex case, including Maharshal (responsum #33 and in *Responsa Rema*, #13), R. Zvi Hirsch of Brisk (*Responsa Rema*, #14), and R. Kalman Wormeiser (*Responsa Rema*, #15). All of them found the woman innocent, for false witnesses had libeled her. Between the lines, it is possible to deduce the position held by R. Shalom Schachna concerning this case, and we can only agree with

---

and we can conclude from his words that the author was also familiar with Rema's opinion, though he may not have seen the actual legal brief. He died before Rema's responsa were first printed in Cracow in 1640.

One should note that the legal brief by Rashash also manifests his aggressiveness: "Hence, I say that all Israel and anyone called an Israelite, who comes close to this betrothed woman … without a valid bill of divorce, with the exception of the husband … shall be put to death, either by being shot or by being stoned according to the Rabbinic law, as it mandates for anyone who cohabits with his fellow's betrothed. He will be smitten by hail stones and the stones of Elgavish, and lose his sanctity among Israel, and will be called a male prostitute, and he will make her into a harlot. And he will not be purified of his excrement until he is banished to the Dinur River [the border of hell]. Any rabbi or rabbinical student who deals with the betrothal of this betrothed woman will be considered a rebellious elder and will be judged with stoning, and will be placed under a ban and excommunicated, and will have no relationship to wisdom and Talmud, and if he is a priest, he will not be among those who bring the meal-offering …" [addendum to *Hidushei Hareaya Lekidushin* (Jerusalem: 1958), 105]. Perhaps his sharp style is meant to deter other sages from disagreeing with him.

what one scholar wrote: "It becomes evident that R. Shalom Shachna had a different opinion."[25] To advance this thesis, the following points should be noted. One of the scholars involved, R. Zvi Hirsch of Brisk, wrote a prologue to his responsum that included a complete description of the case and some interesting details:

> The truth is that my seal, signature, and a line of writing were at the end of the legal decision of the Gaon, our teacher, R. Shachna: "I agree with the words of this Gaon for they are on the side of truth." For I had not made up my mind about this case, and I was not counted as one who agreed to join you rabbis [Rema and his colleagues on the court], as I had not seen nor heard anything but that legal decision. And perhaps that Gaon did not hear the entire true story, but only part of it, which he quoted in his legal decision, and this was the basis of his legal brief. In my haste, due to matters related to the fair, I concurred with the basic thrust, but did not give my [full] consent until I had entered deeply into the issues involved. In order to be guiltless before God and Israel, and to respond to the questioner who asks what I originally thought, and why I changed my mind, and so that I will not be accused of writing like a blind man and then deciding to retract, I offer this apology before all scholars, and he who so chooses should draw closer to [my words].... As Heaven is my witness, this has been my method throughout my entire life, not to flatter any person, but only to testify to the truth as I see it, and all who love me, love me, and all who hate me, hate me.

Certain interesting facts can be gleaned from this introduction: the many apologies, the pressures of time and the Lublin fair, the retraction of his first legal brief on the subject, in which he had agreed with Rashash. R. Zvi Hirsch of Brisk claimed that his reconsideration was the result of greater analysis of the case, and emphasized his never-ending search for the truth. Rashash's responsum on this issue is no longer extant, but parts of it can be reconstructed from quotations found in the body of R. Zvi Hirsch of Brisk's responsum, for example, from the following lines:

> Likewise, what the judges of Cracow wrote, [viz.,] that two proper witnesses testified that the first pair of witnesses were unfit. ... Rashash refuted this by saying that perhaps they thought they were unfit, and it is not so. Perhaps the later witnesses are unfit. ... At first glance, it appeared so to the Gaon [Rashash], since the last pair of witnesses is not mentioned

25 Preshel, n. 7 above, 687. On this incident, see A. Siev, "The Rema as an authority" (Hebrew), *Hadarom* 25 (1967), 213–219.

> at all in the Gaon's legal brief. Rashash did not consider them unfit, since the cause of their unfitness is unclear.... For all these reasons, I concurred with the words of the Gaon... However, when I saw the legal decision of the three judges of Cracow, who certainly knew that the first pair of witnesses were empty and reckless persons.... and thus I joined those who permit this woman to her husband (*Responsa Rema*, #14).

Presented here is the central factor in the legal discussion: the trustworthiness of the first witnesses, who had testified to the alleged adulterous actions of the woman. Rashash tended to be stringent in the woman's case, for he had found no argument to invalidate the first witnesses. In contrast, R. Zvi Hirsch of Brisk concurred with the judges of Cracow, who decided to invalidate them.[26] It should be emphasized that during the entire lengthy and complex discussion, the three Rabbis of Cracow, R. Moshe Landa, Rema, and Rema's brother-in-law, R. Joseph Katz, did not mention Rashash and his legal ruling at all (*Responsa Rema*, #12). Perhaps this was due to their esteem for Rashash and his standing, in addition to the fact that he was their mentor. Moreover, Maharshal, who wrote an extensive and detailed responsum about the matter,[27] hinted at his controversy with Rashash in his lyrical summary of his legal ruling. He determined that the first set of witnesses were invalid, and the woman is permitted to return to her husband, adding: "And the words of the halakhic authority (*more*) who said that the woman is forbidden to her husband due to ugly deeds will be nullified, for he inadvertently erred. ..." If Maharshal was referring to Rashash with the term "the halakhic authority," this would be another link in the chain of controversy between these two great scholars, which lasted until the demise of Rashash in 1559, about half a year

26 However, see the letter by R. Mordechai Gimpel Yaffe of Razinai, quoted in E. Lichtenstein, *The Glorious City: Brisk and Its Great Scholars* (Hebrew), (Warsaw: 1880), 145, who wrote that R. Zvi Hirsch agreed with Rashash on this issue. Siev apparently accepted this view; see Siev, *Rema*, n. 1 above, 131. In my opinion, however, R. Zvi Hirsch retracted his original decision. An additional point is worthy of mention. R. Zvi Hirsch disagreed with other rabbis, including Maharshal and Rema, on at least one point. He accepted the testimony of witnesses that had been given in the absence of the litigants, whereas the other rabbis invalidated this testimony. Nevertheless, he concurred with them regarding the final and decisive legal ruling. See S. Shilo, "Testimony given in absentia of the litigants" (Hebrew), *Shenaton Hamishpat Haivri* 5 (1978), 326–329.

27 *Responsa Rema*, #13 = *Responsa Maharshal*, #23, 98–115.

after this incident. Certainly, this incident was not the primary cause for the ongoing controversy, but part of the series of events that fueled it.

3. It would appear that the methodologies of decision making in Jewish law also contributed to the bitter controversy between the Maharshal and Rashash. This issue was central to their *Weltanshauungen*. Rashash was known for his refusal to author a code of Jewish law, as described by his son, R. Israel:

> And thus I heard as an actual ruling from my master, my mentor, my father, teacher and light of all the Diaspora, R. Shalom, known as Shachna, of blessed memory ... who had many disciples in all corners of the earth, and from whose mouth we live and from his waters we drink. And I declare that often I and many [of his] students had asked him to become a decisor. His response, due to his immense piety and modesty ... was ... 'I know that once my decisions are written down, afterwards they will become the legal norm, since the law is in accordance with the view of the later authority, and I do not want the entire world to depend upon me. ...'
>
> ... And for the same reason, our teacher R. Jacob Pollack also did not author any volume, nor were any of the responsa that were sent abroad [first] copied in the homes of these great rabbis.[28]

Clearly, this description allows us to describe Rashash's position, which was based on the intellectual heritage of his mentor, R. Joseph Pollack. Rashash accorded the rule "the law is decided according to the view of the latest authority" preferential status as the preeminent basis for determining Jewish law. In addition to the tradition of his mentor, it led him to an absolute refusal to author any volume on Jewish law.[29] Rema's well-known argument against the method of legal decision-making employed by R. Joseph Caro, was likely also inspired by the general rules of legal decision-making he had received from Rashash:

> And the third is the most essential in this study, for it is known that the author of the *Beit Yosef*, R. Joseph Caro, would decide the law according to two or three witnesses, R. Isaac Alfasi, Maimonides and R. Asher (Rosh),

28 *Responsa Rema*, #25, 156.

29 R. Israel's explanation for his father's refusal to pen a volume of Jewish law differed from the reason given by a disciple of Rashash, R. Haim b. R. Bezalel of Freiburg, as recorded in his introduction to his *Vikuah Mayim Haim* (Amsterdam: 1712). According to R. Haim, Rashash refused to author any volumes for ideological reasons: the very nature and essence of Jewish law is incompatible with its summation and unification.

> usually two against one. And he usually ignored other great rabbis, determining the law in accordance with the views of two of the abovementioned rabbis. Although they were early rabbis and not later ones, he was not concerned about what the earliest rabbis had declared … that the law is always in accordance with the later rabbis, and one should not rely upon the earlier ones, even where there is a controversy between mentor and disciple. This was the practice of later rabbis, foremost among them rabbis Joseph Colon and [Israel] Isserlein in their sweet responsa.… And through this practice, the *Beit Yosef* contradicted all the customs in these lands, the majority of which are simply and naively based upon this rule, and no one doubts it.[30]

Rema's view is quite clearly that one should accept the rule that the law is in accordance with the view of the later authority as the essential tradition of Ashkenazic Jewry.[31] Hence, he was critical of R. Joseph Caro, whose mode of deciding Jewish law was predicated on the views of the three medieval sages.

In contrast, Maharshal authored a comprehensive volume of Jewish law, the *Yam Shel Shlomo,* the introduction to declares his approach to be the following: "The Talmud decides Jewish law, and clear proofs determine it" (first introduction to *YSS*, Hulin). In his opinion, the Talmud is the basis for all subsequent discussion: it is the exclusive source of authority, and obligates all rabbis and Jewish law scholars throughout the generations. Maharshal harshly criticizes a number of works, and describes the perplexity among some circles of Jewish law experts caused by the clash between different methods of deciding Jewish law.[32]

To this evidence we should add Maharshal's 1552 requests for approbations from some of the scholars of Poland, such as Rema and R. Kalman Wormeiser, who describe him as a bona fide decisor of

30 *Darkhei Moshe*, introduction.

31 Concerning the various opinions concerning this rule and its use and limitations, see my *Halakha*, n. 3 above; I. Ta-Shma, "The law is in accord with the later authority — *hilkhata kebatrai*: historical observations on a legal rule," in H. Ben-Menahem and N. Hecht (eds.) *Authority, Process and Method: Studies in Jewish Law* (Chur, Switzerland: 1998); Y. Yovel, *Rishonim Veaharonim: antiqui et moderni*" (Hebrew), *Zion* 57 (1993), 369–394. See also Israel Ta-Shma, *Ritual, Custom and Reality in Ashkenaz 1100–1350* (Hebrew), (Jerusalem: 1996), 58–78 and S.E. Wozner, "*Hilkhata kebatrai* — a new perspective" (Hebrew), *Shenaton Hamishpat Haivri* 20 (1995–1997), 151–167.

32 See *Maharshal*, n. 1 above, 143–183. See also Reiner, n. 3 above, 55–58.

Jewish law, a teacher of Judaism, and above all, author of a number of significant works. R. Kalman wrote the following:

> And I say that even in these generations, although hearts have been weakened, he [Maharshal] has the power and knowledge to be creative in legal works, and has the intellectual capability to logically deduce from the legal decisions of earlier rabbis, of blessed memory, and commit them to writing, provided his intent is to be honest and forthright, for the sake of Heaven. Therefore, after having reviewed the rabbi's compilation, I can state… [that it is] a new vessel filled with old [wine], [and that] R. Solomon b. R. Yehiel Luria is a public expert and popular teacher whose students will one day be future decisors of Jewish law. Fortunate is he who merits this, and certainly, anything that has left his hand is complete, and it is fitting to rely upon his logical arguments.

From this approbation, one can deduce the nature of Maharshal's request, his desire to justify his general halakhic methodology, and his demand that this methodology be recognized, apparently in contrast to a different approach.[33]

Taking all these facts together, and utilizing them to highlight the different approaches of Rashash and Maharshal, and keeping in mind Maharshal's responsum to Rema cited at the beginning of this article, gives us insight into the nature of Maharshal's complaint. The question posed by Rema dealt with a dying man's will, which was made out to his daughter, who had a disagreement with the other heirs concerning her ownership of part of her late father's house. The case had been brought before Rema, who at that time was still quite young ("my relative, the young and wise genius, R. Moses Isserles"), who decided the case according to the generally accepted halakhic reasoning, using the many sources in the Talmud, and the works of the early medieval sages (*rishonim*) and later ones (*aharonim*), including Rashba, Tur, Mahari Weil. In his conclusion, Rema wrote: "This is what appears to me to be the case regarding these matters. And I rely on my mentors and colleagues to provide further proofs, although the matter seems clear to me, and that there is no need for any further proof. …" This was the issue dealt with in the responsum that Rema sent to

33 See Rabbinovicz, n. 9 above, 63, n. 5. These approbations were published in the wrong place, as appendixes to the introduction to *Hokhmat Shlomo* (Cracow: 1582). According to his sons, Maharshal had originally not intended to publish this work. Note too that by 1552, parts of *YSS*, which Maharshal began to write in 1547, had already been published; see *Maharshal*, n. 1 above, 95–97.

Maharshal for his inspection, and probably also for his comments and guidance.

In his reply, which, in comparison with his other responsa, is unusual, Maharshal complained about the "students who rebelled and transgressed" and "the strength of the Elder and his son." Other exceptional elements in this responsum include its framework, its formulation, and the sources cited. First, there is the bitter complaint about his troubles and his students who transgressed against him. As the responsum unfolds, the normative approach he would have been expected to take is absent — there are no talmudic sources to inaugurate the discussion, and the few that are quoted are lifted from Rema's responsum. Only one other talmudic quotation is given, and it is cited incorrectly, not being found in the tractate Marharshal refers to. Of all the *Rishonim*, commentators, and legal decisors usually quoted by Maharshal, he quotes only R. Asher, who was also been cited by Rema. Unlike any of his other legal discussions, which are based on analysis of the talmudic sources and commentaries, in this responsum Maharshal's only contribution to the discussion is some comments and questions.

It appears that the conclusion to the responsum provides the key to understanding this unusual responsum, and the other issues I have raised in this article. I will therefore quote it once again, this time with some additional sentences:

> And by God, even if his honor will respond with citations from later authorities concerning this incident, I will not pay attention to him, for his honor, with his clear mental faculties, is as important in my eyes as are the other great later rabbis, unless the matter is found in the Talmud or in the legal decisions of the Geonim, in which case I will not be ashamed and will admit [to my mistake]. Because of my many sins, and as a result of the rebellion of my students, who have rebelled and transgressed against me; and they rely upon the strength of the Elder and his son the Gaon, may God preserve them. They have removed me from my quarters and have damaged my body and the health of my mind. And he who does not turn to … of Edom should not … me, or should turn their hearts of stone and cruelty to hearts of flesh, or give me strength and courage to save my soul and the souls of my worthy students from them. And even when I was in the land of my enemies and under their control, the Lord, may He be blessed, did not detest or loathe [me], nor break the covenant with me. And He increased my jurisdiction, [granting me] proper disciples from all four corners of the world, and they are like thorns in [my enemies'] eyes. And may God protect his honor and deliver him from all similar evil events. By God, his honor would not have been able to withstand such a test for even thirty days.

Maharshal has created an association between two matters that appear unrelated. On the one hand, he harshly criticized those who relied solely on later authorities, as seen in the first sentence quoted above. His use of an oath suggests a heated debate, and hence his statement that the Talmud and the legal decisions of the Geonim are the conclusive source for deciding Jewish law. This issue is then linked to the polemics between himself and "the Elder and his son," which appears to refer to Rashash and his son, who had attracted a number of Maharshal's disciples.[34] This affords us a glimpse of the background to the controversy, if not the catalyst that fed its expansion. Maharshal articulates the essentials of the methodology of legal decision-making in Jewish law, its basis being that "the matter must be found in the Talmud or in the legal decisions of the Geonim." This is in contrast to the "citations from later authorities," a phrase that hints at deciding Jewish law according to the rule that the law is in accordance with the view of the later authorities, a rule that Maharshal declares he will not heed. Although Maharshal himself employed this rule in his decision-making, he never viewed it as the only rule by which to determine the law. Generally he used it in conjunction with other rules and principles for determining the law, such as: legal decisions should be stringent (*YSS* on Hulin 1:10); a prohibition should be presumed (*YSS*, Beitza 4:19); those who are expert at determining the law should be followed when their decisions have become widespread in a certain area (*YSS*, Baba Kama 8:29).[35] It must be noted that Maharshal viewed the rule

34 See *Halakha*, n. 3 above, 137–138.

35 For an illuminating example, see *Responsa R. Joseph Colon*, #90: "It is well-known that Maimonides preceded R. Isaac *Or Zarua*, for the latter was the disciple of R. Judah of Paris, as he wrote in his *Or Zarua*.... Thus, R. Judah of Paris preceded R. Isaac *Or Zarua* and was his mentor, whereas Maimonides preceded R. Judah. Thus one may suppose that during the period of R. Isaac *Or Zarua*, even Maimonides would had agreed." Maharshal's reaction can be found in *YSS*, Baba Kama 10:10:

> What he sought to do — to contrast Maimonides to the *Or Zarua* and differentiate between them by their having flourished in different periods, and thereby to decide the law in accordance with the *Or Zarua* — does not seem correct. R. Asher was later than the *Or Zarua*, for the latter was the mentor of R. Meir of Rothenburg who in turn was the mentor of R. Asher, and R. Asher never distinguished between his era and earlier periods. Furthermore, the Tur and R. Nissim, who were much later, cited Maimonides as law to be put into practice.

that the law is decided in accordance with the view of the later authority as a tradition from antiquity whose source is in the Talmud (ibid. 2:15),[36] which became a tool for determining Jewish law within the tradition of Ashkenazic Jewry. Nevertheless, the principal method of decision-making in Maharshal's works is based on the Talmud and its commentaries, especially the *Rishonim*. Certainly, the rule that the law is decided in accordance with the view of later authorities does not have the same authority as conclusions derived from the Talmud. In contrast, Rashash considered the rule overwhelming and granted almost unlimited power to the present-day decisor. Thus, as quoted by his son, he refused to author any legal work, lest it become the sole authoritative determination of the law. He also influenced Rema in using this rule to criticize the *Beit Yosef*, as noted above.

Moreover, parts of *Yam Shel Shlomo* that exemplified Maharshal's methodology of legal decision-making — studying the relevant talmudic passages and commentaries thereon — were either studied or actually compiled in the talmudic academies where he was the dean (*rosh yeshiva*). This is implied in his introduction to *YSS*:

> Thus, I had extensively searched for and analyzed every source for the law, untiringly analyzing them, discussing them with my colleagues and **most of all with my students**, before writing them down. Anyone who reads this volume will see the sources and the proofs, and will understand and realize that I did not ignore any author before arriving at any actual conclusion.[37]

---

> It is also possible that [R. Isaac] *Or Zarua* himself was just reflecting a local custom at his time … [a custom] that had not spread to other areas. And even if you would argue that his legal decision was for all generations, who is to say that we must follow him and not other views, including later ones? Thus, it is clear that the rule that the law is in accordance with the view of the later authorities is not employed alone, but along with another principle: "one should follow other views," which really means, "the law is in accordance with the majority opinion."

36 Cf. *YSS*, *Baba Kama* 1:2 on the application of this rule to controversies after the generation of Abbaye and Rava.

37 Also note the introduction to *YSS*, Baba Kama:"… Therefore, I will not believe any compilers.… Nevertheless, the Talmud is what determines [the law], and clear proofs will justify it." See also *YSS* on Baba Kama 1:8; Jebamot 13:9; Ketubot 1:22; Hulin 8:8. See also *Maharshal*, n. 1 above, 285–293, Reiner, n. 3 above, 68–76.

This is not a metaphor, for *YSS* took about 28 years of Maharshal's life to complete, and he viewed it as worthy of being included in the chain of the tradition of the Oral Law. Thus, its compilation must have found expression in the study hall and in his lectures to his students. A summary of a number of essential points in the work thus sheds light on the methodology of study and legal decision-making that Maharshal taught his students.

It is thus very plausible that the controversy between Maharshal and Rashash flared up over the methodology of legal decision-making, especially when Maharshal published his work, disclosing his views to the wider public, in contrast to Rashash, who refused to author any halakhic work, as we said.

The results of the controversy, or controversies, can be deduced from the responsum cited at the beginning of this essay. Rashash and his son employed various means to incite students to leave Maharshal's yeshiva, and had Maharshal removed from his quarters. Whether this refers to Maharshal's becoming distraught, or hints at exile is unclear.[38] In any case, he was cut off from his yeshiva and his books, and this explains the strange form of the responsum — the lack of talmudic sources and early commentators and decisors, in contrast to the form of his other legal briefs. The methods employed to convince students to leave Maharshal's yeshiva are unknown, and were referred to by Maharshal as "the strength of the Elder and his son the Gaon." We can certainly imagine the type of sanctions employed by Rashash, who as the official Rabbi of Poland had authority and power, the communal institutions being under his jurisdiction. "Strength," in this context, certainly implies not only great Torah knowledge, but also the power to diminish Maharshal's yeshiva and lure away some of the student body.

Ideological issues in deciding and publishing codes of Jewish law, especially taken together with other issues, could certainly have provoked controversy. Nevertheless, all this is no more than educated conjecture.[39]

38 An allusion to exile can be found in responsum #2: "And at this time, when I am wandering in the land ... and the judges have no power, that is, no staff, whip or cornet [to enforce the law], until God will comfort [me concerning] the evil that He said he would do." Thus far, we have no concrete evidence to link this responsum with the "Elder and his son" controversy.

39 See also the analysis in Reiner, n. 3 above, 55–56, which suggests a struggle between the Maharshal and the Elder's academy, over the question of which would prevail: the Polish legal hegemony, represented by R. J. Pollack

The following source should also be noted:

> We, Sigismund Augustus, King of Poland by Divine mercy… make known to all through this writ, to the public and to individuals, now and for the future: Through the good efforts of some of our advisors, and according to the modest request of the Jews of Lublin, with this writ we permit them to establish a yeshiva and an adjoining synagogue with funds provided by the Jewish community. The yeshiva and synagogue will be built on the property of the house of the physician Isaac May, which is found among the Jewish homes in the outskirts of Lublin.… It will be run by someone who will have authority and influence among the teachers, and will be capable of maintaining order and discipline among the students. All the scholars and rabbis of Lublin will form a committee and elect one of themselves as head of the yeshiva. It will be someone who strengthens the Torah and will bring it honor among them. He will have the authority to supervise both teachers and students. With this [writ], we grant him the honorary title of Rector (*rosh hayeshiva*). Not only is he exempt from submission to the authority of Israel b. Shachna, presently Rabbi of Lublin, and other future rabbis, but he is hereby appointed to supervise all the scholars and rabbis [in Lublin].
>
> Horodna, 23 August, 1567[40]

Although supplementary material concerning this document is still lacking, it appears to reflect the struggle of Polish Jewry for a degree of autonomy in the political and judicial realms.[41] Nonetheless, one thing is certain about this document: the authority of R. Isaac b.

---

and R. S. Shachna, or the Ashkenazic halakhic tradition, represented by Maharshal (without necessarily identifying "the Elder and his son" as Rashash and his son). And see above at n. 16.

40 A reproduction of the writ is found in S. Eidelberg, "Two documents on the establishment of the yeshivot in Poland in the sixteenth century" (Hebrew), in S.K. Mirsky (ed.), *Jewish Institutions of Higher Learning in Europe, Their Development and Destruction* (Hebrew), (NY: 1956), 415–417. See also E. Indalman, "The Scroll of Poland" (Hebrew) in *American Jewish Year Book* (NY: 1949), 622, n. 1; Balaban, n. 7 above, vol. 2 (Jerusalem: 1954), 239. See also Siev, n. 1 above, 49, n. 134; D. Assaf, n. 13 above, 42–43, 102. The explanation suggested by H.H. Ben-Sasson, *Scholarship and Leadership* (Hebrew), (Jerusalem: 1959), 224–225, appears to be problematic.

41 See Balaban, n. 40 above, 238, n. 13, re the 1551 document that permits the Jews of Grand Poland to elect a chief rabbi as they desire. Nissenbaum, n. 10 above, 4, cites the license granted to a doctor named Isaac May, in 1557, to buy a plot of land in Lublin. See also M. Balaban, *The Jewish Town of Lublin* (German), (Berlin: 1919), 22–23. I. Schiffer wrote a series of Hebrew

R. Shalom Shachna, the Chief Rabbi of Lublin at that time, was diminished. We can surmise that this writ cleared the way for Maharshal to come to Lublin to serve as head of the yeshiva, for until his death in 1574, he lived in Lublin. Consequently, we can conclude from this document that Maharshal became the highest rabbinical authority in the city at that time. It would be useful to consider other controversies that broke out over the need to clarify the authority of the city's rabbis and the competition between them,[42] but this would be beyond the scope of this essay. Should "the Elder and his son" in fact be R. Shalom Shachna and his son, R. Israel, the sages of Lublin, this article has suggested reasons for the acute controversy between them and Maharshal, reasons that correspond to, and explain, the known facts. Likewise, a significant chapter in the history of Jewish law in Poland during the sixteenth century will have been described.[43]

---

articles on this matter, see *Zefirah* 44 (1919), nos. 41–48. Unfortunately, they were not included in S. Eidelberg (ed.), *Isaac Schiffer, Selected Writings and Appreciations* (NY: 1967), nor were they included in the bibliography of his writings in that volume, 267–282. For his Yiddish articles on this matter, see ibid., 276–277. See also B. Weinryb, *The Jews of Poland* (Philadelphia: 1976), 124–125.

42 On the authority of R. Shalom Shachna as Chief Rabbi, see Preshel, n. 7 above, 685–686.

43 I would like to thank Prof. Berachyahu Lifshitz for his illuminating comments, and Dr. Shlomo Pick for his suggestions.

*The Jewish Law Annual*, Vol. XIV

# KINGS, COINAGE AND CONSTITUTIONALISM: NOTES ON A RESPONSUM OF NAHMANIDES

BERNARD SEPTIMUS*

## 1

Spanish Jewry is celebrated for its passionate politicians and keen thinkers; but its political thinking, its conceptualization of political reality, is insufficiently studied. This article explores the political ideas in a responsum of Nahmanides, the premier talmudist of the thirteenth century.[1] The responsum seeks to delimit the principle that Jewish law in Exile recognizes royal law; or, to quote the talmudic formulation: "the law of the kingdom is law" (*dina demalkhuta dina*).[2] Our focus will be twofold: the historical context of Nahmanides' responsum, and its significance as a document of medieval Jewish constitutionalism.[3]

The question posed to Nahmanides dealt with a royal debasement of the coinage. This was an old issue that had generated extended discussion: how, precisely, were debts contracted before a debasement to be repaid?[4] But as put to Nahmanides, the question had a new twist: is

* Bernard Septimus is Jacob Safra Professor of Jewish History and Sephardic Civilization in the Department of Near Eastern Languages and Civilizations at Harvard University, and works in medieval Jewish intellectual history.

1 Prof. Thomas Bisson read a draft of this article and made valuable suggestions. For its faults, I bear full responsibility.

2 bNedarim 28a and parallels. The discussion of this principle in medieval Spain is well mapped in Shmuel Shilo's superb *The Law of the State is Law* (Hebrew), (Jerusalem: 1975), henceforth, Shilo.

3 Annotated versions of the responsum may be found in Simha Assaf, *Works of Early Authorities* (Hebrew), (Jerusalem: 1935), 87ff.; *Responsa of Nahmanides* (Hebrew), ed. C.D. Chavel (Jerusalem: 1975), #47, 75–78. Numbered excerpts are translated in an appendix to this article, and referred to in the notes throughout.

4 There is a monographic treatment by Shillem Warhaftig, *Currency in Jewish Law* (Hebrew), (Jerusalem: 1980).

a royal decree that the debased coin be accepted as full repayment of loans in the old coin, deemed valid?[5]

The question came from Nahmanides' friend, the wealthy Barcelona scholar R. Samuel Hasardi.[6] He solicited Nahmanides' opinion while working on this question for his civil law treatise, *Sefer Haterumot*. Nahmanides' responsum is cited in chapter 46 of that treatise. Chapter 45 gives the current date as 1222/3. So the question probably dates from about that time.[7]

This dating suggests a likely historical context: in 1222, James I of Aragon, in financial straits, debased the coinage of Barcelona, and decreed that the new debased coins be overvalued by 25 percent in relation to the old, "even though," to quote the king, "it may seem … that … some people are unjustly troubled."[8] Among those "troubled" — unjustly or not — were apparently the Jews, at least the creditors among them.

Among Christians, in both Aragon and Castile, royal debasements led to struggles with the Crown, and stimulated the development of representative institutions.[9] Jews did not engage in power struggles with the Crown. But they did have to decide whether their own courts would enforce a "troubling" royal decree, or, to put it differently, whether that decree came under the talmudic principle, "the law of the kingdom is law."

There was a broad consensus that the principle had its limits, but no consensus on what they were.[10] Some thought "the law of the kingdom is law" held only in matters touching on "the king's [own] business,"

5 The question had come up about a century earlier in northern France, but Nahmanides was apparently unaware of that discussion; see Shilo, n. 2 above, 403–406.

6 On their relationship, see my "Piety and power in thirteenth century Catalonia," in *Studies in Medieval Jewish History and Literature*, ed. Isadore Twersky (Cambridge MA: 1979), 197–230.

7 *Sefer Haterumot* (Jerusalem: 1988), ed. Aryeh Goldschmidt, 2:842, 1060–1062.

8 T.N. Bisson, *Conservation of Coinage* (Oxford: 1979), 118f; idem, *The Medieval Crown of Aragon* (Oxford: 1986), 61.

9 See Antonio Marongiu, *Medieval Parliaments: A Comparative Study* (London: 1968); Bisson, n. 8 above.

10 Notice the subtle shift in the sense of *dina*, in the formula *dina demalkhuta dina*: in its first use, it is qualified (*dina demalkhuta* = royal law) then, unqualified (*dina* = valid [i.e., Jewish] law): it is the latter that grants legitimacy to the former. And what it grants it can certainly limit. The various proposed limitations are discussed in Shilo, n. 2. above.

but not private law.[11] Nahmanides considered this limitation too restrictive. In formulating his own understanding of the limits in question, he addressed a problem central to medieval European political thought: to what degree is royal authority subject to the rule of law?

Nahmanides cited a crucial limitation on "the law of the kingdom is law" formulated by the last great talmudist of Muslim Spain, R. Joseph ibn Migash. Ibn Migash observed that the talmudic rule refers to "the **law** of the kingdom," and a law is, by definition, a general rule, not an arbitrary decree. So ad hoc exactions that target individuals are not royal law, but royal robbery.[12]

Nahmanides accepted Ibn Migash's limitation, and added another. Ibn Migash had focused on the word "law" in the phrase "the law of the kingdom." Nahmanides' further restriction focused on the word "kingdom" (*malkhuta*). Had the principle been, 'the law of the king (*malka*) is law,' it would have recognized all royally-imposed rules. But, he argued, the law of the more abstract "kingdom" refers not to the decree of a monarch, but to the constitution of a monarchy.[13]

Let me quote Nahmanides:

> We say "the law of the kingdom is law" only with regard to laws recognized as the king's [prerogative] throughout his realm, which he and all

11 See Appendix, paras. 2–3; Shilo, n. 2. above, 131–142. Both Nahmanides and Samuel Hasardi attribute this restriction to some of their teachers. Samuel also attributes it to some scholars of *Tzarfat* (probably, northern France). Samuel takes this restriction as putting the regulation of debt payment, a question of private law, outside the purview of *dina demalkhuta*. Nahmanides, as we will see, disagreed.

12 See Appendix, para. 6; Shilo, 109. A distinction of this sort is fundamental to any conception of the rule of law, but also requires considerable clarification. Ibn Migash, rather than attempt a precise demarcation of the boundary between "law" and arbitrary exercise of power, preferred to put forward the principle in broad strokes, presumably leaving individual cases to judicial discretion.

13 Historians of political thought have debated whether the idea of a "state" existed in the Middle Ages. Critical to this controversy is whether medievals conceived of "an apparatus of power whose existence remains independent of those who may happen to control it at any given time." Various terms have been adduced as evidence for the existence of such an idea. See Antony Black, *Political Thought in Europe 1250–1450* (Cambridge: 1992), 186–191. Should we add Nahmanides' notion of a kingdom (*malkhuta*), as distinct from its current king, to the list? I'm not certain. The term *malkhuta* means "kingship" as well as "kingdom." Perhaps Nahmanides

> the kings who preceded him have implemented, and which are recorded in the royal chronicles and statutes. But an ad hoc action of the king, or a new law that he decrees, penalizing the people in a manner that is without precedent in ancestral times, is royal extortion, and we do not adjudicate on the basis of such a 'law'. … [This] can be deduced from the fact that [the talmudic rule] reads, "the law of the kingdom is law," not 'the law of the king is law.' It refers, therefore, to generally recognized law,[14] not actions taken by kings unilaterally and coercively.[15]

Nahmanides' description of "the law of the kingdom" corresponds to the medieval idea of an ancient constitution that has been in force from time immemorial and limits the authority of the king.[16] The appearance of this notion in Hispano-Jewish law is a small symptom of Spanish Jewry's transfer from Islam to Christendom.

Ibn Migash, still writing in al-Andalus, limited royal authority by focusing on the concept of law in the abstract: real constitutionalism was unknown in this Islamic environment.[17] Appeal to an ancient constitution to restrict royal authority was a European phenomenon. It could thus be used by Nahmanides, one of first great Spanish

---

was thinking more of the institution than of the realm. In any event, the two senses of *malkhuta* are not always sharply differentiated, and Nahmanides' understanding of the formula *dina demalkhuta dina* may be a case in point.

14 The phrase in the original is *dina diyedia lekhulhu*.

15 Appendix, para. 5; *Hidushei Haramban*, Baba Batra 55a; see Shilo, n. 2 above, 195.

16 Cf. Shilo, 199ff. The classic study of the medieval notion that law must conform to ancient custom is Fritz Kern, *Kingship and Law in the Middle Ages* (Oxford: 1939). The suggestive term "ancient constitution" is borrowed from J.G.A. Pocock, *The Ancient Constitution and the Feudal Law* (NY: 1967). The importance of Nahmanides' responsum was rightly sensed by Yitzhak Baer, *A History of the Jews in Christian Spain* (Philadelphia: 1966), 1:286ff., but Baer was vague and cursory as to its significance.

17 On the absence of Islamic constitutionalism, see Bernard Lewis, *The Political Language of Islam* (Chicago: 1988), 112ff. Though in theory Muslim rulers could not legislate on their own and were limited to enforcing Islamic law, it was universally recognized that, in fact, they decreed and ruled quite independently of Islamic law; see Lewis, ad loc. Jewish awareness of this fact is, interestingly, expressed in *Ibn Kammuna's Examination of the Three Faiths*, tr. M. Perlman (Berkeley: 1971), 148.

halakhists of the Christian period. It is no coincidence, then, that the authorities he cites are from twelfth century France, not the Islamic world.[18]

Nahmanides' own political environment, the Crown of Aragon, was a hotbed of medieval constitutionalism, rivaled only by England. Something of the defiant spirit of Aragonese constitutionalism is captured in the traditional oath of allegiance sworn by the nobility to a new king: "We who are as good as you and together are more powerful than you, make you our king and lord, provided that you observe our *fueros* [= laws] and liberties, and if not, not."[19]

Medieval constitutionalism cannot, of course, be conceived anachronistically. The ancient constitution was obscure and contentious. (There was certainly no institutional framework for 'interpreting the constitution' or 'striking down' unconstitutional decrees.) But it could be enlisted by powerful vassals struggling to resist their lord-king. Raw power was crucial in such confrontations, but the ancient constitution provided an essential theoretical complement: the claim that the lord-king had trespassed time-honored bounds, and resistance was in order, in defense of long-standing rights.

So constitutional discourse dealt with the relative rights of kings and nobles. It would probably have surprised this ruling elite to learn

18 See Appendix, paras. 8–9. The first important Spanish talmudist of the Christian period, R. Meir Halevi Abulafia (Ramah), does not yet use a constitutionalist argument to delimit *dina demalkhuta dina*. Ramah recognizes royal taxes only if they are determined by a fixed formula *(kitzva)*; see *Yad Rama*, Baba Batra, 3:241. He understood bBaba Kama 113a to teach that taxes that are not determined by a fixed formula *(kitzva)* are robbery, even if imposed directly by the king. See his comment cited in R. Bezalel Ashkenazi, *Shita Mekubetzet*, Baba Kama, ad loc. Ramah, writing in Toledo some twenty years before Nahmanides, was more rooted than Nahmanides in the tradition of Muslim Spain, and more limited in his use of the Tosafists. Furthermore, Castile was less constitutionalist than the Crown of Aragon; see Angus MacKay, *Spain in the Middle Ages* (London: 1977), 96–117. Ramah's distinction, in this context, between royal "law" and royal "robbery," is probably influenced by Ibn Migash. However, in requiring that law (in this case the formula for determining taxes) be consistent over time, Ramah may be taken to anticipate Nahmanides somewhat. See especially the formulation of Ramah's position in *Tur*, HM 369:14, and Shilo, n. 2 above, 197. For Ramah as a transitional figure, see my *Hispano-Jewish Culture in Transition: The Career and Controversies of Ramah* (Cambridge MA: 1982).

19 Cited in MacKay, ibid., 105.

that Jews were subjecting their decisions to constitutional review.[20] What Jews valued in the idea of constitutional limitation was the principle of the rule of law: some, like Nahmanides, esteemed it enough to find it in the Talmud.[21] That they should have adapted a defense of noble rights to the definition of their own may also point to an aristocratic self-image: it is probably no coincidence that a decision, cited by Nahmanides, likens the status of Jews to that of knights (*parashim*).[22]

## 2

The ancient constitution, as understood by Nahmanides, permanently delimits the king's jurisdiction: he can legislate only within its boundaries;

20 Cf. Appendix, para. 8. While Nahmanides' paraphrase speaks of "kings," the case to which he refers involved the "unconstitutional" acts of a feudal magnate (*sar*). See *Tosafot*, Baba Kama 58a s.v. *i nami*; Shilo, n. 2 above, 192.

21 This regard for a theory that protects the nobility at the expense of royal authority is especially striking in light of the practical interest of Spanish Jews in a strong monarchy. In fact, nobles could assert their "rights" to demand anti-Jewish measures; see e.g. Baer, n. 16 above, 1:172ff. Catalonian knights also demanded (and in 1202 received) reaffirmation of their traditional right "to maltreat" their peasants! See T.N. Bisson, "The politicising of West European societies," in C. Duhamel et al. (eds.), *Georges Duby, L'écriture de l'histoire* (Brussels: 1996), 252. It is possible that Nahmanides' constitutionalist interpretation of the talmudic dictum reflects an assumption, on his part, that constitutional monarchy is a universal phenomenon! See below, n. 34. On limited v. absolute monarchy in Hispano-Jewish thought, see further Aviezer Ravitzky, *Studies in the History of Jewish Philosophy* (Hebrew), (Jerusalem: 1991), 105–125; Amos Funkenstein, *Perceptions of Jewish History* (Princeton: 1993), 155–165.

22 Appendix, para. 8. On the term *parashim*, see the Ben Yehuda dictionary. The decision cited by Nahmanides declares limitations on Jewish movement "unconstitutional" on the grounds that Jews are recognized, in this regard, to have the status of knights. This formulation perhaps reflects the threefold division of feudal society into nobles, clergy and serfs; see George Duby, *The Three Orders: Feudal Society Imagined* (Chicago: 1982). Jews, the argument then goes, are like nobles who have freedom of movement, as opposed to serfs, who do not. (For Jews to compare themselves to the clergy was likely uncongenial.) The issue was probably moot in Nahmanides' Spain, but became relevant in the fourteenth century; see Abraham Neuman, *The Jews in Spain* (Philadelphia: 1942), 1:10–11, 231–232.

and these boundaries are immutable.[23] But there is a germ in Nahmanides' responsum that may have suggested the possibility of amending the constitution:

> The words of R. Samuel [= Rashbam] also incline [toward my position]; for he said: "the law of the kingdom is law" — all taxes and imposts and usages sanctioned by the statutes of kings, which the latter customarily implement[24] in their kingdoms, are legally valid. For all the subjects of the kingdom willingly accept the royal statutes and laws."[25]

The idea of consent might have resonated in Nahmanides' political environment, for contractualism featured prominently in the constitutional thought of the Crown of Aragon.[26] Contractualism provides a potential antidote to the rigidity of the ancient constitution: a contractual constitution need not be projected whole onto a mythic past; contracts are subject to renegotiation. By linking the "the law of the kingdom" to a theory of popular acceptance, Nahmanides may have prompted R. Yom Tov al-Ishbili (= Ritva, a student's student) to attribute the following to him:

> One says that "the law of the kingdom is law" only with regard to long-standing, well-recognized royal prerogatives. But if the king establishes some new law, it is not [recognized as] law, **unless all the people of his kingdom agree to it**. That is why [the third century Amora] Samuel did not say, 'the law of the king is law' but referred to "the law of the kingdom". ... Therefore if the king takes a Jew's property without sanction of the established royal prerogatives, it is extortion, and if an Israelite purchases [that property] from him, he does not acquire ownership, and holds it unlawfully.[27] (emphasis added)

23 Thus the devaluation of 1222, a new law, is valid if, and only if, devaluations are within the king's timeless jurisdiction; see below. It is probably incorrect to attribute an absolute rejection of new law to Nahmanides. Cf. Shilo, n. 2 above, 192, 199ff.

24 Cf. Shilo, 60, n. 5.

25 Appendix, para. 9; Rashbam, Baba Batra 54b s.v. *ve ha amar shmuel*.

26 See MacKay, n. 18 above, 104ff. A theory of acceptance does not, in itself, entail a political framework for testing it. So an acceptance theory need not assume constitutional significance. See, e.g., Yaakov Blidstein, *Political Concepts in Maimonidean Halakha* (Hebrew), (Ramat Gan: 1983), 154–160.

27 *Hidushei Haritva*, Baba Batra 55a. That the words I emphasize go beyond what Nahmanides actually says was pointed out by Shilo, n. 2 above, 65ff. Besides the citation from Rashbam, Ritva may have seen a hint of his extension in Nahmanides' own assertion that "the law of the kingdom is law ... does not refer to actions taken by kings **unilaterally** (*meiatzmam*). ..." See above at n. 15.

On this reformulation of Nahmanides, the "law of the kingdom" is subject to ongoing amendment: it includes enactments that were not part of the ancient constitution, but have been subsequently accepted by the people. This 'acceptance' may allude to ratification by a representative body, such as a *cortes*, although this is not entirely clear.[28]

Funkenstein argued that the recognition of new legislation as "the law of the kingdom" resulted from an erosion of early-medieval custom-based law, under the influence of Roman law, which gives the sovereign absolute authority to legislate.[29] Perhaps this was sometimes the case. But recognition of new royal law could also be conditioned on consent, and emerge from **within** a custom-based context. A recent student has observed that

> the feudal element in kingdoms could facilitate the development of representative forms of government. The prime examples were to be found in England and the lands of the Crown of Aragon (Aragon, Catalonia and Valencia). The element of mutual consent, the essence of the feudal relationship, became enshrined in parliamentary institutions representing the community of the realm.[30]

Al-Ishbili's comment accords well with this picture. It conditions the authority of royal legislation on consent, and assimilates this qualified acceptance of new law to Nahmanides' theory of the ancient constitution.

It is hard to say whether other members of Nahmanides' school shared Al-Ishbili's view: they do not address the question directly. But

28 On the legislative role of the *cortes* (or *corts*, as the Catalan version was known), see Joseph O'Callaghan, *A History of Medieval Spain* (Ithaca: 1975), 440–442.

29 N. 21 above, 155–158. Cf. Baer, n. 16 above.

30 J.P. Canning, in J.H. Burns (ed.), *The Cambridge History of Medieval Political Thought* (Cambridge: 1988), 354. It should be noted, however, that many scholars now consider the view that parliamentary life and constitutionalism grew out of feudalism to be untenable, and find the origin of European ideas about limiting power in Roman and canon law. See e.g. Gaines Post, *Studies in Medieval Legal Thought* (Princeton: 1964); Brian Tierney, *Foundations of the Conciliar Theory: The Contribution of the Medieval Canonists from Gratian to the Great Schism* (Leiden: 1998).

consider the following variation on Nahmanides by his student, R. Solomon ibn Adret (= Rashba):

> It is the consensus of all the authors and commentators that "the law of the kingdom is law," applies only to things that are royal prerogatives. But what the king takes forcibly is not law. … If [the king] comes to exact from the inhabitants of his land more than these [prerogatives allow], it is not law. This is the reason [the Sages] say, "the law of the kingdom is law," not, 'the law of the king is law.'[31]

Almost identical language is used by R. Nissim Gerondi.[32]

While drawing on Nahmanides, Ibn Adret has quietly dropped his teacher's assertion that "the law of the kingdom" is the ancient constitution and legal innovation that goes beyond it is therefore baseless. On Ibn Adret's definition, "the law of the kingdom" is not the ancient constitution: it is just the constitution. Ibn Adret, while loath to offer his own view on the sources of constitutional authority, may have realized that his teacher's was becoming obsolete.[33]

## 3

According to Nahmanides, it is not only Gentile kings who are subject to constitutional constraint:

> The same is true of Israel's sacred kings: the laws defining royal prerogative are well known, as set forth in Scripture by the prophet Samuel. And our masters said (bSanhedrin 20b): "everything mentioned in 'the passage on the king' (= I Sam. 8:11–17) is permitted to the king."[34]

31 *Hidushei Harashba*, Baba Batra 55a.

32 R. Nissim Gerondi, *Hidushei Haran*, Baba Batra 55a; see also R. Joseph Haviva, *Nimukei Yosef*, Baba Batra 29b.

33 We may conjecture that Jewish jurists were reluctant to dwell on the role of representative institutions in legitimating new legislation because these institutions excluded Jews, while including clergy and townsmen along with nobles. Nobles were not as protective of the Jews as the king was, and the latter two estates were generally hostile.

34 Appendix, para. 7. This analogy is often repeated in restatements of Nahmanides' position. Thus a fuller citation from the passage by Ibn Adret discussed above reads:

> It is the consensus of all the authors and commentators that "the law of the kingdom is law," applies only to things that are royal prerogatives; but what the king takes forcibly is not law. For royal prerogatives are well known and acknowledged. Know [that this is so],

"The passage on the king" is part of Samuel's response to Israel's demand for a king. Nahmanides' claim that it is a constitution is puzzling, for the passage reads as follows:

> These will be the ways of the king who will reign over you: he will take your sons and appoint them to his chariots and to be his horsemen and to run before his chariots; and he will appoint for himself commanders ... and some to plow his ground and reap his harvest, and to make his implements of war and the equipment for his chariots. He will take your daughters to be perfumers and cooks and bakers. He will take the best of your fields and vineyards and olive orchards and give them to his servants. He will take the tenth of your grain and of your vineyards and give it to his officers and to his servants. He will take your menservants and maidservants and the best of your cattle and asses and put them to his work. He will take the tenth of your flocks and you shall be his slaves.
>
> I Sam. 8:11–17

This sounds more like a warning against kings than a constitution that limits them. Hence the sequel: "And in that day you will cry out on account of your king, whom you have chosen for yourselves; but the Lord will not answer you on that day" (I Sam. 8:18).

It was Maimonides who turned "the passage on the king" into a constitution. Nahmanides cites what must have been a crucial factor in this reinterpretation: the talmudic dictum, "Everything mentioned in 'the passage on the king' is permitted to the king" (bSanhedrin 20b). If one were to follow the plain sense of "the passage on the king," this

---

> for [Samuel] wrote down "the passage on kings" (I Sam. 8:11–17) for Israel ... and [the Sages] of blessed memory said: "Whatever is written in 'the passage on kings' is permitted to the king." All [other] kings have well-known prerogatives as well. But if [the king] acts to exact from the inhabitants of his land more than these [prerogatives allow], it is not law. This is the reason [the Sages] said, "the law of the kingdom is law," not, "the law of the king is law."

It is interesting that Ibn Adret apparently imagines that "all kings" have recognized but delimited prerogatives, i.e., that constitutionalism is a universal phenomenon. See also *Responsa Rashba* 6:254. The same assumption may underlie Nahmanides' interpretation of "the law of the kingdom," a talmudic concept, in constitutionalist terms.

dictum would license despotism. So Maimonides subtly reinterpreted "the passage on the king."[35] On his reading, it gives the king substantial but still delimited powers: these limits afford a measure of protection to the rights of his subjects.[36]

Consider, for example, how the crushing conclusion to "the passage on the king" — "and you shall be his slaves (*avadim*)" — turns into a prerogative to levy taxes:

> The king has the authority to tax the people for his needs or military needs. And he can fix a [proportional] levy, which it is forbidden to evade. He may decree that whoever thieves the levy forfeit property or life. For it is written, "and you shall be his *avadim* [servants]" and elsewhere it is said, "they shall be subject to your tax *vaavadukha* [and serve you]" (Deut. 20:11) — whence his authority to tax and fix a [proportional] levy. His laws in all these matters and their like are law. For everything mentioned in the "passage on the king" is the king's right.[37]

Another example: people and their movables may be conscripted into royal service, but not without payment:

> [The King] can draft whatever craftsmen he needs to do his work and he pays their wages. He can take any animals, menservants or maidservants for his work, **and pays their hire or price**, as it is said: "And some to plow his ground and reap his harvest and to make his implements of war and the equipment for his chariots.... He will take your menservants and maidservants and the best of your cattle and asses and put them to his work."[38]

35 Contrast the solution of R. Tam, who rejects the dictum, "everything mentioned in 'the passage on the king' is permitted to the king," as non-normative; see *Responsa of the Tosaphists* (Hebrew), ed. I. Agus (NY: 1954), #12. This position had Spanish adherents; e.g. R. Joseph Haviva, *Nimukei Yosef*, Nedarim 10a *s.v. veha amar shmuel*. A full treatment of classical and medieval interpretation of "the passage on the king" is beyond the scope of this article.

36 See Blidstein, n. 26 above, 161–168. Blidstein finds Maimonides' reading somewhat less remarkable than I do. Unfortunately, Maimonides does not say what, if any, institutional checks can keep the king from exceeding his legitimate prerogatives; see Blidstein, 189–196.

37 *Code*, Laws concerning Kings 4:1.

38 *Code*, Laws concerning Kings 4:3.

Yet another example: fields can be commandeered, but only if their crops are needed in military emergencies; and then they must be paid for:

> [The king] can take fields, olive trees and vineyards for his servants, when they go out to battle and are encamped in those areas, **if they have no other source of food; and he must pay their price**, as it is said: "He will take the best of your fields and vineyards and olive orchards and give them to his servants."[39]

Thus, "the passage on the king" functions as the constitution of an Israelite monarchy.

But this constitution is not unique to the Israelite monarchy. For Maimonides, the prerogatives granted by "the passage on the king" are precisely those granted by the principle that "the law of the kingdom is law."[40] Limitations on the latter principle (e.g., that of Ibn Migash) apply to Israelite kings as well.[41]

Returning now to Nahmanides, we see that his position bears a twofold resemblance to that of Maimonides: both take "the passage on the king" to be a constitution; and both liken the prerogatives it grants the king to "the law of the kingdom is law."[42] But there is also a fundamental difference between them: they were thinking of different kinds of constitutions.

39 *Code*, Laws concerning Kings 4:6.

40 This point is nicely demonstrated by Blidstein, n. 26 above, 149–154. Note, for example, the final sentence of the excerpt above at n. 37.

41 Blidstein, n. 26 above, 178–181.

42 For Nahmanides, because "the law of the kingdom" is a constitution, it is **analogous** to the "the passage on the king." It is not clear whether he thought the talmudic formula, "the law of the kingdom is law" actually **refers** to Israelite, along with Gentile, kings. Maimonides apparently did; cf. Meiri, *Beit Habehira*, Baba Kama 113a. Maimonides probably understood *malkhuta* as the universal phenomenon of "kingship." Cf. above, n. 13.

According to R. Tam's responsum, cited in n. 35 above, *dina demalkhuta dina* does not apply to Jewish kings: to claim otherwise would compromise the rule of the Torah. Nahmanides' student R. Aaron Halevi of Barcelona reportedly adopted R. Tam's position; see *Responsa R. Isaac b. Sheshet*, Metzger ed., vol. 2, Responsa attributed to the Rivash, #9, 16. Ibn Adret himself mentions this view favorably in *Hidushei Harashba*, Nedarim 28a; see Shilo, 1 n. 2 above, 102ff.

Maimonides recognized one universal constitution upholding the powers all kings are assumed to need to maintain security and order.[43] Any royal edict, Israelite or Gentile, falling within its boundaries, is legal. Living, like Ibn Migash, in the Islamic world, Maimonides knew no real constitutions. His constitution is a legal-philosophical construct. But for Nahmanides, constitutional discourse and praxis were political realities. Constitutions were part of the political landscape, not theoretical constructs. They were, moreover, distinctive institutions: each kingdom's constitution was "the law of the kingdom" in its domain.[44]

## 4

For Nahmanides, therefore, "the law of the kingdom" is something to be determined empirically, by finding out what royal prerogatives are, in fact, generally recognized. This, I believe, explains Nahmanides' position on the royal debasement of 1222. Despite his commitment to constitutional limitation, Nahmanides recognized the legality of the king's decree.

He argued that even were "the law of the kingdom is law" restricted to the "the king's [own] affairs," royal debasements would still be valid; for "there is no matter more royal than this, [kings] being the masters of the coin (*baalei hamatbeia*), who mint it and establish its currency in their domains. If their determination in raising the value of coins were not valid, they would lose all of their profit and all of their right over coinage."[45]

On the face of it, this argument is puzzling. It seems sensible enough that currency be centrally regulated, and kings were, of course, associated with that authority.[46] But it hardly follows that they have

43 See Blidstein, n. 26 above, 149–154.

44 Because Nahmanides accepted Ibn Migash's qualification, he preserved a universal standard as well: while the "kingdom" is an empirical reality, there is still a universal standard for what can be considered "law." It is hard to say how aware Nahmanides was of constitutional variety: he undoubtedly realized that different kingdoms could have diverse constitutions, but it is not clear how much constitutional diversity he would have perceived in thirteenth century Europe.

45 Appendix, para. 3.

46 Thus for Maimonides, the distinction between a king and a thug is that the king's coin is current; see *Code*, Laws concerning Robbery and Lost Property 5:18 (where the context is the definition of a "king" with regard

a right to debase for profit![47] Why, then, did Nahmanides think it manifest that devaluation designed to enrich the treasury is a royal prerogative?

Probably because it was the regnant reality. It was widely believed, in the thirteenth century, that the king had a right to do what he liked with the coinage; that the currency, in fact, **belonged** to him. Nahmanides' claim that kings are the *baalei hamatbeia*, translated non-committally above as "masters of the coin," may mean, in fact, that they are "owners of the coin."

True, many in the Crown of Aragon were "troubled" by royal debasements and struggled against them. But their strategy was to enter into bargains whereby the king promised not to debase the coinage for a specified period in return for new taxes. The assumption underlying these bargains was that exploiting the coinage for profit was the king's proprietary right, a right that, for a yearly price, he agreed not to exercise.[48] Opponents were probably loath to concede such a right openly: even the king was not articulate in asserting it. What Nahmanides did was to spell it out explicitly: debasement is a king's constitutional right, and thus, by definition, "the law of the kingdom."[49]

---

to *dina demalkhuta*.) R. Vidal of Tolosa, *Magid Mishne*, ad loc., remarks only, "this is clear (*mevoar*)" — i.e., self-evident. R. Elijah of Vilna, *Biurei Hagra*, HM, 369:9, alludes to bMegila 14b (top). See also Blidstein, n. 26 above, 154ff.

47 According to Bernard Guenée, *States and Rulers in Later Medieval Europe* (Oxford: 1985), 94ff., not all medieval devaluations were for the ruler's profit: some were fiscally prudent. But Nahmanides' responsum speaks quite openly of the king's profit in devaluation. The debasement of 1222 was, in fact, part of James I's long struggle to restore the Crown's solvency, and had "profitable results." See T.N. Bisson, "The finances of the young James I," in *Medieval France and her Pyrenean Neighbors* (London: 1989), 356. Cf. also *Responsa R. Isaac bar Sheshet*, #197 (Metzger ed.), 1:238.

48 Peter Spufford, *Money and Its Use in Medieval Europe* (Cambridge: 1988), 295–301, 307, 316. Bisson, n. 47 above, 356, notes that James I was able to debase the coinage of Barcelona in 1222, although he had already concluded bargains not to debase in Aragon, because the *monedatge* (money tax) had not yet been approved in Catalonia.

49 Prof. Bisson, in a personal communication, observes: "It looks as if, in a way nowhere comparably documented in Christian discourse, Nahmanides was recognizing coinage as a lordly prerogative. This is just what Jaume I was struggling to retain in the early thirteenth century." It is interesting that Nahmanides himself seems to have viewed royal debasements with a measure of contempt. In his *Commentary on the Torah* on

Ruling on a later debasement, Ibn Adret reaffirmed his teacher's position. But he also reports that, in reaching his decision, he consulted Gentile lawyers, and they confirmed that the "prerogatives of kingship" (*hukei hamalkhut*) do give the king the right to debase.[50] It is clear, then, that when members of Nahmanides' school speak of the "prerogatives of kingship," they are using a political concept that they share with Christian contemporaries. Like his teacher, Ibn Adret identified "the law of the kingdom" with the constitution of the Crown. It was natural, therefore, that he ask Gentile lawyers what constitutional powers they recognized in their king.

## 5

Nahmanides' ruling, though repercussive, met with resistance. Fragments of a commentary by R. Meir Hakohen of Saragossa (written ca. 1235) have been preserved in a sixteenth century anthology. They include comments that look very much like a conscious rebuttal of Nahmanides' constitutional argument:

> If someone lent money ... and the coin was changed ... he is repaid in the coins that he lent ... even if the king said that anyone who has a debt in the old coin should repay it in the new coin.... We do not say "the law of the kingdom is law" in this sort of case, but only regarding royal laws with scriptural warrant. The king has the power to establish coinage, and to penalize anyone who traffics in another coin; for we find that Solomon established coins. ...[51] But he has not been empowered to decree that his coins be accepted for more than their worth. ... Even if someone is of a notion to disagree — on the grounds that the king, having the right to change the coinage, also has the right to decree whatever he likes about it ... — he should at least concede to us that if the king authorized Israelites to litigate among themselves before Israelite judges, no litigant can exempt himself from the laws of Heaven by recourse to the king's decree, since it is not a decree imposed on Israelites.[52]

---

Exod. 30:13, he suggested that the "sacred shekel" was a coin minted by Moses, in his capacity as "a great king." Moses "called that coin 'shekel' [a measure of weight] because the coin was of full weight, without any missing or impure silver." One senses an implied contrast to the coins of contemporary kings.

50 *Responsa Rashba*, 3:34.

51 See bBaba Kama 97b.

52 Cited in R. Bezalel Ashkenazi, *Shita Mekubetzet*, Baba Kama 97b. See Shilo, n. 2 above, 402. For the dating of R. Meir's commentary, see *Shita Mekubetzet*, Baba Kama 5a s.v. *bishlama mefagel*.

For R. Meir of Saragossa, the authority of all kings (Israelite and Gentile) comes under the principle of *dina demalkhuta dina*. It is subject to constitutional limitation, and includes the issuance and regulation of currency. In all this he agrees with Nahmanides. But against Nahmanides, he argues that a right to regulate coinage does not extend to debasement: that remains royal robbery.

R. Meir recognizes a "universal" constitution: all royal powers must have scriptural warrant,[53] and no concession is made to local peculiarities. It is a construct, independent of the constitution of the Crown of Aragon or any other European kingdom, and is, as such, impervious to the kind of empirical data adduced by Ibn Adret.[54]

R. Meir was closer to the tradition of Muslim Spain than his Catalan contemporaries, and less influenced by the constitutionalism of the Tosafists. Perhaps, too, he was further from the royal court than the Catalans, and less sympathetic to royal claims. He may well have shared the economic concerns of the Christian subjects who fought to limit royal debasements. But even Catalans close to Nahmanides, like R. Samuel Hasardi and R. Jonah Gerondi, sympathized with R. Meir's claim that a royal grant of judicial autonomy should be construed as exempting Jews from enforcing royal decrees that do not include them explicitly.[55] Nahmanides' position emerged victorious; but not without a struggle.[56]

## 6

A brief postscript on "the law of the kingdom is law" in the writing of Ibn Adret (which remains in need of fuller historical analysis):

Ibn Adret, we saw, repeated a slightly revised version of Nahmanides' definition. But he also allows that he has struggled long

53 See Shilo, n. 2 above, 65.

54 In its universality, R. Meir's constitution resembles that of Maimonides. But it appears to be based exclusively on scriptural authority and lacks the foundation in political theory that one senses quite clearly in Maimonides.

55 See *Sefer Haterumot*, ch. 46 (Goldschmidt ed., 2:1060); *Aliyot deRabbenu Yona*, Baba Batra 55a (ed. M. Hershler, Jerusalem: 1966), 1:256.

56 *See Shulhan Arukh*, HM 74:7 and *Siftei Kohen* ad loc., §28. Given its basis in the constitutional reality of medieval Aragon, one wonders about the legitimacy of using Nahmanides' ruling as an authoritative precedent in very different times and under very different regimes. Later readers apparently took Nahmanides' ruling to derive from purely halakhic considerations, independent of regional constitutional realities.

and hard with the principle that "the law of the kingdom is law,"[57] and his **responsa** betray unresolved tension on the subject.[58] This circumstance may have a political context.

Nahmanides' responsum was composed about 1223, toward the beginning of a century that would see an ambitious program of codification carried out under royal auspices, in both Aragon and Castile.[59] The result was a significant expansion of what could be construed as "the law of the kingdom," which, in turn, posed a threat to the autonomy of Jewish law.

Ibn Adret continued to press Nahmanides' distinction between kingdom and king, but added another as well: talmudic law, he noted, recognizes the law of the kingdom (*malkhuta*), not the law of the people (*umata*).[60] His likely intent was to deny talmudic authority not only to customary law but also to the new royal codes.[61] The distinction between "kingdom" and "people," though it may seem abstruse, encapsulated an essential postulate of Hispano-Jewish political thought.

Spanish Jewry, in both Aragon and Castile, had always sought space for a secure and autonomous existence in alliance with the monarchy. This strategy could work so long as the monarchy viewed itself as standing above a medley of quasi-autonomous political and ethnic entities.[62] It began to break down toward the end of the Middle Ages — as monarchy began to ally itself with a nascent, though still inchoate, nationalism that had no room for Jews.

Contrast to Ibn Adret's distinction the famous formulation of the fifteenth-century English jurist Sir John Fortescue: "from the **people** there breaks forth a **kingdom**, which is a mystic body governed by one man as head."[63] This sort of junction of kingdom and people is precisely what Ibn Adret was trying to resist. Ultimately, it proved a losing battle.

57 *Responsa Rashba*, 6:254.

58 See e.g., Shilo, n. 2 above, 137f.

59 On royal codification in Castile and Aragon, see O'Callaghan, n. 28 above, 449–452. Nahmanides was young when he wrote the responsum — twenty-eight, on the usual estimate of his birth date (1195). Ibn Adret was not born till about a decade after the responsum was written; see the approximate date of his birth in Baer, n. 16 above, 1:281.

60 See *Responsa Rashba*, 6:149 and 6:264.

61 See, e.g., *Responsa Rashba* 6:254, where an appeal to royal codification is explicitly rejected.

62 Cf. Baer, n. 16 above, 1:181.

63 *In Praise of the Laws of England*; quoted in Black, n. 13 above, 137ff.

*Appendix: Nahmanides' Responsum (excerpts)*

1. As to your question about a king who mutated the coinage, diminishing its content significantly, and then decreed upon all [his subjects], that this [new] coin be accepted in place of the old one in the repayment of debts and [regarding] all the laws of loans,

2. [My] response [is as follows]: I gather from what you have said that you rely upon the opinion of some of the scholars of the previous generation, who ruled that we say "the law of the kingdom is law," only with regard to affairs of the king that pertain to his own needs, like his right to cut down palms and construct bridges to make a road for himself, or … to declare that anyone who pays [the unpaid] taxes on [another person's] land (that is subject to [royal] taxation) gets that land.

3. This opinion has, in fact, been transmitted to us by some of our teachers. But even granting it, I would not concede your application [of this restrictive reading] to coinage; for there is no matter more royal than this — [kings] being the masters of the coin, who mint it and establish its currency in their domains. If their determination in raising the value of coins were not valid, they would lose all of their profit and all of their right over coinage. …

4. But we have already examined this opinion [of the scholars of the previous generation] and found that it crumbles in the face of the talmudic evidence. … Moreover, … the validity of the documents recorded in Gentile registries … rests on "the law of the kingdom"; yet such documents are valid even if they are irrelevant to royal business. … It follows that [royal] decrees are legally valid in all monetary matters. … We may thus conclude that all laws and usages that kings implement in their kingdoms and apply throughout the kingdom are legally valid. I have already written in my novellae … as follows:

5. … It seems reasonable that we say "the law of the kingdom is law" only with regard to the laws known as the king's [laws] throughout his realm, which he and all the kings who preceded him implemented, and which are recorded in the royal chronicles and statutes. But an ad hoc action of the king, or a new law that he decrees, penalizing the people in a manner that is without precedent in ancestral times, is royal extortion, and we do not adjudicate on the basis of such a 'law.'

6. R. Yehosef Halevi [ibn Migash] ruled that if the king robs one of his subjects of his wealth, seeking some pretext against him, it is called royal extortion; whereas what he enacts [uniformly] throughout his land possesses royal authority and is legally valid. This is a correct

ruling, but needs to be supplemented with what I have written. The latter can be deduced from the fact that [the talmudic rule] reads, "the law of the kingdom is law," not 'the law of the king is law.' It refers, therefore, to generally recognized law, not actions taken by kings unilaterally and coercively.

7. The same is true of Israel's sacred kings: the laws regulating royal prerogatives are well known, as stated in Scripture by the prophet Samuel. For our Rabbis said (bSanhedrin 20b): "everything mentioned in the 'paragraph on the king' (I Sam. 8:11–17) is permitted to the king."

8. I have discovered a counterpart to my position that if a king issues a new ruling that is not in consonance with the royal statutes, it is considered extortion. For some of the northern French scholars have written in their works that in some places, when Israelites emigrate from one kingdom to another, the king [of the first kingdom] seizes whatever property they own anywhere in his kingdom [in order to discourage emigration]. If another Israelite then purchases it from that king, it was decided (when such a case, in fact, arose) that [the second Israelite does not gain title]; for this is not the law of the kingdom, but royal extortion. For it is well known in their laws that the legal status of Jews is analogous to that of knights, who are free to dwell wherever they please. If, therefore, there is some monarchy that wishes to change the law and to make its own law, this is not considered "the law of the kingdom." This supports my position.

9. The words of R. Samuel [= Rashbam] also incline [toward my position]; for he said: "the law of the kingdom is law — all taxes and imposts and usages sanctioned by the statutes of kings, which the latter customarily implement in their kingdoms, are legally valid. For all the subjects of the kingdom willingly accept the royal statutes and laws."

10. As to your contention that if the value of the coin was **increased**, and the king decreed that a hundred of the [new] coins be given in payment for [a loan of] one hundred of the old coins, [it would be forbidden to comply] on account of the prohibition on usury: in point of fact, here too [the king's] decree is legally valid. For this addition is paid without the stipulation or will of the parties. Were it not for the "law of the kingdom," such an addition would constitute not usury, but robbery. But because the king's law is law, and his expropriation, a valid expropriation, there is neither robbery nor usury here. [The question], however, [is moot because] kings nowadays are not accustomed to undervalue new coins, but to overvalue them.

*The Jewish Law Annual*, Vol. XIV

# ON THE RELATIONSHIP BETWEEN THE CAPACITY TO PERFORM A LEGAL TASK AND THE CAPACITY TO APPOINT AN AGENT TO PERFORM IT

MICHAEL WYGODA*

## 1 *Introduction*

This article explores the relationship between the principal's capacity to appoint an agent to perform a legal function, and his capacity to perform this function himself.

In consideration of the fact that agency brings about, through the function of the agent, the legal results that would have occurred had the principal himself acted, it is clear that the first condition for permitting the appointment of an agent is that the principal be legally capable of performing the act himself.[1] On the basis of this axiomatic

* Senior Director (Jewish Law), Ministry of Justice, Israel.

1 See A. Barak, *The Law of Agency* (Hebrew), (Jerusalem:1996), para. 437. According to the author, the starting point of the Law of Agency, 1965, is that "if the principal is unfit to perform a given task, there is no possibility of creating an agency relationship with respect to that task, for the agency relationship requires that the act of the agent 'binds and benefits' the principal, which result, in our given case, would be impossible." See also para. 177, 429, 433. Continuing, the author states: "let us be precise: **impossibility of performing the agency does not result from the principal's lack of fitness to appoint an agent**, but rather arises by virtue of the fact that in such a situation the agency lacks any existence whatsoever" (para. 442). From these words, it appears that appointment of an agent is valid even when, at the time of the appointment, the principal was unfit to perform the legal task, provided that the situation had changed by the time the agent actually performed the delegated task. So, for example, one who anticipates relaxation of the currency control laws could appoint an agent in advance to accept foreign currency on his behalf once the new law permitting such acceptance became effective. Below, we will see that the question of the relationship between the ability of the principal to perform the delegated task and his ability to appoint an agent is treated at length in the sources of Jewish law. See also, S. Ettinger, *Agency in Jewish Law* (Hebrew), (Jerusalem: 1999), 39–42.

premise, the Talmud[2] establishes that the *kohanim* who brought sacrifices in the Temple in Jerusalem were certainly not acting as agents of the Jewish people, but rather, as agents of God; after all, if an Israelite (who is not a *kohen*) is himself unfit to bring a sacrifice, how could he appoint a *kohen* as his agent to do so in his stead?[3] That is to say, the first condition for enabling appointment of an agent is that the principal must categorically be one who is "able to act."

But what are the conceptual parameters of being "able to act"? For a principal to be categorized as "able to act," is it necessary that he have the capacity to carry out the specific delegated task himself? Or rather, is it sufficient that the principal have general qualifications needed to perform the task? For example, is there no validity to an agency for the purpose of betrothing a woman who is married at the time the agency is created, on the grounds that at that time the principal himself would not have been able to betroth her? Or is such agency valid, by reason that the principal himself is not unfit to betroth her, and upon the woman's divorcing or becoming widowed, the agent will be able to complete the delegated task? Assuming that such an appointment (i.e., one where performance of the delegated act is impossible at the time) is in fact invalid, the question arises as to whether it is invalid regardless of the basis for the impossibility of carrying it out, or there is reason to distinguish between different types of impediments to performance, such as legal impediments (as in the previous example) and physical impediments, e.g., where the principal has a disability and is physically unable to perform the task himself. Below, we will see that with respect to these questions, the halakhic decisors have a broad range of opinions. We will first discuss physical impediments, then legal impediments.

---

On this matter in American and English Law, see "Agency," 3 *Am Jur* 2d, 516–519; Webb, "The capacity of an infant to appoint an agent," 18 *Mod. L. Rev.* (1955), 461.

2 bKidushin 23b.

3 The question of whether *kohanim* performed their service as agents of the nation or as agents of God is not merely theoretical. Rashi, Kidushin 23b, s.v. *shluhei derahmana,* points out that a distinguishing practical case between the two approaches is presented by one who vows not to benefit from the *kohanim.* Were the *kohanim* acting on behalf of the nation, such a vow would prevent the one expressing it from bringing a sacrifice in the Temple; were the *kohanim* serving as agents only of God, there would be no such limitation. See also *Tosafot* ad loc. s.v. *deamar.*

## 2 *Physical Incapacity*

There are situations where the principal, on account of a physical incapacity, is not fit to perform a task he seeks to delegate. Does this physical impediment deprive him of the ability to appoint an agent to perform the task?[4]

As we will see below, here it is important to distinguish between, on the one hand, an incapacity that prevents the principal from performing the act itself, such that were he physically located in the place where its performance was to take place, he would still lack the physical capacity to perform it ("direct incapacity"), and, on the other hand, an incapacity that only prevents the principal from arriving at the place of performance, but which, had he arrived there, would not have kept him from performing it himself ("indirect incapacity").

### 2.1 Direct Incapacity

Does the direct incapacity of the principal, such as, for example, if he is paralyzed and unable to perform any task whatsoever, render him "unable to act" and deprive him of the capacity to appoint an agent? As we will see, the decisors differ on this question.

There are two apparently-incompatible relevant legal sources. The first is a Tosefta[5] on agency for divorce, where the husband, acting as principal, lacks the physical capacity to write the divorce document

4 There is no doubt that the situation where, at the time of the appointment, the principal is not at the place the delegated act is to be performed, and accordingly is unable to perform it, does not render him "unable to act," even according to the opinion that there is a requirement that the principal be physically capable of accomplishing the delegated act. Indeed, this is the essence of agency: permitting someone to expand the bounds of his legal actions beyond physical limitations. The explanation for this will be provided below at n. 17. Cf. the statements of the *Arukh Hashulhan* (henceforth *AH*), n. 90 below.

It is possible that this premise is at the source of the law of the Mahari Bruna, according to which one who obtains the right to perform a mitzva and goes to a different city (i.e., leaves the town where the mitzva was to be performed) may appoint an agent to perform the mitzva in his name. (This halakha is derived from *Kneset Hagdola, Hagahot Hatur*, OH 146 'b,' in the name of Mahari Bruna). Cf. *Responsa Hikrei Lev*, EH 46 s.v. *veeikh*.

5 Tosefta Gitin 5:1, also cited in bGitin 70b.

himself: "If he was cross-eyed or had gnarled hands, and indicated a divorce document should be written for his wife, it should be written and given to her so long as the husband remains alive." In this instance, the principal's incapacity is direct, but nevertheless, it is established that he has the ability to appoint an agent.

The second source is a talmudic discussion from which it follows that a *kohen* who is incapable of offering sacrifices himself is unable to appoint an agent to do so in his stead, despite the fact that were he healthy there would be no incapacity:

> The rabbis learned as follows: A *kohen* comes and offers his sacrifices at all times and hours that he wishes ... if he is old or sick, he may assign [the activity] to any *kohen* he wishes. ... What is the nature of this old or sick *kohen*? **For if he is unable to perform the service, how can he appoint an agent?**[6] (my emphasis)

This conclusion, apparently, conflicts with that derived from the Tosefta.

As stated previously, the decisors differed over the relationship between these conflicting sources. Some uphold the conclusion derived from the first source, according to which physical incapacity, even if direct, does not render the principal unfit to appoint an agent.[7] In their view, the categorical classification "unable to act" includes only those who are subject to some legal, as opposed to physical, incapacity. So writes, for example, the author of *Responsa Hikrei Lev*: "[One who is] 'unable to act' ... is a purely a legal categorization, comprising persons whom the Merciful One said should not act, and who therefore may not appoint an agent."[8]

As to the second source above, concerning the *kohen* who is legally incapable of appointing an agent when he himself is physically unable to carry out the task of offering a sacrifice, which appears to conflict

6 bBaba Kama 109b–110a.

7 See *Hikrei Lev*, EH 44 (at page 104d), s.v. *ela deakati; Responsa Hokhmat Shlomo* (found at the end of *Har Hamor*), sec. 1. This certainly is also the opinion of the Maharit, as stated below, at n. 33. It appears, too, that this is the view of those decisors who posit that the physical act of writing a divorce document properly may be delegated to an agent, but nevertheless permit appointment of an agent by a husband whose hands have been severed. See below, n. 12. For discussion of the opinions of other decisors who apparently share this view, see below, nn. 46 and 58.

8 See n. 7 above.

with the conclusion that the physically incapacitated are not per se precluded from appointing agents, these decisors explain that if an "old or sick" *kohen* is not able to appoint an agent, it is not because his physical incapacity renders him "unable to act," and therefore unfit to appoint an agent. Rather, the reason is that a condition for the *kohen*'s right to offer a sacrifice is his ability to offer it personally. This is the meaning of the Talmud's bewilderment — if a *kohen* is incapable of offering a sacrifice personally, he lacks any right to perform it, so how can he appoint an agent to benefit from something to which he himself has no right?[9]

In contrast, there are those who adopt the conclusion derived from the second source, according to which a direct physical incapacity deprives the principal of his ability to appoint an agent.[10] In their view,

9 The author of *Hikrei Lev* cites bBekhorot 41a in the explanation he gives in *Hikrei Lev*, OH 40. Of similar thinking is the Netziv of Volozhin in *Haamek Sheeila*, on *Hayei Sarah*, *sheilta* 17:2, where he writes:

> Every *kohen* who is not personally able to perform the work himself, **is not endowed by the Merciful One with the right to work in the Temple**, and is tantamount to a *kohen* who is not serving his appointed watch ... to whom the Torah has granted no rights, except to the extent that he can act himself, and not when he must rely on appointment of an agent to accomplish the task for him. Here too, regarding the Temple service, it is written, "But the Levites shall do the service" (Num. 18:23) implying that so long as he is able to perform the service himself, the Merciful One grants him rights, and he may appoint an agent, but if he is unable to perform the service, **the right is not his**, and he has no right to appoint an agent. (my emphasis)

*Shoel Umeishiv*, 3rd ed., 2:169, s.v. *uvaze meyushav heitev* explains the matter similarly, as does (although in a different context) *Noda Biyehuda*, 2nd ed., EH 69 s.v. *uma dekashya*. It is also the explanation of R. Elhanan Wasserman in his novellae on Gitin 32b, published most recently in the booklet *Divrei Sofrim* (Jerusalem: 1991) 75. I thank Prof. Dov Frimmer for drawing my attention to this source.

10 See *Tosafot Yeshanim*, Eruvin 13a (published in the marginal notes; see n. 12 below); *Beit Meir*, EH 119:6. This is also the opinion of *Responsa Hatam Sofer*, YD 271, which upholds the principle in a more extreme way, arguing that even when the impediment preventing the principal from accomplishing the act himself is only psychological, that suffices to deem him "unable to act." The *Hatam Sofer* asserts that a bastard, who is unfit to write a Torah scroll because he is unable to properly focus his attention while writing the name of God in the sentence, "a bastard shall not enter into

a *kohen* merits partaking in a sacrifice even if "old or sick," but is categorized as "unable to act," and therefore deprived of the ability to appoint an agent. On this approach, in complete contrast to the previous approach, the rule with respect to one who is "unable to act" does not merely refer to legal incapacity, but rather "all those who are unable to act, **whatever the source of the incapacity**."[11] As for the first source, which appears to contradict their conclusion, they explain that it deals with the writing of a divorce document, and on their view, the **writing** of a divorce document is not an act which the husband is required to do himself, but rather, it suffices if the divorce document is written at his direction.[12] The **giving** of the divorce document, in

the community of God" (Deut. 23:3) (a law brought by the *Mordekhai, Halakhot Ketanot* (at the end of Menahot)), is also unfit to appoint an agent to write it in his stead. On this basis, the *Hatam Sofer* reaches the conclusion that a bastard is exempt from the commandment to write a Torah scroll, because he completely lacks the wherewithal to observe the commandment, either on his own or by an agent.

11 Quoting the *Beit Meir*, n. 10 above.

12 The *Rishonim* debated the question of whether the laws of agency apply to the writing of a divorce document. Some of them posit that there is no requirement that a bill of divorce (*get*) be written specifically by the husband, but rather, to satisfy the requirement that the *get* be written specifically for the purpose of divorcing the wife of the man in question (*lishma*), it is important only that it be written at his direction. On this approach, the laws of agency do not apply to the writing of a *get*. *Tosafot Yeshanim*, bEruvin 13a, explain that for this reason someone who has no hands can divorce his wife: "and one must distinguish between the phrases 'and he shall write [a *get*]' and 'he shall give [a *get*]' [which appear in the biblical sentence, "and he shall write for her a severance document and he shall give it into her hand" (Deut. 24:1), the textual source for the laws of divorce], for the giving by someone other than the husband requires agency, but the writing by someone other than the husband does not require agency, for surely the biblical verse acknowledges that every man can divorce his wife, **even one whose hands have been severed**" (my emphasis). In contrast, there are those who posit that the writing of the *get* is an obligation that rests on the husband, and he is thus unable to fulfill his obligation through another, except by the power of the laws of agency. For a summary of the different approaches, see the Talmudic Encyclopedia, vol. 5, "*Get*," 569–570. It should be noted that those *Rishonim* who posit that the laws of agency apply to the writing of a *get*, do so on the view that physical incapacity does not constitute "inability to act" (see *Hikrei Lev*, n. 7 above). If this were not the case, how could they explain the Mishnaic

contrast to its writing, must be performed by the husband or his agent. However, even if the husband lacks the physical power to deliver the divorce document into his wife's possession, he is able to appoint an agent, because his situation is merely an indirect physical incapacity (such that were he in her courtyard, he would be capable of transferring the divorce document to her despite his physical limitations). As we will see below, on all opinions, indirect incapacity does not preclude appointment of an agent.

## 2.2 Indirect Incapacity

It is indisputable that if the physical incapacity only prevents the principal from arriving at the place where a task is to be performed, this does not deprive him of the capacity to appoint an agent. The halakhic sources are replete with examples of principals who were in places distant from the place of performance of the delegated task (such as, for example, "one who sends a *get* from an overseas nation"[13]), and it is not stated that a condition for fulfillment of the agency was the principal's ability to reach the place of performance. It is clear from other contexts as well that an incapacity of this type does not invalidate the act of a principal. Thus, for example, the Mishna speaks of an agent "who brings a *get*" that was entrusted to him by an "old or sick" principal.[14] In situations such as old age or sickness, the principal would not have been up to the demands of traveling to the place of performance, and despite this the agent's act is not invalid.

The thesis that a principal's indirect incapacity does not invalidate the agent's act is consistent not only with the principle that the "ability" requirement relates only to the legal capacity of the principal,[15] but also with the view that it has to do with physical ability as well.[16] While

law that one who has no hands can send a *get* to his wife, for is he not physically incapable of writing it himself? The *Mahane Efraim* reaches this conclusion in his commentary on Maimonides, *Code*, Laws concerning Divorce 3:15, but the issue warrants further investigation. *Hikrei Lev* dismisses any such hesitation.

13 mGitin 1:1.

14 mGitin 3:3.

15 See text at n. 8 above.

16 See text at n. 10 above.

indirect incapacity precludes the principal's performing the act himself, for he lacks the ability to reach the place of performance, arrival at the place of performance is not part of the legal act for which the agent was sent, to which the agent's standing to act relates. In other words, with respect to reaching the place of performance, the agent acts on his own and not on the basis of his principal's ability to do likewise. It is clear, accordingly, that the laws of agency which provide that the agent's ability to act derives from that of the principal do not apply to the physical function of reaching the place of performance, and there is no requirement that the principal be able to reach the place of performance.[17]

## 3 *Legal Incapacity*

### 3.1 Talmudic Sources

Thus far, we have dealt with a principal who is prevented from accomplishing a delegated task himself on account of a physical incapacity. We will now turn to the case of a principal who is prevented from accomplishing a delegated task himself on account of a legal incapacity. It would appear that an incapacity of this type completely deprives him of the ability to appoint an agent, as reflected in the talmudic discussion cited above,[18] with regard to the standing of *kohanim* doing service in the Temple. As mentioned above, the Talmud established

17 This point was noted in the *Beit Meir* on EH 119:6 s.v. *lefikhakh*: "The agent's power to walk is not a function of his agency." And cf. the approach of the *Hatam Sofer* at n. 62 below. He agrees that indirect incapacity does not render the principal "unable to act," but derives this principle from a different claim (namely, that indirect incapacity is merely relative and not absolute. See below).

In light of this, the statements of the *Kreti Upleti*, sec. 61, Pleti, 6, are perplexing. He criticizes those living outside the land of Israel who appoint agents in the land of Israel to purchase on their behalf animals to be slaughtered to give the *matnot kehuna*. In his opinion, appointing an agent under these conditions is not feasible, because the principals are deemed "unable to act." This is perplexing, for, as we have seen, it is clear that distance from the place of performance in and of itself does not render the principal "unable to act," even where the principal has no means of overcoming this distance, for instance, where he is physically disabled and cannot travel to the place of performance. Cf. *Hikrei Lev*, EH 46 s.v. *veeikh*.

18 See text at n. 2 above.

that the *kohanim* are certainly not agents of the nation, but rather agents of God, because it is not possible for the agent to do something, in the name of the principal, that the principal himself is prevented from doing. However, attention to additional talmudic texts reveals that such a determination is too sweeping, insofar as these texts give rise, apparently, to the opposite conclusion.

From the discussion on methods of freeing a Canaanite slave, for example, it becomes clear that not every legal incapacity rules out the ability to appoint an agent.[19] The Talmud cites the opinion of R. Shimon b. Eleazar, according to which a slave is not freed upon receipt of a document declaring his emancipation that is provided him directly by his master. The reason for this is that a condition of his freedom is that the document pass out of the custody of the master, a condition that is not satisfied by the slave's receipt of the document from the master directly, for the general principle is, "the hand of a slave is like the hand of his master."[20]

Despite this, the Talmud establishes that even according to the opinion of R. Shimon b. Eleazar, a slave can appoint an agent for the purpose of accepting the emancipation document on his behalf. The Talmud asks how it can be that a slave can appoint an agent to perform a task he himself is (legally) unable to perform? It answers that a distinction must be drawn between the incapacity of one who is not a *kohen* to bring a sacrifice, and the incapacity of a slave to accept an emancipation document: "Israelites [who are not *kohanim*] have nothing to do with the realm of sacrifices at all; a slave has something to do with documents [of manumission] ... for a slave can accept the document emancipating his fellow from the hand of his fellow's master." In other words, the sacrificial service is completely foreign to one who is not a *kohen*, and for this reason it is clear that a *kohen* cannot be his agent to perform it. In contrast, the legal act of receiving a document of manumission is not foreign to a slave, as he is able to take possession of such a document on behalf of another slave. Similarly, he is able to

19 bKidushin 23b.

20 The opinion of the Sages, which differs from the opinion of R. Shimon b. Eleazar, is that "the document and the hand arrive together" — in other words, because the slave is emancipated upon receipt of the document, he is fit to accept it. On their opinion, then, explaining why a Canaanite slave can appoint an agent to accept the document of emancipation raises no difficulty.

appoint an agent to free him, even though he would not have been able to carry out the task himself.[21] It appears that even when a legal incapacity prevents a principal from achieving the objective of the agency himself, he is not unfit to appoint an agent, so long as the task in question is not foreign to him.[22]

A different talmudic discussion apparently reaches a contradictory conclusion,[23] leading some of the decisors to distinguish between different types of legal incapacity.[24] The Talmud cites a law in the name of R. Johanan, in connection with an agent who was appointed to betroth

21 See *Helkat Yoav*, EH 20, s.v. *umitaam*, where it is pointed out that in jKidushin 1:3 (12b–13a), a different approach is suggested, on which even in this situation, the principal is deemed "unable to act." A more thorough discussion of this matter is beyond the scope of this article.

22 However, it is clear that this conclusion is unacceptable to those who are of the opinion that a direct physical incapacity deprives a principal of the ability to appoint an agent; see the text at n. 10 above. In fact, they declare unfit to appoint an agent even one whose physical incapacities prevent him from accomplishing the delegated task, e.g., an amputee who is incapable of writing a divorce document, but to whom the task at hand is not foreign. See below at n. 54.

23 bNazir 11b–12b.

24 Cf. H. Ben-Menahem, "The judge-agent analogy in the Talmud," in H. Ben-Menahem and N. Hecht (eds.), *Authority, Process and Method: Studies in Jewish Law* (Chur, Switzerland: 1998), 33–58. Ben-Menahem explores the proposition (apparently raised, on his view, in various talmudic discussions) that the judge is the agent of the litigants. He explains that one of the problems with this concept is that a person cannot appoint an agent for an act that he himself is unable to perform, and clearly, a litigant is unfit to judge himself. However, the solution proposed by Ben-Menahem, based on the talmudic discussion of the slave who appoints an agent to accept his bill of manumission (in which case it suffices that the matter be of relevance to the principal), does not address the talmudic discussion we analyze here, bNazir 11b–12b, though Ben-Menahem indeed refers to it in his article. This discussion puts forward a position that conflicts with Ben-Menahem's proposed solution. There is also some doubt as to whether his solution has substance even on the approach of the Maharit, discussed below. The Maharit certainly maintains that at the time of the performance of the delegated task the principal must be fit to accomplish it himself. See the view of *Mirkevet Hamishne* at n. 45 below. Let us also point out that while Ben-Menahem himself dismisses the contemplated solution in light of the discussion in bBaba Kama 110a (the case of the sick *kohen*; see n. 6 above), as we saw above at n. 8, many decisors do not perceive this particular discussion as raising a substantive problem.

an unspecified woman: "One who says to his agent 'go and betroth for me some woman,' and the agent dies [so it is not known which woman he betrothed][25] — the principal is prohibited to [marry] any woman in the world."

The reason for this sweeping prohibition is that every woman is subject to doubt as to whether she is a relation of the woman whom the agent betrothed for the principal, so that it is possible she is the mother, sister, daughter or other close relative of that betrothed woman.[26] Rava qualifies the law of R. Johanan, and establishes that the prohibition does not pertain to a woman who has no female relatives or whose female relatives were married at the time of the agent's appointment (as any such relative was certainly not betrothed to the principal). This qualification applies, emphasizes that Talmud, **even where that female relative was divorced soon after the appointment of the agent**. Even though, as a theoretical matter, it is possible that the agent met with her as an unwed woman and betrothed her in the name of the principal, such a betrothal would have been without authorization and is not binding, because at the time of the appointment she was still a married woman. And in the words of the Talmud: "A man is only able to appoint an agent with respect to something that can be achieved now [the time of the appointment], but with respect to something that cannot be achieved now, he is not able[27] to appoint an agent." From here it would seem that even if, at the time of the agent's appointment, the

25 However, there is no doubt that he in fact betrothed a woman, because "there is a presumption: an agent fulfils the purpose of his agency."

26 In other words, all women are forbidden to the principal as spouses because of the possibility that due to their degree of kinship they are prohibited sexual partners. The *Tosafot*, bNazir 12a s.v. *asur*, explain that the prohibition is a Rabbinic sanction imposed on the principal on account of his failure to specify the woman he was interested in betrothing, but from a purely legal perspective, the principal is permitted to marry any woman in the world by virtue of the principle of "the majority," in that the majority of women are not related to the woman whom the agent betrothed on his behalf. This is not the view of Nahmanides. See the *Magid Mishne*, Laws concerning Marriage 9:6 (but according to Nahmanides, the female relatives of a woman are competent to testify that they were not betrothed by the agent, in which case she is permitted to marry the principal). But cf. Rema, EH 35:11.

27 The word *"matzi"* (able) is not found in all extant texts, for instance, the Vilna edition. See n. 31 below.

matter in question is not foreign to the principal (as he is legally fit to marry), he is nonetheless unable to appoint an agent to betroth a woman who was married at the time of the appointment, because at that time he was unable to betroth her himself.[28]

As stated, this apparently contradicts the conclusion arrived at in the discussion of the Canaanite slave who appoints an agent.[29] There we concluded that it suffices, with respect to the fitness of the principal, that the subject of the agency not be foreign to him, even if under the circumstances he is unable to perform the task himself. The conclusion reached in the discussion of agency to betroth an unspecified woman is that it does not suffice, but rather, the principal must be able to perform the delegated task himself. Many *aharonim* have endeavored to resolve this contradiction, and have suggested various solutions, leading to different juridical developments with regard to the fitness of a principal. We now turn to the solutions that have been suggested. We will begin with the approach of the Maharit, on whose exegesis of the 'agency to betroth an unspecified woman' discussion, there is no contradiction, not even on the face of it, between the two

28 Apparently this is also the conclusion to be derived from bJebamot 52a–b: "One who tells a clerk, 'write a *get* ... to a woman [who is not betrothed to him] — such a *get* has no legal effect, because it is not within his power to divorce her." Here too, since at the time of the appointment of the agent the principal was unable to divorce the woman, as she was not at the time his wife, the *get* has no effect, though divorce is not foreign to the principal. And indeed so the *Tosafot*, s.v. *uleisha*, understood that discussion. But cf. Maimonides, *Code*, Laws concerning Divorce 3:6: "If he said to the scribe, 'write a *get* to such and such a woman and I will have it with me so that when I marry her, I can use it to divorce her,' and if it was written and they were married and then he used that *get* to divorce her — such a *get* has no legal effect, because the woman was not categorically one who could be divorced from him at the time the *get* was written, **and as a result it could not have been written for the purpose of divorce**" (my emphasis). From Maimonides' remarks, it seems that the invalidity of the *get* is not a reflection of some defect in the appointment (the principal's "inability to act"), but rather, is due to its not having been written for the express purpose of divorcing the woman (*lishma*). If so, this source does not conflict with the opinion of the Maharit (below, n. 30), as elucidated by R. Jacob Kuli in his commentary on *Mishne Lamelekh*, Laws concerning Marriage 9:6, s.v. *umai shna*. Cf. *Responsa R. Akiva Eger*, 2:73.

29 The *Orah Mishor* (Kremnitzer) (printed in the Vilna ed.), bNazir 12b s.v. *gemara*, wrote of this contradiction: "and the matter was left unresolved, and in need of further study."

talmudic passages. In his opinion, the fundamental principle is that arising from the emancipation of a Canaanite slave case, and he maintains that the relationship of the principal to the subject of the agency suffices to render the principal fit to appoint an agent.

### 3.2 The Maharit's Proposal

In the talmudic discussion of the appointment of an agent to betroth an unspecified woman, the Maharit's[30] text of the Talmud does not read, "one who is unable to act **is unable to** appoint an agent," but rather, "one who is unable to act **does not** appoint an agent."[31] In the opinion of the Maharit, the intent of the Talmud is not to establish a halakha, or legal norm, according to which a principal is unable to authorize an agent to carry out an act that, at the time of the appointment, the principal is unable to carry out. The intent of the Talmud is only to establish a presumption as to the principal's state of mind, namely, that the principal does not intend to authorize his agent to carry out an act that he is unable to perform at that time. In other words, as a matter of principle, there is nothing to prevent someone from appointing an agent to betroth a woman who is still married at the time of the appointment, provided that the principal's intent is clear from the language of the authorization.[32] It is understood that the agent will not be able to perform the delegated task until after the woman is divorced or widowed, but that does not detract from the validity of the appointment.

30 *Responsa Maharit*, 2, HM 23, s.v. *ukvar*; and see also EH 43.

31 The *Rif* had this text as well. See Kidushin, ch. 2 (page 21b in the *Rif*): "But where he is unable to betroth her, he does not appoint an agent." In his *Haamek Sheeila* on the *Sheiltot*, *Hayei Sarah*, *sheilta* 17:2, the Netziv of Volozhin elucidates the matter of the variant texts: "But it is known that the language of tractate Nazir is unusual, and there are a number of variant texts that are not from talmudic sources, but from a Gaon."

32 Maimonides, *Code*, Laws concerning Marriage 9:6, writes: "One may only appoint an agent to betroth for him a woman whom he could have betrothed at the time of the appointment." In the opinion of the Maharit, s.v. *umihu*, "the statements of Maimonides are weighty," as if to say, it is difficult to tell whether Maimonides concurs with the Maharit or with the prevailing opinion (which we examine below) that this is a law, and not merely a legal presumption. Cf. *Haamek Sheeila*, n. 31 above. In the opinion of the Netziv, the *Rif*, Maimonides, and Rabbenu Yeruham (22:2) concur with the Maharit. But cf. *AH*, n. 43 below.

With respect to the validity of the appointment, the only relevant principle is that set out in the discussion of the Canaanite slave, viz., that it suffices that the subject matter of the agency not be foreign to the principal.[33, 34]

As we will see, many decisors dismiss the Maharit 's proposal, on three grounds: textual, exegetical and legal. Those decisors[35] who dismiss it on **technical** grounds cite as the authoritative text: "he is unable to appoint an agent." On the basis of this text, it is apparent that the Talmud does not establish only a legal presumption, but rather a normative standard.[36] The **exegetical** reason is that the flow of the talmudic discussion about the betrothal of an unspecified woman is inexplicable unless one posits the existence of a norm according to which it is impossible to appoint an agent to accomplish a task that the

33 It goes without saying that if a legal inability to act does not render the principal "unable to act," a physical inability certainly does not.

34 Compare *Noda Biyehuda*, 2nd ed., EH 69–70. He cites an explanation that he wrote in his youth (an apparent reference to his *Doresh Letzion*, *drush* 13 (51:4), according to which he also is of the opinion that for the principal to be fit to appoint an agent, it suffices that the subject of the agency not be foreign to him (in his words, it must "have relevance"). The crux of the explanation is that the "ability" requirement in the discussion in tractate Nazir (delegating an agent to betroth an unspecified woman), does not pertain to the principal, but rather **to the agent**. If there is no requirement that the principal himself be able to fulfil the delegated task, it becomes clear how a slave can appoint an agent to accept an emancipation document on his behalf though he himself cannot accept it.

In any event, with respect to the matter of the fitness of the principal, it is sufficient if the matter is deemed of relevance to him. See *Noda Biyehuda*, 1st ed., EH 64 s.v. *kvar*, which considers the question of whether a minor is deemed one for whom marriage "has relevance" (since in the future he will presumably marry).

35 Nahmanides; the Ritva (on bNedarim 24a, in the pages of the *Rif*); the *Mordekhai*, on Kedushin, *Haish Mekadesh*, 519; the *Rosh*, on Kidushin 2:18 (and bNazir 12b, published in the marginalia); R. Azriel, cited in the *Shita Mekubtzet* on Nazir 12b, s.v. *umeshani ki*; the *Ran* on Nedarim 72b s.v. *veha lo shmia lei*.

36 This is the view of the *Tosafot* on bNazir 12a s.v. *mai taamei* and bJebamot 52a s.v. *uleisha*, as well as the following authorities: *Sheiltot, Hayei Sara, sheilta* 17; *Rosh* on Nazir 12b; *Beit Habehira* on Nazir 12a s.v. *haomer; Shita Mekubetzet* on Nazir 12b s.v. *amri; Mahane Efraim*, Laws concerning Agency and Partnership 10; *Piskei Halakhot, Yad David* 2:24, A n. 3; *Ketzot Hahoshen*, 126:16, 123:1.

principal cannot carry out at the time of the appointment.[37] And the **legal** reason is that the essence of agency is the transfer of rights from principal to agent. How is it possible for the principal to transfer to the agent rights that he does not possess at the time of the appointment? In the words of the *Beit Meir*, "**He must possess the power at the time of the agent's appointment, for what will he give and what will be added by any power that he acquires after the appointment?**" (my emphasis).[38, 39]

This is not the place to further expound the textual and exegetical reasons.[40] As to the legal reason, it is worth noting that the Maharit

37 See *Mishne Lamelekh*, Laws concerning Marriage 9:6, s.v. *umai shena rabeinu*. Even though his text, like the Maharit's, does not read, "he is unable to appoint an agent" but rather "he does not appoint an agent," he nonetheless concludes, from scrutiny of the remainder of the discussion, that the intent of the Talmud is that the principal **is unable** to appoint an agent, and not merely that he does not **intend** to do so. The Talmud dwells on the apparent contradiction between the principle that "with respect to something that he cannot do now — he does not appoint an agent," and the law of R. Josiah, according to which it is **mandated by biblical decree** (*gzeirat hakatuv*) that a husband cannot appoint an agent to annul vows his wife will make in the future. The Talmud asks: if the correct rule is that one does not appoint an agent to perform a task he himself could not have performed at the time of the appointment, R. Josiah would not have needed to base his legal decision on the textual mandate of the Torah, for the opinion of the Sages is that a husband cannot annul future vows of his wife. (The Talmud answers that perhaps R. Josiah follows the opinion of R. Eliezer, on which one can annul his wife's future vows, in which case it is apparent why he needs the textual mandate of the Torah). In the opinion of the *Mishne Lemelekh*, the Talmud's query proves that the opinion of the Maharit is unacceptable. On the Maharit's approach, the Talmud should not have been troubled by the fact that R. Josiah based his ruling on the textual mandate of the Torah. According to the Maharit, even on the opinion of the Sages, were it not for the textual mandate of the Torah, there would have been nothing preventing the husband from appointing an agent (for the key is the principal's state of mind at the time of the appointment, and there is no need that he be fit to perform the task at that time).

38 *Beit Meir*, EH 119:1.

39 The question arises whether, on this approach, it is possible to overcome the fitness requirement by means of an appointment that takes effect only at a later time, when the principal is able to perform the task himself. But this is not the place to clarify the matter.

40 On the variant texts, see *Haamek Sheeila* on *Sheiltot*, *Hayei Sara*, *sheilta* 17:2.

may have had a different conception of the essence of agency. He held that the purpose of agency is not to transfer to the agent the capacity of the principal, but rather to create a legal identity between the principal and his agent. On this conception, the difficulty mentioned by the *Beit Meir* is resolved, for following the appointment, the legal capacity vested in the principal is similarly vested in the agent, by virtue of the identity created between them *ab initio*.[41]

Although there are decisors who side with the position of the Maharit,[42] it appears that the law to be applied (*halakha lemaase*) is not in accord with his opinion.[43] From this point on, therefore, we

---

On attempts to answer the exegetical issue arising from the talmudic discussion (see n. 37 above), see: *Mirkevet Hamishne*, 1, Laws concerning Divorce 6:3 (3rd answer); *Haamek Sheeila*, n. 31 above, "And I know that on the text we have ... it is unsatisfactory. But it is known that the language of tractate Nazir is unusual, and there are a number of [variant] texts that are not from talmudic sources, but from a Gaon." That is, he agrees that the talmudic discussion does not accord with the approach of the Maharit, but raises the possibility that it was not in the original text, but added in the Geonic period; *Responsa Shoel Umeishiv*, 3rd ed., 1:73; 2:169, s.v. *vehinei hamarahit*.

41 See also *Responsa Hatam Sofer*, EH 1:11 s.v. *mitokh*. Although he dismisses the approach of the Maharit, his argument against the Maharit is based on the textual mandate (*gzeirat hakatuv*) that the principal must be "able to act" already by the time of the appointment and not only at the time of performance: "The laws of agency are learned from the beginning of the chapter *Haish Mekadesh* from the cases of *teruma* (the heave offering), betrothals and divorces, and we require a full analogy with those cases — the principal must be able to act at the time of the appointment. And even if he was explicit [in his instructions], they are ineffective." Hence the Hatam Sofer did not see the Maharit's approach as conflicting with the legal essence of agency, and dismissed it solely on the grounds of the textual mandate.

42 See: *Mirkevet Hamishne*, 1, Laws concerning Divorce 6:3 (though it is not clear beyond doubt that he in fact upholds the approach of the Maharit); *Responsa Shoel Umeishiv*, 3rd ed., 1:73; 2:169; 3:106. See also *Sde Hemed*, Rules, *kaf*, rule 88, who cites decisors who uphold the Maharit's approach.

43 In the words of the *AH*, HM 182:4: "As a matter of practical halakha, because the *Tosafot* are explicit that he cannot appoint an agent, and similarly Nahmanides, the Rosh and the Ritva cite this talmudic portion in the tenth chapter of Nedarim and their textual version is: 'One cannot appoint an agent' [see n. 35 above], and [conversely] the opinion of *Maimonides* [see n. 32 above] is not clear, we uphold their view."

will only take up suggestions for resolving the conflicting talmudic discussions that were proposed by decisors who do not uphold this position.

### 3.3 The *Mirkevet Hamishne* and Others on the Nature of the Impediment

As we said, many decisors reject the Maharit's approach, and are of the opinion that in order for the principal to appoint an agent, it is not sufficient that the subject matter of the agency not be foreign to him,[44] but it is required that he be able to perform the delegated task himself. Accordingly, even though betrothal is not foreign to the principal, he is unable to appoint an agent to betroth for him a woman who is still married at the time of the appointment. However, for the principal to be deemed "unable to act," and deprived of the power to appoint an agent, it is necessary to examine the essence of the factor preventing him from performing the delegated task himself. There are cases where, as in the example of agency for the purpose of betrothing a woman who already is married, that which precludes agency is fundamental and a matter of principle (the doctrine that betrothal of a married woman is ineffective), and therefore suffices for the principal to be deemed "unable to act." But there are cases where the impediment is only secondary, such as that of the slave who is unable to bring about his own emancipation. This latter impediment does not arise because the slave, as a matter of principle, cannot be set free, but out of an secondary legal impediment — the principle that "the hand of a slave is like the hand of his master" — which prevents him from accepting the bill of manumission. And this explains the relationship between the seemingly-contradictory talmudic discussions. The distinction is implicit, for example, in the words of the *Mirkevet Hamishne:*

> For there, surely, emancipation documents have some relevance to the slave, **and this emancipation document too he can, in principle, accept**, and only because of some other factor that arises, namely 'what a slave takes possession of, his master takes possession of,' he was prevented… which is not the same with respect to our case [agency to betroth a married woman], for here there is no principle on which to base betrothal of

44 Or, in other words, that he come "within the scope of the matter."

the woman, for she is a married woman, and therefore he is unable to appoint an agent.[45, 46] (my emphasis)

One of the practical questions which arose over the generations regarding the principal's fitness, is that of the validity of what is referred to as a "*get kushta*."[47] The question is the correctness of the custom that a man whose wife becomes of unsound mind, is able and required, prior to marrying another woman, to appoint an agent to divorce his first wife, after she regains her sanity.[48] Or are the rabbis of Constantinople, who came out against the custom, correct in claiming that since at the time the husband is prevented from divorcing her,[49] he

45 *Mirkevet Hamishne*, part 1, Laws concerning Divorce 6:3 (p. 4:3).

46 It seems that a similar distinction is the focus of *Responsa Avnei Nezer*, EH 8 *lamed* and *Helkat Yoav*, EH 20 s.v. *umitaam*. They, however, formulate the distinction slightly differently. They say that the principal is deemed "unable to act" when, even after he performs all the tasks necessary for its accomplishment, he does not achieve the desired legal result. But if the principal's inability to achieve that result is due to inability to carry out all of the necessary tasks, he is not deemed "unable to act." As stated, it seems to us that at the core of this formulation lies the distinction between a fundamental impediment, and a secondary impediment, which we cited in the name of the *Mirkevet Hamishne*. Compare R. Shimon Shkop, Responsum on the matter of the woman who came to be of unsound mind (published at the end of his novellae on Kidushin), s.v. *veha dehiksha*.

We should note that all the decisors who draw this distinction accept the approach of the *Hikrei Lev* (n. 7 above), that a physical incapacity, even direct, does not render the principal "unable to act," as all physical incapacities are only secondary, and not fundamental.

47 This term comes from the testimony of R. Jacob Kuli in his glosses on the *Mishne Lamelekh*, Laws concerning Divorce 6:3, about an incident that arose with respect to this matter in Constantinople (Kushta). See below.

48 The following authorities so ruled: *Bah* (*Bait Hadash*), EH 1 and 119; *Beit Shmuel*, EH 1:23. (Indeed, a husband whose wife becomes of unsound mind is permitted to marry a second wife, and does not, in so doing, transgress the "edict of Rabbenu Gershom" that one who marries more than one wife is to be banned. See the *Rema*, EH 1:10, in the name of the Rashba. However, for the benefit of the woman, in the event that her mental faculties return, "it is an accepted tradition among the great scholars of the world" — to use the language of the *Bah* — that the husband is required to set aside her bill of divorce at the outset.)

49 For it is known that the law does not permit divorce of a woman of unsound mind.

is deemed "unable to act," and the appointment has no validity?[50] The *Mirkevet Hamishne*, in line with his approach, justifies the custom. He explains that the case differs from betrothing a married woman, where the impediment is a matter of principle, for in principle there is no impediment to divorcing a mentally unsound woman, since the reason she cannot be divorced is but secondary (as in the matter of the emancipation of the Canaanite slave), namely, the lack of a "hand" to accept the *get*. Accordingly, appointment of an agent is possible even prior to her recovery, and there is no reason to oppose the custom.[51]

50 See *Mirkevet Hamishne*, Laws concerning Divorce, 1, 6:3, which attests that the rabbis of Lissa were also of this opinion. The *Mirkevet Hamishne* is angered by these rabbis: "Why are they not apprehensive about the honor of the *Rishonim*, and the offense [it would cause] to the many women who recovered from being of unsound mind, and thereafter married and gave birth to children, on the strength of divorce documents that had been delivered to an agent when they were still of unsound mind, and then delivered to them after they recovered their sanity? And on the opinion of the sages of Constantinople, are children born to those women suspected of illegitimacy?!"

51 Compare *Noda Biyehuda*, 1st ed., EH 3. He too is of the opinion that the custom should not be abolished: "We did not want to abolish the custom of the early authorities, who did not lift the ban [on marriage to a second wife] of Rabbenu Gershom, the light of the exile, until the husband transferred a bill of divorce to an agent for delivery, for perhaps Rabbenu Gershom, at the time that he established this ban and gave permission to allow [remarriage] where a mitzva was involved [e.g., procreation], did so on condition that remarriage would be permitted only upon deposit of the bill of divorce, this being the reason for the spread of the aforesaid custom, in which case it is impossible to lift the ban except in this manner."

Nevertheless, he was of the opinion that as law to be applied, the opinion of the rabbis of Constantinople should be taken into account, and the woman, upon recovering, should not be permitted to remarry without a new bill of divorce (i.e., one drawn up after her recuperation). He adds, "and even though in the responsum I dealt with this at length [referring, apparently, to his having dealt at length with the statements of the sages of Constantinople, and raised doubts as to their correctness], in any event, our speculation alone does not allow us to permit a married woman [to remarry] where there are such repercussions." It is unclear to what responsum he refers, and what doubts he raised regarding the approach of the sages of Constantinople. Cf. the approach of R. Akiva Eger (n. 65 below), who also ruled, for different reasons, that as law to be applied both opinions should be taken into acount.

It goes without saying that if we accept the approach of the Maharit,[52] the question of the validity of the *"get kushta"* does not come up at all. As we saw above, according to the Maharit, the fact that divorce is not foreign to the principal suffices to validate the agency, even for a task that he cannot accomplish at the present time, so long as it is clear, as in the case of the *"get kushta,"* that he intended to include such an act in the authorization he gives the agent.[53]

### 3.4 The *Beit Meir* on the Source of the Impediment

Another approach to resolving the apparent conflict between the cited talmudic discussions, and to defining the concept of "inability to act," is proposed by the *Beit Meir*.[54] We have already mentioned the explicit statements of the *Beit Meir*, according to which the requirement that the principal be able to himself carry out the delegated task at the time of the appointment follows from the very nature of agency: "it does not make sense that he can delegate power to an agent when he lacks such power."[55] This is the reason it is impossible to appoint an agent to betroth a woman who is married to someone else at the time of the appointment (even though the explicit intent is for the agent to betroth her after she is divorced): "He has to possess the power at the time of the agent's appointment, for what will he give and what will be added by any power that he acquires after the appointment?"

This same logic entails that we restrict the "ability to act" requirement to those tasks that the agent carries out by virtue of the principal's mandate, and not apply it to tasks that the agent carries out on his own. This is why a Canaanite slave can appoint an agent to accept the document of his manumission, even though he himself cannot be set free by accepting the document with his own hand. In this case, the task which

52 See sec. 3.2 above.

53 So opined, among others: *Mirkevet Hamishne*, 1, Laws concerning Divorce 6:3; *Responsa Shoel Umeishiv*, 3rd ed., 1:73.

54 *Beit Meir*, EH 119:6 s.v. *lefikhakh*. We saw a similar approach on the part of R. Shimon Shkop in the responsum on the woman who came to be of unsound mind (see n. 46 above), s.v. *haole; Shaarei Yosher*, 6:17 s.v. *ubeha*. And see n. 58 below.

55 Let us mention that on the opinion of the *Beit Meir*, this statement refers not only to a legal lack of power to act, but also to a physical lack of power. See nn. 10 and 17 above.

the agent must accomplish through the power delegated by the principal is acceptance of the document of manumission, and carrying out this task is within the power of the principal. The proof of this is that the principal can accept a document of manumission on behalf of another Canaanite slave. Thus, had the slave accepted his emancipation document from his master with his own hand, the emancipation would have had no validity, as the document would not, legally speaking, have left the domain of the master. But this does not impinge on the validity of the appointment, because, for the purpose of taking an emancipation document from the master's domain, the agent's power to act derives not from the principal but from himself. To what is this analogous? To a principal who cannot physically reach the place where a task is to be performed; this impediment too, as we saw above,[56] does not render the principal "unable to act," because reaching the place of performance is not part of the agency that exists by virtue of the principal's power. Just as the agent does not arrive at the place of performance by virtue of the principal's power,[57] so the "domain" into which the agent accepts the emancipation document does not derive from the principal's "domain." This is why the fact that the principal has no "domain" of his own does not deprive him of the capacity to appoint an agent to accept the emancipation document in his stead.[58]

On this reasoning, we can say that appointment of an agent is possible when the source of the impediment is the third party's lack of power to accept the delegated task, and not a lack of power to perform the task on the part of the principal. Hence, the agent is able to act as soon as the legal status of the third party changes. Accordingly, the

56 See n. 17 above, and accompanying text.

57 And for this reason, the principal's inability to reach that place does not deprive him of the capacity to appoint an agent.

58 The explanation given by R. Shimon Shkop (see n. 54 above) differs. He states: "The fact that he does not accept the emancipation document himself is not because of some deficiency in himself, but because of a secondary deficiency, namely, that he has not left his master's domain." It must be determined whether this difference in their explanations is merely semantic, or reflects a difference of opinion regarding physical incapacity. As mentioned above, the *Beit Meir* maintains that a direct physical incapacity is sufficient to render a principal "unable to act." It is possible that R. Shimon Shkop disputes this, since a physical incapacity is a secondary incapacity, not a fundamental one. This matter requires further examination.

*Beit Meir* also justifies the custom that a man whose wife has come to be of unsound mind appoints an agent to divorce her once she recovers.[59] He explains that the principal does not lack the power to divorce her (for he could divorce her were she of sound mind), but rather, the wife is the one who has no power to accept the *get*.[60] Accordingly, there is no impediment to the principal's transferring his power to an agent, even when his wife is of unsound mind. The *Beit Meir* argues that the wife

> 'has no hand' to accept it [the *get*], and when she will 'have a hand,' the husband's agent will divorce her, **for then no further power will be conferred on him by his appointer** … from the time of the original appointment he had all the husband's power, and as his power was then, so his power is now, without any need to add to the power of the agency.[61] (my emphasis)

Nevertheless, it must be pointed out that the *Beit Meir* ends his remarks with some hesitation, stating, "but note that at any rate, further study of the matter is necessary."

### 3.5 The *Hatam Sofer* on the Degree of the Impediment

A third approach to resolving the apparent contradiction between the talmudic discussions and defining the concept of "inability to act" is

59 See the text at n. 47 above.

60 There is, however, reason to challenge this: Were this argument sound, why would it not apply to the case where one appoints an agent to betroth a woman who is still married at the time of the appointment? There too the problem is not the power of the principal, who is able to betroth a woman who is not married, but rather, resides in the woman, who is unable to accept the betrothal because she is a married woman. R. Shimon Shkop (n. 54 above) raises this question, and answers: "the matter is not comparable to the case of the betrothal of a married woman, because the betrothal is performed by the one who betroths, and when the object of the betrothal [that is to say, the woman] is not fit for the matter [because she is still married to another], it is something that does not come into existence. But one of unsound mind is fit for divorce, as she may be divorced through her father [when she is engaged and a minor], and when she has no father, and has no way to accept the *get*, that does not impinge on her power to be divorced." And cf. the approach of the *Hatam Sofer* below at n. 64.

61 And cf. the *Mirkevet Hamishne*, 1, Laws concerning Divorce 6:3 (p. 5b), who makes a similar distinction (in addition to the distinction already cited in his name, above at n. 45).

suggested by the *Hatam Sofer*.[62] He contends that whether the principal is deemed "unable to act" is not a function of the nature of the impediment (that is, whether it is fundamental or secondary), as suggested by the *Mirkevet Hamishne*, nor a function of the source of the impediment (that is, whether it is an impediment of the principal or of some other party), as suggested by the *Beit Meir*. Rather, the determining criterion is the degree of the impediment itself: the principal will not be deemed "unable to act" unless the impediment (even if secondary)[63] is **absolute**, namely, would have existed (in him or in a third party) in any event. But if the impediment does not exist except in the context of the relationship between the principal and a third party, and would not have existed between the principal (or the third party) and other parties, this indicates that it is not absolute but only **relative**, in which case the principal should not be considered "unable to act."

This distinction follows, in his opinion, from the talmudic law that a Canaanite slave can appoint an agent to accept a document of manumission from his master. Indeed, the slave cannot accept the document of manumission himself (for he does not have his own separate "domain"). But the fact that he can receive an emancipation document on behalf of another slave proves that we are not speaking of an absolute impediment but only a relative one, that arises specifically with respect to his relationship with his master, and does not reflect a complete lack of power with respect to agency.

In contrast, as we said, if the impediment is absolute, the principal will be deemed "unable to act" even though the impediment is not in him, but exists only by virtue of some third party. An example is the matter of the appointment of an agent to betroth a married woman. Even though the impediment does not reside in the principal (who has the power to betroth), but rather, the woman (who cannot be betrothed),[64] since the legal result [betrothal] will not be achieved in any event (whether to the principal or someone else), she cannot be the object of the agency arrangement. Applying this criterion, the *Hatam Sofer* concludes that there is no possibility of appointing an agent to

62 *Responsa Hatam Sofer*, EH 1:11, s.v. *ela*.

63 And as we saw above, in n. 10, the *Hatam Sofer* also categorizes the principal as "unable to act" when he has a physical impediment that is only secondary. See too n. 17 above, on indirect incapacity.

64 See n. 60 above, the approaches of the *Beit Meir* and R. Shimon Shkop.

divorce a woman who is of unsound mind,[65] for someone of unsound mind is absolutely precluded from accepting a *get*, and this impediment is entirely unrelated to her relationship with her husband.

Note that the approach of the *Hatam Sofer* is no more restrictive, with respect to appointing an agent, than the other approaches we have surveyed. There are circumstances in which this approach would validate appointment of an agent where the others would reject it. Consider, for example, the following situation: while his wife is alive, a man appoints an agent to betroth her sister for him upon his wife's

65 See the text at n. 47 above, on the "*get* Kushta." Despite this, as law intended for implementation the *Hatam Sofer* recognizes the validity of such a *get*, not on the basis of the laws of agency but on the basis of the principle "*zakhin leadam shelo befanav*" ["one can bestow a benefit on someone who is not present"], that is, it is possible to give the *get* to a woman on behalf of the husband even when the appointment was flawed, because this certainly is the husband's intention and interest. (On the principle "one can bestow a benefit on someone who is not present," see the Talmudic Encyclopedia, vol. 12, 135). The *Mirkevet Hamishne*, 1, Laws concerning Divorce 6:3, dismisses this argument, because the principle is only that "one can bestow a benefit on someone" (*zakhin leadam*) and not "one can have a benefit bestowed **by** someone" (*zakhin miadam*). In other words, here, where the husband is not the recipient, but is, rather, the grantor of the *get*, it does not apply. Others dismiss the approach, because it is uncertain whether it is in fact a benefit to the husband to divorce his wife after her recovery, for perhaps he would want to be reunited with his first wife.

See also *Responsa R. Akiva Eger*, 2:73. Like his son-in-law, R. Eger is of the opinion that there is no possibility of appointing an agent to divorce a woman of unsound mind, for the principal is deemed "unable to act" in this context. At the same time, he justifies the enactment that one whose wife has come to be of unsound mind transfers a *get* to an agent, on the ground that it is difficult to assess the severity of the mental illness of the wife, and it is possible that as a matter of Torah law she is permitted to be divorced, and the prohibition against divorcing her is only a matter of Rabbinic law. Since the divorce of a woman who is not deemed to be of unsound mind except as a matter of Rabbinic law, is legally effective after the fact, the husband, in light of this, is deemed "able to act" (see below at n. 67). In R. Eger's opinion, it was due to this doubt as to whether her incapacity is a matter of Torah or Rabbinic law that the enactment mandating deposit of a *get* with an agent was established. However, since it also is possible that the wife is deemed by Torah law to be of unsound mind, such a *get* alone cannot be relied on, and one must also give an additional *get* once she has recovered. Cf. n. 51 above. See *Otzar Haposkim*, EH 1:10 *lamed*, on the many decisors who concur.

death. On the approach of the *Mirkevet Hamishne*, the appointment is invalid, for the principal himself is precluded as a matter of principle from betrothing his wife's sister. This is also the conclusion that would be reached by the *Beit Meir*, as the principal lacks power to betroth his wife's sister, and since, on his view, the source of the impediment resides with the principal, he is deemed "unable to act." In contrast, on the approach of the *Hatam Sofer*, there is no flaw in the appointment, for betrothing the woman in question is not forbidden except to that particular principal, as she is his wife's sister, but is not forbidden with respect to any other man. Accordingly, the appointment need not be invalidated, as the principal is not deemed "unable to act."[66]

### 4 *Prohibition*

Thus far we have dealt with different physical and legal limitations that deprive the principal of the capacity to achieve a desired legal outcome himself. In this section we ask, what is the law concerning a task, the legal outcome of which the principal can achieve by himself, but which is prohibited? Does this fact in itself deprive him of the capacity to appoint an agent?[67]

66 It should be pointed out that this law was not stated explicitly by the *Hatam Sofer*, but our claim is that it appears to follow from his approach. Cf. *Haamek Sheeila*, n. 31 above. There appears to be an affinity between his approach and the approach of the *Hatam Sofer* discussed here, and he cites this law explicitly. But the relationship between their approaches merits further study.

67 At first glance, there is no apparent reason to ask this question, because it is a well-known principle that "there is no agency to perform a forbidden act." But see M. Wygoda, "The meaning and scope of the 'there is no agency to perform a forbidden act' rule" (Hebrew), *Kol Miheikhal* 3 (1996), 53, where we showed that there are opinions according to which this principle only applies when the task is forbidden to both the principal and the agent. It appears that on these opinions, one could certainly inquire whether a principal can appoint an agent to carry out a task that is forbidden only to the principal. Or is it perhaps the case that the task's being forbidden to him suffices to render him "unable to act," and thereby invalidates the appointment? The article also points out that some decisors are of the opinion that the principle "there is no agency to perform a forbidden act" is meaningful only in the criminal context (that is, the principal is not punished for the deed of the agent), but not in the civil (that is, the legal results of the agent's deed are attributed to the principal). For those who hold these views, there is no doubt that the question we raised here must be answered in the negative, that is, the fact that the delegated task is forbidden

The *Mahane Efraim*[68] deals with the case of a principal who vowed not to betroth a certain woman, and despite his vow, appointed an agent to betroth her. This therefore presents an example of a forbidden act (breaking a vow) which an agent was appointed to carry out, and the question is: is the appointment valid? On the opinion of the *Mahane Efraim*, since, after the fact (*bediavad*), the betrothal would have been binding had it been carried out by the principal himself, the appointment is not invalid. The *Mahane Efraim* brings a compelling proof for his position from the talmudic discussion about 'agency for something forbidden.'[69] In that discussion, the opinion of Ravina is that a betrothal between a priest (*kohen*) and a divorcee is valid, **even when carried out via an agent.**[70] It is evident, therefore, that a prohibition that pertains to the principal with respect to the object of the agency does not detract from the validity of the appointment, and apparently this is so because had the principal violated the prohibition himself, his act would have been legally valid after the fact (as in the example of the *kohen*, for though it is forbidden to him to betroth a divorcee, the act has validity after the fact).[71] However, we also have found

to the principal, of itself, does not invalidate the agency, for were there no validity to the appointment, how could those decisors claim that the agent's deed has legal impact on the principal? We pose our question, therefore, only to those who dispute the position taken by these decisors.

It goes without saying that on the approach of the Maharit, n. 30 above, there is clearly no basis for the question.

68 *Mahane Efraim*, Laws concerning Agency and Partnership, 9. See also *Sde Hemed*, Rules, *kaf*, rule 85.

69 bBaba Metzia 10b. See Wygoda, n. 67 above.

70 For he maintains that the principle, "there is no agency to perform a forbidden act" does not apply when the agent is not obligated to observe the relevant commandment (*bar hiuva*), as is the case here, where betrothing the divorcee is only prohibited to a principal who is a *kohen*, and not to the agent.

71 There appears to be a simpler way to make the point that the fact that the delegated task is prohibited does not suffice to render the principal "unable to act": the Talmud, in bKidushin 42b, grounds the principle, "there is no agency to perform a forbidden task" in different sources: logic ("given the statements of the teacher and the statements of the student, which should be heeded?"), and various halakhic midrashim (see Wygoda, n. 67 above, and the literature there cited). If the fact that the delegated task was prohibited were sufficient to render the principal "unable to act," there would be no need for those sources, since appointment of an agent to perform a forbidden act would have no validity whatsoever!

those[72] who argue with the *Mahane Efraim* and invalidate the appointment of an agent to perform a forbidden act,[73] even when the act would have been valid *bediavad*, had it been performed by the principal

---

This appears to be the thrust of *Miknei Avraham* (Sirano), *kaf*, 159 s.v. *kol*. The *Mahane Efraim*'s insight is that although with respect to the principal's fitness to appoint an agent, the appointment is valid even when the object of the agency is a forbidden task, such fitness depends on whether performance of the task would have been effective if carried out by the principal himself, for if not, the principal would be deemed "unable to act," which would suffice to invalidate the appointment.

72 See *Responsa Mayim Amukim (Raanah)*, 2:18 s.v. *tzarikh* (cited by the *Mahane Efraim* himself as a dissenting opinion); R. Akiva Eger, in his notes on *SA*, EH 35:3 (cited in *Pithei Teshuva* ad loc., 13). In a case similar to that dealt with by the *Mahane Efraim* (someone who appointed an agent to carry out a task he had forbidden himself to do by a vow), the *Mayim Amukim* and R. Akiva Eger ruled that in principle there is no validity to the appointment. However, it is possible that there is no real difference of opinion here between the *Mahane Efraim*, on the one hand, and the *Mayim Amukim* and R. Akiva Eger, on the other, and the latter only ruled as they did out of concerns about the opinion that there is no validity to an act carried out in breach of a vow. (On this, see bTemura 4b, on "Any act that the Merciful One forbade — if it has been performed. … it has no legal effect" (*kol milei deamar rahmana lo taavid, i avid. … lo mehanei*), and consult the differing opinions among the *Rishonim* on the question of whether this rule also applies to an injunction one thinks up himself.) See *Responsa Hikrei Lev*, EH 24, on how to explain their opinion. (See also E. Shochetman, *Action by Way of Transgression* (Hebrew), (Jerusalem: 1981), 131–154, who proves that in truth, the matter is not in dispute among the *Rishonim* at all, and an act carried out through the breach of a vow is valid according to all opinions. The *Aharonim* believed erroneously that the matter was in dispute, because they had in their possession a partial and fragmentary text of the words of one of the *Rishonim*.)

One additional decisor who explicitly disputes the approach of the *Mahane Efraim* is the Maharsham, in his *Responsa*, 3:47. The Maharsham relies on a talmudic source (bBaba Kama 110a), which establishes that a ritually impure *kohen* is unable to send an agent to offer sacrifices in his behalf, because he himself is unable to perform the service. This law apparently contradicts the principle established by the *Mahane Efraim*, for it is a law that the service of a ritually impure *kohen* is valid after the fact (see *Tosafot*, Yoma 7b s.v. *dam shenitma*). As to the Maharsham's source and his approach, note the following:

1 The source upon which he relies to refute the approach of the *Mahane Efraim* is not conclusive, for it is possible that the impediment to appointment of an agent in the said talmudic discussion does not arise because the principal is deemed "unable to act," but rather for a different reason, as noted in n. 9 above. See *Responsa Shoel Umeishiv*, 3rd ed., 1:68, who refers to the remarks of *Mefarshei Hayam* on the

himself. Despite this, it appears that the view of the *Mahane Efraim* is the accepted view.[74]

---

passage in bBaba Kama. (But see *Sde Hemed*, Rules, *kaf*, 86, s.v. *uma*, who finds the explanation in *Shoel Umeishiv*'s problematic.)

2 The approach of the Maharsham is itself problematic, for how does he come to terms with the "agency for a forbidden task" discussion, which seems to clearly prove the correctness of the *Mahane Efraim*'s approach? Regarding the matter of a *kohen* who dispatches an agent to betroth a divorcee for him, one possible explanation why the agency has validity is that the betrothal of a *kohen* and a divorcee is not in and of itself forbidden, but rather it is their living together as a married couple that is forbidden (as noted by the *Noda Biyehuda*, see Wygoda, n. 67 above, n. 20). However, what would he have answered with respect to the second example cited by the Talmud there, regarding a principal who sends his wife to shave the sideburns of a child, where the appointment itself is similarly valid, since there, the shaving of sideburns is certainly a task forbidden to him? And what would the Maharsham have answered as to the point we raised in n. 71 above?

3 The continuation of the discussion in bBaba Kama apparently contradicts the approach of the Maharsham, for it is established there that a *kohen* who is an *onen* (one whose recently deceased close relative has not yet been buried) can appoint an agent to do his service in his stead even though, as an *onen*, the principal is forbidden to perform the service. The Maharsham raises this question himself, and in explanation of his position, cites the opinion of the *Mishne Lamelekh*, Laws concerning the Temple 2:6, who explains that perhaps a *kohen* who is an *onen* can appoint an agent because he is only prohibited from the service by virtue of a Rabbinic prohibition, and **in the context of a Rabbinic prohibition, the principal is not deemed "unable to act**." (As an aside, note that from these statements of the *Mishne Lamelekh* it appears that he also disputes the approach of the *Mahane Efraim*, for according to the *Mahane Efraim*, even in the context of a Torah prohibition, the principal is not deemed "unable to act" so long as the prohibited task is valid *bediavad*. This has been noted by the *Minhat Hinukh*, mitzva 151, and *Responsa Beit Yitzhak*, EH, I 3:4. On the approach of the *Mishne Lamelekh*, see also *Sde Hemed*, Rules, *kaf*, rule 86.)

73 However, some maintain that there is a distinction between acts forbidden by the Torah and acts forbidden by the Rabbis, so that in the context of a Rabbinic prohibition the principal is not deemed "unable to act."

74 See: *Responsa Hikrei Lev*, EH 24; *Yad David, Piskei Halakha*, part 2, *Darkhei David*, 4, n. 4; *Responsa Shoel Umeishiv*, 1st ed., 1:115; (and so too in his letter of approbation for *Zikhron Tzvi Menahem* (*Mayzlish*)); *Sde Hemed*,

## 5 *Non-Permanent Impediment*

### 5.1 An Impediment that Can Be Removed by the Principal ("Lacking Action")

An important qualification made by those decisors who dispute the approach of the Maharit is that the principal may appoint an agent even when the circumstances that constitute the basis of the principal's interest in delegating the agent do not yet exist; **provided that had the principal so desired, he could have accomplished the delegated task himself at the time of the appointment.** This arises from the following discussion in Jebamot: "If one said to a clerk, Write me a *get* to give to the woman I have betrothed [through the ceremony of *erusin*], so that when I marry her, I can then divorce her — the *get* is in fact proper, **because it was within the principal's power to divorce her** [because even severance of the *erusin* relationship requires a *get*]."[75] Even though the intent of the husband is to divorce his wife only after they are married (under the *hupa* in the *nesuin* ceremony), a state that does not yet exist, he can appoint the clerk as an agent to write a *get* for him, because it is already within his power to divorce her, as she is his betrothed.[76]

---

Rules, *kaf*, rules 86 and 89. (But cf. *Responsa Shoel Umeishiv*, 3rd ed., 1:68, which appears to take issue with the *Mahane Efraim*, although his words are unclear and require further study. See too the sharp comments in *Sde Hemed*, Rules, *kaf*, rule 86. But it seems he attributes to *Shoel Umeishiv* ideas that the latter never held. The matter requires further study.) *Sde Hemed* also cites many other decisors who so rule.

75 bJebamot 52a. See above, n. 28. For a full account of this talmudic discussion, see below, at n. 84.

76 There are situations where the impediment to the principal's performing the delegated task himself stems from his lack of knowledge, that is, he is unaware of how a certain task is performed. Such, for example, is the situation of a principal in the case of agency for divorce, since most people do not know how to write a *get* (assuming the writing of a *get* calls for agency; see n. 12 above). So too with respect to agency for the writing of a Torah scroll, since most people are not scribes. However, because it is within his purview to study and learn the skill, the principal is not categorized as "unable to act." So first explained *Responsa Hikrei Lev*, EH, 46 s.v. *veeikh*. The implication of this approach is that were the principal unable to study and learn such skills he in fact would be deemed "unable to act." We should note that this explanation is only required by those who hold

What is the scope of the concept "something within his power" (*davar shebeyado*)? Does it encompass the situation where the object of the agency does not yet exist ("something not in existence"), but is within the province of the agent? For example, can the principal appoint an agent to sell a house that has not yet been built, even though the law is "one cannot alienate something that is not in existence?"[77] The question is whether it is sufficient that it is within the principal's power to build the house at the outset for him to be deemed, from a legal perspective, one who can delegate to an agent the task for which he seeks to appoint him ("able to act")?[78] There is a difference of opinion

that a physical impediment can render the principal "unable to act" (see above at n. 10). Those who hold that the principal is deemed "unable to act" only by virtue of a legal impediment (see above at n. 7), do not need this argument, because a lack of knowledge is not a legal impediment. And this is the ultimate conclusion of the *Hikrei Lev* himself s.v. *ela deakati*. See also *Sde Hemed*, Rules, *kaf*, rule 87.

An interesting application of the principle of "something within his power" (*davar shebeyado*) appears in connection with the laws of Hanukah. The *Pri Megadim*, *Eshel Avraham*, 679:1, raises the following question: "Is one able to appoint an agent to light Hanukah candles for him after having already ushered in the Sabbath for himself, given that the established rule is that anything that he cannot do, he cannot appoint an agent to do? After all, since he has already ushered in the Sabbath himself, he cannot light the candles. [Further, if he does so, he will not fulfill his obligation to light Hanukah candles at any rate, because such an act would be 'a precept observed through performance of a prohibited act.' See also text at n. 68 above, concerning an impediment arising from a prohibition]. This matter requires further study." The author of *Rashei Besamim* (the author of *Beit Aharon*), vol. 8, 79, responds that since ushering in the Sabbath prior to its prescribed time of arrival only mandates observance of the Sabbath as a function of a vow to begin it early, there is no basis for deeming the principal in such a situation "unable to act," for he can be asked to, and may, annul the vow retroactively.

77 See Maimonides, *Code*, Laws concerning Sales 22:1; *SA*, HM 209:4.

78 The decisors put this question as follows: "Is not one who has it in his power to act unlike one who lacks such power?"

We should point out that this has not been the case in the instances we have looked at thus far, in which the principal anticipates that his situation will change in a way that would permit the delegated task to be carried out, but the anticipated change is beyond his control. So, for example, one who sends an agent to betroth a woman who is still married at the time of the appointment hopes that the woman's status will change and she will-become available (she will become divorced or widowed), but such a change, which would alter her status so that she falls within the ambit of the agency — is not within his control.

on this matter.[79] Some[80] posit that in such a case the appointment is valid.[81] Others[82] restrict application of the concept of "something within his power." They do agree that if **the object of the agency is in existence** but the principal is impeded from performing the delegated task due to some other reason, which he has the ability to overcome, he is deemed "able to act." This is the reason, for example, a husband can appoint an agent to divorce his wife even before a *get* is written. Despite the fact that it is impossible to divorce one's wife without a *get*, this is not because the object of the agency does not exist (for the wife is alive), but rather due to a different impediment (absence of a *get*). Similarly, the fact that the principal has it within his power to overcome the impediment and to write the *get*, is enough to render him, even at

79 But see *AH*, HM 182:5. We should point out that this argument is not confined to the delegation of agents, but applies to the general principle that "one cannot alienate something that is not in existence." The question is, does this rule apply as well to something whose existence is within the control of the party seeking to alienate it? See *Netivot Hamishpat*, 243:6, who explains that this is the source of the dispute discussed in the *SA*, HM 11, regarding someone who is interested in giving a present to his friend. To this end, he appoints an agent to write the document deeding the gift for the benefit of the friend and to accept the gift on the friend's behalf. Those who rule that from the time the document is written the giver loses his ability to retract the gift, are of the opinion that since the writing of the document is "something within his power," the document is considered something already in existence, and that there is thus validity to the directive bestowing the item as a gift even if it was issued before the document was drawn up. In contrast, those who rule that even when the document is written, the giver can retract the gift, are of the opinion that though at the time the principal gave his directive to bestow the gift it was "within his power" to write the document, nevertheless, since, at the time of the appointment, the document "lacked an action" (namely, was not actually written), the law that governs it is that governing someone who gave a directive to alienate "something not in existence," and he can retract his directive.

80 See *Mordekhai*, Kidushin, *haish mekadesh* 519; *Sefer Yereim*, 118 s.v. *tenan* (see also the explanation of his remarks in the *Sefer Mitzvot Gadol*, positive commandment no. 141, p. 202d). On this view, see *Beit Yosef*, YD, 327 s.v. *vekatav haram; Responsa Hikrei Lev*, EH, 46 s.v. *akh et ze kashe*.

81 In their view, this is the reason for the custom relating to the separation of *hala*, according to which one can appoint an agent to separate *hala* even before the flour is made into dough. Despite the fact that as long as the dough is not formed, the requirement of separating *hala* does not apply to the flour, since the principal has the power to turn the flour into dough, he can appoint an agent to separate *hala* even at the outset, before it is actually carried out.

82 See *Tosafot*, Nazir 12a s.v. *mai taama*, in the name of Rabbenu Tam. Below, we adduce the statements of Rabbenu Tam, in line with the interpretation of the *Shaar Yosher*, 6:17. See also *Netivot Hamishpat*, 243:6.

the outset, "able to act."[83] However, if the principal is prevented from performing the delegated task by virtue of the fact that **the object of the agency does not yet exist**, even though he has the power to bring it about, this does not suffice to render him "able to act."[84] Therefore, even though the principal has the ability to build the house that is the

83 However, one who upholds the view that only a legal impediment renders the principal "unable to act," need not accept this account, because the case here is one of an empirical physical impediment (a *get* cannot be given before it is written), which is not a legal impediment. See *Responsa Hikrei Lev*, EH, 46, s.v. *ela dakati*. Cf. *Mahane Efraim* (on Maimonides), Laws concerning Divorce 3:15; *Responsa of R. Akiva Eger*, 141; *Keren Ora*, Nazir 12a (see too the explanation of *Keren Ora*, found in *Kehilat Yaakov* (Kanievsky), Gitin, 28:4); *Doresh Letzion*, sermon 13 s.v. *lakhen*.

84 The *Tosafot* bring a proof for this approach from the continuation of the discussion in Jebamot cited above at n. 75. After the Talmud establishes, on one hand, that the husband may appoint an agent to divorce the woman he has betrothed following their marriage (since he is already able to divorce her at the time of the betrothal), and on the other hand, that one may not appoint an agent to divorce a woman whom he has not yet betrothed (since he cannot divorce her at the time of the appointment, given that she is still a single), the Talmud asks: "Rami bar Hama asks: What is the law with respect to a woman with whom he would be obligated to enter into *yibum* [that is, levirate marriage to the wife of his deceased brother, who has died without fathering a child]? Since she is related to him [by virtue of the law that imposes a relationship between them pending either *yibum* — through which the relationship comes to fruition — or *halitza* — through which it is dissolved], is she considered his betrothed? Or is it perhaps the case that because he has not betrothed her, she is not considered his betrothed? The question remains unanswered." In the opinion of the *Tosafot*, the fact that the Talmud leaves the question open to further study proves that even when it is within the power of the principal to bring into existence the object of the agency (for in principle a woman can be married through *yibum* even against her will), this does not suffice to render him "able to act." (Note that this proof is not accepted by those who dispute the view of the *Tosafot*, apparently because on their view this is not considered "within his power," for the woman who is subject to *yibum* can run away or evade it. See *Mahane Efraim* (on Maimonides), Laws concerning Divorce 3:15, s.v. *ibra dekashe* (at the end); *Responsa Hikrei Lev*, EH, 46 s.v. *akh et ze kashe li; AH*, HM 182:5)

R. Shimon Shkop explains that on the approach of Rabbenu Tam, the following is the essence of the Talmud's doubt with respect to agency to divorce a woman subject to levirate marriage: On the one hand, since, even prior to the *yibum*, the woman is related to the levir, there is some reason to treat the agency as an agency the object of which already exists (as is the case with the betrothed woman). Hence, the *yibum* does not create the object of the agency, but rather removes the impediment that prevented the divorce. Thus the fact that the principal has it within his power to enter into levirate marriage against the woman's wishes is sufficient to render

object of the transaction, he cannot appoint an agent to sell it so long as it has not actually been built, for were he to do so, he would be selling "something that is not in existence."[85, 86]

---

him "able to act." On the other hand, since so long as the levir has not betrothed the woman, she is not his wife, it is necessary to treat the agency as an agency whose object has not yet come into existence (as in the case of a single woman), and the levirate marriage, therefore, is the act that creates the object of the agency. Hence, the fact that it is within the principal's power to perform *yibum* against the woman's will and thereby create the object of the agency has no bearing on the situation.

85 The question then arises how it is possible to justify the custom according to which, "a woman can say to her friend: knead flour for me and separate out *hala* for me." For the fact that the woman is able to prepare the dough, and so to create the object of the agency, does not suffice to render her "able to act"! In other words, because the dough does not yet exist, she should not have the ability to appoint an agent to separate *hala*. Cf. n. 81 above. Indeed, Rabbenu Tam suggests another explanation for the validity of such an appointment: "**She has the power to bring prepared dough** and to say that this dough should be the *hala* for the flour that is going to be kneaded; and what is within her power to make is considered to be real, and not considered that which is not in existence, since it is within her power to knead and work the dough, and it is rightly considered something in existence, because it is within her power to do it." In other words, it is possible to appoint an agent for the purpose of separating *hala* even before kneading the dough, because according to the law, it is possible to **separate *hala* on flour** (as the *Biur Hagra*, YD 327:1, also explained: "And Rabbenu Tam says… **it is because he can set aside *hala* now** [on this flour] **from** [other] **prepared dough**" (cited by R. Shimon Shkop)). While one must take the *hala* from a different batch of dough, a batch that does not yet exist, this only constitutes a different type of impediment (which does not result from absence of the object of the agency); and since it is possible to overcome this impediment by kneading another batch of dough, the agent is deemed "able to act."

(Cf. the approach of Rabbenu Tam to that of the Ri, which appears in *Sefer Mitzvot Gadol*, positive commandment 134 (p. 197:3–4). From his remarks, it appears that in principle he accepts the position of Rabbenu Tam, which is that the mere fact that it is within the principle's power to create the object of the agency is itself insufficient to render him "able to act." At the same time, with respect to agency to separate *hala*, he proposes an explanation that differs from that of Rabbenu Tam. In his opinion, the validity of the agency to separate *hala* from as yet unkneaded flour is due to the fact that the principal can already at that time transfer the flour to the agent, who can then function independently. Because such potential already exists, the appointment is valid. The logic and legal significance of this approach merit further study.)

86 The *Aharonim* were critical of Rabbenu Tam's explanation. See *Responsa Hikrei Lev*, EH, 46, which analyzes the statements of Rabbenu Tam at

### 5.2 An Impediment that Will Disappear by Itself ("Lacking Time")

Sometimes the principal cannot remove the impediment on account of which he is unable to perform the delegated task himself, but the impediment will disappear in and of itself with the passage of time. This, for example, is the situation with respect to the redemption of the first-born son before thirty days have passed from the day of his birth. Is the father able to appoint an agent to redeem his son before the prescribed time of redemption, or unable to do so? This situation is referred to as "lacking time." From one perspective, since, in this case, the impediment is not set, but rather stands to disappear in and of itself, there is room to argue that it is not a true impediment and the principal should be deemed "able to act." On the other hand, since removal of the impediment is completely beyond the power of the principal, from this perspective his position is worse than that of someone who has the power to overcome the impediment himself. The decisors are divided on this as well.

The author of the *Noda Biyehuda*[87] ruled that the father cannot appoint an agent until the thirty days have elapsed.[88] That is, on his

length. He cites the explanations of those who came before him, dismisses them, and offers his own explanation. However, his statements are unclear and require further study. See also *Orah Mishor*, Nazir 12a s.v. *mideamar*. It seems that the *Aharonim* had difficulty understanding the remarks of Rabbenu Tam — some even said that Rabbenu Tam negates the validity of agency for the separation of *hala* from flour (see the opinion of *Bnei Yaakov*, cited by the *Hikrei Lev*, and see *Orah Mishor*) — because they mistook his phrase, "because it is within her power to knead and work the dough," to apply to the unkneaded flour that was to be rendered fit by separating the *hala*, and not to the second batch of dough. Were this really Rabbenu Tam's understanding, it is unclear what this possibility has to do with the second batch of dough, which he mentions at the very beginning of his comments. On the interpretation offered by R. Shimon Shkop, n. 85 above, these difficulties vanish.

87 See *Dagul Mirvava*, YD 305:10 (indeed, as we mentioned above, n. 34, in the opinion of the *Noda Biyehuda*, being "able to act" pertains to the agent and not to the principal, but here there is no practical difference between the two). See also *Sde Hemed*, Rules, *kaf*, rule 90, s.v. *umidei*, who scrutinizes the views of the *Dagul Mirvava*.

88 But cf. *Responsa Oneg Yom Tov*, YD 101, who takes issue with this and posits that it is possible to appoint an agent even before the thirty days have elapsed. However, his point is that one can redeem the son early, hence this is merely an example of "something within his power."

view, "lacking time" has the same legal import as "lacking action," and since the principal is unable to overcome the impediment, he is deemed "unable to act," and his appointment lacks validity. In contrast, the opinion of the *Hatam Sofer*,[89] with respect to the appointment of an agent to betroth a woman who is a minor at the time of the appointment, is that the appointment is valid, because "lacking time is tantamount to ability to act."[90] In other words, the fact that the time for the act is not ripe does not impact the principal's being deemed "able to act."

## 6 *Conclusion*

What arises from our discussion is that a strict practical limitation governs the institution of agency in Jewish law. For according to the

89 *Responsa Hatam Sofer*, EH 1:11.

90 Ibid., s.v. *amar rava*. He so concludes from scrutinizing bNazir 12a. It would seem that proof could be adduced for this position from the Talmud's discussion in bGitin 29b, which addresses the case of an agent appointed to convey a bill of divorce to a woman, on condition that he will hand the bill of divorce over to her only after thirty days have elapsed. It is established there that even before thirty days have elapsed, the agent can appoint an agent to perform the task in his stead. It follows that the law with respect to one who "lacks time" is tantamount to that of one who is "able to act." But this proposed proof can be refuted on the basis of *Pithei Teshuva*, EH 141:40, in the name of the *Mishne Lamelekh*, Laws concerning Divorce 6:3 (however, I did not find the reference there). From his remarks there, it follows that the law with respect to a subagent is tantamount to the law with respect to an agent appointed directly by the principal, and the latter is by no means one who "lacks time." See too *Ein Yitzhak*, OH 28, *alef*.

The *AH*, YD 305:9, too, adopts this approach, but his explanation requires further study. He writes: "There is a view that even though one may appoint an agent [to redeem a first born son], that pertains in any event to his appointing an agent after thirty days, when it is within his power to redeem him himself. ... and in my humble opinion ... "lacking time" is not like "lacking action" ... for were this not so, in every agency entered into for the purpose of betrothal or divorce, when the woman is in a far-off place, we would say that he is unable until she arrives here, or he arrives there. ... However, "lacking proximity" is not like "lacking action" ... and so too "lacking time" is not like "lacking action." The comparison made here by the *AH* between "lack of proximity" and "lacking time" is surprising: how is it possible to compare an indirect physical impediment [distance, see the text at n. 17 above], with a direct legal impediment (even if only temporary)?

prevailing opinion, it is not possible to appoint an agent for commerce when the object of the agency is "something that is not in existence" or "something that is not within the possession" of the principal. And certainly many, if not most, other categories of agency are alike in this respect. The question then arises as to how the halakha coped with such severe limitations on the economic and practical effectiveness of the institution of agency. Our purpose in this article has only been to delineate the problem, and not to consider solutions. We will just point out that, in our opinion, one way to address the matter appears to lie in transforming the agent into a hired worker, that is, paid agency. As hired workers fall under the principle "the hand of the worker is like the hand of his master," most of the limitations we examined above can be overcome.[91, 92]

91 See *Responsa Even Harosha*, 26: "with respect to one who is paid, we do not say anyone who is unable to act is unable to hire a worker"; *Responsa Turei Even*, 35 (these sources are cited by the *Sde Hemed*, Rules, *kaf*, rule 90, s.v. *vesham*).

And cf. B. Lifshitz, "*Assignment and agency*" (Hebrew), *Tarbiz* 58 (1989) 1, 17–19. Lifshitz suggests the theory that at its inception, the institution of agency viewed the agent as one who is beholden to the principal. On this theory, at the outset, the practical difficulties we have mentioned here would not have arisen. However, once the connection between agency and ownership was severed (or in Lifshitz's words, when the institution of agency underwent a transition "from ownership to representation"), the aforesaid problems did arise. If his assertions are correct, there is some irony in the fact that the way to resolve these problems was to reinstate the concept of possession 'through the back door,' so to speak, in the form of the hired agent whose legal position was that of the worker, which made possible revival of the principle, "the hand of the worker is like the hand of the master of the house" with respect to the agent. That is to say, the worker is considered an extension of his employer's domain and not one who acts on his own. Use of the construct of the paid employee, therefore, alleviates the problems incurred when the physical, legal or other link between the principal and his unpaid agent is severed. (This is so despite the fact that the status of the worker also changed over time from an arrangement akin to servitude, in which the employer was perceived to have rights in the employee, to a contractual arrangement. See B. Lifshitz, *Employee and Independent Contractor — Acquisition and Obligation in Contrast* (Hebrew), (Jerusalem: 1994).) However it appears that this matter requires much additional study.

92 I would like to thank R. Eliezer Heisherik, who assisted me in researching this article, and Daniel Rosenthal, who translated it.

# PART TWO

# CHRONICLE

*The Jewish Law Annual*, Vol. XIV

# "SOMETHING THERE IS THAT DOESN'T LOVE A WALL"

Robert Frost, "Mending Wall"

MARTIN EDELMAN*

Religion has always had a prominent place in the political culture of the United States. The framers of the Constitution and the First Amendment's religious clauses believed that the nation they sought to establish could not long endure without a widespread concern for the public good, what they called "republican virtue." In the words of James Madison, "If there be not [republican virtue], no form of government can render us secure. To suppose that any form of government will secure liberty or happiness without any virtue in the people is a chimerical idea."[1] Religion, the founders believed, was a principal factor, if not **the** primary means, for instilling the values, attitudes and behaviors associated with republican virtue.[2]

According to Alexis de Tocqueville, the framers were admirably successful: "Religion in America takes no direct part in the government of society, but it must be regarded as the first of their institutions; for if it does not impart a taste for freedom, it facilitates the use of it. ... I am certain that they hold it to be indispensable to the maintenance of republican institutions. This opinion is not peculiar to a class of citizens or to a party, but it belongs to the whole nation and to every rank in society."[3]

For all its importance in shaping republican virtue, however, the framers were well aware that religion could be the source of societal strife.

* Political Science, Rockefeller College of Public Affairs and Policy, The University at Albany.

1 Quoted in Robert N. Bellah et al., *Habits of the Heart* (Berkeley: 1985), 253–254.

2 James Madison, *Memorial and Remonstrance Against Religious Assessments* (1785), reprinted as the appendix to Justice Wiley Rutledge's dissent in *Everson v. Board of Education*, 330 U.S. 1, 63–74 (1947).

3 Alexis de Tocqueville, *Democracy in America* (NY: 1960), vol. 1, 316.

The European history of religious wars was never far from their consciousness. Therefore they developed a particular way to shape the arrangements between religion and the state. Religion was to be removed from the public sphere (the Establishment Clause) and privacy in matters of religion was to be protected (the Free Exercise Clause).[4]

The Establishment Clause was designed to remove any incentive for religious entanglement in the political life of the nation. Since the government could enact **no** law **relating to** the establishment of religion, all sorts of aid to religious groups was thought to be precluded. Government could not be used to impose the beliefs of one religious group on others. Competition among religious groups for financial resources from the public treasury would be eliminated. Even the competition among organized religions for the status that had previously been associated with the state's imprimatur would be eliminated. Instead, each religion would compete for members and support in the "free market" associated with the private sphere. Not only would religious strife be removed from the public sphere, but religion in general would escape both the overt and the subtle corruptions of government influence, and American citizens would escape discrimination based upon religious belief.

The framers reinforced their belief in the private nature of religion by the Free Exercise Clause, which was designed to preclude government intervention in this area. Excluding governmental action would permit American citizens to freely develop their own beliefs about the fundamental values of human existence. As with other matters of conscience, American citizens would come to their own conclusions on the basis of such private experiences as family and education. These values, the framers believed, would nurture republican virtues and enable American citizens to function effectively in the public sphere.

Yet precisely because religion deals with the fundamental values of existence, it could not be walled off from the public sphere. In a democracy, like-minded individuals organize themselves to create the type of society they desire. Government agencies and the policies they implement are frequently utilized for this purpose. American citizens want government agencies, like schools, to adopt policies that reflect their values, many of which are rooted in religious beliefs. Among the groups pressing for such policies there are bound to be religious organizations.

4 The First Amendment: "Congress shall make no law respecting an establishment of religion, or prohibiting the free exercise thereof. … "

Thus the societal pattern put in place by the framers of the Constitution creates a perpetual tension central to the American scheme of liberty. On the one hand, they wanted to create a wall of separation between religion and the state. On the other, they wanted and expected religious groups to nurture and develop the values that American citizens would utilize when they acted in the public square. The difficulty of defining the boundary between religion and the state with precision inheres in this tension, a tension that defeats any attempt to create, in the words of Jefferson, "a wall of separation between Church and State."[5] Both the issues that will be discussed in this article reflect the fact that no firm walls can be erected between religion and the state.

## I *Kiryas Joel Redux*

Readers of this journal will recall the long struggle to establish a public school district in the Village of Kiryas Joel in the Town of Monroe, Rockland County, New York.[6] All residents of the village are Satmar hasidim. Most children are educated in the group's private religious schools. But these schools do not provide for the education of handicapped children, who are entitled, under federal and state laws, to governmentally-funded special services. Prior to 1985, the Monroe-Woodbury Central School District provided educational services to the handicapped children of Kiryas Joel in a building annexed to one of the religious schools. In that year, the United States Supreme Court held that publicly-funded classes on religious school premises violated the Establishment Clause,[7] so the public school district ceased offering on-site schooling to the handicapped Satmar children of Kiryas Joel.

5 Thomas Jefferson, "Letter to a committee of the Danbury Baptist Association," Jan. 1, 1802, in Saul Padover, *The Complete Jefferson* (NY: 1943), 518–519. Jefferson's phrase was quoted with approval in *Reynolds v. United States*, 98 U.S. 145, 164 (1878) and in *Everson v. Board of Education*, 330 U.S. 1, 16 (1947).

6 Martin Edelman and Christopher M. McMahon, "*Grumet v. Board of Education of Kiryas Joel*: towards a lemon-aid theory of the First Amendment's religious clauses," 9 *Jewish Law Annual* (1994), 207–220; idem, "Lemon peels: the unraveling of a constitutional law doctrine," 13 *Jewish Law Annual* (2000), 241–265.

7 *Aguilar v. Felton*, 473 U.S. 402 (1985), *Grand Rapids School District v. Ball*, 473 U.S. 373 (1985).

Thereafter, the Monroe-Woodbury School District provided the required educational services in its public schools. That was unacceptable to the Satmar hasidim. The very last thing they wanted was to have any of their children educated with children from the larger society; that was why the Satmarer had established their own village, with its own religious schools, in the first place. So the Satmar community turned to the legislative arena. In July 1989, the New York Legislature created the Kiryas Joel Union Free School District, the geographic boundaries of which were completely coterminous with those of the village.

In *Kiryas Joel I*, the New York courts[8] and, ultimately, the U.S. Supreme Court,[9] held that the legislation contravened the Establishment Clause.[10] Four days after the Supreme Court decision, the New York Legislature enacted another statute to correct the constitutional defects in the 1989 law. But the New York courts found that the 1994 law was also unconstitutional.[11] In *Kiryas Joel II*,[12] the state's highest court, the Court of Appeals, unanimously held that the 1994 statute violated the Establishment Clause's neutrality principles in two ways. First, notwithstanding its facial neutrality, the law had the non-neutral **effect** of allowing the religious community of Kiryas Joel, but no other group at the time and probably ever, to create its own school district. Because the statute was limited to municipalities in existence as of its effective date, any other group subsequently incorporated as a municipality was effectively precluded from its benefits. Second, the conferral of that special benefit on the Village of Kiryas Joel alone, as against virtually all other groups — religious or non-religious — effectively conveyed a message of impermissible governmental endorsement of that Satmar community.[13]

8 *Grumet v. New York State Education Dept.*, 579 N.Y.S. 2d 1004 (Sup. Ct. 1992); *Grumet v. Board of Education of the Kiryas Joel School District*, 592 N.Y.S. 123 (App. Div. 3d Dept. 1992); *Grumet v. Board of Education of Kiryas Joel School District*, 618 N.E. 2d 94 (NY Ct. of Appeals 1993).

9 *Board of Education of Kiryas Joel School District v. Grumet*, 512 U.S. 687 (1994).

10 See Edelman and McMahon articles, n. 6 above, for a detailed discussion of the constitutional doctrines utilized by the various courts and judges.

11 In *Grumet v. Cuomo*, 625 N.Y.S. 2d 1000 (Sup. Ct. 1995), the law was declared constitutional, but both higher courts held it invalid. *Grumet v. Cuomo*, 647 N.Y.S. 2d 565 (App. Div. 1996); *Grumet v. Cuomo*, 90 N.Y. 2d 173 (NY Ct. of Appeals 1997).

12 *Grumet v. Cuomo*, 90 N.Y. 2d 57 (1997).

13 Ibid., 69.

Three months later the Legislature enacted yet another law to maintain the Kiryas Joel Union Free School District. The New York Court of Appeals had indicated that the Legislature might achieve a constitutionally-acceptable result if it enacted a law of "general applicability" so that the Village of Kiryas Joel was just "one of a broad array of eligible municipalities."[14] The 1997 law was the Legislature's effort to satisfy those criteria. But in *Kiryas Joel III*, the New York courts once again held that the Legislature had failed to satisfy the requirements of the Establishment Clause.[15]

The law was indeed written in terms of general applicability.[16] Yet in a 4-3 decision, the Court of Appeals held that "both the origin and operation of the statute" led to the "inescapable" conclusion that it had the "primary effect of advancing religion and constitute[d] an impermissible accommodation."[17] "The events surrounding the [law's] enactment" indicated that it was intended to achieve "what previous legislative efforts had failed to accomplish: provide the residents of Kiryas Joel with an exclusively Satmar 'public school' environment, at taxpayer expense, in which to educate their children."[18] While the legislative history of "Kiryas Joel No. 3," as it was called in the legislative debates, could not be dispositive, it added force to the fact that "only the Village of Kiryas Joel and one other of the State's 1,545 municipalities" could meet the statute's "neutral" criteria.[19] And the majority, unlike the minority,[20] was plainly unwilling to speculate about the future: "the eligibility requirements" were "still limited in such a way that permit[ted] the statute's benefits to flow almost exclusively to the religious sect it was plainly designed to aid."[21] Thus the majority concluded that "a statute so narrowly drawn that it delegates significant governmental power almost exclusively to a single religious group, and provides no assurance that the statute's benefits will be equally available to others, is unconstitutional."[22]

14 Ibid., 75.

15 The N.Y. State Supreme Court granted summary judgment against the State; the Appellate Division affirmed, *Grumet v. Pataki*, 675 N.Y.S. 2d 662 (1998); and the Court of Appeals agreed, *Grumet v. Pataki*, 93 N.Y. 2d 677 (1999).

16 *Grumet v. Pataki*, 93 N.Y. 2d 677, 686–687 (1999).

17 Ibid., 696.

18 Ibid., 695–696.

19 Ibid., 689.

20 Ibid., 701.

21 Ibid., 691.

22 Ibid., 694.

The Court of Appeals majority was also puzzled as to why the Legislature believed there was still a need for any special enactment to help handicapped Satmar children receive educational services.[23] In June 1997, the U.S. Supreme Court had overruled the 1985 decision that had triggered the whole incident. Under *Agostini v. Felton* (1997),[24] the Monroe-Woodbury Central School District could once again provide the services in an exclusively Satmar setting. Thus one month after *Kiryas Joel II*, and two months before the Legislature enacted the 1997 law, legal developments had made it unnecessary.

There was, of course, no puzzle. The Court of Appeals majority was simply utilizing traditional judicial language to point out the obvious. The leaders of both New York political parties were eager to ingratiate themselves with the Satmar hasidim and like-minded Orthodox Jews. At the very least, the elected leadership was unwilling to offend those groups. A century ago, a New York congressman requested that President Grover Cleveland reconsider his decision to veto a bill by pleading "what's the Constitution between friends?"[25] Apparently, New York Democrats and Republicans still adhere to that position, at least where votes are at stake.

The Satmar hasidim and their allies are not interested in votes. They are interested in obtaining the maximum government funding possible for their religious schools. That is why the Satmarer keep pressing for the establishment of a union free school district in Kiryas Joel. The authorization of a general school district would enable the Satmar hasidim to obtain a wide variety of governmental funds to administer the district, as well as to provide the special educational services for the handicapped children. Ultimately, some of these administrative funds could be shared with the village's plainly religious schools. The sharing of administrative costs is a common practice in New York among religiously-affiliated institutions of higher education that receive state aid under the Bundy Law.[26] In Albany, it has long been believed that the Kiryas Joel controversy could have been resolved if the Satmar hasidim had been willing to settle for the creation of a special school district designed solely for the education of their handicapped children.

23 Ibid., 696–697.

24 521 U.S. 203.

25 Timothy Campbell, as quoted in Antony Jay (ed.), *The Oxford Dictionary of Political Quotations* (Oxford: 1996), 74.

26 Maureen Manion, "State aid and sectarian education," *Review of Politics* 48 (1986), 264.

The foregoing analysis of the underlying interests involved in the Kiryas Joel saga is further strengthened by subsequent events. In the wake of the *Kiryas Joel III* decision, the New York Legislature enacted yet another law to establish a union free school district in the village. By modifying the criteria that a municipality would need to establish its own general-purpose school district, the August 1999 law applies, it is estimated, to approximately 29 existing local governmental units. If all these localities exercised the option to create their own school districts, it would reverse a long-standing state educational policy promoting the consolidation of small school districts. Moreover, it might encourage other insular minorities to "secede" from the larger body politic, to create their own local governmental units, each with its own school district. Thus the latest law establishing a union free school district in Kiryas Joel has a potentially destructive impact on state educational policy. It also has the potential to bring about a sizable increase in state costs, as fragmented school districts increase administrative costs. Most importantly, the 1999 law, like its predecessors, sends the wrong message. In opting once again to accommodate the Satmar hasidim, New York's politicians reveal their willingness to pay the social costs — as defined by the framers of the First Amendment — involved in abandoning governmental neutrality toward religion.

As of this writing, the New York School Boards Association — the plaintiff in all the previous litigation over the Kiryas Joel school district — has not chosen to contest the 1999 law. Apparently, the 4-3 decision in *Kiryas Joel III*, when the law applied to only two existing municipalities, has made them reluctant to challenge a law applying to approximately 29 existing (and a much larger potential number of) local governmental units.

Nonetheless, the 1999 law has not escaped legal challenge. While the village's residents are all Satmar hasidim, a minority has always opposed the creation of a publicly-funded school in Kiryas Joel. These dissidents believe that the need to utilize a secular curriculum to educate the handicapped children — a condition of public funding — violates God's law. They have filed suit in New York State Supreme Court, Orange County, to enjoin the expenditure of any state funds for the Kiryas Joel Union Free School District.[27] The dissidents claim that the

27 "Birnbaum v. Board of Education of the Monroe-Woodbury Central School District," *New York Law Journal* (Jan. 24, 2000), 1.

village does not meet the 1999 law's requirement that the organizing municipality have at least 10,000 residents.[28]

The dissident Satmar hasidim insist on separating their religion from even seemingly-beneficent governmental acts. In so doing, these religious extremists are acting to protect important First Amendment values. For Roger Williams and the framers of the Establishment Clause, avoiding the subtle corruptions involved in any governmental entanglement of religion and the state was a basic reason for their separation.[29] Moreover, the approach of the dissident Satmar hasidim is better suited to preventing competition for financial resources from the public treasury between various religious groups. Avoiding such religious strife was central to the framers. It is ironic that the protection of these important public values now appears to reside in the actions of a tiny, otherworldly religious group rather than in those of New York's elected officials.

## II *The "Yale Four"*

Yale College, the undergraduate division of one of America's oldest and most prestigious universities, requires first and second year students to live in university housing. In the autumn of 1997, five Orthodox Jewish students sought an exemption from this policy on the grounds that it violated their religious beliefs. When Yale refused to accommodate them, four[30] of the students filed suit in Federal District Court, claiming that their constitutionally protected rights under the Free Exercise Clause, federal statutes, and the common law, had been violated. In July 1998, the court granted Yale's motion to dismiss on all counts.[31] At this writing, the decision is on appeal to the U.S. Court of Appeals for the Second Circuit.

28 According to the 1990 census, the last official count, there were 7,437 inhabitants in Kiryas Joel, ibid.

29 Mark DeWolfe Howe, *The Garden in the Wilderness* (Chicago: 1965).

30 Although the media continued to refer to this case as the "Yale five," one student was granted an exemption because she was soon to be married. As discussed in the text below, Yale allows married students an exemption from its residency requirement.

31 *Hack v. President of Yale College*, 16 F. Supp. 2d 183 (D. Conn. 1998). The students' arguments under the Federal Fair Housing Act, Federal anti-trust laws, and the common law will not be discussed here.

The text of the First Amendment applies only to the Federal government. The two religious clauses were "judicially incorporated" in the Due Process Clause of the Fourteenth Amendment and thereby made applicable to the States.[32] Since the *Civil Rights Cases* (1883),[33] the Supreme Court has consistently held that the Fourteenth Amendment applies only to state action, as distinct from private action. Thus had the students been objecting to a comparable housing policy at an acknowledged state institution, such as the University of Connecticut, there is a good possibility that their suit would have been successful.[34] For a private institution like Yale, a First Amendment claim requires significant governmental involvement in the alleged violation, that is, the institution must be found, in reality, to be a state actor or to have acted under the color of state law.[35] The District Court held that Yale was a private, rather than state, actor, and that it had not acted under the color of state law.[36]

The court's analysis is persuasive. The public perception is plainly that Yale is a private institution, as distinct from a public institution such as the University of Connecticut. Yale University does indeed have a long history of close relations to the State of Connecticut, going back to 1701, when it was incorporated by an act of the colonial assembly. And since 1818, Yale's charter has been recognized in the state constitution. But permission to incorporate (establish) a college, and its recognition in the state constitution, cannot be confused with state control of an institution.[37] The state does not appoint a majority of the directors of the Yale Corporation. While the Governor and Lieutenant Governor are *ex officio* members of the governing board, they are only two of the nineteen directors. In addition, there is no evidence that state officials control the decisions of one of the nation's most famous

32 The Free Exercise Clause was explicitly incorporated in *Cantwell v. Connecticut*, 310 U.S. 296 (1940); and the Establishment Clause was incorporated in *Everson v. Board of Education*, 330 U.S. 1 (1947).

33 109 U.S. 3.

34 In *Rader v. Johnston*, 924 F. Supp. 1540 (D. Neb. 1996), the District Court required the University of Nebraska to allow a devout Christian freshman to live off-campus because the life style in the university dorms conflicted with his religious beliefs and practices.

35 The continuum of state action ranges from the obvious — e.g., legislation — to actions found to be taken "under the color of state law." *United States v. Classic*, 313 U.S. 299 (1941); *Screws v. United States*, 325 U.S. 91 (1945).

36 *Hack v. President and Fellows of Yale College*, 16 F. Supp. 2nd, 183, 189 (1998).

37 Cf. *Dartmouth College v. Woodward*, 4 Wheat. 518 (1819).

private institutions of higher education. Moreover, the District Court's understanding of the Supreme Court's unwillingness at this moment to adopt a broad reading of the "state actor" concept is plainly correct.[38]

To act "under the color of state law," one need not be an employee of the state.[39] But there does have to be some indication that the policy of the private entity "was itself based upon some rule of conduct or policy put forth by the State."[40] There are no Connecticut laws or regulations suggesting that it compelled or even encouraged Yale's housing policy. Moreover, there is no evidence that the state could influence Yale's policy through the power of the purse. Since 1882, Yale has not had a specific, designated line in the state budget. In sum, there was no indication of the significant governmental involvement in Yale's housing policy necessary to sustain a First Amendment claim.

Contrary to popular perception, the Yale students were also unable to invoke Federal civil rights statutes.[41] These laws are designed to protect individuals from private acts of discrimination. But the laws banning discrimination in education deal only with racial and gender bias, not with religion.[42] Until Congress amends the civil rights statutes to prevent discrimination on the basis of religion by private entities, students like the "Yale Four" will have no federal remedy available.

Even were Congress to add that sort of amendment to the applicable laws and thereby make them comparable to other civil rights provisions, current Supreme Court doctrine might still preclude students like the "Yale Four" from vindicating their Free Exercise claim, given the Supreme Court's 1997 decision that Congress' Religious Freedom Restoration Act (RFRA) was unconstitutional.[43]

In *Employment Division, Department of Human Resources v. Smith* (1990),[44] the Court held that neutral, generally applicable laws may be applied even where such enforcement burdens an individual's exercise

38 Compare *Burton v. Wilmington Parking Authority*, 365 U.S. 715 (1961) with *Lebron v. National R.R. Corp.*, 513 U.S. 374 (1995).

39 *United States v. Price*, 383 U.S. 787 (1966).

40 *Rendell-Baker v. Kohn*, 457 U.S. 830, 844 (1982).

41 The Civil Rights Acts of 1964 and 1968 are the basic statutes.

42 Joshua Weinberger, "Religion and sex in the Yale dorms: a legislative proposal requiring private universities to provide religious accommodations," 147 *University of Pennsylvania Law Review* (1998), 205.

43 *City of Boerne v. Flores*, 117 S. Ct. 2157 (1997).

44 494 U.S. 872.

of religion, and that the government's refusal to accommodate religion does not trigger strict judicial scrutiny.[45] This was a significant change in the Court's standard for interpreting the Free Exercise Clause. The previous standard required courts to consider whether a governmental action substantially burdened an individual's religious practice, and, if so, whether that burden was nonetheless justified as the least restrictive means for serving a compelling governmental interest.[46] Congress enacted RFRA in direct response to the *Smith* decision, in order to restore the previous standard for interpreting the Free Exercise Clause.

In *City of Boerne v. Flores* (1997), the Court held that Congress' power under Section 5 of the Fourteenth Amendment[47] does not extend to defining the substance of constitutional rights; Congress only has the power to deter or remediate violations as defined by the Supreme Court.[48] Since, according to the current Supreme Court, an individual's right is not violated by a **neutral, general governmental policy** that burdens the exercise of religion, Congress could not transform a comparable **private entity's policy** into a constitutional violation. Under current doctrine, such a law would involve the Legislature in exceeding two Fourteenth Amendment limitations: the Amendment protects individual rights only against governmental actions, and Congress can only provide remedies for rights as defined by the Supreme Court.

There is, of course, no necessity for interpreting Congress' authority under the Fourteenth Amendment in so constricted a manner. In the *Civil Rights Cases* (1883),[49] the first Justice John Marshall Harlan, in dissent, indicated a variety of ways in which Congress could be understood as having the authority to protect civil rights as attributes of U.S. citizenship.[50] There are problems with Harlan I's suggestions, as his grandson, Justice John Marshall Harlan, pointed out in his separate opinion in the *Sit-In Cases* (1963).[51] But these problems do not, in themselves, mean that Congress may not expand (as opposed to restrict) the

45 See the discussion in Martin Edelman, "Limits without walls: constricting religious freedom in the United States," 10 *Jewish Law Annual* (1992), 247, 251–257.

46 *Sherbert v. Verner*, 374 U.S. 398 (1963).

47 "Congress shall have the power to enforce the above with all appropriate legislation."

48 *City of Boerne v. Flores*, 117 S. Ct. 2157, 2164–2165.

49 109 U.S. 3.

50 Ibid., 26.

51 373 U.S. 244–375, at 249.

guarantees secured by the Fourteenth Amendment beyond those recognized by the Supreme Court.[52] The existence of the power of judicial review does not require that the Constitution always be equated with the Supreme Court's view of it.[53] The Court could be seen as protecting the minimal, core nature of constitutional rights, with Congress having the authority to grant, at its discretion, more expansive protections of these rights.[54] Under a different interpretation, the power of Congress under Section 5 of the Fourteenth Amendment could be treated as equivalent to its power under the Commerce Clause.

This interpretation would permit Congress to extend the protections it incorporated in RFRA to private entities; the free exercise of religion could then receive the same sort of protection as race.[55] Then, and only then, would the "Yale Four" have a strong argument. The students claimed that the university's housing policy burdened their religious convictions and obligations as Orthodox Jews. Yale's dormitories are all co-educational. Since even single-sex floors — and their bathrooms — are fully accessible 24 hours a day to other dormitory residents, the students claimed that Yale's housing policy violated Orthodox Judaism's strict code of sexual modesty. The policy might well expose the students to undressed, or immodestly dressed, members of the opposite sex. Under a RFRA-like standard, there would be little doubt that Yale's housing policy burdens the students' genuine religious practices. The argument would then shift to whether Yale's policy is nonetheless justified as the least restrictive means of serving a compelling objective.

Yale argued that its students, particularly its freshmen and sophomores, gain immeasurably by the experience of living together with people from diverse backgrounds. But married students and students over the age of 21 are routinely granted exemptions; these students are not required to make persuasive counterarguments. As a result, Yale's housing policy treats religion-based claims for exemption less favorably

52 See the opinion for the Court by Justice Brennan in *Katzenbach v. Morgan*, 384 U.S. 641 (1966).

53 Walter Murphy, James Fleming and Sotirios Barber, *American Constitutional Interpretation* (New York: 1986, 1995), part 3.

54 See, for example, William Cohen, "Congressional power to interpret due process and equal protection," 27 *Stanford Law Review* (1975), 603.

55 But see *United States v. Morrison*, 120 S. Ct. 1740 (2000), where the Supreme Court called into question Congress' authority to utilize the Commerce Clause to protect individual rights.

than certain secular claims. Thus whether Yale's argument could survive the strict judicial scrutiny required by a RFRA-like statute is an open question.

As indicated, under the Supreme Court's current interpretation of both the Free Exercise Clause and Congressional Power under the Fourteenth Amendment, all this is sheer speculation. It only indicates the obstacles confronting suits such as that brought by the "Yale Four." These obstacles also indicate the strength of the religious convictions at play. The prominent lawyers acting on behalf of the "Yale Four" were surely aware at the outset how much law would have to change if their clients were to prevail, yet all involved believed it important enough to undertake the effort nevertheless.

Thus both the "Yale Four" and the Kiryas Joel actions demonstrate once again the vast and varied forces that religious beliefs unleash. The framers of the Constitution and its First Amendment were well aware of the great strengths, and great dangers, such strong, passionate beliefs posed for the American democracy they were creating. The founders sought to protect both religion and the state from the dangers inherent in their entanglement, in a manner that recognized the importance of religion to the fibre of democratic life. In the end, the founders simply provided a framework within which to resolve issues relating to religion. While the framers believed it essential to separate religion and the state, they did not provide an immutable formula. They certainly did not write constitutional provisions creating a fixed wall to demarcate the boundaries. In the words of Chief Justice Warren Burger: "Judicial caveats against entanglement [of religion and the state] must recognize that the line of separation, far from being a 'wall,' is a blurred, indistinct and variable barrier depending on all the circumstances of a particular relationship."[56]

56 *Lemon v. Kurtzman*, 403 U.S. 602, 614 (1971).

*The Jewish Law Annual*, Vol. XIV

# JEWISH LAW IN ISRAEL AND AROUND THE WORLD

DANIEL B. SINCLAIR

## 1 *The Validity of a Gift Made with the Intention That It Take Effect Only upon the Donor's Death*

In the case of *R. Abergel* v. *Estate of Moshe Ben-Yair*,[1] the Supreme Court dealt with the validity of a deed purporting to make a gift of property in such a way that it would not be construed as a will, but would, nevertheless, only take full effect upon the donor's death. The deed was intended to be valid under both Jewish and Israeli law, and a clause to this effect appeared in the document. The facts of the case are as follows. Moshe Ben-Yair, a widower, died childless in a Jerusalem old-age home, leaving an apartment worth about $120,000. His legal heirs discovered that shortly before entering the home, he had signed a deed of gift transferring the apartment to the appellant, Rabbi Abergel, who had known Ben-Yair and his wife for many years. The relationship between the appellant and the deceased began when the former started preaching on a regular basis at a synagogue one of whose founding members was Ben-Yair. Over the years, the Ben-Yair's spent many Sabbaths and Festivals in the Abergel home, and the rabbi was a regular visitor during the time that Ben-Yair lived in the old-age home. The deed explained that the gift to the rabbi was a sign of appreciation of the many years of kindness and consideration shown by the rabbi and his family to the Ben-Yair's. In contrast to the warm relationship between Ben-Yair and the appellant, his family relationships had always been frosty and strained. The deed of gift was drawn up by a notary chosen by R. Abergel, and the witnesses were two of his rabbinical colleagues. On Ben-Yair's death, the home contacted R. Abergel, who arranged the funeral and delivered the eulogy. Shortly after the funeral, R. Abergel used the notarized document to transfer the apartment to his name in the Land Registry.

1 C.A. 2555/98, P.D. 53 (5) 673.

The deed of gift purported to be valid under both Jewish and Israeli law. Ben-Yair's legal heirs contested its validity under both systems, and the District Court ruled in their favor in terms of both halakha and Israeli law. It should be noted that under the doctrine of freedom of contract in Israeli law, the parties to an agreement are free to make it subject to Jewish law, provided that such a step does not run counter to any existing law, moral principle or the public good.[2] Since the parties chose to make their agreement in accordance with Jewish law, the District Court was perfectly entitled to question its halakhic validity. In the wake of the District Court decision, R. Abergel appealed to the Supreme Court. The Supreme Court also ruled against him, in a decision written by Englard J., with Heshin J. and Orr J. concurring.

Englard J. began his judgment with the issue of the validity of the gift under Jewish law. From a halakhic perspective, the crucial clause in the agreement was the one which stated that Ben-Yair gave the apartment to R. Abergel "from now and one hour before my death." Now Jewish law does not permit a person to bequeath his possessions to a stranger, thereby depriving his legal heirs of their inheritance.[3] On the other hand, a person may make a gift of his property during his lifetime to anyone he wishes. Such a gift, however, may not be made on condition that it only take effect upon the donor's death.[4] To deal with a situation in which a person wishes to make a gift of land to a stranger in his lifetime, but also wishes to retain a legal right to the property until his death, the Talmud separates the transfer of the land from that of the usufruct. The legal title in land may be passed to the recipient during the gift-giver's lifetime, but the latter retains the sole right to its use until his death. In order to create this type of gift, the deed must state that the land is transferred to the recipient "from this day," but the fruits only accrue to him "after my death." Jewish law, therefore, adopts a two-track approach to ownership, to allow people to make gifts of property in such a way that they both retain their right to use it for the duration of their lifetime, and succeed in avoiding the laws of inheritance.[5] Since R. Abergel was not Ben-Yair's legal heir, and Ben-Yair did not want to totally divest himself of his only significant asset until his death, it would have been expected that the phrase "from this day and

2 *Contract Law* (*General Part*) 5733-1973, § 24, 30, 61(b).
3 *Shulhan Arukh* (henceforth *SA*), HM 282:1.
4 *SA*, HM 281:7.
5 mBaba Batra 8:7; *Tur*, *SA*, HM 257.

after my death" would have been used in the deed. The phrase used by R. Abergel, however, was "from now and one hour before my death." It was on the basis of this divergence from the accepted terminology that the District Court declared the deed invalid under Jewish law.

Englard J. held that from a halakhic standpoint, the difference in terminology was not critical. The phrase "from now and one hour before my death" originates in the context of divorce law,[6] and was employed by many halakhic authorities in relation to deeds of gift.[7] In a decision by a Rabbinical Court on this matter, it was specifically stated that there is no difference between the phrase "from this day and after my death," and the phrase "from now and one hour before my death." In both cases, the effect of the sentence is to transfer ownership of the land as of the date of the deed, and the use of its fruit after death.[8] The phrase used in the present deed also figures in academic writings in this field of Jewish law.[9] The District Court, therefore, erred in invalidating the deed under Jewish law on the grounds of its deviation from the standard formula.

Englard J. then observed that other halakhic problems may arise as a result of the use of this more unusual phrase. For example, a deed of gift drawn up using the standard formula would not normally require a *kinyan* — a formal act of acquisition by the beneficiary — to ensure the legal validity of the gift. In the present case, the use of the less well-known phrase may necessitate the making of a *kinyan* to ensure that the gift is legally binding. The absence of such a *kinyan* is not, however, sufficiently significant to nullify the deed under Jewish law.

As far as Israeli law is concerned, section 8 of the *Succession Law*, 5725-1965, provides that "a gift given on condition that legal title passes to the recipient on the giver's death is only valid if it fulfils all the requirements of a will as specified in this law." According to the District Court, there was no doubt that the intention of the parties was to create an agreement under which legal title would pass to the appellant upon Ben-Yair's death. R. Abergel himself admitted that the force of the phrase "one hour before my death" was to allow Ben-Yair to return from the old-age home to full occupancy of the apartment at any time

6 Tosefta, Gitin 4:11.

7 See *Responsa Rosh*, 74:4; 84:5; Rema, *SA*, HM 281:10; *Hokhmat Shlomo, SA*, HM 257; R. Ezra Batzri, *Dinei Mamonot* (Jerusalem: 1990), 3, 186.

8 *P.D.R.* 1, 354.

9 See Y. Rivlin, *Inheritance and Wills in Jewish Law* (Hebrew), (Ramat Gan: 1999), 172–173, 296–298.

prior to his demise. Clearly, there was no intention that the rabbi would become the legal owner until Bar-Yair passed away. Moreover, the very expression "one hour before death" is clear evidence that the agreement is a will and not a gift *inter vivos*, since the hour in question can only be determined retroactively from the moment of death.

Having established that the deed was a will and not a gift, the District Court proceeded to declare it invalid, on the grounds that R. Abergel had played an active role in drawing it up. Under section 35 of the *Succession Law*, the involvement of a beneficiary in drawing up a will makes it invalid. In addition, section 20 of the Law requires the witnesses to affirm that in this type of situation, the deceased declared his intention that the deed of gift would serve as his will. Needless to say, this was not done, since any reference to a will would have rendered the deed halakhically invalid.

In his appeal to the Supreme Court, the appellant argued that the use of the phrase "from now" in the deed of gift was totally inapplicable to a will, and the District Court had erred in neglecting this essential phrase, and in placing the entire emphasis on the words "and one hour before my death." The main thrust of the language employed in the deed was to make the recipient the full owner at the time the deed was drawn up, and this was also the true intention of the parties. They were simply following the two-track approach of Jewish law to gifts made in contemplation of death, and the deed, therefore, should be interpreted as a gift and not as a will.

Englard J. accepted that splitting the ownership of land into an "abstract" right to the property, which cannot be realized in practice, and a "concrete" right to its use, is indeed the correct approach under Jewish law. Under Israeli law, however, the major constitutive aspect of land ownership is registration in the Land Registry, and the apartment was only registered by R. Abergel in his name after Ben-Yair's death. It is also evident that neither R. Abergel nor Ben-Yair ever intended to register the apartment in the former's name until the demise of the latter. The reason for this is that registering such an "abstract" right to land, although possible, is a very complicated process, and it is far simpler to register full ownership than such partial ownership. In terms of Israeli law, therefore, the conduct of the parties indicated that the deed in question was a will and not a gift.

In fact, it is not necessary to take this line of reasoning to defeat the validity of the deed in Israeli law. According to Englard J., the correct approach in this case is to pay attention to the essential nature of the deed, rather than its wording. This is the approach adopted by Israeli law when dealing with the classification of foreign wills for the purposes of succession law, and the same criterion should apply to deeds drawn up in accordance with halakha. Since the essential nature of the split ownership construction in Jewish law is that of a will, the deed is to be construed as such. Religious Jews wishing to make halakhic "wills" by employing the form of a gift of deed need encounter no problem having such a deed honored in the secular system, provided they ensure that their arrangements correspond to the provisions of the *Succession Law,* including that barring the involvement of the beneficiary in the drafting of the document. Since R. Abergel was closely involved in the preparation of this "will," however, it is invalid under Israeli law, and the appeal must be rejected.

Englard J. noted that on his approach, an oral gift made by a dying person (*matnat shekhiv mera*),[10] which is valid under Jewish law, would also be valid under secular law. This is because section 23 of the *Succession Law* recognizes an oral death-bed will. The Israeli *Gift Law,* 5728-1968, however, has no provision for oral gifts; a gift must be in writing to be valid. In this respect, the approach based on a deed's essential nature, rather than its wording, is more advantageous for religious Jews than the formal approach on which, in accordance with the halakhic construction, the oral death-bed gift is classified as a gift, with the result that it would be invalid under secular law. On Englard J.'s approach, however, the oral death-bed "gift" would be treated as a will, and would be acceptable as such under secular law.

Finally, Englard J. cited the talmudic statement warning that those who are inexpert in the laws of marriage and divorce ought not get involved in drawing up documents in these areas.[11] The same warning applies to wills.

## 2 *Does Showing Films Featuring Orthodox Jews on* Shabat[12] *Infringe Their Basic Rights?*

The facts of *Gur Aryeh* v. *Second T.V. and Radio Authority*[13] were summarized by Barak J., the President of the Supreme Court, as follows. The petitioners were Orthodox Jews who had agreed to take part in

10 See M. Elon (ed.), *The Principles of Jewish Law* (Jerusalem: 1974), 453–455.

11 bKidushin 6a.

12 The Jewish Sabbath. The terms *Shabat,* Sabbath and Saturday are used interchangeably in this case-note.

13 H.C. 1514/01, P.D. 55 (4) 267.

a short documentary film about social tensions in Israeli society. The film was slotted for a program that regularly aired on Saturday afternoon. At the end of the filming process, the petitioners discovered that the film would be shown on *Shabat*, and upon consultation with their rabbi, were informed that if the film did indeed air on *Shabat*, they would become accomplices in the act of Sabbath desecration involved in the showing of the film. They then turned to the Second T.V. and Radio Authority with a request that the film be aired during the week. Their request was turned down on the grounds that it was extremely difficult, from a logistic point of view, to switch slots, and that any such change would involve extra costs. The Authority did, however, offer to display a notice to the effect that the film had been made on weekdays and the petitioners objected to its being shown on the Sabbath. This offer was refused, and the matter came before the Supreme Court sitting as the High Court of Justice. The petitioners claimed that in refusing their request for a weekday showing, the Authority offended their religious sensibilities, and interfered with their freedom of religion.

The issue of the Sabbath screening was not specifically raised by either party prior to the making of the film. The petitioners claimed that they did not know that it was to be shown on *Shabat*, and had assumed, on the basis of the fact that some of the respondents were Orthodox Jews, that there was no question of its being screened in violation of the Sabbath laws. The respondents argued that the appellants knew the name of the program for which the film was being made, and could easily have established that it was shown on Saturdays only. Also, many films screened on the Sabbath feature observant Jews. On occasion, there is a request that a notice be displayed to the effect that the filming was done during the week. This option was offered to the appellants, but they turned it down.

Barak J. began his judgment with the issue of the petitioners' religious sensibilities. The law protects the religious sensibilities of its citizens as part of its desire to promote tolerance in society. In the words of Landau J., in the leading case of *Kenan v. Film and Theatre Censorship Board*,[14] the obligation to avoid offending people's religious sensibilities in Israeli law, "stems directly from the need for mutual tolerance in a society made up of different faith communities. In the absence of such an obligation, democracy could not survive in a society as varied as ours."[15] In the present case, this right was in conflict with that of the

14 H.C. 351/72, P.D. 26 (2) 811.

15 Ibid., 814.

respondents to freedom of expression, and the right of the public, as a statutory corporation, to a free media. The question of the proper balance between these two rights was dealt with by the Supreme Court in earlier cases, the answer being that freedom of expression overrides the protection of religious sensibilities, unless the damage to religious feelings is sufficiently substantial and serious to "shake the very foundations of mutual tolerance"[16] in Israeli society. In the present case, the damage to the petitioners' religious feelings does not reach this degree of seriousness. Interviews with religious Jews, especially politicians, appear on Saturday television frequently. The image of a religious Jew on television on the Sabbath is not, therefore, so shocking to Jewish religious sensibilities as to threaten the foundations of religious tolerance in Israeli society. In these terms, the petition must fail.

In view of the long-standing and widespread trend in the media to feature observant Jews in films shown on Saturdays, Barak J. pointed out that a finding for the petitioners in the present case might very well lead to a total ban on all Saturday TV and radio. This is clearly too heavy a price to pay for the preservation of individual religious sensibilities, the infringement of which does not amount to a threat to the very existence of Israel as a tolerant society. In a democratic society, there will be cases in which individual religious feelings will have to give way to the public good, and this is one of them. A religious person featured in a media item in Israel, and wishing to retain his religious integrity in terms of *Shabat* screening, has the option of protecting himself by specifically stipulating that the material not be broadcast on Saturdays. In the absence of such a condition, free speech overrides religious sensibilities.

Freedom of religion is a fundamental right in Israeli law, and in that of any enlightened democracy.[17] It includes the right of an individual to believe in and act in accordance with his faith, and its rules and customs.[18]

16 *Horev v. Minister of Transport*, H.C. 5016/96, P.D. 51 (4) 50. Also see *Temple Mount Faithful v. Government of Israel* H.C. 7128/96, P.D. 51 (2) 509; *Universal City Studios v. Film and Theatre Censorship Board*, H.C. 806/88, P.D. 43 (2) 22; *Sutzkin v. State of Israel*, C.A. 697/98, P.D. 52 (3) 289.

17 A. Rubinstein, *Constitutional Law in the State of Israel* (Hebrew), (Tel-Aviv: 1993), 1, 175; *Yosipof v. Attorney General*, C.A. 112/50, P.D. 5, 481; *Morad v. Government of Israel*, H.C. 866/78, P.D. 34 (2) 657.

18 H. Cohn, "On freedom of religion and religious integrity" (Hebrew), in A. Barak and A. Maoz (eds.), *Essays in Honor of Moshe Landau* (Hebrew), Tel-Aviv: 1995, 813; *Rubinstein v. Minister of Defense*, H.C. 3267/97, P.D. 52 (5) 528; *Gabarin v. Minister of Education*, H.C. 4928/93, P.D. 48 (5) 199.

Unlike the right to the protection of religious sensibilities, which is derived from the public good, the freedom of religion is a purely individual right. As such, it is only overridden by a serious threat to the welfare of society, for instance, to national security,[19] or to the preservation of the integrity of the legal system.[20] In the absence of this type of threat, conflicts involving fundamental individual rights are resolved in such a way that a maximum of individual freedom is preserved.[21] In the present case, however, it is not the freedom of religion of the petitioners that has come under attack. Showing the film on *Shabat* does not interfere with the petitioners' freedom to believe in their faith or practice its tenets; rather, it is their desire to prevent others from breaking the Sabbath that is the real essence of their petition. The Supreme Court has already rejected this type of claim,[22] as it has the claim that the importing of non-kosher meat into Israel, and its consumption by non-observant Jews, encroaches upon the freedom of religion of observant Israeli Jews.[23] Similarly, Barak J. ruled that permitting vehicular traffic on a road in a religious neighborhood on the Sabbath did not constitute a violation of the constitutional right of each and every resident living on the road to the freedom to practice his or her religion.[24] The real essence of the claim in that case, as in the present one, is the damage to the petitioners' religious sensibilities, and not to their freedom of religion.

Now it is true that in this case, the petitioners are claiming that the airing of film segments containing their images and interviews on *Shabat* is contrary to their religious beliefs. Nevertheless, the fact remains that it is the conduct of others that underlies their petition. In the same way that the Court would reject a claim by a religious author that reading his book on the Sabbath in a manner contrary to the laws of *Shabat* constitutes an infringement of his freedom of religion, an observant Jew may not claim that showing, on the Sabbath, a film in which he appears, encroaches on his freedom of religious. The petition, therefore, also fails in terms of the argument from freedom of religion.

Dorner J. disagreed with Barak J., and held that showing the film on the Sabbath would, indeed, constitute an infringement of the

19 *Dahar v. Minister of the Interior*, H.C. 448/85, P.D. 40 (2) 708.
20 *Disenchik v. Attorney General*, Cr.A. 126/62, P.D. 17, 169.
21 A. Barak, *Interpretation in Law* (Hebrew), (Tel-Aviv: 1993) 2, 688.
22 *Miron v. Minister of Labour*, H.C. 287/69, P.D. 24 (1) 337.
23 *Mitreal v. Prime Minister and Minister of Religion*, H.C. 3872/93, P.D. 47 (5) 500.
24 *Horev v. Minister of the Interior*, H.C. 5016/96; P.D. 51 (4) 1.

petitioner's right to freedom of religion. She began by adopting a more generous attitude to the petitioners than did Barak J., and pointed out that the petitioners were both young and inexperienced as far as dealing with the media was concerned. They were, indeed, genuinely unaware that the program would be shown on *Shabat,* until a chance remark by one of the producers at the end of the filming revealed this fact to them. Upon expressing their deep anxiety over this, they were promised by one of the producers that the problem would be solved. The producer was unable to carry out his promise, and the Second Channel refused both oral and written requests for a change in the scheduling of the program. The petitioners' rabbi was adamant in his insistence that if the film was shown on *Shabat,* they would be directly implicated in an act of Sabbath desecration. Dorner J. also found that it would not be too difficult for the respondents to move the film to another day, and thereby preserve their freedom of speech at no cost to the petitioners' freedom of religion.

The issue of freedom of religion is determined in accordance with the expert opinion of a religious authority; it is not up to the Court to establish the nature and scope of religious obligations.[25] This is also the position in the United States, and in the words of Burger C. J., "It is not within 'the judicial function and judicial competence' to determine whether the Amish or the Government has the proper interpretation of the Amish faith: courts are not arbiters of scriptural interpretation."[26] The petitioners' rabbi ruled that they would be personally implicated in Sabbath desecration were the film to be shown on *Shabbat,* and as their local halakhic authority (*mara deatra*), he alone is authorized to rule on whether the petitioners will be in breach of their religious obligations if the film is shown on a Saturday. Now it is true that there are more lenient rulings on this matter,[27] however, there is also a considerable body of rabbinical opinion in favor of the position taken by the petitioners' rabbi.[28]

25 H. Cohn, *The Law* (Hebrew), (Jerusalem: 1992) 525; *Shavit v. Rishon Lezion Burial Society*, C.A. 6024/70, P.D. 53 (3) 600.

26 *United States v. Lee*, 455 U.S. 707 (1982) 716. Also see *Hernandez v. Commissioner*, 490 U.S. 680 (1989) 699.

27 R. D. Stav, "Filmed on a weekday, screened on *Shabat*" (Hebrew), *Nekuda* 211 (1998), 52–53.

28 R. S.Z. Auerbach, "Repeat radio broadcasts on *Shabat*" (Hebrew), *Tehumin* 17 (1997), 13.

Dorner J. took issue with Barak J.'s argument that the essence of the petitioners' claim was that they objected to the non-halakhic conduct of the respondents, and that their individual rights to religious freedom had not been violated. This was patently wrong. The petitioners' claims do not relate to the screening of films on the Sabbath *per se*, or even the screening of the particular program for which they were interviewed. Their sole claim is that screening a film in which they appear on *Shabat* renders them Sabbath-breakers, and that is what they object to so strenuously. Forcing them to transgress the precepts of Jewish law is undoubtedly a breach of their right to freedom of religion, and not merely an attack on their religious sensibilities.[29]

As concerns the conflict between the petitioners' right to freedom of religion, and that of the respondents to freedom of expression, Dorner J. held that the correct approach to such conflicts between individual rights is to minimize, as far as possible, the infringement of the rights of all the parties involved.[30] If it is not possible to arrive at a compromise, then the right, which, if infringed, will cause the greatest damage to the individual concerned, is the one that must be allowed to prevail.[31] In the present case, it is not possible to reach a compromise between the petitioners' right to religious freedom, and that of the respondents to freedom of expression, since the former have been told in no uncertain terms by their rabbi that the screening of the film renders them Sabbath-breakers. The respondents, however, are in a position to move the film to a weekday slot. The damage to their freedom of expression is, therefore, much less serious than that which will be suffered by the petitioners in terms of their right to religious freedom.

29 The present case may be compared to two German decisions, the first of which found that the presence of a cross in court infringed the religious freedom of a Jewish lawyer (35 *BverfGE* 35), and the second struck down a state law requiring crosses to be hung on schoolroom walls, on the grounds that their presence encroaches upon the religious freedom of non-Christian students (93 *BverfGE* 1). In both cases, the religious tenets of the non-Christians made it impossible for them to go about their business in the same room as the cross. The issue was not the hanging of crosses per se, but the way in which the petitioners were affected by the presence of the crosses in their places of work and study.

30 I. Zamir and M. Sobol, "Equality before the law" (Hebrew), *Mishpat Umimshal* 5 (2000), 214–215.

31 *Lishkat Menahalei Hashkaot Beyisrael* v. Minister of Finance, H.C. 1715/97, P.D. 51 (4) 422-423; *Tnufa v. Minister of Labor and Welfare*, H.C. 450/97, P.D. 52 (2) 452.

In Dorner J.'s opinion, the temporary injunction ought to be made permanent, and the film taken off the Saturday program.

As concerns the fear for the future of Saturday TV and radio expressed by Barak J., Dorner J. pointed out that there is a clear difference between this case, and the screening of films featuring Orthodox Jews who are not aware that they are in the footage, or public figures whose images regularly appear on television on the Sabbath. The present case deals with a particular couple who agreed to participate in a particular film and did so without being aware of the possibility of its being screened on *Shabat*. A decision to shift the film to a weekday slot would apply to this type of case alone.

S. Levin J. concurred with Barak J., and judgment was given in favor of the respondents.

### 3 *When One Life Overrides Another: Separating Conjoined Twins in English and Jewish Law*

Mary and Jodie, the conjoined twins in the present case, were born at St. Mary's Hospital, Manchester, England on August 8. Mary's heart was barely functional, and she depended on Jodie's normal heart for her blood supply. The twins' physicians were unanimous in their prognosis that unless the twins were surgically separated, neither would survive for more than six months. The proposed surgery involved separating the twins' blood vessels, with the result that Mary would die within seconds of the operation. The physicians believed that Jodie's chances of surviving, and enjoying a normal life, were good enough to justify carrying out the surgery. They were also of the opinion that any delay in carrying out the operation would result in a much less favorable outcome for Jodie. The parents, who were devout Catholics, objected to the separation on religious grounds, and the matter went to the Family Division of the High Court, which overruled the wishes of the parents and permitted the surgery.

In September 2000, the Court of Appeal upheld the decision of the Family Division and also permitted the separation, notwithstanding the fact that only one twin would survive.[32] In effect, the court held that under certain circumstances, it was legally permissible to kill one innocent person to save the life of another. One of the main grounds for so

32 *Re A (Children)* 2 WLR (2001) 480.

doing was the doctrine of necessity.[33] On this doctrine, there are certain situations in which a killer may plead the defense of necessity to a charge of murder. The classic and generally uncontroversial example of necessity is self-defense. Here, the killing is justified both in terms of the attacker's intention to inflict a serious bodily injury on the intended victim, and the respect society accords the basic instinct of self-preservation. Another, more controversial, example, cited in the older works on the common law of England,[34] but specifically rejected in later works,[35] is the killing of one innocent person to save the life of another innocent person. The justification for applying the doctrine of necessity in this type of situation is of a purely objective nature, and depends upon the circumstances of the case. Typical examples of justifying circumstances are sacrificing the few for the sake of the many, and killing someone who will definitely die even if no action is taken, for the sake of saving someone who has a chance to survive. The decision of the Court of Appeal is, therefore, groundbreaking, in that it officially restores a defense that has not been part of English criminal law for some 400 years, albeit in the limited circumstances of the surgical separation of conjoined twins.

To support their departure from the previously held view regarding this type of objective necessity, the judges cited positive recommendations for its acceptance in the reports of various Law Commissions on the necessity defense, the opinions of learned writers on its application to cases similar to that of the conjoined twins and, in particular, the halakhic argument that in a case where one conjoined twin was "designated for death" by virtue of its physical inability to survive, it was permissible to kill that twin to save the life of the potentially viable one.[36] The halakhic argument was made in relation to a case decided in Philadelphia in 1977, in which the parents were Orthodox Jews, and their consent to the separation of their conjoined twins was conditional on halakhic support for the procedure, which was indeed forthcoming. The reasoning upon which the halakhic ruling was based was that one of the twins could be identified as "designated for death," and hence killing it to save the other's life was permitted. In this

33 For a recent analysis of this doctrine in the context of the criminal law, see F. McAuley and J. McCutcheon, *Criminal Liability* (Dublin: 2000), ch. 17.

34 See F. Bacon, *Elements of the Common Laws of England* (London: 1630) in Montague (ed.), *Works* (London: 1831), vol. 13, 160.

35 See the sources cited in n. 46 below.

36 See nn. 56–58 below.

respect, Jewish law played a part in expanding the doctrine of necessity in modern English criminal law, and also made an important contribution to contemporary bioethics.

## The Facts of the Case and the Decision of the Family Division of the High Court

Jodie and Mary were born connected to each other in the lower abdominal region. Each possessed a complete set of limbs and organs. Mary's heart, however, was much weaker that that of Jodie, and the medical view was that Mary was, in fact, being kept alive by Jodie's heart. Had Mary been born a singleton, she would not have survived. Mary's lungs were also much weaker than those of Jodie, and there was some evidence that her brain was less developed than that of her sister. Without surgical intervention to separate the two children, both would die within a period of about six months. The physicians did not wish to wait for a complication to occur before doing surgery, since that would greatly lessen the chances of its success. The separation of this type of conjoined twins is a long and complex procedure, entailing a much follow-up surgery and other treatments. The considered medical opinion, therefore, was to perform the operation as soon as possible.

The legal issue that gave rise to the case was the fact that Mary would die as a direct result of the separation. Her own heart was far too weak to maintain a proper blood supply, and within seconds of severing the connection between her circulatory system and Jodie's aorta, Mary would be dead. In effect, the doctors would be killing Mary in order to allow Jodie a chance to survive. This is certainly not an easy idea to countenance, from either a legal or a moral perspective. Indeed, it was not acceptable in terms of the twins' parents' religious convictions. The parents, both of whom were practicing Catholics from a small island near Malta, refused to consent to the separation, on the grounds that it conflicted with their religious beliefs. It was because of their opposition to the doctors' decision to separate that the case came to court.

The first court to hear the case was the Family Division of the High Court, which overrode the parents' wishes and held that that the separation was perfectly legal. The court reiterated the well-established principle, in both family and medical law, that the proper basis for resolving conflicts between parents and doctors over the treatment of a child is to consider the child's best interests.[37] In this case, the court found that it was in the best interests of Jodie to live. Somewhat surprisingly, it also found that it was in the best interests of Mary to die. Among the arguments used to downgrade Mary's interest in living was that because she was attached to her normal sister, her retarded development would cause her to suffer. Jodie, in expanding her own contact with the world, would pull her around. Mary's world would always be much narrower, and she would become a mere appendage of Jodie, lacking any capacity for the realization of her own much more passive will. This would result in distress and frustration on Mary's part and, as a result, it was in her best interests to die.

In terms of the criminal law issue of killing one innocent twin to save the life of the other, the judge drew an analogy to someone's being kept alive through artificial nutrition. In the latter case, the House of Lords ruled that it was permissible to disconnect an individual in a persistent vegetative state[38] from his source of artificial nutrition, if it could be shown that this course was in the best interests of the patient.[39] Similarly, it was permitted in the present case to disconnect Mary from Jodie's heart, since it was not in her best interests to remain connected.

## The Decision of the Court of Appeal and the Necessity Defense

The court began by emphasizing that conjoined twins were not to be regarded as monsters or sub-humans, but as perfectly human individuals entitled to the full protection of the criminal law. It is noteworthy that a similar approach is found in the halakha. According to R. Jacob Reischer, an early eighteenth century authority, such twins are to be regarded as full and separate individuals for all halakhic purposes.[40] R. Reischer cites a talmudic view that Adam and Eve were originally created as fully-formed conjoined individuals and only later separated.[41]

37 See *Children Act*, 1989, ch. 1, sec. 1; *Re B (A minor)* (1981) 1 WLR 1424.

38 This term is used to denote someone who has lost all brain function with the exception of the brain stem, which controls the so-called vegetative functions, i.e., breathing, regulation of heart beat, the sleep cycle, digestion and reactions to light.

39 *Airedale National Health Trust v. Bland* (1992) 1 All ER 821.

40 *Responsa Shvut Yaakov* 1:4. See J.D. Bleich, *Bioethical Dilemmas* (Hoboken: 1998), ch. 11, for a full discussion of conjoined twins in Jewish law.

41 bEruvin 18a.

Since the Bible specifically refers to them in their joined condition in the plural — "male and female did He create them... and he called their name Adam,"[42] it is evident that conjoined twins are separate individuals.

The Court of Appeals also found for the physicians, and overrode the wishes of the parents. However, the grounds for the decision were entirely different from those of the court of the first instance. Indeed, the court specifically rejected the grounds offered by the first instance judge for his decision. Regarding the application of the criterion of the child's bests interests, the Court of Appeals held that it was not up to a court of law to decide that a particular life was not worth living and that death was in that person's best interests. The only question that may legitimately be answered by a court in this type of case is whether or not the treatment being proposed is for the benefit of the patient.[43] In medical terms, it was quite clear that killing Mary would not, and could not, be of any benefit to her. On the other hand, it was in Jodie's best interests to be separated, since that was the only way she might be able to realize the prospect of long term survival. The only way of resolving this clash of best interests between two children was to "choose the lesser of the two evils and so find the least detrimental alternative."[44] Since Jodie alone possessed the potential to survive, her life and interests overrode those of her sister Mary, who, in the words of the rabbinical scholars in the Philadelphia case, was "designated for death," given that her capacity to live was "fatally compromised." The correct course, therefore, was to separate the twins.

As to the criminal issue of murder, the first instance judge was wrong in comparing the situation to that of a patient attached to an artificial respirator. There is no analogy. Artificial respiration is a medical procedure governed by medical law, which permits its removal once it is established that the procedure is no longer in the patient's best interests. It was nature that joined Mary to Jodie and made her life dependent on her sister's. Separating the twins and killing one of them

42 Genesis 5:2.

43 "The question is always whether the treatment would be worthwhile, not whether the patient's life would be worthwhile. Were one to engage in judgments of the latter sort, and to conclude that certain lives were not worth living, one would forfeit any principled basis for objecting to intentional killing" (J. Keown, "Restoring moral and intellectual shape to the law after *Bland*," 113 *Law Quarterly Review* (1997), 485).

44 *Re A*, n. 32 above, 525.

is, therefore, no different, in principle, from any other act of murder. The question that then arises is how the court justified its decision to go ahead with the separation.

According to Lord Justice Brookes, the answer lies in the above-mentioned aspect of the doctrine of necessity that justifies killing one innocent person to save the life of another, when objective circumstances dictate who will be the victim.[45] In the present case, the objective fact that justified killing Mary was that it was she who was in any event "designated to die." The separation of Jodie and Mary did not, therefore, constitute an act of murder.

However, as already observed, the use of this form of the necessity defense in the criminal law has not been part of English common law since the mid-seventeenth century. Since then, it has been specifically rejected by both learned authors[46] and leading precedents. In the seminal case of *R v. Dudley and Stephens* in 1884,[47] three mariners and a cabin boy were shipwrecked on their way to Australia. After eighteen days in an open boat, their supplies of food and water having run out, the two accused suggested killing and eating the boy in order to survive. Two days later, the boy, who at this stage was extremely weak, was killed. The three men then fed on the boy's flesh. Four days later, they were rescued. The accused were indicted for murder, the third mariner having turned Queen's evidence. Dudley and Stephens were found guilty of murder and sentenced to be "hanged by the neck until dead." They were, nevertheless, promptly pardoned by Queen Victoria, who commuted their death sentences to six months' imprisonment.[48] It is noteworthy that the Court was not prepared to accept a necessity defense, even in the form of the well-established "custom of the sea" according to which lots would be drawn to select a mariner who would be sacrificed to save the lives of the rest of the crew.[49] This approach

45 See n. 33 above.

46 See M. Hale, *Pleas of the Crown* (1763) 151; W. Blackstone, *Commentaries on the Laws of England* (1857) 4, 28.

47 (1884) 14 QBD 273.

48 For a detailed account of the facts, the trial and the aftermath, see B. Simpson, *Cannibalism and the Common Law* (Chicago: 1984).

49 See Simpson, ibid., 249 and N. Hanson, *The Custom of the Sea* (London: 1999). The practice of drawing lots has a biblical precedent, see Jonah 1:7. This practice was, apparently, fully condoned by the Admiralty and the Board of Trade prior to the case, and it is noteworthy that Dudley and Stephens made no attempt to conceal their cannibalism. It would appear that the main reason the case came to court was to discourage a practice that did not sit well with Victorian moral sensibilities.

was concisely summed up by Justice Cardozo, who wrote that there is no "principle of human jettison" in the common law.[50] The precedent in *Dudley and Stephens* was followed by the House of Lords in 1987 in the leading case of *R v. Howe*.[51]

It is also important to note that the Queen did pardon the sailors. Dudley eventually made his way to Australia, settling in Sydney. Clearly, the killing of the cabin boy was not regarded by the public as a heinous act, and the necessity doctrine did, indeed, manifest itself at the level of royal clemency, even if it did not find expression in the law. As one commentator pointed out, "the most persistent English attitude to the problem raised by the necessity plea — intellectually unsatisfying though it may be — is that hard cases are best dealt with by the prerogative of mercy."[52]

In support of his departure from precedent, Lord Justice Brookes cited a number of suggestions made by various Law Commissions to the effect that this type of necessity ought to be recognized as a defense in special circumstances, such as, where many lives could be saved by killing one individual, or in a medical situation of the type under discussion in the conjoined twins case.[53] He also referred to academic writers and, in particular, to the discussion of a case in which a ferry capsized in the North Sea and a group of survivors waited in the water to climb a ladder to safety. A young man froze halfway up the ladder, probably as a result of a combination of cold and fear, and no one was able to continue climbing to safety. Realizing that they could not last much longer in the icy waters, one of the survivors, an ex-soldier, pushed the unfortunate youth off the ladder to certain death. As a result of his action, the rest the group survived. In the opinion of the academic writers, the ex-soldier's action did not constitute murder under the common law, since it was justifiable in terms of the necessity defense.[54] These writers also sought to distinguish the ferry case from that of the shipwrecked mariners. In the latter case, Lord Justice Coleridge had based his opposition to the necessity defense on two

50 *Law and Literature and Other Essays and Addresses* (NY: 1931), 113.

51 (1987) 1 AC 417.

52 P. Glazebrook, "The necessity plea in English criminal law," *Cambridge Law Journal* (1972a), 118–119.

53 See *A Criminal Code for England and Wales*, 1989, Law Commission no. 177, 1, 4(4), 45c; *Offences Against the Person and General Principles*, 1993, Law Commission no. 218, 35:6.

54 See J. Smith, *Justification and Excuse in the Criminal Law* (London: 1989), 77–78; A. Ashworth, *Principles of Criminal Law* (Oxford: 1999), 153–154.

main arguments. The first was that there was no objective reason that necessitated choosing the cabin boy rather than another sailor. The second was the threat to the principle of the value of human life posed by a lenient decision.[55] Neither of these arguments applied in the ferry case. There was a clear, objective reason for causing the death of the frozen youth, and the circumstances were so unusual that a lenient decision could not be said to be a threat to the value of human life and its preservation. Lord Justice Brookes applied the same reasoning in the conjoined twins case. He began with the halakhic concept that Mary was "designated for death," and went on to argue that her killing was an objectively-justifiable necessity. He relied on the highly unusual nature of the case to avoid any charge that his decision would result in a lowering of the value of human life.

Lord Justice Ward chose a different line of argument to justify the separation. In his view, not intervening to save Jodie's life was just as much a matter of murder as cutting the aorta that provided Mary's lifeblood. Murder may, after all, be carried out by omission as well as commission. This approach, however, led him to the conclusion that, if, in a hypothetical case, parents at the gates of a concentration camp were offered the possibility of saving one of their two children, they would be guilty of murder if they refused to choose and entered the gates with both their offspring. The judge immediately pointed out that the parents would not actually be prosecuted, but in terms of strict legal logic, they would still be murderers. This conclusion follows logically from Lord Justice Ward's approach. It is, however, rather harsh, and his reference to the non-prosecution of such parents indicates that he himself is aware of the emotional harshness of his position. In the present writer's view, therefore, Lord Justice Brooke's necessity-based approach is the more attractive. Now, Lord Justice Ward also used the notion of Mary's being "designated for death" in his judgment, and it is to a full discussion of this concept and its halakhic basis that the following section is devoted.

## Separating Conjoined Twins in Jewish Law: The 1977 Philadelphia Case

In this case, conjoined twins with joined hearts were born to an orthodox Jewish couple living in Lakewood, New Jersey. One of the twins

55 In the words of the Home Secretary, Sir William Harcourt, "We cannot give carte blanche to every ship's captain, when he runs low on provisions, to eat his cabin boy."

had a normal four-chamber heart, whereas her sister's heart had only two chambers.[56] As in our case, one heart was sustaining two babies, and without the separation and sacrifice of the weaker sibling, neither twin would survive. The physician in charge of the case was Dr. Everett Koop, who was later to become Surgeon General of the United States. He recommended separation, and assembled a large team of experts for what was then, and still is, a highly complex and uncertain procedure. The operation was due to be performed at the Children's Hospital in Philadelphia. The parents, however, would not consent to the separation without halakhic approval, and the medical team waited until the late R. Moses Feinstein, the leading halakhic authority in North America at the time, issued a ruling to the effect that the procedure was halakhically permitted. The operation was a success, but unfortunately, the surviving twin died some two months after the separation from hepatitis contracted from a blood transfusion.[57]

R. Feinstein did not leave a written responsum detailing his decision, but the halakhic cases upon which he based it were widely reported at the time,[58] and his son-in-law, R. Moses Tendler, published a reconstruction of his late father-in-law's reasoning.[59] R. Bleich also discusses the details of R. Feinstein's ruling in his article on conjoined twins in Jewish law.[60] We will begin with an account of the two cases on which R. Feinstein's decision was based, and proceed to offer our own analysis of that decision.

The first is a talmudic case concerning a group of defenseless travelers faced with a choice between certain death for the entire company, or the survival of the majority at the cost of handing over one group member to be killed. The ruling in this case is that if a victim is named by those threatening the group, that is, is "designated for death," then that individual may be handed over.[61] This is the source of the concept of "designation for death" that the English judges found so useful in

56 For purposes of the decision it was assumed that the defective heart could be assigned to one twin, and the non-defective one to the other, and there was no question of a common organ shared by two individuals, see Bleich, n. 40 above, 297.

57 See D. Drake, "The twins decision: one must die so one can live," *Philadelphia Inquirer*, October 6, 1977.

58 See Drake, ibid.; G. Annas, "Siamese twins: killing one to save the other," *Hastings Center Report* 17 (1987), 27–28.

59 See R. Moses Tendler, *Responsa of Rav Moshe Feinstein*, vol. 1 (NY: 1996), 209.

60 N. 40 above.

61 Tosefta, Terumot 7:20; jTerumot 8:4.

dealing with the separation of Mary and Jodie. The second case is hypothetical, involving a pilot who ejects from a burning plane and successfully opens his parachute. As he is sailing to the ground, a second pilot, whose parachute failed to open, passes him and grabs hold of his leg. The parachute is only capable of bringing one person safely to the ground, and if both of them maintain their grip, neither will survive. According to R. Feinstein, the first pilot is permitted to dislodge the second and send him hurtling to certain death in order to save his own life. The English judges appear to have understood this case to be a variation on the theme of "designation for death," and another illustration of the principle that in certain cases, Jewish law recognizes that one life does, indeed, override another. Our conclusion will be that the two cases deal with different aspects of the problem, and both are necessary for a complete understanding of the halakhic approach to this type of tragic choice.

Both cases, however, require deeper analysis to grasp their proper significance for the halakhic position on the separation of conjoined twins. With regard to the case of the travelers, there is a view in the talmudic sources that even if a particular individual is "designated for death," he may not be given up unless he is also deserving of death, that is, guilty of a capital crime. This view is adopted by Maimonides in his codification of the halakha,[62] and followed by many authorities.[63] Clearly, in both the Philadelphia case and the case dealt with by the Court of Appeal, the weaker twin was not guilty of any capital crime, and the relevance of the case of the travelers is, therefore, questionable. This problem, however, may be resolved by following the opinion of R. Menahem Hameiri and creating a new category of designation for death, defined in terms of the absence of physical viability rather than the existence of a judicial death sentence. In commenting on the case of the travelers, R. Hameiri states that in his view, "it is quite evident that if one of the members of the group is stricken with a fatal medical condition, then that individual may be sacrificed for the sake of the rest of the company."[64] Under Jewish law, a person whose medical prognosis is certain death within twelve months is known as a *treifa*. There is no death penalty for murder of a *treifa*,[65] but it is nevertheless a serious

62 *Code*, Laws concerning the Fundamental Principles of the Torah 5:5.

63 See *Bayit Hadash*, YD 157; *Turei Zahav*, YD 157:7.

64 *Beit Habehira*, Sanhedrin 74a.

65 Sanhedrin 78b; Maimonides, *Code*, Laws concerning Murder and the Preservation of Life 1:8.

moral offense punishable by divine sanction.[66] However, where there is a sound moral justification for sacrificing a *treifa* for the sake of saving viable life, then the halakha would appear to permit it, the case of the travelers being an instance where there is such a justification.[67] The same may be said of the case of the conjoined twins. The weaker, non-viable twin may be justifiably sacrificed for the sake of saving her potentially viable sister. In both the Philadelphia and the English cases, the twin with the defective heart has less than twelve months to live, and is a *treifa*. In both cases, therefore, the life of the *treifa* may be given up for the sake of her potentially viable sibling.

There is, however, another complication. The case of the traveler involves handing over an individual, not direct killing. In the conjoined twins cases, the issue is the direct killing of one sibling in order to save the other. Once again, it would appear that the case of the travelers is not analogous to the conjoined twins situation.[68] To resolve this problem, we must turn to the parachute case, and it is probably for this reason that R. Feinstein used both cases in his decision. In the parachute case, the second pilot is, in halakhic terminology, a pursuer or *rodef*. Under Jewish law, it is permitted to kill, in a direct manner, anyone who is pursuing someone else with intent to kill. The threat to the pursued person must be direct and immediate, and all other means of preventing the killing must have been tried prior to taking the pursuer's life.[69] There are, however, situations in which the law of the *rodef* applies even where the pursuer does not intend to kill the person being pursued. Maimonides, applying it to therapeutic abortion, justifies killing a foetus for the sake of saving the mother on the grounds that the foetus is "like a pursuer threatening its mother's life."[70] Thus, therapeutic abortion comes within the ambit of the law of the pursuer, notwithstanding the fact that the foetus has no intention whatsoever of killing its mother. The same, presumably, goes for the conjoined twins. The weaker one is considered "like a pursuer" in relation to the stronger

66 Maimonides, ibid. Also see D. Sinclair, *Tradition and the Biological Revolution* (Edinburgh: 1989), ch. 3.

67 See Sinclair, ibid.

68 This problem is raised by the commentators; see *Responsa Noda Biyehuda* 2, HM #59.

69 Deuteronomy 25:12; mSanhedrin 8:7; bSanhedrin 72b; *Code*, Laws concerning Murder and the Preservation of Life 1:6; Elon, n. 10 above, 474.

70 *Code*, Laws concerning Murder and the Preservation of Life 1:9.

one, and may therefore be killed in a direct manner in order to keep her sister alive.

There is, however, an obvious distinction between the two cases. According to the halakha, a foetus is not a legal person until birth.[71] The reason for dispensing with the element of intention in relation to a foetus, therefore, is that its mother is a full person under Jewish law, whereas the foetus is not.[72] Hence, it would be halakhically acceptable to make the life of the foetus subordinate to that of its mother, even without the pursuer argument. There is no halakhic basis for dispensing with the element of intention in the parachute case, since both pilots are legal persons under Jewish law. The parachute case, therefore, does not appear to be capable of providing a complete solution to the question raised above regarding the direct killing of the weaker conjoined twin to save her potentially viable sibling.

To resolve this, we must return to the case of the travelers. In (the Meiri's variant of) that case, the rationale for giving up the party being sought was his lack of viability. It could be argued that in the parachute case, the second pilot is treated as a pursuer, notwithstanding the absence of any intention on his part to kill the first pilot, because he is not viable and would have been dead had it not been for the first pilot's parachute. The two cases complement each other, and both are necessary to understand the resolution of the conjoined twins issue. The case of the travelers provides the rationale for sacrificing the non-viable twin for the sake of her viable sister, and the parachute case illustrates how the direct killing mandated by the law of the *rodef* can be applied to the case of the twins.

Both cases are necessary for a full understanding of the halakhic approach to the separation of twins conjoined in such a way that one must die so that the other may live. The major theme in the halakhic discussion is the notion that the one who is "designated for death" by purely objective circumstances may be given up to save his or her potentially viable sibling. In this respect, the Court of Appeal certainly applied the halakhic principle appropriately in a legally complex and emotionally wrenching case.

71 Rashi, bSanhedrin 72a; Ramban, bNida 44b; *Beit Habehira* 72b; *Responsa Radbaz* 1, #695.

72 R. Hayim Halevi, *Novellae,* Laws concerning Murder and the Preservation of Life 1:9.

# PART THREE

# SURVEY OF RECENT LITERATURE

# SURVEY OF RECENT LITERATURE

**Contributors**: Stephen M. Passamaneck (SMP), an anonymous editorial board member, and the following students from the J. Reuben Clark Law School, Brigham Young University, who provided abstracts, under the coordination of Prof. J.W. Welch: D. Belnap, V.A.G. Celaya, T.R. Christiansen, W.R. Dennert, K.H. Flindt, D.K. Geilman, S. Lambert, M.R. Mumford, M.L. Nielsen, M.L. Quist, S.M. Setzer, R.S. Woodbury.

## BIBLICAL LAW

1755. David Instone Brewer, "Deuteronomy 24:1–4 and the origin of the Jewish divorce certification," *Journal of Jewish Studies* 49 (1998). — The author carefully analyzes the biblical pericope in light of both early rabbinic material on the text of the instrument of divorce and Ancient Near Eastern laws and institutions pertaining to "divorce documents." He concludes that the passage is understandable in the social and literary context of the second millennium BCE. A husband who had abandoned his wife and children might at any time appear and reclaim them. This right to reclaim was occasionally relinquished in marriage or (less frequently) divorce documents. The biblical version of Ancient Near Eastern divorce law made this relinquishment of a right to reclaim mandatory. The divorcee was then absolutely free to remarry.

SMP

1756. R.G. Kratz, "Der Dekalog im Exodusbuch," *Vetus Testamentum* 44 (1994), 205–238. — This article demonstrates how comparison of the Decalogue found in Exodus 20 and Deuteronomy 5 with singular commandments given by various prophets may be useful in reconstructing the original Decalogue. Kratz focuses primarily on stylistic and grammatical evidence from the Hebrew Bible, observing that the Decalogue can be organized according to "*Gottesrecht*" and "*Menschenrecht*," and presenting Hebraic stylistic and tense examples supporting this division of the tablets.

K.H. Flindt

1757. B.M. Levinson, "Recovering the lost original meaning of ולא תכסה עליו (Deut. 13:9)," *Journal of Biblical Literature* 115 (1996), 601–620. — Levinson argues that the current understanding of ולא תכסה עליו as "nor shall you conceal/shield him" in Deuteronomy 13:9 does not fully express the meaning of the כסה in the *piel* + עַל. Noting the internal inconsistency in this verse, as well as the origin of the present understanding of this phrase, Levinson suggests a new translation by analyzing the other attestations of כסה in the *piel* + על in the Hebrew Bible and related legal terminology found in Hittite and Neo-Assyrian treaties. He concludes that the phrase should best be rendered as "nor shall you condone him."

D.K. Geilman

1758. T. Meacham, "The missing daughter: Leviticus 18 and 20," *Zeitschrift für die Alttestamentliche Wissenschaft* (1997), 254–259. — Laws prohibiting incestuous relationships are most inclusive in Leviticus 18 and 20; however, in each of these chapters there is an obvious omission: there is no specific prohibition against relations between father and daughter. Meacham asks: "why was the most obvious incest situation not explicitly prohibited"? After reviewing the "incomplete" rationales that have been given by others, Meacham proposes that the incest lists are a "type of apologetic literature, a reaction against the actions of the patriarchs, heads of tribes, and leaders of the nation." Because "there are no instances of father–daughter incest among [these Israelite leaders]," Meacham suggests, there was no "need to address that prohibition in Leviticus." According to Meacham, the only biblical account of father–daughter incest is that of Lot and his daughters in Genesis 19:30–38. The absence of father–daughter incest in the Leviticus lists, Meacham concludes, not only "allowed the redactors of the book of Genesis to use it as a form of denigration of their enemies, Moab and Ammon," but also "reflects an internal Jewish polemic between the priestly families seeking to control the people and the Davidic line which was blemished by several fruitful but forbidden sexual liaisons."

M.R. Mumford

1759. C. Patton, "'I Myself gave them laws that were not good': Ezekiel 20 and the Exodus traditions," *Journal for the Study of the Old Testament* 69 (1996), 73–90. — Patton analyzes Ezekiel's use of the Exodus motif to argue that the exile of Israel was a result of the sins of the exiles themselves, and not of their parents. The Exodus motif includes elements of sojourn, deliverance, wilderness and conquest found in pre-exilic Israelite traditions. The author contends that the law of child sacrifice, presented as part of Israelite tradition, was given by YHWH as punishment for the Israelites' sins in order to guarantee the people's ultimate destruction while preserving YHWH's righteousness. Laws in the book of Ezekiel that resemble those in the Holiness Code and the Covenant Code attest to the assertion that the author of Ezekiel knew some of the legal corpus of pre-exilic Israel. Patton asserts that the law codes in Ezekiel most closely relate to the Holiness Code but also resemble the Deuteronomic tradition. In chapters 40–48, Ezekiel is led to a high mountain where he receives a plan of sanctuary to take back to the people, as Moses did. Major elements in this vision include the permanence of the restoration, indicating YHWH's intention never to leave again, and a complete reorganization of Israelite society.

M.L. Quist

1760. C. Schroeder, "'A Love Song': Psalm 45 in the light of Ancient Near Eastern marriage texts," *Catholic Biblical Quarterly* 58 (1996), 417–432. — In this article, Schroeder divides Psalm 45 into two strophes, and, after comparing the second strophe with other ancient Near Eastern marriage texts, concludes that the psalm is not so much a description of legal aspects of the king's marriage as it is a description of the activities immediately preceding its consummation. This is further emphasized by the series of rituals associated with the consummation: (1) the anointing with the "oil of gladness"; (2) the instruction given by the mother-in-law; and (3) the procession to the palace. This strophe, when paired with the first, which concerns the king's fortunes in war, is used by the writer to show how God has validated and favored his servant, the king, and guaranteed the future of the royal dynasty.

D. Belnap

1761. J. Watts, "The legal characterization of God in the Pentateuch," *Hebrew Union College Annual* 67 (1996), 1–14. — Watts discusses the character attributes of YHWH that can be derived from YHWH's speeches in the Pentateuch concerning YHWH's giving of commandments, the covenant relationship between Israel and God, and the content of YHWH's law. Just as Mesopotamian law codes illustrated the lawgiver's right to rule (because the laws are just), so too the laws of the Pentateuch depict God as the ideal judge and ruler. Through the laws found in the Pentateuch, God is established implicitly as king, legislator, judge and executive. Contradiction among divine commands allows God to be the "instigator of change within law," thus solidifying judicial principles. God is interpreter, giver and reformer of law;

still, YHWH shares administration with humans who are obligated to meditate and use reason when dealing with legal matters.

M.L. Nielsen

1762. J.W. Watts, "The legal characterization of Moses in the rhetoric of the Pentateuch," *Journal of Biblical Literature* 117 (1998), 415–426. — Watts analyzes the legal characterization of Moses in the Pentateuch to explain the different voices found in the text. He argues that Moses is portrayed in the Pentateuch as a type of the ideal king, prophet and scribe of ancient Israel. To support these assertions, Watts compares the statements ascribed to Moses to those attributed to King David, Hosea and Isaiah.

T.R. Christiansen

1763. G.J. Wenham, "The gap between law and ethics in the Bible," *Journal of Jewish Studies* 48 (1997), 17–29. — Wenham asserts that failing to distinguish between three different "worlds" — the world of the writers, the world of the law, and the world of the actors themselves — in biblical texts results in misreading of the texts concerning ethics. The author describes the law as a minimum standard of behavior below which a person cannot fall without incurring society's intervention. Ethics, according to Wenham, is more than keeping the law: in biblical texts, ethics is often independent of the law. Wenham addresses the legal and ethical implications of idolatry, homicide and adultery, which illustrate the demanding nature of biblical ethics, and are set out most clearly in the opening chapters of Genesis and in the wisdom literature.

M.L. Quist

1764. R. Westbrook, "The Deposit Law of Exodus 22, 6–12," *Zeitschrift für die Alttestamentliche Wissenschaft* 106 (1994), 390–403. — In this article, Westbrook finds the laws in Exodus 22:6–12 dealing with bailor/bailee relationships to be coherent, with no need for interpolation or editing. Verses 6–8 deal with goods lost from the bailee's house. Westbrook asserts that verse 8 is not, as some argue, an oath imposed on a single party and the sole factor in deciding the outcome of a case, but more likely an oracular decision, involving both parties. Conversion by a bailee differs from ordinary theft: verse 8 specifies double repayment in all cases, while theft laws in the Covenant Code indicate that the punishment depends on the type of chattel stolen. Exodus 22:9–12 describes the responsibility of a herdsman/bailee herding another's animals. Verse 11 clearly makes the herdsman strictly liable for theft; verse 12 just as clearly exempts him from loss due to wild animals, unless he cannot provide the remnant of the animal as proof. Westbrook suggests that verses 9 and 10 describe a situation where the animal has been lost and the herdsman/bailee's defense is that the owner secretly took back his own animal and is pressing a fraudulent suit. Here there is a claim (the herdsman/bailee took the animal) and a counterclaim (the bailor took his own animal), each of which is settled separately by the exculpatory oath procedure.

S.M. Setzer

1765. R. Westbrook, "Riddles in Deuteronomic law," in G. Braulik (ed.), *Bundesdokument und Gesetz* (Herders Biblische Studien, 1995), 159–174. — This article explores the collection of special laws in Deuteronomy 12–26 and suggests that classification structures used in other ancient legal codes, such as chronological sequence, status of individuals in society, and the traditions of ancient scientific literature, may be used to understand the organizational structure of Deuteronomy 12–26. Unifying these ancient classification structures is the idea that it is difficult to categorize ancient legal codes according to modern legal methodology.

S. Lambert

1766. M. White, "Naboth's vineyard and Jehu's coup: the legitimation of a dynastic extermination," *Vetus Testamentum* 44 (1994), 66–76. — In I Kings 21:19 and 21:21, Elijah prophesies that Ahab will be punished severely for his murder of Naboth: Ahab will die and his progeny will be destroyed. White contends that I Kings 21:21–29 is an integral part of the story running through I Kings 21 and II Kings 9 (Jehu's destruction of Ahab's line) and is not a Deuteronomistic interpolation. Rather, the "fulfillment" of Ahab's personal death in I Kings 22 is itself Deuteronomistic and actually refers to a later king. The differences between the story in I Kings 21:1–16 and its retelling in II Kings 9:25–26 correspond directly to the parallels between Ahab's murder of Naboth as recounted in I Kings and David's murder of Uriah. White posits that I Kings 21 and II Kings 9:25–26 are an integrated whole written at the time of Jehu's reign to justify the destruction of Ahab's line by showing that Ahab's sin corresponded to David's.

S.M. Setzer

## HALAKHIC LITERATURE

**a** Medical/Bioethics

1767. J. David Bleich, "Survey of recent halakhic periodical literature," *Tradition* 32:2 (1998). — The author briefly reviews the halakhic problems associated with surrogate motherhood, which he believes to be a misnomer, since a surrogate is in fact a natural mother. The problems noted are infertility and the requirement of procreation, artificial insemination, semen procurement, artificial insemination and paternity, suppression of maternal identity, and baby selling. The author concludes by criticizing legislation in the United States that holds sperm donors immune to later claims, e.g., for support, from progeny from this sperm. If surrogacy is now to be discouraged, the laws should be modified to remove such immunity from persons who have entered into either written or oral surrogacy agreements.

SMP

1768. J. David Bleich, "Survey of recent halakhic periodical literature," *Tradition* 32:3 (1998). — The author discusses at length the matter of cloning, from a halakhic perspective, and also draws attention to general problems involved in cloning. On his view, tampering with natural processes is not part of the biblical mandate to fill the earth and conquer it. Thus, society has both the right and the obligation to regulate cloning experimentation so that only societal benefit, and not harm, may accrue from such an undertaking.

SMP

1769. J. David Bleich, "Survey of recent halakhic periodical literature," *Tradition* 34:1 (2000). — In light of the growing possibility of genetic screening presaged by the human genome project, the author calls for a destigmatization of genetic testing, which has become feared in the Orthodox community. He asserts that as the science of genetics develops, more and more people will be identified as carriers of links to disease or disability. These persons are not, in the author's opinion, to be stigmatized. He writes that there is a point beyond which the future remains unknown, and one cannot prevent the unpreventable. At that point one needs to recognize that over-concern and over-protection for oneself and one's offspring is a very dangerous path to follow.

SMP

1770. John D. Loike and Avram Steinberg, "Human cloning and halakhic perspectives," *Tradition* 32:3 (1998). — The authors briefly review the scientific background relating to human cloning, and raise some of the halakhic problems attendant upon it, such as whether clones would be halakhically human or would have the status of *golem*, and who the "parents" of a cloned child would be. In view of the continuing advance of technology in this area, and the serious halakhic problems lurking behind this advance, the authors call for an international committee, composed of rabbinical and scientific experts, to explore and clarify the legal issues, so that the foremost rabbinical authorities could then go on to answer the complex questions raised.

SMP

1771. Edward Reichman, "The halakhic chapter of ovarian transplantation," *Tradition* 33:1 (1998). — The author, an assistant professor of emergency medicine, opens a new and most interesting area of medical halakha heretofore largely omitted from medical-halakhic research: the connection between medical history and medical halakha. The author maintains that although halakhic principles have not altered from age to age (a proposition he basically accepts without question), scientific understanding has clearly evolved, and it is thus important to understand earlier rabbinic sources on medical-halakhic topics in the light of their contemporaneous medical-historical world. Employing a contextualized comparative approach to the assessment of medical-halakhic texts, he explores issues arising from modern reproductive technologies and infertility.

SMP

1772. Fred Rosner and David Weinberger, "Jewish concerns about gifts to physicians and drug companies," *Tradition* 32:3 (1998). — The authors contend that the gifts and favors that drug companies offer physicians may well involve serious halakhic problems, including taking bribes, deceit and unfair competition. The halakhic literature does not presently have much to say about these specific matters, which are clearly major concerns in the ethical conduct of physicians, hospitals, and the like.

SMP

### b Marriage and Divorce

1773. J. David Bleich, "Survey of recent halakhic periodical literature," *Tradition* 33:1 (1998). — The author critiques three arguments that claim that *agunot* may have their marriages annulled by declaring them based on *kidushei taut*. Although on the author's view finding a solution to the plight of *agunot* is "an imperative," he disapproves of this particular approach, and, apparently, the court that proposed it, which is composed largely of individuals not recognized by Prof. Bleich as expert in this sensitive area of halakha.

SMP

1774. J. David Bleich, "Survey of recent halakhic periodical literature," *Tradition* 33:2 (1999). — The author examines the concept of *derekh kidushin* as an alternate approach to actual marriage in the modern context of relaxed moral standards. The examination is by way of continued critique of an article by Prof. Meir Feldman, which argued that a relationship *derekh kidushin* would be tantamount to a marriage yet not require a *get* in the event it was dissolved.

SMP

c Professional Ethics

1775. J. David Bleich, "Survey of recent halakhic periodical literature," *Tradition* 33:3 (1999). — The author examines the halakhic problems raised by a late 1998 New York State Supreme Court ruling in which, inter alia, a rabbi was held liable for damages resulting from the violation of a congregant's confidence. There is a detailed review of confidentiality as it appears in the halakha, and a careful exploration of the civil law clergy-penitent privilege with respect to rabbis. The author holds that in some situations a rabbi, for reasons of conscience, will need to reveal a confidence. At length, a solution to the matter is proposed: a suggestion that states in which a confidentiality privilege is held only by the congregant, so that only he or she may waive it, amend their codes to allow a member of the clergy a similar privilege of waiver, though the clergy are not compelled to testify. The author argues that such an extension of waiver would better accord with the original intent of the privilege of confidential communication, which, in his opinion, was intended to protect religious liberty of both priests and penitents rather than to foster free communication between them.

SMP

1776. Aaron Levine, "False goodwill and halakha," *Tradition* 34:1 (2000). — The author uses a case study method to explore various ethical issues faced by rabbis in their professional duties, which require an atmosphere of good will that the rabbi attempts to engender in various ways. The problem with respect to good will is that it may be produced by "false impressions." The author attempts to draw the parameters for generating good will, which is then the "proper entitlement" of the person who created it. A further matter considered is when and why even properly generated good will must be eschewed.

SMP

**d** Other

1777. A. Sagi and Z. Zohar, *Circles of Jewish Identity, a Study in Halakhic Literature* (Hebrew), Tel Aviv: 2000. The authors analyze the halakhic problem of the legal status of wine of a person known to desecrate the Sabbath, a problem addressed throughout the ages. They seek to reveal the different underlying attitudes to the question of whether Jewish identity is determined by ethnic or by religious factors.

## HELLENISTIC AND ROMAN PERIOD

1778. Robert Brody, "Evidence of divorce by Jewish women?" *Journal of Jewish Studies* 50 (1999). — In this brief article the author takes issue with the opinion of Hannah M. Cutton and Elisha Qimron that a passage in a Dead Sea papyrus indicates that a Jewish woman gave a bill of divorce to her husband, contrary to the overwhelming evidence in other early material that only the husband could issue the instrument of dissolution. The author interprets the clause in question so that word "from me" in the bill of divorce refers to the husband, not the wife. The author does not assert that his understanding of the text is the only possible one, but that his reading, coupled with the evidence from the cultural context, argues strongly against a revisionist understanding of the passage.

SMP

1779. R. Goldenberg, "The Septuagint ban on cursing the gods," *Journal for the Study of Judaism in the Persian, Hellenistic and Roman Period* 28 (1997), 381–389. — In this article, Goldenberg draws upon the writings of Philo to explain the translation of Exodus 22:27 in the Septuagint as "Do not speak ill of gods." Philo gives three possible reasons the Jews, who were traditionally against idolatry, promoted this ban: (1) those who malign beings whom others consider divine may lead those people to malign the true divine being; (2) the name "God" deserves respect no matter how it is used, thus this commandment is not intended only to avert blasphemy, but irreverent talk in general; and (3) speaking positively of others' gods will induce them to praise the true God. These explanations lead Goldenberg to conclude that the translation of the Septuagint served in part to convince Gentiles living near Alexandria of Jewish goodwill toward them. The small amount of commentary on this verse suggests that the project soon failed and was abandoned, as evidenced in the mockery of idols found in later Rabbinic literature.

D. Belnap

1780. E. Nodet, "Josephus and the Pentateuch," *Journal for the Study of Judaism in the Persian, Hellenistic and Roman Period* 27 (1997), 154–194. — Nodet evaluates Josephus' role as a first-century source of information on the Bible and concludes that Josephus most likely used a Hebrew version of the Pentateuch from the sacred library, though the copy probably was put at his disposal in a much less impressive manner than Josephus suggests. Though Nodet places Josephus in an honorable position among early sources of information about the Bible, he admits that Josephus used sloppy paraphrasing and often boosted his "own usual vanity."

V.A.G. Celaya

1781. S. Pearce, "Josephus as interpreter of biblical law: the representation of the high court of Deut. 17:8–12 according to *Jewish Antiquities* 4.128," *Journal of Jewish Studies* 46 (1995), 30–42. — Pearce analyzes the apparent discrepancy between Josephus' description of the high court in *Jewish Antiquities* and the biblical description of the court in Deut. 17:8–12. Josephus states that the high court is composed of "the chief priest and the prophet and the senate." According to the biblical text, however, the court is only composed of two elements: the "Levitical priests" and "the judge who will be in those days." Pearce asserts that because Josephus desired to leave the law "written as [Moses] left it" and wanted his readers to "learn what was the nature of our laws from the first," Josephus' high court is to be understood in terms of an ancient model attributed to Moses, comprising the High Priest Eleazar, Joshua the prophet, and the elders. Pearce describes these as "ideal members of an ideal constitution on the Mosaic pattern." The fact that Josephus does not name Eleazar or Joshua, Pearce concludes, "may be motivated by the desire to represent this body as valid for a timeless present."

M.R. Mumford

1782. C. Werman, "The rules of consuming and covering the blood in priestly and rabbinic Law," *Revue de Qumran* 16 (1995), 621–636. — Scholars have commented that the Book of Jubilees, the Temple Scroll, the Aramaic Levi Document, and the Damascus Covenant all devote special attention to the laws of consuming and covering blood in ritual ceremony. However, Werman believes this subject has not yet been considered deeply enough. The author demonstrates the profound legal conflict between the rabbinic and priestly views on the subject of eating and covering blood. Under priestly law the soul is in the blood, so blood must be treated with reverence. According to Jubilees, a person who eats blood commits a crime on a par with murder and should be sentenced to death. In contrast, while rabbinic law prohibits the consumption of blood, it imposes the penalty of being cut off from the people only in specific circumstances. Jubilees emphasizes the requirement that all blood be put on the altar to cover it; in rabbinic law, however, only the blood of venison and birds is covered. These opposing religious outlooks may be explained by the different approaches to be found in the Bible itself, in Leviticus 17 and Deuteronomy 12.

W.R. Dennert

## NEW TESTAMENT

1783. J.A. Glancy, "Obstacles to slaves' participation in the Corinthian church," *Journal of Biblical Literature* 117 (1998), 481–501. — Calling into question Paul's assertion that the gospel message breaks down walls between slaves and the free (1 Cor. 12:13; Gal. 3:28; cf. Col. 3:11), Glancy argues that Paul's teachings on sexuality in 1 Corinthians 5–7 would have complicated and likely even prevented slaves' participation in the early Christian community. Relying on ancient literary texts, manumission inscriptions, tax codes, contracts and anecdotes, as well as recent scholarship on the subject, Glancy concludes that Greco-Roman masters in the first century BCE had extensive control over the sexual behavior of their slaves, making contradictory Paul's statements that servile status was no impediment to full fellowship within the Christian community and that the only sexual relations tolerated by that community were those within the bonds of marriage. Admitting that the New Testament is silent as to the sexual obligations of slavery, and that one cannot know precisely how Paul responded to the situation of slaves, Glancy nevertheless encourages contemporary scholars and readers to carefully reconsider these issues.

R.S. Woodbury

## TALMUDIC PERIOD

1784. S. Valler, *Women in Jewish Society in the Talmudic Period* (Hebrew), Tel Aviv: 2000. This study seeks evidence of a liberal attitude toward women in the public sphere and in social life, and with respect to their status in court and their involvement in the world of knowledge and information, in the talmudic period. Based upon the facts (cases) and stories in the Talmudim, it uses a rigorous philological methodology to arrive at its conclusions, which are cautious.

STYLE SHEET

# STYLE SHEET

In preparing your manuscript, please conform to the following guidelines. Manuscripts not so prepared will be edited by JLA staff or returned for revision.

Please provide a line or two of information about yourself, such as an institutional affiliation, before the first footnote.

Manuscripts should be submitted in hard copy and by e-mail; submissions should be in Word 2000 or less, or WordPerfect 2000 or less. Papers should be double-spaced (text and footnotes).

All papers are to be submitted in English. Hebrew should be transliterated wherever possible, as follows:

| | | | |
|---|---|---|---|
| alef | a | lamed | l |
| bet | b | mem | m |
| vet | v | nun | n |
| gimel | g | samekh | s |
| dalet | d | ayin | a |
| hei (pronounced) | h | pei | p |
| vav | v | fei | f |
| zayin | z | tzadi | tz |
| het | h | kuf | k |
| tet | t | reish | r |
| yod | y | shin | sh |
| kaf | k | sin | s |
| khaf | kh | tav | t |

| | |
|---|---|
| patah; kamatz | a |
| hirik | i |
| shva (pronounced) | e |
| segol | e |
| shuruk; kubutz | u |
| holam | o |
| tzeire | ei |

No diacriticals, apostrophes, hyphens, doubling of consonants or capitalization should be used as elements of the transliteration or to indicate prefixes and the definite article.

These transliteration guidelines are not intended to apply to papers addressing linguistic or philological issues.

Names should be spelled according to accepted usage, and not transliterated or otherwise altered, thus R. Moses Isserles (Rema), R. Elijah b. Solomon, Mizrachi Organization, Kiryas Joel.

Authorized Version abbreviations for books of the Bible, listed in dictionaries and style guides such as *The Chicago Manual of Style,* should be used. In referring to the Talmud, tractate names should not be abbreviated. m, b or j prefixed to the tractate name should be used to indicate whether the Mishnah, the Babylonian Talmud or the Jerusalem Talmud is being referred to.

## CITATION STYLE

Hebrew titles should be translated into English. Where an English translation of the title is given in the original, please provide it. If no English title is given, please provide both the (transliterated) Hebrew title and a translation, and indicate to us that the translation is yours.

## HALAKHIC LITERATURE

*Beit Yosef,* OH 156, YD 147.
Maimonides, *Code,* Laws concerning Robbery and Lost Property 11:1.
Rashi on bBaba Kama 27a s.v. *lemikah umimkar.*
*Responsa Beit Shlomo,* OH #57.
*Responsa Mabit,* #37.

## BOOKS

W.C. Kaiser, *Toward Old Testament Ethics* (Grand Rapids, MI: 1978), 99.
E. Urbach, *The Sages: Their Concepts and Beliefs,* trans. I. Abrahams, (Jerusalem: 1987), vol. 1, 343.

## JOURNAL ARTICLES

A. Shaffer, "Cuneiform tablets from Palestine I: the letter from Shechem" (Hebrew), *Beer-Sheva* 3 (1988), 163–169.
Joseph Raz, "Legal principles and the limits of law," 81 *Yale L.J.* (1972), 823–834.

## ARTICLES IN EDITED VOLUMES

B.S. Jackson, "Legalism and spirituality," in E.B. Firmage, B.G. Weiss and J.C. Welch (eds.), *Religion and Laws: Biblical, Judaic and Islamic Perspectives* (Winona Lake, IN: 1990), 243–261.

D. Sinclair, "Defending the lives of the mortally ill, the embryo and the non-Jew" (Hebrew) in G. Frishtick (ed.), *Human Rights in Judaism* (Hebrew), (Jerusalem: 1992), 37, n. 19.

## CROSS-REFERENCES IN NOTES

23 A. Sagi and D. Statman, *Religion and Morality* (Amsterdam: 1995); henceforth, Sagi and Statman 1995.
24 See Englard 1991, n. 11 above, 67.
25 Ibid., 121.
26 See Sagi and Statman 1995, chs. 6–7.

For Product Safety Concerns and Information please contact our EU representative GPSR@taylorandfrancis.com
Taylor & Francis Verlag GmbH, Kaufingerstraße 24, 80331 München, Germany

www.ingramcontent.com/pod-product-compliance
Lightning Source LLC
LaVergne TN
LVHW011107300926
849160LV00008B/298
*9781138973787*